Why Fathers Count

The Importance of Fathers and Their Involvement with Children

Edited by

Sean E. Brotherson
Joseph M. White

Why Fathers Count:
The Importance of Fathers and Their Involvement with Children

Edited by Sean E. Brotherson and Joseph M. White

 Men's Studies Press, Harriman, Tennessee 37748
Copyright 2007 by the Men's Studies Press, LLC.

James A. Doyle, Acquisition Editor
Sally Ham Govan, Designer, Production Editor
Cover photo: Comstock

First Edition
ISBN-13: 978-1-931342-05-6 (paperback)
ISBN-13: 978-1-931342-06-3 (casebound)

Library of Congress Cataloging-in-Publication Data

Why fathers count : the importance of fathers and their involvement with children / edited by Sean E. Brotherson, Joseph M. White.
    p. cm.
Includes bibliographical references and index.
ISBN-13: 978-1-931342-06-3 (casebound : alk. paper)
ISBN-13: 978-1-931342-05-6 (pbk. : alk. paper)
ISBN-13: 978-1-931342-07-0 (electronic)
1. Fathers. 2. Fatherhood. 3. Father and child. I. Brotherson, Sean E., 1967- II. White, Joseph M., 1963-
HQ756.W49 2007
306.874'2--dc22
                                    2006049922

Table of Contents

Contents

Dedication

To our wise and wonderful parents, Jack and Karen Brotherson, Joseph and Loretta White, Ms. Judith White, and foster parents Dick and Penny Wilkens, for their wisdom and strength and love in our lives; to our bright and beautiful wives, Kristen Walch Brotherson and Alice Marie White, for their care, generosity, and loving support; to our children who are the light in our lives, Ellen, Ethan, Mason, Bryn, London, and Bronwyn Brotherson, and Sarah, Isabella, Alexandria, Hannah, Victoria, Joseph, Jr., and Olivia White, for letting us be fathers and bringing us lasting joy; to our siblings, family members, and friends, for encouragement and support; and to our mentors and friends, David Dollahite, Alan Hawkins, Anisa Zvonkovic, Karen Hooker, Jim Deal, Karen Zotz, Richard Wampler, Randy Jones, Ron Fesler, Scott Gardner, John Schipper, Bob Chell, Daryl Nygaard, Dennis Gill, and the late Bill Iron Moccasin for guiding us and giving us inspiration and opportunities to learn about what we love—families.

Foreword

Jay Fagan

In the past decade, there has been a flurry of research on fathers, some of it calling into question whether fathers are even *essential* to the healthy growth and development of their children.[1] Some of these questions have actually had a positive influence on the fathering field. The implementation of projects such as *Why Fathers Count* is one such positive influence. While there is still much debate about whether mother and father roles are interchangeable, the research literature is filled with examples of how fathers influence children differently than mothers. For example, researchers have found that fathers have distinctive play styles that differ from those of mothers and that fathers' play has an especially important influence on child outcomes.[2] On the other hand, some have questioned the magnitude of these differences. Research with preschoolers, for example, suggests that there may be more similarities than differences in mothers' and fathers' interaction patterns with children.[3]

An important outcome of this scholarly debate has been the recognition that both mothers and fathers need to be included in research designs in order to better examine the relative impact of each parent, let alone the interactive impact of both parents together. It is important that we temper our view and not exaggerate the impact of father influences on children. There are many mothers who are successfully raising their children without the presence of an active father and who may be subsequently left feeling guilty because they are not providing their offspring with an involved father. It is my hope that books such as *Why Fathers Count* will present a positive and realistic picture of fathers' influences on their children.

We are in a period of rapid social change in which fathers are needed more than ever to assume the father role. Women with children have joined and stayed in the labor force in unprecedented numbers. Fathers are needed to fill the gap in children's lives as a result of mothers' multiple roles. Far too many men have withdrawn from family life and are no longer involved with their children. Books such as *Why Fathers Count* are needed not only to present a realistic picture of how fathers influence children but also to articulate the role fathers play in relation to families, communities, and society. We are beginning to learn in the fathering field that changes in families have far-reaching impacts on all other systems throughout society.

There are many reasons why this book is desperately needed. One of the most important may be that it is designed to reach a broad audience from the general public to the practitioner, from parents to policymakers, and from social service providers to academics. Far too often researchers have written critical articles or books read only by other researchers. These important articles are seldom read by those who work directly with fathers and families. As a consequence, professionals who work with fathers are not provided with access to important knowledge. *Why Fathers Count* addresses that gap and provides a well-needed bridge between "the town and gown," that is to say, between the general public and family professional. As such, it is a timely and welcome addition to the growing literature on fathers and families.

Endnotes

1. Silverstein, L.B., and Auerbach, C.F., 1999, "Deconstructing the Essential Father," *American Psychologist*, 54, 397–407.

2. Paquette, D., Carbonneau, R., Dubeau, D., Bigras, M., and Tremblay, R.E., 2003, "Prevalence of Father-Child Rough-and-Tumble Play and Physical Aggression in Preschool Children," *European Journal of Psychology of Education*, 18, 171–189; Roggman, L.A., Boyce, L.K., Cook, G.A., Christiansen, K., and Jones, D., 2004, "Playing with Daddy: Social Toy Play, Early Head Start, and Developmental Outcomes," *Fathering: A Journal of Theory, Research, and Practice about Men as Fathers*, 2, 83–108.

3. Lewis, C., 1997, "Fathers and Preschoolers," in *The Role of the Father in Child Development*, 3rd ed., edited by M.E. Lamb, NY: Wiley, pp. 121–142.

Acknowledgments

We appreciate the invitation of Jim Doyle, our editor at Men's Studies Press, to edit this volume on fathering and its importance in contemporary family life. He has been generous with his trust, exemplary in his feedback, and fatherly in his willingness to let us explore the terrain of fathering. We would like to thank Sally Govan, also from Men's Studies Press, for her important and expeditious efforts in the final editing process. Her timely questions and reminders from an editorial perspective helped bring this project to completion. We are grateful to Ken Canfield of the National Center for Fathering for his counsel and feedback on early drafts of the project. We wish to thank the many outstanding contributors to this volume, who have provided us with great material and been highly responsive to our editorial suggestions. We have learned from them and their tremendous insights.

We extend our gratitude also to the many fathers we know, the men we have spent time with in interviews, seminars, and family settings, who have convinced us that fathering is indeed a man's most important work. And, finally, we are most appreciative of the constant encouragement of our wives and families, without whose support we could not work and without whose love we would not know the joy and importance of fathering.

Introduction

Sean E. Brotherson and Joseph M. White

When Jim Doyle picked up the phone and called us about doing a book on the importance of fathers in the lives of children and families, it was a leap of faith. We had never met. We were (and still are) two young, unknown family scholars located in the obscure upper Midwest. We were already relatively busy with research projects, work responsibilities, family relationships, and other life projects. Jim's call was a bolt from the blue, and yet that call initiated an opportunity and a continuing desire to make available a clear, compelling case for why fathers count in the lives of children and families and to make that case to an important general audience, one that goes beyond the ivory tower.

Making the case for why fathers count from an empirical, statistical perspective is fairly easy. The data overwhelmingly demonstrate the positive impact fathers have when they are involved in the lives of their children and the negative outcomes when fathers are absent. Many of these findings will be discussed in Chapter 1 and throughout the book.

Making the case for responsible fatherhood from a political perspective is also fairly easy. The most prominent political leaders in our country have recognized the importance of this issue. The social concern over fatherhood, in fact, led former President William J. Clinton to authorize a 1995 executive order in which he instructed all federal departments and agencies to review their programs "that pertain[s] to families to ensure" those programs would "seek to engage and meaningfully include fathers."[1] This attentiveness to supporting fathers' roles in family life elevated the issue and prompted greater awareness of the need for encouraging responsible father involvement. Further, in an address at the National Fatherhood Summit in 2001, President George W. Bush articulated a clear perspective on fathers:

> Nearly every man who has a child wants to be a good father, I truly believe that. It's a natural longing of the human heart to care for and cherish your child. But this longing must find concrete expression. Raising a child requires sacrifice, effort, time, and presence. And there is a wide gap between our best intentions and the reality of today's society. More than one-third of American children are living apart from their biological fathers. Of these, five out of six do not see their fathers more than once a week. And 40 percent of the children who live in fatherless households have not seen their fathers in at least a year. Some fathers are forced away by circumstances beyond their control. But many times when a couple with children splits up, the father moves away or simply drifts away. We

know that children who grow up with absent fathers can suffer lasting damage. They are more likely to end up in poverty or drop out of school, become addicted to drugs, have a child out of wedlock, or end up in prison. Fatherlessness is not the only cause of these things, but our nation must recognize it is an important factor.[2]

The gap between "our best intentions and the reality of today's society" is genuine, but too great a focus on the problems in family life can leave us without energy to pursue necessary solutions. Attentiveness to the broad scope of the issue is required. President Bush went on to say:

There is a familiar litany that behind every statistic is a child, and a compassionate society can never forget the large place a father occupies in that child's life. Children look to their fathers to provide—even imperfectly—and nurture protection, provide discipline and care, guidance and, most importantly, unconditional love. Fathers are the object of a young child's admiration. . . . The absence of a father can shatter a child's world. One 14-year-old girl put it this way: "My father left me when I learned to say 'daddy.' Even though my father is not around, in my heart he's always there. Every birthday, every Christmas, I cross my fingers in hopes that my father will come home. Does my wish come true? No. But I never quit looking and hoping." When children quit looking and stop hoping, something terrible happens to them, and to us. Over the past four decades, fatherlessness has emerged as one of our greatest social problems.[3]

It was clear to us that continued attentiveness to understanding and encouraging responsible and caring father involvement is important. Deciding how to make the case for why fathers count to a diverse, general audience, however, proved interesting and challenging.

After a good deal of conversation and a flurry of e-mail activity, we launched the project and set sail for distant shores. We hope this brief introduction will serve as an outline of our journey and an invitation into the pages of this book on your own voyage of discovery about fathers and fathering. While our main qualification for editing this volume was enthusiasm, we also were guided and gifted by four other elements that we felt would make this book a meaningful contribution to the growing body of work on fathering.

First, we have a personal and professional *passion* for the topic of fathering. We sincerely think that healthy, caring, and involved fathers are the most important and untapped resource in the world today. Second, we believe in *people* and what they can bring to such a book. We felt that, if given the opportunity, a wide range of scholars, community professionals, and family practitioners would respond to the opportunity to share their vision of how fathers make a meaningful difference in specific areas of family life. We were not disappointed. Third, we have a profound respect for *parenting* and its importance not only for families but for society. Whether parenting is done by a mother or a grandfather or a caring teacher; in a family of Mexican, Anglo, or Hawaiian ancestry; on a rural farm or in an urban city—it is of vital importance. As children of caring parents, as parents ourselves, and as observers of parenting in family life, we think parenting ought to be greatly appreciated, that its importance should be examined and better understood. And fourth, we are confident in the *promise* of such a book, in the belief that we could harness the collective insight and wisdom of many contributors to paint anew a vision of the importance of fathers in family life. Ideas are powerful, so we started with one idea: fathers make a difference.

Exploring the Terrain of Fathering

It can be surprising how difficult the task of articulating and agreeing upon a basic vision for an edited book such as this can be. In the early stages, we talked and planned and outlined and started over again, stuck on the initial question of what we wanted to accomplish. Did we need to define the boundaries of responsible fatherhood and healthy father involvement? Did we wish to document the ongoing academic investigation of fathers in family life? Did we want to enter the sometimes vociferous debate about the roles of men in contemporary society and family life? These and other questions shaped our discussions, but in the end, we agreed that ours was a voyage of discovery more than anything else. Most of all, we wanted to explore the worlds and experiences of fathers and those who work or live with them and to invite others to journey along with us.

One of the first and most important questions we settled early on was whether a journey of exploration into the worlds of fathering was worth taking in the first place. After all, there are those who think and write about fathers from a perspective of skepticism. In other words, they wonder aloud whether fathers are genuinely important and question the emphasis on father involvement. These are important questions that deserve consideration, and we have dealt with them in our own scholarly work elsewhere.[4] However, for this project, we were less interested in an "ivory tower" debate about the legitimacy of father involvement and much more interested in a learning dialogue about the contributions of fathers to family and community life. As fathers ourselves, it struck us that our relationships with our own children do not begin with a question about whether we are important in their lives. Instead, interactions with our children consistently engage and challenge us to make meaningful and lasting differences in their lives. In other words, this journey does not focus on the question of whether fathers make a difference but instead begins with the assumption that fathers and father figures make a difference, and we are on an expedition to learn how and why. To us, this is the important and logical next step in exploring the terrain of fathering since we have determined there is sufficient evidence for the importance of father involvement to warrant making such a journey.

In developing a book focused on the topic of why fathers count in the lives of children and families, we wished to not only identify fathers' contributions but explore their experiences, share their voices, highlight key principles, provide ideas and insights, and suggest best practices related to fathers and family life. We wanted not only to facilitate an understanding of fathers but to encourage better fathering and improved efforts to engage and support fathers in family life. Hawkins and Dollahite have previously suggested that "a perspective of fathers as generally deficient in their paternal role is not the best place to begin to understand and encourage better fathering."[5] We agree with this sentiment. We have thus sought to develop a focused collection of articles centered on the assumption that fathers can and should be meaningfully involved with their children and families.

In the process of recruiting contributors for this book, we asked potential authors to explore their particular area of expertise or special content area with an emphasis on the importance and value of meaningful father involvement in that context. We asked them to provide examples of how and why fathers made a difference in their given area, examples that were practical and personally relevant or that came from their research experience. We also wanted relevant suggestions that scholars, practitioners, fathers, and families themselves could use in personal and professional settings. Finally, we asked that each chapter essay be addressed not solely to an academic audience but to the broader community of interested readers who would like further information and insight on the specific topic of how and why fathers are important in the lives of children and families.

Objectives of the Book

What did we hope to accomplish with this book? After considering whether to pursue a "universal handbook of fatherhood" that would address everything from Caribbean fathers to fathers in contemporary literature, we opted to focus more on conceptual simplicity and address central elements of fathers' experiences with their children and families. These elements include (1) relationships and relationship processes (Sections I and II), (2) domains of development (Section III), and (3) contexts of influence, involvement, and support (Sections IV, V, and VI). The defining objectives of our book were:

- to explore key topics in fathers' involvement and experience and introduce others to what has been and is being discovered in these areas;

- to focus on the generative capacities or strengths that most fathers can and do bring to their engagement with children and how these qualities make a meaningful difference for children and families;
- to base articles in research and highlight key important findings from relevant research while writing in an accessible style;
- to acknowledge the complexity of family experiences while also addressing the core elements of how fathers can make a difference in the well-being of children and families;
- to focus on what is common across all fathering situations—relationships and relationship processes, domains of development, and contexts of caring, involvement, and support;
- to highlight the key points with principles from research, practical examples, or personal narratives from the lives of real men, fathers, families, and communities, and their children; and
- to provide a respectful approach to issues of diversity and contextual differences in fathering throughout the text.

"Why Fathers Count" Outline

Each chapter written for this volume addresses certain dimensions of the fathering experience, many of which are common across family relationships and some that are unique. As mentioned, we chose to focus generally on aspects of fathering experience that are common to most or all fathers and asked contributors to make their chapters informative, insightful, and practical. Each section includes a short discussion outlining the chapters of that section in further detail:

- The opening chapter addresses the fundamental issue of the book, why fathers count, and the vital importance of healthy father involvement to the future of our children, families, and society.
- The five chapters in Section I, "Fathers and Family Relationships," explore fathering in different family relationship contexts, including becoming a father (transition to parenthood), fathers and mothers, fathers and marriage, father-daughter relationships, and grandfathering.
- Section II, "Fathers and Family Interaction," introduces several topics concerning how fathers influence their children through different processes of family interaction, including play, reading with children, building parent-child connections, and love and sacrifice in family life.
- In Section III, "Fathers and Domains of Development," four chapters illustrate how fathers influence children in varying aspects of development and growth, highlighting the developmental journey from birth to young adult-

hood, psychological development and well-being, moral development, and spiritual development.

- Section IV, "Fathers and Contexts of Influence," includes three chapters addressing contextual influences that may shape the interactions or experience of fathers and their children, including race and ethnic background, divorce and non-residential fathering, and incarceration.
- The six chapters that make up Section V, "Fathers and Contexts of Involvement," highlight a variety of contexts in which fathers are involved with and influence their children and families, including work, early childhood education and care, mentoring, education, religion, and leadership.
- Section VI, "Fathers and Contexts of Support," attends to varying contexts of support for fathers as they seek to engage in being and becoming better parents, including community-level engagement, small group involvement, and parent and family education.
- Finally, Section VII concludes our book with a final chapter that looks at the most important setting and context in which fathering occurs, within the walls of his own home. It is here that fathers "really" father by the way they treat their children, spouses, parents, ex-spouses, and others. It is here that fathering comes to life. It is *where* fathers are born. We close with this chapter because it speaks to the heart of fathering. It offers enjoyable and sacred experiences that highlight how and where fathers count the most in the lives of their children.

The Fathering Journey

We strongly believe fathering must be understood and acknowledged as a developmental journey in the life of a man. Men enter the experience of fatherhood at differing points in time and through varying passages. Some men become fathers in less than ideal circumstances, some come to fatherhood by marrying and having a child with a woman they love, some enter fatherhood by taking on the role of stepfather, and some become father figures in the lives of children they love as uncles, grandfathers, mentors, teachers, or other caring figures. Healthy fathering can benefit children, but it also tends to act as a balancing experience for men and can aid them in developing into more mature, sensitive, and caring individuals.

As we have explored the fathering journey, we have been led to see the experiences of men, women, and children in family life from new vantage points and fresh perspectives. We have been led to consider the critical role that mothers play in facilitating father involvement and the dance steps that occur as fathers raise their daughters. We have learned how fathers can influence children by playing on the floor or shaping a child's moral thinking. We have more deeply understood how race or a life behind bars can influence a father's outlook and experience. We have come to see how fathers can contribute to family life through harmonizing work and family experiences, volunteering as a mentor in the community, or engaging in servant leadership at home. All this has guided us on this learning journey of fathers' influence in many areas of life. It is our hope that you, too, will enjoy this journey and grow in your understanding of why fathers count. We hope it will add to your personal and professional life experience in new and unexpected ways. We hope you enjoy the voyage.

Endnotes

1. Clinton, W., 1995, *Memorandum for the Heads of Executive Departments and Agencies: Supporting the Roles of Fathers in Families,* Washington, DC: The White House.

2. Bush, G.W., 2001, *Remarks by the President to the Fourth National Summit on Fatherhood*, Washington, DC: The White House.

3. Ibid.

4. Brotherson, S.E., Dollahite, D.C., & Hawkins, A.J., 2005, "Generative Fathering and the Dynamics of Connection between Fathers and Their Children," *Fathering: A Journal of Theory, Research, and Practice about Men as Fathers*, 3(1), 1–28; Brotherson, S.E., Yamamoto, T., and Acock, A.C, 2003, "Connection and Communication in Father-Child Relationships and Adolescent Child Well-Being," *Fathering: A Journal of Theory, Research, and Practice about Men as Father*s, 1(3), 191–214; Brotherson, S.E., and White, J.M., 2002, "Federal and State Policy Initiatives to Strengthen Fatherhood: Issues and Implications for Practitioners," *Professional Development: The International Journal of Continuing Social Work Education,* 4(3), 16–34; Dollahite, D.C., Hawkins, A.J., and Brotherson, S.E., 1997, "Fatherwork: A Conceptual Ethic of Fathering as Generative Work," in *Generative Fathering: Beyond Deficit Perspectives*, edited by A.J. Hawkins and D.C. Dollahite, Thousand Oaks, CA: Sage Publications, 17–35; White, J.M., Godfrey, J.G., and Iron Moccasin, B., 2006, "American Indian Fathering in the Dakota Nation: Use of Akicita as a Fatherhood Standard," *Fathering: A Journal of Theory, Research, and Practice About Men as Fathers*, 44(1), 49–69; White, J.M., Hoyt, D., Whitbeck, L., and Johnson, K., 2005, "American Indian Father Involvement: Predictors of Youth Prosocial Outcomes," submitted for publication.

5. Hawkins, A.J., and Dollahite, D.C., 1997, "Beyond the Role-Inadequacy Perspective of Fathering," in *Generative Fathering: Beyond Deficit Perspectives*, edited by A.J. Hawkins and D.C. Dollahite, Thousand Oaks, CA: Sage Publications, pp. 3–16, at 3.

Author Joseph M. White with two of his daughters, Hannah and Victoria

Why Fathers Count:
Fatherhood and the Future of Our Children

Sean E. Brotherson and Joseph M. White

atherless America! thundered the title of a provocative book, followed by the subtitle's pressing tone: *Confronting Our Most Urgent Social Problem.*[1] The most urgent social problem in the United States today, according to some scholars, is the increasing number of fathers who either are not in the home or are ineffective parents while at home. A variety of studies, publications, and social programs in recent years have focused attention on the issue of fathering.[2] Efforts to encourage better fathering have been underway in this country for some years due to such social concerns, resulting in hopeful appraisals of the "new father" or the "androgynous father." However, it has been pointed out that the "conduct of fatherhood" does not necessarily keep pace with the "culture of fatherhood,"[3] and the efforts to create a culturally ideal father are not always exemplified by real fathers. One limitation of efforts to reengineer the role of fathers has been that they often arise from a "deficiency model of men," a perspective that emphasizes men's deficiencies in fulfilling a socially defined father role.[4] And yet it is men's strengths—their capacity to care, protect, and give—that are needed by children, women, and men themselves. In a culture that questions the value of men in family life, we need a fresh perspective on what men can contribute to their families and communities as well as insight into the ways in which fathers and father figures make a meaningful difference.

Why is fathering an important issue on the nation's agenda? How did we get to a point in history when fathering is consuming a large portion of the debate over child well-being? Perhaps because, as one researcher has written:

> Increasingly, more children do not live with their fathers, relate to their fathers on a regular basis, or enjoy the economic support of their fathers. In my view, this situation is a rending of the moral fabric of family life and thus of society as a whole, as a generation of men fail to engage in responsible generativity toward the next generation.[5]

Because children are largely dependent on caring adults for their support and well-being, the question of how adults are responding to the needs of the coming generation is critical for communities. William Doherty's assessment that the current situation is "a rending of the moral fabric of family life and thus of society as a whole" is a serious charge. Two leading family scholars, Paul Amato and Alan Booth, have examined family upheaval in America and titled their book on the subject *A Generation at Risk*.[6] Are future generations of Americans truly at risk due to the concerns that exist about fathers in family life? Erik Erikson, the pioneering developmental psychologist, asserted in his work that caring for the next generation is among the most profound responsibilities that rest upon humanity. It seems, then, that we should be very concerned about fatherhood and the future of our children.

Fatherhood and the Future of Children

In addressing the issue of fatherhood and the future of our children, it is challenging to settle on the best approach to engaging others with the issue. We could present a deluge of statistics from research-based studies that provide evidence of fathers' positive contributions to child well-being and the negative consequences that can occur due to father absence or lack of involvement. We might work on an attention-getting media campaign that splashes images of fathers in family life across magazines, television screens, and the Internet. We could offer a menu of programs and policy prescriptions designed to lower barriers to father involvement and strengthen men in their efforts to be responsible and committed as fathers. Yet, and perhaps most important, we could simply capture and communicate the simple idea that a father counts in the life of a child.

There is nothing quite as powerful as a good idea. There is nothing quite as compelling as the smile of a baby, the outreached arms of a toddler, or the laughter and love of a teenage son or daughter to kindle love in the heart of a father. Too many men, however, have learned to limit their responses to a child's love, and too many children have faced life without the loving arms of a father to guide, nurture, and protect them. More must be done to address the issue of fatherhood and the future of our children. Therefore, we hope that one of the contributions of this book will be its ability to communicate the power of a father's love in the life of a child.

An important point must be made about fathers and their involvement in family life. In all that we do to promote enhanced quality of life for children and their families, this concept may be an important factor in capturing the "heart of a father."[7] While many men don't need to be cajoled or coerced into spending more time with their children, some men do need greater encouragement and support. Men can do better. We do not need to be satisfied with attitudes that accept limited involvement, abusive behavior, or lack of responsibility as the status quo for men in family life. Men are most likely, we believe, to respond to moral invitations that ask them to give the best of themselves to parenting the children in their lives.

A key issue is that, in addition to benefits for children, mothers, and the community, men themselves ultimately benefit when they fulfill their paternal obligations and responsibilities.[8] Such "fathering work" is, therefore, also important to a father's personal development and will directly affect his health, happiness, and satisfaction. Fathers meaningfully involved in their children's lives are participating in an important aspect of adult development called generativity. They are caring for the next generation. Substantial and worthwhile involvement at this stage of life is an important precursor to an issue in the last stage of adulthood called integrity, when men begin to question how meaningful their life's efforts have been.[9] Without adequate emphasis on their children during the formative years of childhood and adolescence, men may struggle in resolving the impending issues of the final stage of life. Therefore, the case should also be made that, in general, most men need to do the work of fathering for their own happiness, health, and peace.

Do Fathers Really Count?

As scholars of fathering and fathers ourselves, we sometimes face the question of whether a father's involvement in the life of his family is really important. What does the evidence truly suggest? We can only believe that some individuals who would dismiss the evidence of fathers' importance simply choose a kind of selective ignorance in which there is a willing disregard for an ever-increasing body of scientific research that documents the power and significance of a father's caring and involvement in the lives of children. Those who blatantly choose to ignore the facts about father absence and the devastating impact it often has on children and family life are often the first to scream at the band because it did not "play on." The band, of course, was on the upper end of the Titanic before it sank. Ignorance may be bliss until it brings everyone down with it!

Nearly three decades ago, child psychologist Michael Lamb shared a description of fathers as the "forgotten contributors to child development." Today it would be hard to make such a claim. Other commentators have recently written:

> Over the past decade, burgeoning interest in fatherhood by family scholars has produced a body of research impressive in its size, breadth, and depth. Moreover, interest in fatherhood has not been limited to researchers and academics, but has spread to policymakers, social service providers, politicians, community and religious organizations, social commentators, and others. At no time in American history have so many been paying so much attention to fathers and the institution of fatherhood.[10]

With so much attention being given to fathers and family life, what has been learned? Increasingly, it is both acknowledged and accepted that the involvement of a loving, committed father brings many positive elements to the growth and development of children, the stability of families, and the well-being of communities. It is our view that both parents count: mothers *and* fathers. Our work focuses on fathers and does not, in any way, minimize the tremendous contributions of mothers to the lives of their families.

A brief sampling of random findings related to the contributions of fathers in family life illustrates the theme of why fathers count:

- Data from the National Study of Families and Households showed when fathers were positively involved, children experienced fewer behavior problems and anxieties, got along better with others, and were more responsible.[11]
- A study on empathy in adulthood found that the strongest predictor of empathy for others was the level of care and support by fathers in childhood. This applied to both men and women.[12]
- Summarizing a series of early studies on fathers' influence on young children, researchers indicate that fathers' interest and involvement in the early years is strongly associated with higher cognitive functioning and greater academic achievement among school-age children.[13]
- Childhood poverty in America is affected by fathers' ties to the family. Only 9 percent of children living in married-couple families lived below poverty level, while 42 percent living in single-mother families lived below poverty level in 2004. This finding becomes even more significant for children born to mothers outside of marriage, dramatically increasing the poverty rate for such children.[14]

■ Data from the National Longitudinal Survey of Youth indicate that a father's absence significantly increases the likelihood of difficulties with peers, depressive behavior in boys, and other behavioral challenges for girls.[15]

Getting along with others, empathy, academic achievement, childhood poverty, and depression in childhood—all issues that reflect differing aspects of a child's well-being and development—are significantly affected by a father's presence and involvement. The list could be significantly expanded. The simple point is that a mounting wave of scholarship suggests fathers count in a variety of ways in the lives of children and their contributions inevitably shape the future of a child's life.

Beyond the research on family life, the most compelling evidence for a father's love and involvement can be seen in the eyes of a child. Watch a child who has a caring, involved father in his or her life interact with him. Notice the laughter and the warmth. In the eyes of a child, a father's love and acceptance can count for everything. John Snarey, who tracked the contributions of fathers to children across generations in a four-decade study, surveyed this vast research and summarized: "Good fathering, it seems, really does matter. It matters over a long time, over a lifetime, and even over generations."[16]

A Brief Historical Portrait of Fatherhood

Since we have arrived at a point in American history where the question of fatherhood and the future of our children is a central concern, it can be useful to look back and see how fathers in family life have been viewed over time. A brief historical overview of some of the culturally dominant themes and perspectives on fathering in the United States can be informative. We should note that such themes often fail to account for divergent patterns in family life that often occurred due to variations in race, culture, or social class, but they provide a somewhat useful perspective on general themes.

In writing about fatherhood over time in American history, two of the field's scholars commented:

In the conventional wisdom, over four centuries of American history the stern patriarch of the colonial settlers changed into the involved father of today, as the hierarchical model of domestic government gave way to the modern democratic ideal. Gone was the moral guide, distant and cold, rod in one hand and Bible in the other. In his place stood the playmate, pal, coach, child development specialist, diaper changer, chauffeur, and childbirth attendant of modern film and advertisements.[17]

It hardly needs to be said that images of fatherhood, while representing a form of reality, generally fail to do justice to the many dimensions that represent the true diversity of fatherhood. The colonial father of European descent, represented as "distant and cold" from his children, was likely surrounded by other men who, like fathers today, varied widely in their motivation and involvement with their children.

Significant challenges in addressing the fatherhood issues of today involve capturing the diversity of fathering experiences across culture, ethnic group, and social class as well as understanding the multiple paths by which men father children and interact with them. We need look no further than efforts to understand and support Native American fathers to see that they do not fit the cold image of the colonial father. For example, among the northern Plains tribes that live in the Midwest, where we reside, men were never seen as the stern patriarchal disciplinarians espoused by European settlers. In fact, men in these native cultures were described by outsiders as lazy because they were gone for extended periods of time to hunt, fish, or trap. It was culturally appropriate for others to assume the responsibility of raising their children.[18] Other men in the extended family network, typically uncles, filled the role of father figure. Native American fathers we interviewed identified characteristics of good fathers and noted their most important quality was "forgiveness." This may or may not be considered the supreme characteristic of good fathers within mainstream American culture, but it certainly has adaptive value within theirs. Relationship interaction styles within families may adapt over time to the needs of a given culture and should be appreciated within differing cultural and historical contexts.

Elizabeth and Joseph Pleck provide an overview of the culturally dominant ideals of fatherhood across four different periods of American history.[19] Although little attention is given to cultural variations, a review of culturally dominant themes is valuable in providing a general understanding of predominant cultural ideals and what mainstream society seemed to think about fathers at a given time. It is important to note that most children of African American, Native American, or other minority groups have lived in and witnessed mainstream conceptions of the involved, breadwinning father and its opposite, the failed provider. This commingling of cultural ideals has serious consequences for how family relationships are understood not only within dominant cultures but within other related or minority cultural groups. Although ideas of what has constituted the "good dad" have varied across time and context, the basic perceptions of the "bad dad" have remained constant across historical trends.[20] He was the father who failed to provide for his family.

The four historical fatherhood trends that have been identified in America include the "stern patriarch" of the colonial period, the "distant breadwinner" of the 1830s–1900s, the "genial dad" and sex-role model from 1900–1970, and the "co-parent" from 1970 to the present day.[21] The stern patriarch of the colonial period represented the largely Protestant, European, and rural majority of the North. These American colonists believed, in general, that fathers were important as models and conveyors of good moral character, rationality, self-control, and theological understanding. Later, the distant breadwinner ideal emerged in the time period of 1830 to 1900, in which the mother emerged as the primary parent and fathers began to be viewed as taking more of a back seat in parental respon-sibilities (aside from setting moral standards and administering discipline). This ideal was associated with developments from the Industrial Revolution, in which many men moved off the farm and into business settings, and also with a greater emphasis on the superiority of maternal love and instinct in child development.

The time period from 1900 to 1970 reflected a cultural trend back toward a closer and more involved father, with the ideal father being more genial and mod-eling sex-role patterns.[22] In addition to the provider and disciplinarian roles, fathers were seen as being able to express affection, participate in child-rearing activities, and actively engage children in fun activities. Also, concerns about juvenile delin-quency were attributed to father absence. Cartoons about the "bumbling father" emerged during the 1920s as a stereotype of the bad father, seemingly as a reflec-tion of the new cultural mores that emphasized fathers' good points. A new and noteworthy rationale for father involvement emerged later in this period (during the 1950s) that suggested involved fathering was good for men and that it could be more enjoyable and rewarding than occupational endeavors.

From the 1970s to the present, a new trend has emerged that focuses on an ideal of fatherhood emphasizing the nurturant and equal co-parent who partici-pates fully in nurturing children and shares child-rearing tasks equally with the mother.[23] Two trends combined to facilitate this ideal, the women's movement and the emergence of the dual-income family, with many mothers entering the work-force outside the home. This trend called for men to become equally involved in sharing the tasks of childcare and other parenting responsibilities and also empha-sized the nurturing aspects of parenting often associated with maternal care. The rate at which women work outside the home has steadily increased, so that today a significant majority of children under the age of six have mothers who work out-side the home. Some question whether the ideal of the co-parent father has actu-ally been realized or is only an upper middle-class image; however, evidence suggests that fathers' participation in childcare and family work has substantially increased over the past three decades.

Additional trends that have influenced fatherhood have emerged in the past three decades, shaping a new cultural discourse about fatherhood and how it affects the future of our children. One image that has emerged is the opposite of the nurturing co-parent and instead characterizes many men as "deadbeat dads" who live apart from their children, avoid involvement, and fail to support them.

This father image has gained new relevance and is no longer associated simply with men of lower socioeconomic status but with men of all ethnic and class backgrounds. This image has been fueled by changing family structures, which have corresponded with a rise in the divorce rate and out-of-wedlock childbearing, thus making fathers' ties to their children more tenuous. The contemporary images of fatherhood in America range from the bumbling father to the new, nurturant father to the deadbeat dad, with some voices insisting on a return to traditional, patriarchal family types while others advocate change in social patterns without concern for the impact on children.

Developments of the past few decades in the United States have led to a proliferation of images about fatherhood and a vigorous dialogue about the best approaches to supporting men in the lives of children and families. The continuing dialogue is being shaped anew by social forces such as 9/11 and the War on Terror, with thousands of American men being drawn into conflicts across the world and leaving their families behind for months or years at a time. Fatherhood is at the top of the national agenda for reasons that include child support, employment, military deployment, incarceration, divorce, delinquency, and the influence of these issues on the well-being of children. Father absence is a national epidemic, and the empirical evidence suggests that the antidote, father involvement, is central to optimal child development outcomes. In reviewing the emergence of fatherhood as a major social concern in the 1990s, scholars commented:

> Heated public debates emerged over numerous issues relevant to fatherhood, including divorce and single parenthood, "deadbeat dads" and "androgynous" fathers, welfare reform, teenage pregnancy and nonmarital childbearing, fathers' rights and responsibilities, the definition of "family," and fathers' potentially unique contributions to child development. Discussions of these issues often make reference to serious social problems assumed to arise from the diverse conditions of fatherlessness and father absence.[24]

We are compelled to believe that families deserve not just lasting debate but actual decisions that reflect a desire to help fathers embrace their responsibilities and become architects of a positive future for the children in their lives. To achieve such change will require sustained attention, effort, and commitment to the ideal that fathers count and their contributions shape the future of generations yet unborn.

Turning the Hearts of Fathers to Children

In the past decade, scholarly and public discourse has moved toward the formation of a different, more holistic approach to encouraging fathers in the care of their children.[25] In essence, there is much dissatisfaction with the inherited models and images that reflect negative thinking about men in family life. A primary critique of the deficit model of fathering is that it limits our conceptual understanding of fatherhood. Some scholars argue that "to the extent that the deficiency model of men in families dominates our perspective, we will surely not see enough or see clearly all that should be viewed."[26] Another major critique is that deficit-oriented ideas inhibit attempts to promote good fathering by scholars, practitioners, and community leaders. For example, an assumption by a school principal that most fathers would not take time to come and read in the classroom with a child may lead the principal never to extend the invitation in the first place. Effective intervention and support must be combined with helpful and growth-promoting assumptions about fathers' potential, and such assumptions are wanting in deficit approaches to thinking about men in family life.[27] Inadequate thinking breeds inadequate research, policy, and intervention—in short, inadequate action.[28] Understanding the link between ideas about fatherhood and how we support fathers in family life can help us develop a more helpful set of ideas for motivating men in their fathering endeavors.

We acknowledge that, while it is desirable to advance an understanding of men that focuses on their abilities rather than their inabilities, there are a great number of men who perpetuate the negative views of fathers in family life: fathers who are uninvolved and uncaring. However, as we accept this negative reality that some men reflect poorly on fatherhood by their abuse or abandonment, we must not abuse or dismiss the contributions of most men to their children and families or abandon hope for responsible fatherhood. Children, women, and men deserve our best efforts to assist fathers in opening their hearts to family life and being committed to their children.

It is evident that research and thinking on fatherhood must not only assess the past but look openly toward the future. Promising new work on fatherhood has begun to focus on men's capabilities rather than their deficiencies.[29] The challenge facing most fathers today, as in the past, is to develop the skills and insights necessary to nurture the rising generation—a concept known as generativity. John Snarey framed generativity as "any caring activity that contributes to the spirit of future generations."[30] In other words, fathers who are generative engage in those caring activities that aid in establishing physical, emotional, and spiritual health and well-being for the children of the next generation. The concept of generativity first emerged primarily in the work of developmental psychologist Erik Erikson, who wrote, "Parenthood is, for most, the first, and for many, the primary generative encounter."[31] Generativity can occur in a variety of caring activities, including direct care of infants, teaching values to children, and creating a healthy community atmosphere for adolescents.

In developing a format for this book, we hoped to capture the many ways in which fathers and father figures are a generative force in the lives of children and families. Alan Hawkins and David Dollahite have built upon the work of Erikson to propose a conceptual framework known as generative fathering, which embraces men's capabilities and highlights the developing ethical relationship between fathers, families, and children.[32] Their thinking about fathers includes some of the following emphases: developmental growth and potential; a broad, inclusive definition of nurturance; fathering as generative work rather than social role-playing; personal transformation rather than social change; emphasis on ethical obligations and the needs of children; and a focus on capabilities rather than inadequacies. The starting point for this view of fathering has its roots in the idea of a generative ethic, an idea akin to the moral imperative recorded in the biblical record to "turn the heart of the fathers to the children, and the heart of the children to the fathers" (Malachi 4:5–6).[33] The focus of such thinking is not simply to document the relationships between fathers and children but to help men become better fathers and family citizens.

Fatherhood can be conceptualized as an ethical relationship between generations. To speak of generative fathering necessarily entails a connection between generations, since the concept of generativity has been conceptualized as those caring activities that nurture such connections, foster growth, and enable the transmission of values and norms.[34] The formation and maintenance of family relationships across generations is, in itself, an ethical challenge and has been characterized as the challenge to "create, care for, and promote the development of others, from nurturing the growth of another person to shepherding the development of a broader community."[35] The relationship between a father and a child naturally occurs in the context of a generational connection predicated on caring, kindness, and moral responsibility. How can fathers best be encouraged to accept the responsibility of such a relationship and "turn their hearts" to fathering so that, likewise, the hearts of their children will turn to them?

The responsibilities and positive capabilities of men to care for and connect with their children must be appreciated and emphasized in order to encourage generative fathering. Of course, this assumes that the responsibility to be a good father exists and that men have the capacity to fulfill it. As a father becomes a parent, he assumes responsibility for another individual, a responsibility that cannot be transferred to others without difficulty.[36] Jean Bethke Elshtain has written of parenthood, "Being a parent isn't just another lifestyle choice. As parents well know, it's an ethical vocation. It is a vocation of the weightiest sort."[37] Fatherhood involves a responsibility to work for a child's well-being in a caring, committed manner. In essence, the development of a father-child relationship asks for a morally committed, actively involved devotion on the father's part. Terry Warner, a philosopher, has described this process of human relationships and declares that one person calls on another "out of his or her hopes and fears, to render service, to share whatever" they have and that relating to someone from the heart means to respond "*ethically, as one who is called upon*" (emphasis added).[38] Each father is called to the work of generativity that spans generations and makes possible the continued labors and loves of family life.

The Vision of Fathers and Family Life

For too many men, women, and children, the vision of a meaningful and happy family experience is blurred, cloudy, or simply missing, and yet for many others the vision is clear. They speak from personal experience about the bonds of love and mutual support that can exist in a family's experience. When there is no vision of a father's meaningful involvement with his children, then the hopes of children for their own future are challenged and may even perish.

How can we understand the impact of a father's absence in a child's life? The work of Pauline Boss on ambiguous loss suggests some powerful ideas for understanding this phenomenon. Her theory of ambiguous loss suggests that individuals who experience loss of a person or object in an ambiguous way will often anticipate that person's existence and long for a return.[39] Because most children grow up wanting a loving and involved father in their lives, this approach is helpful because it provides a framework for understanding the impact of a father's absence in their lives. Of course, no child wants the difficulties associated with an abusive or abandoning father, and yet even in such circumstances a child will maintain hope for a father's love and influence. All children grow up with the knowledge that they have a father or father figure, whether they can physically see him or not. Ambiguous loss suggests that children who cannot see a father who has abandoned his family will anticipate his existence and long for his return, creating its own set of challenges. On the other hand, children who physically see a father who is not present and involved in their lives in a positive way will also experience ambiguous loss and a desire to have him involved. Both situations create damaging concerns for a child. A subtle message may be sent to the child that he or she is not important enough for that father to have been involved in his or her life, whether the father's actions were intentional or associated with other circumstances. Such a sense of loss can be extremely troubling for children. Pauline Boss's research has shown that families of victims of 9/11 or conflicts in Vietnam or South America often meet their loss with denial.[40] So, too, may many of those who have experienced a father's absence or neglect struggle with its impact and face questions about what might have been in their lives.

Each child seems to intuitively want both parents involved in his or her life. We submit that it would be very difficult to find a child who sincerely wishes he or she could grow up without a father or father figure in his or her life, assuming that abuse or neglect has not tarnished that desire. However, when fathers fail to live up to the needs and wishes of their children, the children can be left without the perspective that makes a healthy future generation more possible.

One night driving through a small town on the way to Pierre, South Dakota, Joseph met a couple of young teenage boys, Matthew and Chris, who were skateboarding in an empty grocery store parking lot with their car stereo cranked up. It was about 9:30 p.m. He stopped and explained that he used to skateboard as a teenager and wondered why he didn't see kids doing "360s" on their boards these days. Both teenagers said they didn't know how to do one and asked him to show them. After a brief demonstration, Joseph explained that he was going to a meeting about fathers and was curious about theirs. Both Matt and Chris were willing to talk about their fathers, though neither lived with them. One said he had seen his father once in the past two months, and the other said he saw his father about once or twice a month. Joseph asked if they thought fathers were important. Both agreed they were. He next asked how life would be different for them if their fathers were around. They said they had no clue—they didn't know that life. Finally, Joseph asked how they would do things differently for their children to make sure they were involved in their lives, and they responded that they had no idea since it was not part of their experience.

In America, there is a whole generation of youth with no clear idea about what fathering and family life is all about. Their models are likely received from television, the movies, or other sources. There are many reasons that fatherhood is an important issue, but perhaps none more important than concern for what another generation of children without fathers will become as they move into adulthood. We know all too well about the impact of father absence on a child's life. What does it suggest when millions of children go to bed each night without a father to kiss them goodnight or affirm his love for them? In point of fact, fatherhood shapes the future of our children. As one prominent fatherhood scholar, David Popenoe, put it: "We are at a major fork in the road in America."[41] He explained that we have to make a choice individually and as a nation:

> It is imperative that we take one path—the path that requires a shift of direction—and not the other. For in the words of an ancient Chinese proverb: "Unless we change direction, we're likely to end up where we're headed." And that would be a social disaster—for our children, our families, and our society. The act of being a good father, now so cavalierly discounted, is an essential building block of every successful society. Just as a multitude of personal failings becomes a major public crisis, so does a multitude of personal contributions add up to an enormous public gain. In the final analysis, every father counts.[42]

Endnotes

1. Blankenhorn, D., 1996, *Fatherless America: Confronting Our Most Urgent Social Problem*, New York: HarperPerennial.

2. See Biller, H.B., 1993, *Fathers and Families: Paternal Factors in Child Development*, Westport, CT: Auburn House; Blankenhorn, D., 1996, *Fatherless America: Confronting Our Most Urgent Social Problem*, New York: HarperPerennial; Canfield, K., 1996, *The Heart of a Father: How Dads Can Shape the Destiny of America*, Chicago: Northfield Publishing; Day, R.D., and Lamb, M.E. (Eds.), 2003, *Conceptualizing and Measuring Father Involvement*, Mahwah, NJ: Lawrence Erlbaum Associates; Doherty, W.J., Kouneski, E.F., and Erickson, M.F., 1998, "Responsible Fathering: An Overview and Conceptual Framework," *Journal of Marriage and the Family*, 60, 277–292; Fagan, J., and Hawkins, A.J. (Eds.), 2001, *Clinical and Educational Interventions with Fathers*, Binghamton, NY: The Haworth Press; Hawkins, A.J., and Dollahite, D.C. (Eds.), 1997, *Generative Fathering: Beyond Deficit Perspectives*, Thousand Oaks, CA: Sage Publications; Lamb, M.E. (Ed.), 1997, *The Role of the Father in Child Development*, 3rd ed., New York: Wiley; Marsiglio, W., Amato, P., Day, R.D., and Lamb, M.E., 2000, "Scholarship on Fatherhood in the 1990s and Beyond," *Journal of Marriage and the Family*, 62(4), 1173–1191.

3. LaRossa, R., 1988, "Fatherhood and Social Change," *Family Relations*, 37, 451–457.

4. Doherty, W.J., 1991, "Beyond Reactivity and the Deficit Model of Manhood: A Comment on Articles by Napier, Pittman, and Gottman," *Journal of Marital and Family Therapy*, 17, 29–32; Hawkins, A.J., and D.C. Dollahite (Eds.), 1997.

5. Doherty, W.J., 1997, "The Best of Times and the Worst of Times: Fathering as a Contested Arena of Academic Discourse," in *Generative Fathering: Beyond Deficit Perspectives*, edited by A.J. Hawkins and D.C. Dollahite, Thousand Oaks, CA: Sage Publications, pp. 217–227, at 221.

6. Amato, P.R., and Booth, A., 1997, *A Generation at Risk: Growing Up in an Era of Family Upheaval*, Cambridge, MA: Harvard University Press.

7. Canfield, 1996.

8. Palkovitz, R., 2002, *Involved Fathering and Men's Adult Development: Provisional Balances*, Mahwah, NJ: Lawrence Erlbaum Associates.

9. Erikson, E.H., 1963, *Childhood and Society*, New York: W.W. Norton.

10. Horn, W., and Sylvester, T., 2002, *Father Facts*, 4th ed., Gaithersburg, MD: National Fatherhood Initiative, at 10.

11. Mosley, J., and Thomson, E., 1995, "Fathering Behavior and Child Outcomes: The Role of Race and Poverty," in *Fatherhood: Contemporary Theory, Research, and Social Policy*, edited by W. Marsiglio, Thousand Oaks, CA: Sage Publications, pp. 148–165.

12. Koestner, R., Franz, C., and Weinberger, J., 1990, "The Family Origins of Empathic Concern: A 26-Year Longitudinal Study," *Journal of Personality and Social Psychology*, 58, 709–717.

13. Biller, H.B., and Kimpton, J.L., 1997, "The Father and the School-Aged Child," in *The Role of the Father in Child Development*, 3rd ed., edited by M.E. Lamb, New York: Wiley, pp. 143–161.

14. Child Trends, 2004, "Children in Poverty," accessed January 18, 2006, at www.childtrendsdatabank.org/indicators/4poverty.cfm.

15. Mott, F., 1993, "Absent Fathers and Child Development: Emotional and Cognitive Effects at Ages Five to Nine," Ohio State University.

16. Snarey, J., 1993, *How Fathers Care for the Next Generation: A Four-Decade Study*, Cambridge, MA: Harvard University Press, at 356.

17. Pleck, E.H., and Pleck, J.H., 1997, "Fatherhood Ideals in the United States: Historical Dimensions," in *The Role of the Father in Child Development*, 3rd ed., edited by M.E. Lamb, New York: Wiley, pp. 33–48, at 33.

18. Pleck, E.H., and Pleck, J.H., 1997, pp. 33–48.

19. Ibid.

20. Furstenberg, F.F., Jr., 1988, "Good Dads—Bad Dads: Two Faces of Fatherhood," in *The Changing American Family and Public Policy*, edited by A.J. Cherlin (Ed.), Washington, DC: Urban Institute Press, pp. 193–218.

21. Pleck, E.H., and Pleck, J.H., 1997.

22. Ibid.

23. Ibid.

24. Marsiglio et al., 2000, at 1174.

25. Doherty et al., 1998; Hawkins and Dollahite (Eds.), 1997.

26. Hawkins, A.J., and Dollahite, D.C., 1994, invited essay/book review—of Gerson, K., 1993, *No Man's Land: Men's Changing Commitments to Family and Work*, New York: Basic; Hood, J.C. (Ed.), 1993, *Men, Work, and Family*, Newbury Park, CA: Sage; Rotundo, E.A., 1993, *American Manhood: Transformations in Masculinity from the Revolution to the Modern Era*, New York: Basic; Schoenberg, B.M., 1993, *Growing Up Male: The Psychology of Masculinity*, Westport, CT: Bergin and Garvey; Snarey, J., 1993, *How Fathers Care for the Next Generation: A Four-Decade Study*, Cambridge, MA: Harvard University—in *Journal of Marriage and the Family*, 56(3), 772–776, at 774.

27. Hawkins and Dollahite (Eds.), 1997.

28. Lavee, Y., and Dollahite, D.C., 1991, "The Linkage between Theory and Research in Family Science," *Journal of Marriage and the Family*, 53(2), 361–373.

29. Doherty, W.J., Kouneski, E.F., and Erickson, M.F., 1998; Dollahite, D.C., Hawkins, A.J., and Brotherson, S.E., 1997, "Fatherwork: A Conceptual Ethic of Fathering as Generative Work," in *Generative Fathering: Beyond Deficit*

Perspectives, edited by A.J. Hawkins and D.C. Dollahite, Thousand Oaks, CA: Sage Publications, pp. 17–35.

30. Snarey, 1993, at 19.

31. Erikson, 1963, at 130.

32. Hawkins, A.J., and Dollahite, D.C. (Eds.), 1997.

33. Dollahite, D.C., 2003, "Fathering for Eternity: Generative Spirituality in Latter-Day Saint Fathers of Children with Special Needs," *Review of Religious Research*, 44, 237–251.

34. Erikson, E.H., 1975, *Life History and the Historical Moment*, New York: Norton.

35. Snarey, 1993, at 19.

36. Levinas, E., 1985, *Ethics and Infinity*, Pittsburgh, PA: Duquesne University Press.

37. Elshtain, J.B., 1993, "Families, Communities, and Habits of the Heart," presented at the Annual Conference of the National Council on Family Relations, Baltimore, MD, at 3.

38. Warner, T.C., 1993, *Bonds of Anguish, Bonds of Love*, Provo, UT: Brigham Young University.

39. Boss, P., 1999, *Ambiguous Loss*, Cambridge, MA: Harvard University Press.

40. Ibid.

41. Popenoe, D., 1996, *Life without Father*, Cambridge, MA: Harvard University Press.

42. Ibid., at 228.

I

Fathers and Family Relationships

The five chapters in this section explore the topic of fathering in different family relationship contexts, including becoming a father (transition to parenthood), fathers and mothers, fathers and marriage, father-daughter relationships, and grandfathering.

In Chapter 2, "Transitions to Fatherhood," Rob Palkovitz suggests that becoming a father prompts most men to search for a "how to" manual and job description at first and then goes on to outline how the fathering experience initiates an ongoing series of life changes and transitions for most men. He describes how transitions tied to fatherhood include both the changes in thinking and behavior that occur for men as well as the multiple paths a man may take to fatherhood (biological father, stepfather, adoptive father, etc.). He discusses some key elements of becoming a father, including individual decisions, preparation, the birth experience, providing for a family, and maintaining healthy relationships.

In Chapter 3, which addresses "How Mothers and Fathers Help Each Other Count," Erin Holmes, Tera Duncan, Sherri Bair, and Alice White explore how mothers and their expectations contribute to good fathering. The authors share perspectives on how mothers influence men's understanding of their roles as fathers and facilitate their active involvement. They also furnish concrete suggestions for how mothers and fathers can influence each other positively, including maintaining a positive climate in the home, accepting help from one another, making parenting decisions together, and responding to each other's needs.

The topic of marriage and fathering is explored in Chapter 4, "Better Marriages Make for Better Fathering," and H. Wallace Goddard presents new insights on marriage from recent research findings. He outlines a fresh and practical set of principles for establishing healthy marital relationships that also support active and caring father involvement. His careful exploration of key principles such as growth, understanding, solutions, and service in the marital and parenting context, as well as related key practices, gives insight into approaches that can strengthen men as both husbands and fathers.

In Chapter 5, "The Daddy-Daughter Dance: Insights for Father-Daughter Relationships," Scott Hall and Neil Tift share their accumulated knowledge and practical experience to illumine the relationship dance that occurs as fathers raise and interact with their daughters. As family scholars and fathers of daughters themselves, they discuss portrayals of father-daughter relationships in media and history, address research findings that show the importance of fathers to daughters, and provide suggestions for fathers and daughters to help develop and enhance their relationship. Issues that emerge from their discussion of the father-daughter relationship dance include learning from each other's diverse perspectives, promoting healthy individual development, creating a template for close relationships, and influencing a positive female identity.

A final relationship context is addressed in Chapter 6, "Grandfathers—Rediscovering America's Forgotten Resource," and Alan Taylor argues for the significance of grandfathers in linking families together over generations and nurturing their growth. He describes how grandfathers exert influence in family life through shaping a child's sense of identity, transmitting family values, and serving as an example of caring and respect. Roles that grandfathers play range from family historian to role model, and Taylor gives an overview of themes that emerge from his research on how grandfathers work to fashion stronger intergenerational relationships.

This first section of the book grounds the experience of fathering in primary family relationships, showing how a variety of relationships give substance to and shape the experience of fathering for men and the children they seek to care for and love.

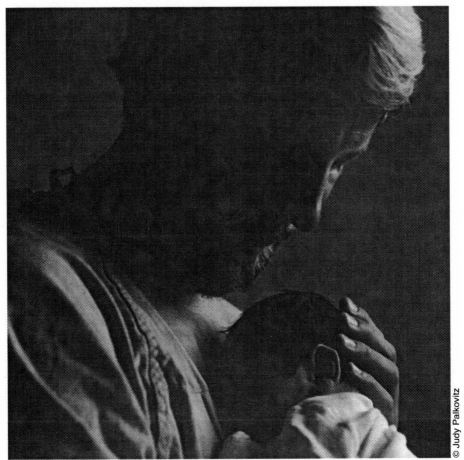

Author Rob Palkovitz holds his son, Nathan, within a few minutes of his birth.

Transitions to Fatherhood

Rob Palkovitz

My transition to fatherhood took place a little more than 25 years ago. I still vividly remember the excitement, the fears, the concerns, the self-searching, and the changes ushered in by this life-transforming event. Over a quarter of a century later, after the birth, growth, and development of four sons, I can still recall the monumental nature of becoming a father for the first time.

I was a student enrolled in a Ph.D. program in developmental psychology. I had completed my master's degree training and all of my coursework for the Ph.D. and was well on my way to becoming an expert in child development. My wife and I had dated for five years through high school and college and had been happily married for three and a half years. We were in a good place as a couple. However, upon hearing the news of our pregnancy, I came to the sudden and disconcerting realization that, though I was a fledgling expert in child development, I knew little about fathering. I felt a desperate urgency to read the professional literature on fathering to get a clear "how to" manual and job description. Unfortunately, in 1979, there was not much professional literature on fathering. Most important, I knew there were areas of my life in which I needed to change significantly, take on greater responsibility, and mature if I were to be in a position to be a "good dad" in a few short months.

Looking back today, I can see that choosing to be an involved father has provided me with an unending string of transitions that have facilitated my adult development in ways I never anticipated—even as a student of human development. The transition to fatherhood initiates a series of subsequent changes that follow as both children and parents grow and develop through various stages and contexts of life. Fathers spend their time and money differently than nonfathers. Men's thoughts and emotions are focused differently, the importance they place on work changes, they often revisit concepts of spirituality, and they consider health and nutrition differently once they have children. Fathers view their lives, their family experiences, and world conditions and events through the eyes of their children, and thus their understandings, priorities, and decisions are different from those of childless men. As children grow and develop through different stages of interests and abilities, involved fathers experience a constantly changing set of events and emotions.

With the certainty of experience and expanding support from empirical research, I can now attest to the fact that the transition to fatherhood is truly a life-changing event with lasting import. This is true not only for me personally but for virtually every man who has ever participated in a study of fathering—and, presumably, for all fathers who have not!

"The Child is Father to the Man"

Based on his keen observations, the British poet William Wordsworth wisely stated that "the child is father to the man." This eloquently describes the dramatic steps toward maturity that fathers commonly take. Any man can tell you when he first became a father. This attests to the fact that the transition to fatherhood serves as an important marker in the life of a man.[1] It represents a dramatic and life-changing occurrence not only for fathers and their children but also for their families, friends, and fellow community members.

As men make the transition to fatherhood, they take on a new status not only in their own eyes but also in the eyes of their families, friends, coworkers, and neighbors. Fathers are regarded as having greater responsibility and therefore are expected to exhibit different qualities and character than men who are not fathers.[2] Men who embrace the role of father experience some prescriptive challenges that dictate important changes in their lives. For example, they typically no longer run with their buddies to the bowling alley or the sports bar at a moment's notice. They may change their partying lifestyle and reduce risk-taking behaviors. As they become fathers, men are challenged to rise to a new, higher level of functioning in relationships, work, and personal conduct.[3]

Therefore, the transition to fatherhood often serves as a threshold to maturity, fulfillment, generativity, and a feeling that one is making a lasting mark.[4,5] The transition to fatherhood launches men into an adventure that lasts for a major portion (if not all) of adult life.[6] This adventure of parenting ushers in a lifetime of change and development that men not making the transition to fatherhood do not experience.[7] Fathering provides a different environment for men's growth intellectually, physically, socially, emotionally, and spiritually. It is like an engine that drives growth and development in men.

After the transition to fatherhood, men think about things they have never focused on from new and different points of view. Fathers frequently change their eating habits, substance use, and exercise routines. They tend to spend more time with other parents and extended family members and less time in men-only settings. Fathers experience a new intensity and quality of feelings that can be experienced only in the context of being a dad. Fathers also place a new importance on spirituality. Therefore, fathering represents a meaningful and challenging developmental context for men. Being a father is typically given priority, time, attention, energy, and other resources in a unique way and to a greater extent than most other life contexts. Thus, fathering has the potential to usher in a great degree of developmental change for men who are engaged in it.[8] The transition to fatherhood requires a readjustment of tasks and priorities, transforms couples into "families," and typically provides a high degree of satisfaction to fathers.[9] In short, the transition to fatherhood plays a uniquely challenging and potentially monumental role in men's lives as they adjust to the joys, dreams, challenges, and needs represented by the role of father.

Diversity in Transitions to Fatherhood

The title of this chapter uses the plural form of transition explicitly— acknowledging that there are multiple paths to fatherhood.[10] These paths may include becoming a biological father, a stepfather, an adoptive father, or a father figure. Within these general categories, men may be "on time" in regard to the social clock, or they may make the transition to fatherhood "early" or "late" (ahead of or behind socially prescribed appropriate times).[11] The degree of planning, readiness, and desire for a child can vary greatly among men and within couples. It is critical to understand the reality that the transition to fatherhood occurs in a multitude of contexts that reflect the diversity of men's lives.

Some men have tried to have children for years, some want children someday but do not feel ready at the time of an unplanned pregnancy, and some feel that having a child will be their undoing as a person. Their wives or partners may be feeling similarly, or they may be in a completely different place in their desire and readiness for a child. New fathers may be married or unmarried. The unmarried men may be fathers as the result of brief or casual sexual encounters or cohabitations of varying duration; they might be separated, divorced, or widowed. In addition, men making the transition to fatherhood may be residential or nonresidential dads. Nonresidential dads may live near their children or at a distance and may vary greatly in the amount of their ongoing contact and involvement with their children. Further, though there is considerable overlap in fathering roles across cultural contexts, different cultures and subcultures emphasize different elements of fathering roles to different extents.[12] Men with different levels of economic assets have access to different resources. Men make the transition to fatherhood at a wide array of ages and in different states of personal, career, and relational development.[13]

The main point of this discussion is that there are many ways to approach the transition to fatherhood, in a variety of contexts and always within the framework of ongoing relationships and life changes. Each man making a transition to fatherhood brings to it a unique set of characteristics, strengths, and weaknesses. Every man making the transition to fatherhood assumes a new role, redefines old roles, and faces new challenges and questions that he may have never before considered.[14]

Virtually all men who make the transition to fatherhood view it as a monumental step, changing many aspects of their daily lives, and ultimately altering the person they were becoming before being a dad. However, not all men who are legally or otherwise recognized as fathers actually make the transition to fatherhood. Conversely, some men who are not recognized with official fathering status do make the transition to fatherhood. What does it mean to make the transition to fatherhood, and what are the factors that facilitate and hinder that transition?

What Is the Transition to Fatherhood?

The transition to fatherhood is not signaled simply by the event of a child's birth. It also encompasses the psychological and behavioral adjustments men go through in response to the presence of a child in their lives who needs fathering. In and of itself, the physical act of having a child does not propel one into the transition to fatherhood. Also, just going through the motions of behaviors associated with being a dad does not reflect this transition. A transition to fatherhood requires both cognitive restructuring (changes in role identities, priorities, etc.) and appropriate accompanying behavioral changes.[15] In other words, men making a transition to fatherhood begin to both think differently about themselves and act differently in their lives and relationships.

The cognitive restructurings of the transition involve issues such as consideration of the meanings of fathering and how fathering roles are envisioned and feared.[16] These mental shifts shape fathers' behavior through both modeling (attempting to make one's life conform to the patterns of positive examples set by fathers) and reworking (attempting to make one's life diverge from the patterns of negative examples set by fathers).[17] In short, a transition requires a change in behavior, in roles, and in thinking about the self in relation to the new role.[18] The bottom line is that fathers think thoughts of different kinds and frequency than nonfathers. For example, they engage in a high degree of contingency planning that men without children do not need to consider (such as what to do if the baby sitter cancels). They have a new set of roles that are central to their identity such as child's playmate and provider for family members. Fathers consider what it means to be a dad as well as a husband, a worker, or a board member. Fathers have an extra layer of expectations and commitments to weigh in their choices and behavior. It is in considering and balancing these various, and often competing, needs that fathers experience a different daily reality than those who are not fathers.

Transitions Take Time

It is important to recognize that transitions are not instantaneous. By definition, they entail processes that take time. There is no specific marker that can be applied for assessment of having attained the transition to fatherhood. A Chinese proverb states, "Be not afraid of going slowly; be afraid only of standing still."

The many changes associated with the transition to fatherhood take time, though some men seem to immediately "snap" into the role of father.[19] For most men, fathering is a role they grow into slowly and gradually. In reality, transitions are not "all or nothing" events. They involve multiple aspects, and because fathering is a complex role consisting of many different components, it is possible to exhibit fatherly behavior or attitudes in some areas but not in others. Fathers frequently ask themselves, "How am I doing as a dad in regard to work? Providing for my family? Protecting my kids? Being a role model? Being a spiritual guide?" Some men may make the transition to fatherhood earlier in some of those areas than others. Some men make fathering transitions in some but not in all of the areas mentioned. This adds to the diversity observed in men's transitions to fatherhood.

Transitions, by definition, cause disequilibrium, require change, and represent both an opportunity for new development and the risk of failing to rise to the

---

What Happens in Becoming a Father?

It is often the case that assuming the role of father causes a man to become reflective and take stock of how he is doing in a broad range of areas. This self-examination takes place in the new context of what it means to be a father and entails a different level and kind of motivation than prior introspection. What does becoming a father spur men to think about?

- Fatherhood causes men to reflect on how they were raised and to make conscious decisions about how they want to be as a dad.
- Fatherhood motivates men to think about provision, protection, moral guidance, friendship, marriage, work, teaching, and living in a new and often unfamiliar context.
- Fatherhood typically triggers changes in men's degree of responsibility, maturity, settling down, and risk taking.
- Fatherhood prompts men to examine the consistency or hypocrisy in their values, morals, and behaviors.
- Fatherhood encourages men to reconsider their health practices in terms of substance use, food preferences, exercise, and the general manner in which they take care of themselves.
- Fatherhood sometimes initiates for men a sort of deadline to bring about changes they had been hoping to facilitate for some time. They feel the need to get things in order before their children are old enough for their own harmful behaviors to negatively affect their children's development.

Becoming a father brings new importance to these issues as well as a deadline for compliance with the goals or standards they adopt. Making the transition to fatherhood puts a "developmental pull" on men to rise to the occasion to become good dads, and the net result is that they become better people. In many practical ways, Wordsworth was right: the child is father to the man.

---

occasion. Therefore, transitions are often portrayed as crises or obstacles to an otherwise stable existence. Many people understand the term *crisis* only in negative terms, but it simply means a turning point—not necessarily a difficult or stressful event. It actually signals change, and without change, there is no development. While all transitions are characterized by a degree of uncertainty and associated stresses, they represent true developmental opportunities. Becoming a father represents a genuine opportunity for men to grow and develop in ways that affect both themselves and their children.

Key Factors and Processes in Transitions to Fatherhood

Fathering is seldom something that is stepped into instantly. Most men making the transition to fatherhood are aware of this impending reality and work with some specific goals and focused energy to accomplish their goals in becoming a father. Though it is possible to be unexpectedly informed that one has fathered a child and is now being asked to take on some level of responsibility for that child, the most common route to fatherhood involves conceiving a child and becoming aware of the pregnancy at some later time. This typically allows time to adjust to the idea of being a father. Adoption similarly requires a process of filing paperwork, meeting with officials, completing home studies, and navigating myriad obstacles that take time. Becoming a stepdad involves the development of a relationship that spans time and phases whereby one becomes recognized as a father (both to oneself and to any number of stepchildren of various ages and developmental levels). So, while transitions require change, most new dads have time to implement changes and to develop in a manner that is consistent with the role of father. A variety of key factors and processes involved in transitions to fatherhood include (1) the timing of becoming a father, (2) the decision to make the transition, (3) preparation for fatherhood, (4) the birthing experience, (5) personal changes in the transition to fatherhood, (6) providing for a family, and (7) relationships and a support network for fatherhood.

Timing of Transitions to Fatherhood

Transitions to fatherhood can take place in any number of social contexts and at different ages. A 19-year-old Hispanic man in urban Chicago may become a father at the same time as a 57-year-old farmer in rural Georgia. Men undergoing the transition to fatherhood experience vastly different challenges. The transition experience for each father comes with its own timetable, trajectory, and set of tasks.

Men who are "early timing" fathers may still be attempting to figure out who they are as people, establish stable relationships with a significant other, and select and launch a career track. Conversely, men who are "late timing" fathers often have dealt with many of the issues of maturity, responsibility, relationships, and careers but find challenges in negotiating the multitude of changes ushered in by having an infant or child in an otherwise stable, familiar, and predictable lifestyle. It can be very disconcerting for an older father who is used to relating to mature people to have to change his scheduled, ordered world to fit the unpredictable and often messy world of feedings, diapers, and emotional variability of an infant. Men who make the transition to fatherhood "on time" tend to exhibit a greater degree of psychosocial readiness to become fathers than early-timing dads. They also tend to have the largest group of friends and peers who can offer various kinds of social support as they become fathers.

The timing of a man's transition to fatherhood is important because men of different ages have different levels of maturity, expectations for behavior, sets of resources, and personal needs. Teens have different levels of maturity, educational and career attainment, and practical experience in establishing and maintaining households and relationships than 40-year olds. Thus, early- and late-timing fathers experience different kinds of shifts in their lives as they become dads. The "easiest" transitions to fatherhood are experienced by on-time dads because supports are geared toward their circumstances and they have the largest number of peers also making the transition to fatherhood. However, men of any maturity level can make positive transitions to fatherhood with enough support and resources.

Individual Decisions and Transitions to Fatherhood

As men navigate the changes associated with becoming a father, in reality the transition to fatherhood does not so much depend on others' support, encouragement, or other contributions. It is most facilitated by the decision the individual father makes to embrace the role of father, give it high priority, engage the role with a sense of awe and adventure as well as responsibility, and build a relationship with his children one day at a time. Men who are dissatisfied with the level of relationship they have with their children at any given time and endeavor to improve upon it in sensitive, caring, and developmentally appropriate ways build positive relationships with their children and are viewed as good dads. Though there is legislation to sequester wages and enforce paternal responsibility, such efforts really have little to do with the transition to fatherhood. The transition involves a volitional decision to be involved with children, to engage in behavior that will support their development, and to provide them with opportunities, experiences, and resources that will foster their growth. The transition to fatherhood cannot be legislated. Though behavioral compliance may follow court orders, men who require such measures may have become "legal fathers" without having made the more important transition to "social fathers" or "daddies."

Preparation for Becoming a Father

The process of making the transition involves numerous small but significant steps that prepare the way for fathers to accept their new roles and responsibilities. These may vary depending on the route to fatherhood a man experiences. For example, important junctures in the transition for biological fathers may include:

- plans and communication with spouse/partner regarding having children,
- learning of the partner's pregnancy,
- adjusting to concordance or discordance between the timing of the pregnancy and plans for parenting,
- feeling the baby's movement,

- seeing an ultrasound image of the child,
- attending childbirth preparation classes,
- attending the baby's birth,
- holding the baby, and
- having time with the baby both together with one's spouse and alone.

Individual or multiple steps in the progression of events may be missed, but each represents an opportunity for cognitive and behavioral adjustments important in the transition to fatherhood. Men who become adoptive or step fathers have a different but parallel set of important encounters with their children that stimulate the cognitive and behavioral changes associated with the transition to fatherhood.[20] Such preparatory steps assist men to more fully assume the responsibilities associated with parenting a child.

The Birthing Experience and Fatherhood

The actual birth of a child marks a key point in the transition to biological fatherhood. Some people place undue attention and importance on the birthing experience. Though it is a unique and often wonderful and transforming event to participate in, an objective review of the "bonding" literature indicates there is no empirical evidence that men who witness the birth of their children have enduringly more positive relationships with them.[21] In fact, prior research has shown that men who are excluded from the birth of their children (men who desired to attend but were prevented from attendance by policies or circumstances) actually are more involved with their children at five months of age than men who attended the birth, at least in the presence of their wives.[22] These findings demonstrate that it is not so much participation in a particular event that makes the difference in the transition to fatherhood; rather, it is a desire to be involved in the ongoing relationships, life, and development of a child that marks men as "daddies." Men should be encouraged, however, to plan for and participate in their child's birth experience if at all possible as a meaningful step in their transition to fatherhood.

Personal Change in Transitions to Fatherhood

Becoming a father imposes a sort of deadline for many kinds of changes that men may want to make in their lives. Such changes may relate to their health, lifestyle, work, or relationships. For example, knowing a child will be born in seven months (a real-time event) provides a time frame (within some level of predictability, plus or minus a number of months) and target dates for ushering in the perceived needed changes. It may be that a father wants to stop smoking immediately because of the effects of secondhand smoke on his partner and their unborn child. Alternatively, he may decide that smoking cessation could wait until his child is two or three. He may reason that if he smokes outside or only in well-ven-

Practical Tips on the Transition to Fatherhood

These recommendations are geared toward men who are becoming fathers to infants, but many of the suggestions apply to men becoming stepdads or father figures to children of different ages, with minor adaptations.

Thinking and Talking about What Fathering Means to You
- Talk with others about fathering and what it is like to experience the joys and challenges of fathering.
- Go out to eat with a friend who is a dad whom you admire for his fathering relationships and ask him what fathering is like. Talk about the joys and challenges of fathering.
- Talk with your own dad to find out what he viewed as the biggest challenges of becoming a new dad. What worked for him?
- Discuss what you view to be your greatest strengths as a dad as well as the biggest challenges for you.
- Talk with your partner about what she needs from you as a co-parent.
- Discuss the kinds of support you may need from your partner.
- Watch some films that portray good dads and talk through the films with your partner or a close friend.
- Go online or to the library and read basic information about the development of infants and children. Discuss the material with your wife or partner.
- Go on the Internet and find some fathering websites. Use the search terms "fathering," "father involvement," or "fathering forum" to find current sites.

Preparing for the Birth
- Go to childbirth preparation classes with your wife or partner.
- Talk with your partner about her pregnancy and how you can help her to adjust and prepare for the birth.
- Discuss ways you can be involved with your infant. Ask for information about areas in which you feel unprepared.
- Attend the birth if you can.
- Be part of preparing the nursery and gathering the supplies and equipment necessary for your baby.

When the Baby Comes Home
- Get involved with infant care as soon as you can: change a diaper; bathe the baby.
- Spend some time alone with your child.

- Be involved in picture taking, and share in visits with friends and family. Talk with them about yourself as a dad.
- Think about a fathering goal for each day and grade yourself at the end of the day. Did you accomplish your goal? How well? What could you do differently to be an even better dad tomorrow?

Planning for and Envisioning the Future
- Plan now for your baby's financial future: start a savings plan, no matter how small. Try to contribute regularly (including every birthday).
- Set some specific goals for your first year of fathering. These may be specific things to do, ways to be, or caregiving plans.
- Set a rough five-year plan for being a good dad. List some specific objectives or characteristics you can try to develop. Talk about these with your partner. Review the list every six months with her.
- Think about your own life and your child's life with a big picture in mind. See yourself as a "person builder," and think about what your child needs to become the best possible person. Position yourself to provide those things.

tilated areas he can wait to make this change until modeling for the child becomes an issue. The point is that different men will have different adjustments to make in their behavior, lifestyle, or personalities and will approach the transition to fatherhood with diverse sets of needs, expectations, and timetables. Experts in behavior change recommend setting specific goals for change, in reasonable increments and with appropriate supports and rewards in place. It is important for planned changes to be undertaken in a reasonable time frame and in doable steps. Becoming a father itself is an enormous change, but men also need to remember the transition is a process and not an event, and other personal changes that accompany this transition can help them to navigate the transition successfully.

Providing for a Child

Providing for a child represents one of the important markers of the transition to fatherhood and signals a new level of responsibility for many men. New fathers need to feel they are capable of providing for the material needs of their children and that they can contribute significantly to their child's ongoing care and nurturance. Men who make positive transitions to fatherhood either sense a goodness of fit between what is needed by their families and what they can provide or see a lack of fit but determine appropriate ways and means to obtain what is needed. What happens to men who may feel they are incapable of providing for the material needs of their children? Unfortunately, some "cut and run" because they view providing to be such a large part of fathering. They reason that, if they cannot adequately provide for their child's needs, they must not be good fathers, and they abandon efforts to make the necessary changes. In contrast, some men may feel responsible to develop capacities for care and provision and thus seek out educational or work opportunities that will enable them to develop such capacities. Such abilities come only through effort and experience across time. Fortunately, transitions take time, and parenting allows for growth in this and other important areas of caring for children.

Facilitating Positive Relationships and Fatherhood

Making a positive transition to fatherhood can help to get your relationships and roles off to a good start, but it is not the end of the successful fatherhood recipe. Some men experience a "jolt" in their thoughts, feelings, or lifestyles when they learn that they are expecting children.[23] Other men accept this role gradually and take time to adjust to new expectations and responsibilities. However, no matter where a man is in his perceived readiness for fatherhood or in his relationship with his child, he can set goals for more positive and developmentally facilitative relationships. A child is born into a community of relationships, and so fathers must work to care for and maintain those relationships. It helps to remember that transitions take time, that they are continuous, and that it is only possible to build from where one is. The transition to fatherhood brings changes into existing relationships and creates ones that did not exist before.[24] New fathers often comment on the need to share time and attention with their child. They most notably feel they receive diminished attention from their spouse or partner.[25] Men must adapt not only to the relationship with a new child but also to how this relationship changes their other relationships.

Fathers note that being a father carries a different degree of responsibility than does being a husband or partner.[26] They recognize that their partner is in a voluntary relationship and is their peer. It is not the same with children: their children didn't select them, have little choice about remaining in their care until adulthood, and are not peers. Being a father also places greater responsibility on men as a spouse or partner because fathers are modeling behavior in such intimate relationships for their children. Parents may work harder than couples without children to present a unified front because they feel an obligation to shield children from arguments and serious disagreements. Affirmative, ongoing communication with a spouse or partner is an important factor in facilitating a positive transition to fatherhood. The communication should ideally include discussion of hopes, dreams, fears, thoughts, and feelings associated with fathering.

As men make the transition to fatherhood, they can also discuss the changes happening in their lives with members of a support network beyond the spouse or partner. A support network can include other family members (parents, siblings, aunts, uncles, etc.) and friends. Many of the people in the extended support network have practical parenting experience and advice that can be shared. Other people can facilitate the transition to fatherhood through providing information, encouragement, respite, examples, instruction, and companionship. Paying attention to and valuing the constructive help of a support network can facilitate positive relationships as fathers make this transition.

Conclusion

Perhaps fathering can best be understood as a process through which men demonstrate care and support for their children on an ongoing basis over time.[27] Men are fathers only in relation to a child. The transition to fatherhood thereby implies the existence of and ongoing relationship with another, intergenerational, developing individual. Doing what is necessary to fulfill the role of father to children requires continual adjustment, empathy, understanding, connection, communication, work, time, adjustment, and care. That is why the transition to fatherhood is such a monumental marker in the lives of most men. Simply stated, most men perceive that being a dad significantly changes their lives. They somehow recognize that, to fulfill the hopes and dreams of being a good father, they will need to rise to much greater heights. In this way, fathering exerts a developmental influence on men and can enhance their growth.

It has not been uncommon for some professionals to criticize the literature on fathering as providing a "deficit" perspective (that is, the literature often focuses on the inadequacies of fathers), and much of that criticism is warranted. However, it is also true that most men will readily admit that, no matter how good a father they may perceive themselves to be, there is always room for improvement. Therefore, fathers themselves work from deficit models, seeing the distance between their ideal levels of functioning and their real levels of performance to date. Fatherhood scholars have discussed this as a gap between the culture of fatherhood (the socially prescribed expectations and roles for dads in a culture or subculture) and the conduct of fatherhood (the actual behavior of real fathers).[28] There is always a gap between the ideal and the real. Faced with the discrepancy between the two, some men make concerted efforts and plans to improve and narrow the gap until their ideals are achieved. Others see the gap as unbridgeable and just accept the difference, continually feeling they are not good dads. Still others see the gap as unbridgeable and the differences as unacceptable and so choose to withdraw from active engagement in fathering in minor or major ways. In the most drastic cases, there is complete separation of the father from the family. In less drastic cases, work, volunteer work, or social commitments keep the father from confronting his gap between the ideal and the real.

In conclusion, the transition to fatherhood represents a monumental turning point in a man's life. There are countless ways to make the transition and many components to the changes that occur. The transition involves numerous processes that take time and a series of ongoing changes that continue across the span of the father-child relationship. It is inappropriate to place undue emphasis on any one event or context of the transition to fatherhood, because it represents a broad-based and multifaceted set of adjustments with repeated opportunities for change. Men who embrace an active role in the ongoing and developing relationship with their children experience a developmental draw that is qualitatively distinct from other contexts of adult development. Therefore, the transition to fatherhood represents what may be potentially among the greatest change agents in a man's life and development as a person.

Endnotes

1. Cowan, P.A., 1991, "Individual and Family Life Transitions: A Proposal for a New Definition," in *Family Transitions*, edited by P.A. Cowan and M. Hetherington, Hillsdale, N.J.: Lawrence Erlbaum and Associates, pp. 3–30; Fawcett, J.T., 1988, "The Value of Children and the Transition to Parenthood," in *Transitions to Parenthood*, edited by R. Palkovitz and M.B. Sussman, New York: Haworth Press, pp.11–34.

2. Hoffman, M.L., and Manis, J.D., 1979, "The Value of Children in the United States: A New Approach to the Study of Fertility," *Journal of Marriage and the Family*, 41, 583–596; Newman, P.R., and Newman, B.M., 1988, "Parenthood and Adult Development," in *Transitions to Parenthood*, edited by R. Palkovitz and M.B. Sussman, New York: Haworth Press, pp. 313–338.

3. Palkovitz, R., 2002, *Involved Fathering and Men's Adult Development: Provisional Balances*, Mahwah, NJ: Lawrence Erlbaum Associates, Inc.

4. Hoffman and Manis, 1979; Newman, P.R., and Newman, B.M., 1988, pp. 313–338.

5. Snarey, J., 1993, *How Fathers Care for the Next Generation: A Four-Decade Study*, Cambridge, MA: Harvard University Press.

6. Rossi, A.S., and Rossi, P.H., 1992, *Of Human Bonding*, New York: Aldine deGruyter.

7. Palkovitz, R., 1988, "Trials and Triumphs in the Transition to Parenthood," *Marriage and Family Review*, 12, 1–5.

8. Ibid.

9. Hoffman and Manis, 1979; Newman, P.R., and Newman, B.M., 1988; Palkovitz, 2002.

10. Marsiglio, W., 1998, *Procreative Man*, New York: New York University Press.

11. Cooney, T.M., Pedersen, F.A., Indelicato, S., and Palkovitz, R., 1993, "Timing of Fatherhood: Is 'On Time' Optimal?" *Journal of Marriage and the Family*, 55, 205–215.

12. Hewlett, B.S., 2000, "Culture, History, and Sex: Anthropological Contributions to Conceptualizing Father Involvement," *Marriage and Family Review*, 29, 59–73.

13. Cooney et al., 1993.

14. Palkovitz, 1988.

15. Cowan, 1991.

16. Daly, K.J., 1995, "Reshaping Fatherhood: Finding the Models," in *Fatherhood: Contemporary Theory, Research and Social Policy*, edited by W. Marsiglio, Thousand Oaks, CA: Sage, pp. 21–40.

17. Palkovitz, 2002; Snarey, 1993.

18. Cowan, 1991.

19. Daniels, P., and Weingarten, K., 1988, "The Fatherhood Click: The Timing of Fatherhood in Men's Lives," in *Fatherhood Today: Men's Changing Role in the Family*, edited by P. Bronstein and C.P. Cowan, New York: Wiley, pp. 36–53.

20. Brodzinsky, D.L., and Huffman, L., 1988, "Transition to Adoptive Parenthood," in *Transitions to Parenthood*, edited by R. Palkovitz and M.B. Sussman, New York: Haworth Press, pp. 267–286.

21. Palkovitz, R., 1985, "Fathers' Birth Attendance, Early Contact, and Extended Contact with Their Newborns: A Critical Review," *Child Development*, 56, 392–406.

22. Palkovitz, R., 1984, "Parental Attitudes and Fathers' Interactions with Their Five-Month-Old Infants," *Developmental Psychology*, 20, 1054–1060.

23. Palkovitz, 2002.

24. Palkovitz, 1988.

25. Cowan, C.P., and Cowan, P.A., 1988, "Who Does What When Partners Become Parents: Implications for Men, Women, and Marriage," in *Transitions to Parenthood*, edited by R. Palkovitz and M.B. Sussman, New York: Haworth Press, pp. 105–131.

26. Palkovitz, 2002.

27. MacDonald, D.A., and Almeida, D.M., 2004, "The Interweave of Fathers' Daily Work Experiences and Fathering Behaviors," *Fathering*, 2, 235–251.

28. LaRossa, R., 1988, "Fatherhood and Social Change," *Family Relations*, 37, 451–457.

Author Erin K. Holmes with her husband, Chris, and daughter, Elena

How Mothers and Fathers Help Each Other Count

Erin K. Holmes, Tera B. Duncan, Sherri Bair, and Alice M. White

When Erin watches her husband and daughter giggle together, listens to him gently sing their daughter a lullaby before bed, or watches his patience grow with their daughter's expanding sense of adventure—she is impressed by the love and care he offers their daughter. She is also grateful that her husband desires to foster a close relationship with their child. Though she pondered parent-child relationships and fathers' roles in families for years as a family scholar, she and her husband did not fully appreciate the responsibilities of parenthood until they held their first child in their arms. Now she is discovering firsthand that she needs her husband's help to be a good mother, he needs her support to be a good father, and their daughter needs both parents to develop well. Needing each other enhances the fact that good parenting requires a healthy balancing act, which includes managing childcare, juggling work schedules, and maintaining closeness. This chapter is meant to encourage parents to share the demands of raising children together. It is also an invitation to fathers and mothers to commit to cooperating and collaborating with each other as they nurture their children into adulthood—and beyond.

How do mothers contribute to good fathering? How does being a good partner help a man to be a good father? How do mothers and fathers successfully come together to parent their children well? We, the authors of this chapter, seek to answer these questions as we study ways mothers and fathers meet their needs as parents and as partners. Though we are all mothers, we write this chapter for women and men alike, believing that without a strong connection between mothers and fathers, parenting is more challenging. Throughout the chapter, we offer research, case studies, and personal experiences to show how mothers and fathers can help each other to parent better. We first present ways that good mothering is connected to good fathering. We continue with a discussion about satisfying marriage as an important component of high-quality parenting. We close with ways that mothers and fathers collaborate. Though this chapter focuses on fathers who live with their children, we also include examples and research for those who do not.

The Link between Good Mothering and Good Fathering

In a model of factors affecting responsible fathering, William Doherty and his colleagues suggested that "fathering cannot be defined in isolation from mothering, [or] mothers' expectations."[1] Why might these authors make such a bold statement? One answer comes from evidence that women's ideas about fatherhood influence the way men parent.

For example, women who believe that men can be good parents, that children need a father figure, and that men should participate in childcare and housework are more likely to have partners who display these qualities.[2] Conversely, women who believe that they are better suited to meet children's needs than men are, that women should be primarily responsible for child bearing, and that men cannot develop the skills necessary to effectively care for children are more likely to have partners who are not involved fathers. Though these correlations could be due to the fact that people choose marriage partners with similar ideas about fatherhood, a deeper look at processes in families shows that fathers feel more competent and capable when mothers believe that men can be as good at parenting as women can.[3] Simply stated, women's ideas about men's skills affect the way men think about their capabilities as fathers.

Mothers' attitudes and expectations about fatherhood are related to men's behaviors and ideas about parenting skills. Two studies conducted during the transition to parenthood concluded that mothers' views about fathers were the best predictors of fathers' interactions with their children.[4] When researchers observed mothers, fathers, and infants playing together, mothers' perceptions about fathers' roles were even more reflective of fathers' behaviors with their infants than fathers' own ideas about their roles were. Even when fathers and infants played without mothers present, mothers' ideas about fatherhood were statistically significant predictors of fathers' behaviors with their babies.[5] A woman's expectations, attitudes, and ideas about fatherhood make a difference to fathers. The way most fathers understand their role as parents, the way men think about their competence in parenting, and the way fathers actually act with their children are all related to women's perceptions of fatherhood. For women, there is a central message in these findings: tell men what they do well, tell them that you want them to be involved, and patiently allow them to improve their skills.

Another reason Doherty and his colleagues argue that fathering and mothering are linked is the consistent finding that if men are not living with the mother of their children, they are less likely to financially support their children or to visit their children.[6] In the 1990s, statistics showed that within one year after divorce 18 percent of children sampled did not see their nonresident father at all, and 50 percent said they saw their nonresident fathers less than once a month.[7] The likelihood that fathers will maintain ties with their children and pay child support is even lower if men never marry the mother of their children.[8] Fathers need to pay child support and actively cooperate with mothers to promote their children's well-being. Children whose parents do not cooperate and whose communication is conflict-ridden are more likely to have problems with depression, aggressive behavior at school, and lower academic success.[9] Children whose fathers do not pay child support are much more likely to live in poverty and therefore live in unsafe neighborhoods, display behavior problems, have lower educational attainment, and bear a child as a teen or unmarried adult.[10] These statistics demonstrate persuasively that maintaining a good relationship with the mother is one valuable way that fathers build relationships with their children.

Finally, mothering and fathering are connected because the quality of a man's marriage influences the amount of time he spends with his children.[11] The more satisfied a man reports being with his marriage, the more likely he is to spend time taking care of his children. While the quality of a woman's marriage may influence how well she parents her children on a given day, her reports of overall marital satisfaction do not predict whether or not she will spend time with her children. In fact, some women may turn to their children more when their marriages are going sour.[12] For men, however, there is a clear and distinct link between the quality of their relationships with women and their involvement with children.

What is it about marriage that would make a man more likely to be involved with his children when his marital satisfaction is high but less likely when his marital satisfaction is low?

The Link between Marriage and Good Fathering

Not all mothers and fathers who share children are married to one another. However, research shows that the dynamics in a marital relationship strongly affect both mothers and fathers in their parenting. Healthy marriages tend to strengthen father involvement, troubled marriages tend to diminish father involvement, and the relationship quality between mothers and fathers is critical to a father's involvement following divorce.

Strong Marriages and Increased Father Involvement

Research suggests that when marital satisfaction is high, fathers are more engaged with their children, more satisfied with their role as fathers, and less likely to experience stress about parenting.[13] Men with strong, positive marital relationships also feel more confident in their skills and are happier to be fathers.[14] Over time, good spousal relationships lead to fathers' optimism and sense of control regarding parenting.[15] Finally, dads in close marriages are more sensitive to their infants' needs.[16] All of these findings suggest that a close marriage provides a context for increased positive feelings about the work of fathering. These results are consistent with more recent findings that strong identification with the paternal role, mothers' perceptions of fathers' parenting skills, and marital satisfaction all predict paternal involvement.[17] A good marriage tends to be a supportive environment for meaningful father involvement.

Troubled Marriages and Decreased Father Involvement

Marriage itself is not the answer to helping men become better fathers, and marriage itself will not help women support their partner's parenting. Researchers emphasize that low marital satisfaction, emotional distance between partners, and high conflict in relationships undermine father involvement. Fathers who do not feel emotionally supported by their partners during the transition to parenthood are much more likely to withdraw from their children and participate less in child-care tasks than fathers who feel emotional support from their spouse.[18] Father-child relationships suffer more than mother-child relationships when parents report high conflict or divorce due to it.[19]

To demonstrate how these processes work, Jason, a married father of three daughters, gave this example:

> If for some reason I am not feeling too happy with [my wife] during the day, then we may shy away from each other, and it makes it harder for us to work together as a team. This causes aggravation between us because now I'm trying to keep my distance and remove myself from the picture,

which instantly involves making her deal with the kids a little bit more, which causes her stress.[20]

Frustrations with each other cause barriers in relationships between partners. Each feels more stress, less desire to work together, and less motivation to help the other with everyday responsibilities. Some men avoid coming home, spend later hours at work, or go out with their buddies to avoid conflict with a spouse.[21] When there is conflict between parents, fathers report a lack of desire to participate in household chores and one-on-one childcare.[22] A man's avoidance of difficulties or withdrawal from his child's mother thus also tends to mean avoidance of or withdrawal from children and family work in the home.

Tera (the second author of this chapter) has experienced similar patterns of both avoidance and closeness in her marriage as she and her husband try to find ways to deal with conflict in their relationship. When she and her husband are upset with each other, both find it difficult to focus on other family members' needs. The anger and hurt they feel becomes a barrier and keeps them from noticing each other's feelings. Negative feelings also distract them from listening to their children or meeting each other's needs. In order for fathers to be emotionally present with their children, they need to overcome and work through distracting, negative emotions due to conflict from marital issues. The same often holds true for mothers.

Fathering after a Divorce

Sharing parenting after divorce is difficult. Researchers find that small numbers of divorced couples are able to effectively co-parent. This is one reason that many fathers do not stay involved in their children's lives after a divorce. Couples who divorce have to commit to staying in touch with each other, resolving past problems, avoiding criticism and hostility when discussing the other parent with their children, and cooperating in regular child-rearing strategies that benefit their children.[23] They must work together as parents in some ways that they may have had difficulty doing as married spouses. Effective co-parenting is not impossible, but divorce tends to heighten the challenges for fathers and mothers who need to work together to benefit their children.

As difficult as this may be, some divorced or never-married parents find ways to care for their children and maintain amicable relationships with their ex-spouses or ex-partners. Researchers committed to helping families work through tough transitions like divorce show that collaborative, mutual, joint parenting is difficult but not impossible to maintain. One example of this comes from Keith, a divorced father, and his ex-wife, Elaine. In an interview, Keith explained, "I think Elaine recognizes that both of us need to be involved with our son, A.J. I think you need to have that understanding to be active as a father." His ex-wife helps him by believing that, although Keith lives in another state, it is still important for him to be involved in A.J.'s life. She supports his parenting by calling or e-mailing him to talk about their son's progress. In turn, he calls her to ask whether she or A.J. needs anything. Keith lives six hours away. Without Elaine's expectation of Keith's involvement and help in making it possible, Keith would not be as active in his fathering role.

Mothers and Fathers Working Together for Children

We would like to suggest six specific ways that men and women work together as parents: (1) maintaining a positive emotional climate at home, (2) appreciating each other, (3) offering instruction and accepting help, (4) making parenting decisions together, (5) unselfishly responding to each other's needs, and (6) sharing personal feelings with each other. These ideas are based on research, interviews with parents, and our own experiences as parents. We hope the specific examples we use will give readers ideas about how to navigate their jobs as parents and nurture their relationships.

Maintaining a Positive Emotional Climate
The general emotional climate of a home is related to the way people feel about their family life. Both positive and negative cycles of emotions affect how individuals respond to each other in families. The mood of one family member can affect the mood of all the others. One example comes from an interview with Andrew, who says he is more prone to be happy, affectionate, and kind when his wife portrays these qualities. His description below shows how effective his wife's efforts to maintain a positive attitude can be in their home:

> Sometimes if I come home, even if I'm in a bad mood, if Sara comes flying toward me and gives me a kiss, boom! I'll be in a good mood. Soon I'll see that Seth [our son] is bugging her in the kitchen, so I'll take him out, and she'll recognize that. So she'll rub my feet or give me a backrub while I'm watching football…. But also that synergy is evident in the kid. He's grumpy, but then he sees mommy kiss dad, and you know he'll be in a good mood.[24]

When people are able to be affectionate, supportive, and kind, their family members are more able to follow suit. The positive feelings one has with a spouse extend into relationships with one's children. Andrew was not the only father interviewed for this study who addressed the emotional climate of his home as an important influence on his fathering. Other men reported feeling a sense of unity, a sense of direction and purpose in their parenting, and a desire to be part of a "family team" when things are going well in their relationship with their wives.

Because the work of maintaining the emotional climate in a home often falls to women,[25] we encourage women to foster these feelings and invite men to respond in kind. We believe that men are equally capable of doing emotional work that builds the family team. Thus, we encourage men to be loving, generous, gentle, and kind as they contribute to unity and togetherness in their families. A positive emotional atmosphere in the home not only benefits mothers and fathers but also allows children to be raised in a nurturing environment that helps them feel secure.

Appreciating Each Other

When fathers talk about the things mothers do to support the fathering role, they say they need to know their contributions as fathers are appreciated.[26] Appreciation motivates fathers in their parenting efforts. Statements such as "I like it when you..." and "Our children are lucky to have you as their father" give fathers extra incentive to be involved. Men say they feel more capable when their fathering is gratefully received. Praise for a job well done fuels their desire to be a better husband and father on the challenging days when, after putting in significant effort, their children still need more. For example, Tera's husband is more likely to play with his children or read to them at bedtime when he knows that Tera appreciates it. He is also more likely to come up with fathering ideas on his own and participate if she lets him know that she is thankful for his efforts.

As mothers ourselves, we appreciate men's roles as nurturing fathers, caring husbands, good financial providers, advice givers, and logical thinkers. Men and women can appreciate their partners with a small "thank you" note, a favorite dinner, a kiss on the cheek, or any other way they see fit.

Offering Instruction and Accepting Help

While cultural ideas promoting the importance of fathers' nurturing have led to slight increases in men's time spent caring for their children, the general consensus among researchers is that mothers still spend more time with children than fathers do.[27] This means mothers typically have more experience caring for their children. Mothering expertise can be viewed as both harmful and helpful to fathering. The manner in which mothers offer their expertise as parents and the manner in which fathers accept such offers are keys to how a mother influences a father's involvement.

Harmful effects on a father's involvement may at times occur from what researchers term "maternal gatekeeping." This concept suggests that mothers play an important role as keepers of the gate to involvement in a child's life and may either limit or enhance a father's involvement by their ideas, expectations, and behaviors. Mothers who close the gate on a father's efforts or desire to be involved limit men's opportunities to learn and grow as they care for their children.[28] Briefly defined, gatekeeping may include a woman's need to maintain very high standards for household work and childcare, a woman's desire to be in charge at home, and the suggestion that fathers' efforts in rearing children are secondary to mothers' importance.[29] As an example, if a mother bases her esteem on well-groomed children and a sparkling-clean house, it may be difficult to share childcare with a father, particularly if she feels that men just cannot meet the same standards of cleanliness that women can. Ask yourself if any of these ideas resonate with your experience. We note that it is unrealistic for women to expect men to learn to keep these same standards if women do not allow men to practice and make a few mistakes before women expect perfection.

Kristen, a mother of three, mentioned in an interview that she struggles to balance her desire for her husband to be involved at home with her concern that he will not meet the same standards she sets for herself. The following experience taught her that when mothers explain their expectations fathers can grow in their parenting skills. One evening her baby daughter, Anna, sat on the floor, crying. Kristen had to attend to other responsibilities, so she asked her husband, Dale, to pick the baby up. He grabbed Anna and sat her squarely in his lap. Anna kept crying. Frustrated that the baby was still crying, Kristen went over to take Anna from Dale. As she walked toward him, she wondered, "How hard is it to hold a baby?" Then Dale looked at Kristen and said, "She never wants me to hold her." Kristen stopped. She realized that Dale was holding the baby, just not the way Kristen expected. Instead of taking Anna, she told Dale that the best way to comfort the baby was to cuddle her, pull her body close to his, and let her rest her head on his shoulder. Once he understood what "holding" the baby meant, he tried it, and it worked.

When my husband first read this, he asked, "Can't fathers have high standards for a tidy house and well-groomed children?" His comment highlighted my own thinking that if women are willing to share the load and adjust their high standards to allow men in their lives to experience more of parenthood, their partners will be better able to learn and grow in their fathering roles. Women may even discover that men often share the same high standards and just need extra time and experience to learn how to meet them. Additionally, fathers may bring their own valuable standards and insights into parenting, allowing children to grow and parents to learn from each other.

While negative maternal gatekeeping limits fathers' relationships with their children, maternal expertise in parenting can also open the gate for fathers to enter. For example, women can still have authority in household and childcare matters but choose to use their knowledge to help men be more involved with their children and in their homes. Many men say they have learned how to be a parent with the counsel and help of their partners.[30] One father, Abe, shared his experience that instruction from his wife, Jenny, helped him connect with his three-year-old son, Joseph. Jenny taught Abe that telling Joseph what to do was much less effective than giving him a few choices and letting him choose for himself. Abe also learned about Joseph's developing abilities from Jenny. For example, Jenny told him that she taught Joseph to tie his shoes by himself. Once Abe knew this, he could encourage Joseph's new shoe-tying skills.

Could Abe learn these things on his own as a father? He probably could. The point here is that he valued Jenny's knowledge and her willingness to share it with him. Her guidance helped him become a better parent. My husband confided in me that he feels I always know the best things for our daughter, so he trusts and turns to me when he feels troubled about how he is doing as a father. My advice and mothering skills are important to him.

While we focus on fathers who live with their children in this chapter, we note that nonresidential fathers typically depend heavily on their child's mother to tell them about their child's progress. Without information and guidance from the mothers of their children, nonresidential fathers may feel particularly distant from their children. For example, Keith lived in a different state from his eight-year-old son. This meant he could not get to know his son's teacher by attending regular parent-teacher conferences, get to know his son's friends, or easily monitor his son's behavior. He needed his ex-wife to tell him about his son's progress in school, friendships, and behavior with his peers. Mothers who have custody of their children have a unique responsibility to share this information with fathers unless there are circumstances that make this unsafe for the child.[31] This is not the sole responsibility of the custodial parent. Nonresident fathers can also ask for advice and encourage their ex-partners to share information.

Making Parenting Decisions Together

When couples are satisfied with decision making and share household tasks, fathers are more likely to spend time with their children.[32] This eases mothers' burdens and decreases their stress. Our personal experiences match this research. We find that when husband and wife reach an agreement on a decision regarding their children, it is easier for both to follow through and achieve their goals. For example, when Tera and her husband decided together what time to put their children down for bed, her husband was more invested in getting the children to bed on time. When Tera was the only one to set the rules, she was the only enforcer of those rules. Parents can carry out family rules much more easily when they are on the same team.

Supporting each other's decisions about discipline is also an important part of making decisions together as parents. When one parent corrects a child, the other parent needs to stand by those decisions, trusting that the spouse has their child's best interests in mind. If parents disagree with the discipline or guidance provided, then that discussion should be held privately. Children recognize disagreements between parents. Sometimes this leads to frustration for children. At other times it causes children to pit one parent against the other. However, when parents avoid directly contradicting each other or undermining each other's authority in front of their children, children will more likely learn the family rules, expect consistent guidance, and respect their parents' rules.

How can parents be more effective at showing children they support each other's decisions? Parents can display support by making comments to their chil-

---

How Mothers and Fathers Can Work Together for Their Children

- **Maintain a positive emotional atmosphere at home.** Be affectionate. Be supportive. Be kind. This fosters family togetherness and helps children feel secure.

- **Appreciate each other.** Let your child's other parent know you appreciate him or her. Write him a little note. Give her a little kiss. Tell each other "Thank you" or "You did a great job helping Tommy with his homework today." We all feel more capable when we receive praise for our efforts.

- **Offer instruction when needed, and be willing to accept help when it is offered.** Sometimes you will know something about your child that the other parent might not. Share this information with your spouse. It will help both of you be better parents and help your child thrive as he/she develops new skills. When your partner offers this kind of information, gratefully accept it. If your partner is not as skilled or does not share the same standards for parenting, this may be an opportunity for each of you to practice patience, discuss expectations, and give each other room to grow.

- **Make parenting decisions together.** Parents carry out decisions much more easily when they are on the same team. When one parent makes a decision, the other should help enforce that decision. Make sure you follow through with guidance and discipline developed by the other parent. Avoid criticizing your partner or undermining his or her authority in front of the children.

- **Be less selfish and more responsive to each other's needs.** You express commitment to each other when you recognize your partner's needs above your own. Be giving. Be sensitive.

- **Share personal feelings with each other.** This reminds each of you that you matter in each other's lives. It rekindles closeness in a couple and regenerates the resolve to work together to strengthen the family.

dren such as "Your dad loves you and gives you these rules to help you" or "I trust your mom's choices and hope you will try harder to obey her." Sometimes parents dispel their child's anger toward the disciplining parent with unified comments.

Finally, you can follow through with guidance or discipline as a parent even though you did not offer the consequence. Alice (the fourth author) has two daughters, Sara and Isabella, who are currently learning to play the piano. Because practice is so important, Alice sometimes finds herself nagging them to practice. After nagging, contention will inevitably follow. She shared her frustration with their father, who agreed that practice was important. He came up with a practice schedule complete with rewards for minutes practiced. Alice continued to enforce the schedule. It was just the motivation her daughters needed but would not have been as effective if both Alice and her husband had not maintained it.

Unselfishly Responding to Each Other's Needs

Another important aspect of co-parenting is the recognition of and unselfish response to needs. Like support, a pattern of recognizing needs and responding to them allows for the understanding required of husbands and wives in caring situations. Fathers can express the commitment they have for their wives as they try to recognize their wives' needs above their own. Harold, a father I interviewed, said:

> What's hard to realize is that if I'm doing all that I can to take care of my wife and her needs, then my needs will be taken care of. You forget that, but that's the truth. If I make her happy, my life is much happier. If I will concentrate on taking care of her, I'm much better off.[33]

Harold explains that, ultimately, as men and women take care of each other, their feelings of closeness and love increase. The close feelings are not unique to husbands. When asked how her husband's care for her makes her feel, Julie said:

> Joe is very sensitive and caring. With me and the kids, he is very giving and unselfish. When Joe does things like that, it helps me try to be more caring for him and reciprocate because [the things he does to care for me] are very valuable to me.[34]

The love partners feel invites them to be better people—more loving and caring with their children. Caring for each other reminds people that they belong to each other and that they enjoy loving each other. Experiences of love and care make couples resilient in hard times that may have potential to break up the intimate connection they have built together.

Sharing Personal Feelings with Each Other

An important part of working together as parents is finding ways to refuel your energy as a couple. Sharing personal feelings is one way couples can remind themselves how much they matter to each other. Though this can be a challenge for some men, husbands who share their personal feelings with their wives know that it brings the two of them closer. Harold shared this story:

> About a week after Shawn [our son] passed away, I came walking into the living room, and my wife [Marjorie] was standing, staring out the window and crying. She just had tears rolling down her face. My initial reaction was that I wanted to go up to her and say, "It's okay, Marjorie, you don't need to cry. Everything will be fine." But this time I just went up and held her, and we cried together. Then we sat down and had the best heart-to-heart talk we'd had in years. It was a time of sharing our emotions, our feelings, and letting each other know that we were the most important persons in each other's lives again. That was a time to start anew. To let her know "I am here for you" and "I can feel what you're going through; use me if you can."[35]

Harold knew that Marjorie needed him. Instead of closing down their communication by telling Marjorie to stop crying, he acknowledged her feelings by holding her and crying himself. Notice, too, that this was not just a nice conversation between two married people. It was "the best heart-to-heart talk" they had had in years. They shared personal feelings and verbalized just how much they meant to each other. Opportunities to rekindle closeness, express how much you love each other, and give unselfishly will regenerate the resolve to work together in strengthening your family.

Conclusion

In this chapter we offer some advice, expertise, and case studies that exemplify ways women and men can work together to strengthen their families. In conclusion, we reiterate the following key points:

- Good mothering and good fathering are connected. We hope that recognizing this connection will help mothers and fathers want to work together.
- Strong marriages provide an important environment for supportive parenting. Stay close to each other while embarking on the challenges of parenting.
- If marriages dissolve, divorced parents should strive to resolve conflict, respect each other's parenting skills, and cooperate to keep fathers involved in their children's lives.

■   Mothers and fathers successfully raise their children together by appreciating each other's hard work, maintaining a positive emotional climate at home, avoiding harmful gatekeeping, sharing parenting expertise, supporting each other's parenting decisions, unselfishly responding to each other's needs, and sharing intimate feelings with each other.

We hope our advice will help parents to recommit to working together to strengthen their families. We know that shared parenting is not always easy but well worth the effort.

As I, Erin, finish this chapter, I can hear my daughter squealing as my husband playfully chases her upstairs. He is playing with her partly so I can finish

---

How Fathers Can Support Children by Supporting Mothers

■   **Relieve Mom's load.** Encourage her to take time out on her own to recharge her batteries. For example, you can watch your children while she takes a night class, develops a hobby, spends time with friends, or does whatever she needs to relax. This gives children one-on-one time with Dad and lets their mother know you care about her needs.

■   **Do a few household chores without being asked.** How many times have you heard women say they just want their husbands to pitch in without being asked? When you willingly do housework before your wife asks, you show her that you care about her. You also set an example for your children as they observe the performance of unsolicited kind acts.

■   **Support her mothering choices.** Whether that means supporting her desire to stay at home or to work outside the home, women appreciate knowing their children's father respects their mothering decisions and sustains their mothering efforts.

■   **Provide for your family's financial needs.** Financial support is an important part of fathering. It can possibly allow women to stay home when they want to be with their children. It also gives children financial security that accompanies a host of positive outcomes for school achievement, social skills, and emotional security.

■   **Treat your children's mother with love and respect.** This teaches children how to relate to other people and that their parents value their relationship and are willing to invest whatever is needed to maintain it. It has been said that the greatest thing a man can do for his children is to love and respect their mother.

this chapter. To me, his time with her represents the fact that when we are both committed to helping each other our entire family benefits. I feel less stress and more appreciation for his efforts to work with me in raising our daughter. He enjoys the opportunity to develop his fathering skills, he knows that I support him in his efforts, and he appreciates the work I do as a mother even more because he participates in that work. Finally, our daughter enjoys a more fulfilled and loving home environment with two parents focused on improving her well-being and the overall quality of our family life. Good mothering, at its heart, acknowledges the important influence of fathers and provides a steady, consistent foundation for fathers to truly count in the lives of their children.

Endnotes

1. Doherty, W.J., Kouneski, E.F., and Erickson, M.F., 1998, "Responsible Fathering: An Overview and Conceptual Framework," *Journal of Marriage and the Family*, 60, 277–292, at 278.

2. Arendell, T., 1996, *Co-Parenting: A Review of the Literature* (LR-CP-96-03), Philadelphia, PA: National Center on Fathers and Families; Barnett, R.C., and Baruch, G.K., 1987, "Determinants of Fathers' Participation in Family Work," *Journal of Marriage and the Family*, 49, 29–40.

3. Holmes, E.K., 2001, "When Mom's Happy Everybody's Happy: Fathers' Perceptions of Mothers' Influences on Fatherhood," research presented at National Council on Family Relations Conference, Rochester, NY.

4. Fagan, J., and Barnett, M., 2003, "The Relationship between Maternal Gatekeeping, Paternal Competence, Mothers' Attitudes about the Father Role, and Father Involvement," *Journal of Family Issues*, 24, 1020–1043; Palkovitz, R., 1984, "Parental Attitudes and Fathers' Interaction with Their 5-Month-Old Infants," *Developmental Psychology*, 20(6), 1054–1060.

5. Ibid.

6. Seltzer, J.A., 1991, "Relationship between Fathers and Children Who Live Apart: The Father's Role after Separation," *Journal of Marriage and the Family*, 53, 79–101; Doherty, W.J., Kouneski, E.F., and Erickson, M.F., 1998.

7. Ibid.

8. Forty percent of children with never-married parents did not see their non-resident fathers for an entire year; 22 percent saw their nonresident fathers less than once a month during the year.

9. Amato, P.R., and Gilbreth, J.G., 1999, "Nonresident Fathers and Children's Well-Being: A Meta-Analysis," *Journal of Marriage and the Family*, 61, 557–573.

10. McLoyd, V.C., 1998, "Socioeconomic Disadvantage and Child Development," *American Psychologist*, 53(2), 185–204.

11. Cowan, C.P., and Cowan, P.A., 1987, "Men's Involvement in Parenthood: Identifying the Antecedents and Understanding the Barriers," in *Men's Transitions to Parenthood: Longitudinal Studies of Early Family Experience*, edited by P.W. Berman and F.A. Pedersen, Hillsdale, NJ: Lawrence Erlbaum Associates, pp. 145–171; Cox, M., Owen, M., Lewis, J., and Henderson, V.K., 1989, "Marriage, Adult Adjustment, and Early Parenting," *Child Development*, 60, 1015–1024.

12. Amato, P.R., 1994, "Father-Child Relations, Mother-Child Relations, and Offspring Psychological Well-Being in Early Adulthood," *Journal of Marriage and the Family*, 56, 1031–1042.

13. Feldman, S.S., Nash, S.C., and Aschenbrenner, B.G., 1983, "Antecedents of Fathering," *Child Development*, 54(6), 1628–1636; see also endnote 11.

14. Cowan, C.P., and Cowan, P.A., 1988, "Who Does What When Partners Become Parents: Implications for Men, Women, and Marriage," *Marriage and Family Review*, 12, 105–131.

15. Frank, S., Hole, C.B., Jacobson, S., Justkowski, R., and Huyck, M., 1986, "Psychological Predictors of Parents' Sense of Confidence and Control and Self- versus Child-Focused Gratifications," *Developmental Psychology*, 22(3), 348–355.

16. Cowan, C.P., and Cowan, P.A., 1987.

17. McBride, B.A., and Rane, T.R., 1998, "Parenting Alliance as a Predictor of Father Involvement: An Exploratory Study," *Journal of Family Issues*, 47(3), 229–237.

18. Berman, P.W., and Pedersen, F.A., 1987, "Research on Men's Transitions to Parenthood: An Integrative Discussion," in *Men's Transitions to Parenthood: Longitudinal Studies of Early Family Experience*, edited by P.W. Berman and F. A. Pedersen, Hillsdale, NJ: Lawrence Erlbaum Associates, Inc., pp. 217–242.

19. Amato, 1994.

20. Please note that all names have been changed to protect the privacy of those participating in this study. See endnote 3 for full citation.

21. Holmes, 2001.

22. Doherty, W., and Beaton, J., 2004, "Mothers and Fathers Parenting Together," in *Handbook of Family Communication*, edited by A. Vangelisti, Hillsdale, NJ: Lawrence Erlbaum Associates, pp. 269–286.

23. Margolin, G., Gordis, E.B., and John, R.S., 2001, "Coparenting: A Link between Marital Conflict and Parenting in Two-Parent Families," *Journal of Family Psychology*, 15, 3–21; McHale, J.P., 1997, "Overt and Covert Coparenting Processes in the Family," *Family Process*, 36, 183–201.

24. Holmes, 2001.

25. Erickson, R.J., 1993, "Reconceptualizing Family Work: The Effect of Emotion Work on Perceptions of Marital Quality," *Journal of Marriage and the Family*, 55, 888–900.

26. Holmes, 2001.

27. For a full review, see Parke, R.D., 2002, "Fathers and Families," in *Handbook of Parenting, Vol. 3: Being and Becoming a Parent*, edited by M. Bornstein, Hillsdale, NJ: Lawrence Erlbaum, pp. 27–74.

28. Allen, S.M., and Hawkins, A.J., 1999, "Maternal Gatekeeping: Mothers' Beliefs and Behaviors That Inhibit Greater Father Involvement in Family Work," *Journal of Marriage and the Family*, 61(1), 199–212.

29. DeLuccie, M.F., 1995, "Mothers as Gatekeepers: A Model of Maternal Mediators of Father Involvement," *Journal of Genetic Psychology*, 156 (1), 115–131.

30. McBride, B.A., and Darragh, J., 1995, "Interpreting the Data on Father Involvement: Implications for Parenting Programs for Men," *Families in Society: The Journal of Contemporary Human Services*, 76, 490–497.

31. Holmes, 2001.

32. Ibid.

33. Holmes, E.K., 2002, "Uniting Men's Work as Husbands and Fathers: Another Look at the Theory of Generative Care," research presented at National Council on Family Relations Conference, Houston, TX.

34. Ibid.

35. Ibid.

Author H. Wallace Goddard with his wife, Nancy

Better Marriages Make for Better Fathering

H. Wallace Goddard

A bad marriage is bad for parenting. When a marriage is strong, both mother and father are more likely to be effective parents. As one commentator has observed, "promoting marital satisfaction promotes good parenting."[1] How can strengthening the marital relationship become an avenue to better fathering? For men, in particular, marital quality counts in helping them to become good parents and sustaining their involvement with children.

Marriage as a Support to Father Involvement

The quality of a marriage relationship can profoundly influence a father's motivation, efforts, and involvement as a parent. My wife and I have experienced a personal and painful example of this with some good friends—two good-hearted, much-loved people married to each other. They seemed like a perfect match in spite of their different backgrounds: she was intense and optimistic; he was gentle and personable. Over the years they added children to their family. And over the years, their differences on various style issues became an irritation in the relationship.

The more irritated the wife became with her husband, the less contact she wanted him to have with their children. As she became more irritated with him, he became more stubborn about his choices. They polarized. She considered him a bad influence on the children because his work ethic was different from the one she preferred. Irritation grew into exasperation, and they grew apart. After more than 20 years of marriage, they divorced.

But long before the divorce, the marital stresses influenced their children. The stress itself spilled into all family relationships and many activities. The children often felt tense and unhappy because of the conflict between the parents. In addition, the chronic conflict over time likely influenced the children's view of healthy marriage—including the belief that such a thing is even possible. Further, in their day-to-day interactions, the mother limited the father's contact with the children, both to punish him and to insulate the children from a father whose easygoing ways had become annoying to her. A troubled marriage had substantial effects on the amount and quality of his time spent fathering.

In contrast, when couples have a strong relationship, they use their differences to complement each other. They draw on each other's strengths and welcome each other's influence on the children. Even their conflicts can be instructive as the children observe two loving people resolving problems in healthy ways. A healthy marriage provides both a safe place for children and a classroom for learning about relationships. In this context, fathers are also more able to connect with their children and benefit from a supportive partner. William Doherty and his colleagues, in a report for the federal government on responsible fathering, noted that "the family environment most supportive of fathering is a caring, committed, collaborative marriage."[2] They also noted that research indicates "if [a man] has a wife but does not get along with her, he may be present as a father, but the quality of his relationship with his children is apt to suffer."[3] This does not suggest that fathers cannot connect with and care for their children outside of marriage but that a healthy marriage is a strong support system for fathers who are married and wish to be good parents.

New Ways of Thinking about Marriage

One major challenge for improving marital satisfaction for both men and women is ignorance. Many marriage partners with good intentions misunderstand the processes necessary to improve their relationships. Doing the wrong things will not strengthen a marriage, just as taking the wrong steps to fix a car engine will not make it run more smoothly. However, understanding and doing the right things can make a marriage stronger and help fathers to improve their parenting.

Over the past two decades, there has been a revolution in the way people think about marriage. Many scholars who study marriage have moved from a *medical* approach (watching for symptoms, considering diagnoses, treating disease) to a *wellness* approach (cultivating strengths, tolerating some limitations, preventing problems). One result of this revolution is less of a focus on problem-centered communication and increased emphasis on relationship building and problem management. It is not unusual for men to withdraw from an approach that identifies their weaknesses and focuses on them, while they are more likely to appreciate a wellness approach that honors their contributions and invites them to grow as husbands and fathers.[4]

Some outdated approaches to improving couple relationships have recommended that partners "fight fair." For example, the idea was to "let your partner know your discontents—but do it fairly." There are a variety of problems with this approach. For example, men in particular are likely to experience relationship discussions as an attack.[5] When people feel attacked, they are not likely to use fair fighting skills, even if they have been trained in them.[6] In fact, men's heart rates commonly skyrocket when their spouses initiate a relationship discussion.

Another problem with the "fair fighting" approach is that it is commonly built on the assumption that one's partner needs to change and it is one's job to engineer that change. Some of the problems with that assumption will become evident in the pages ahead. In any case, such efforts often do not correspond well with how men process relationship issues and too often result in withdrawal from both the marital relationship and parenting efforts.

Extensive research by many scholars recommends a more positive approach to strengthening marriage that also is beneficial to fathering.[7] Some scholars even recommend shifting the focus away from changing each other toward accepting each other.[8] Does this mean that spouses should not change? No. It simply suggests the process of how to approach change needs a new and better starting point.

While debate continues about the balance between the communication and acceptance approaches to strengthening marriage, it is not too early to start translating some of the new discoveries about marriage into practice. This chapter will suggest a variety of ways these discoveries can connect to specific processes and activities for couples and especially for men as fathers.

A Model for Healthy Couple Relationships

Any self-respecting program to help families starts with a model or a state-ment of underlying principles. For example, in the area of parenting, a group of scholars developed the National Extension Parent Education Model (NEPEM) in 1994,[9] which has been used to guide the development of many parenting pro-grams. The closest thing to a model for marriage and couple relationships may be John Gottman's "Sound Marital House."[10] However, this is quite different from the NEPEM model in that it merely lists processes (love maps, fondness and admira-tion system, turning toward versus turning away, positive sentiment override, etc.) for strong marriages without describing the key practices. An optimal model might list both essential processes and key practices in a simple, practical way.

I have elsewhere proposed just such a model (see Table 1).[11] While the model has not yet been fully tested by research, it is based on the work of numerous scholars in the field of marriage and family (see Goddard and Olson, 2004, for more information on the research basis of the model).[12] Table 1 provides a clear outline of six core principles and related key practices that can strengthen men both as husbands and fathers. These six core principles are to:

- *Commit.* Commitment is the willingness to dedicate time and energy to the success of a relationship. It also includes the willingness to set boundaries on intrusions from outside the relationship.
- *Grow.* This principle entails the recognition that a marriage is better when both partners are growing and learning. Healthy marriages open the windows of experience to allow fresh air and sunlight into their common experience.
- *Understand.* The best kind of understanding includes the humility to recog-nize that we never fully comprehend someone else's view of the world. It also includes the willingness to notice and listen to our partner in an effort to be tuned in to his or her preferences, personality, and history.
- *Nurture.* Nurturing focuses on building the connection between partners. It is not necessarily romance. It may be shared time, shared hobbies, and anything that helps two people feel like one.
- *Solve.* All human relationships have challenges. There are sensible ways to deal with those challenges. This principle describes the processes for dealing with challenges and differences.
- *Serve.* Sweet companionship involves more than looking into each other's eyes: working jointly in support of valued purposes, whether those purposes are raising children, serving in the community, or caring for the environment.

In this chapter each of the six principles for healthy relationships is described, and practical suggestions for applying the principles are provided. Why is this

Table 1. A Marriage and Couples Education Model (M/CEM)

Dimension	Practices
Commit	■ Make the relationship primary. ■ Make couple time a priority. ■ Set limits on intrusions. ■ Build in rituals of connection.
Grow	■ Continue development of personal strengths. ■ Support partner's use of signature strengths. ■ Support partner's growth. ■ Show respect for fundamental rights as a human being.
Understand	■ Understand partner through his or her worldview. ■ Make allowances for continuing differences. ■ Accept and value differences. ■ Understand and appreciate partner's pressures and needs.
Nurture	■ Find and cultivate common interests and activities. ■ Develop affectional synchrony with partner (languages of love). ■ Keep relationship positive: five positives for each negative. ■ Supplement and balance rather than compete and criticize.
Solve	■ Stay calm in the face of differences. ■ Be open to other views. ■ Consider multiple courses of action. ■ Accept some differences as a part of the relationship. ■ Allow time for changes.
Serve	■ Develop a couple mission ■ Pursue and practice involvement in common purposes. ■ Build relationship on values as well as feelings.

(Adapted from Goddard and Olson, 2004)

important? As marriage relationships improve, the motivation and involvement of fathers with their children tends to improve also.

As we think about ways to strengthen marital relationships, it is also important to have a fitting metaphor for marriage. Most dating in contemporary society is much like a day in an amusement park. However, establishing and strengthening a marriage is more like cultivating a garden. The image of cultivating a garden fits well with principles of healthy marriage, including such elements as commitment, growth, nurturance, and solving problems.

Marriage and gardening both require time and patience. There are inevitably problems that arise. Weeds, storms, and insects may trouble a garden. Financial difficulties or personal storms regarding health or stress may affect a marriage. There are surprises that take place in gardening and marriage. For example, there might not be enough sun for the hollyhocks, but the sunflowers might be flourishing! A person who works wisely and patiently in gardening and in relationships is likely to find many rewards, yet the work never ends. Both marriages and gardens require continuing care. The principles and practices that can nourish and enrich marital relationships can also strengthen fathers in their efforts to be good parents.

Marital Principle 1: Commit

Can a relationship flourish in the absence of commitment? It hardly seems likely. A garden cannot flourish without commitment to its care, and neither can a marriage flourish without commitment by its partners to care for the relationship they share. For those considering a relationship, there are sensible ways of assessing the potential partner's willingness to make and keep commitments. Has that person shown commitment to family, organizations, and values over time? Naturally, we do not want stubbornness in potential partners, but we do value the kind of commitment that enables a person to honor core values and promises—important in both marriage and fatherhood.

But how do we cultivate and maintain commitment in an existing relationship? Key practices include making the relationship primary in our thinking and continuing our efforts over time, setting limits on intrusions, and remembering and cherishing the good aspects of a relationship.

The heart of commitment, whether as a marriage partner or a parent, lies in making family relationships primary and dedicating time and energy to their success. Many people give up on their marriages when difficulties arise. William Doherty has perceptively observed:

> I think of long-term marriage like I think about living in Minnesota. . . .
> You move into marriage in the springtime of hope but eventually arrive
> at the Minnesota winter with its cold and darkness. Many of us are
> tempted to give up and move south at this point. We go to a therapist for

help. Some therapists don't know how to help us cope with winter, and we get frostbite in their care. Other therapists tell us that we are being personally victimized by winter, that we deserve better, that winter will never end, and that if we are true to ourselves we will leave our marriage and head south. The problem, of course, is that our next marriage will enter its own winter at some point. Do we just keep moving on, or do we make our stand now—with this person, in this season? That's the moral, existential question. A good therapist, a brave therapist, will help us to cling together as a couple, warming each other against the cold of winter, and to seek out whatever sunlight is still available while we wrestle with our pain and disillusionment. A good therapist, a brave therapist, will be the last one in the room to give up on our marriage, not the first one, knowing that the next springtime in Minnesota is all the more glorious for the winter that we endured together.[13]

Commitment means not selling off the garden because it needs fertilizer. It means a willingness to invest of ourselves and to see beyond the bad times. The practice of making the relationship primary in your life and working each day for its future is a cornerstone of commitment. It reflects commitment not only to present needs but to future hopes. Fathers must also commit to both the present needs and the future development of their children. Marital commitment can help men to learn and practice this critical lesson.

A second key facet of commitment entails a willingness to set boundaries on intrusions to the relationship. For example, Shirley Glass, a recognized authority on infidelity and reconciliation in couple relationships, recommends that marriage partners keep a window open between them while building a wall between them and those who threaten the relationship.[14] This "walls and windows" philosophy protects the relationship from others while keeping the connection between partners strong. "Innocent" flirtations and intrusive relatives can come between marriage partners. For men, it can be particularly helpful to recognize that they must limit distractions from work, friends, or other sources that can either interfere with the marriage or undermine their involvement with their children.

For committed couples, marriage means that neither partner flirts with others. It means that neither partner considers himself or herself on the market for another relationship. (You may admire someone else's garden, but you do not steal the flowers!) Those who have experienced years of dating and lived in a culture that overemphasizes romance and promotes quick fixes to relationship concerns may find commitment to be a rare commodity. However, men will learn that women are more likely to support and appreciate them when they make such commitment clear.

A third practice that helps to strengthen commitment involves the way partners think about each other. Commitment, a process that is rooted in our thinking and emotions, can be strengthened by remembering and cherishing the good. John Gottman, a leading scholar on marriage, has written that "nothing foretells a marriage's future as accurately as how a couple retells their past. The crucial factor is not necessarily the reality of a marriage's early days but how husband and wife currently view their joint history. . . . Rewriting history may begin well before you become aware that your marriage is in serious danger."[15]

Gottman's counsel is to "find the glory in your marital story."[16] This suggests that partners in a relationship can and should monitor and modify their ways of thinking about their relationship. How, then, might you think about relationship challenges? Difficult times can be interpreted as an opportunity for new growth. Good times can be celebrated and remembered with appreciation.

The practice of commitment in marriage prepares men to show commitment in fathering. A man who has learned to weather storms, accept challenges, and celebrate victories in marriage is more likely to be an effective father.

Marital Principle 2: Grow

Strong relationships are built by healthy people. Encouraging and working for continued growth is part of cultivating a garden, and it is also part of cultivating a healthy relationship. Healthy people continue to grow in their relationships. Growth in healthy relationships is characterized by partners who cultivate development of personal strengths and also support each other's use of signature strengths. Allowing for growth and focusing on strengths are important principles for marriage and also for men wanting to be effective in fathering efforts.

A central practice that can facilitate growth, both as a marital partner and a parent, is to continue to cultivate your personal strengths and support your partner's growth. In addition to those activities and interests that we may share with our partners in marriage, most of us also have interests that are not shared. This is also true for fathers and their children. When we are actively discovering, developing, and using our gifts, we bring more life and energy to our family relationships. For that reason it is important to actively cultivate our own talents and to encourage our partners' talent development. For example, a woman may notice that her husband likes to play softball in a city league during the summer and encourage this activity. Her encouragement of this area of interest may be important to a future time when her spouse spends time playing catch with a son or daughter in the backyard. Personal strengths can become parental strengths.

An additional key practice centered on growth is to actively support a partner's use of signature strengths. Martin Seligman, who has studied human potential and fulfillment extensively, has described three levels of happiness.[17] The first comes from savoring, enjoying, and appreciating life experiences. This certainly applies to marriage. Those who notice, savor, and remember their good couple experiences are likely to have more of them. This also applies to fathering. A spirit of appreciation and celebration makes family life better for partners and children, and children thrive when fathers notice their activities and encourage them.

Seligman's second level of happiness comes from regularly using one's unique talents, which he calls "signature strengths." When people discover, develop, and regularly use their signature strengths, they are likely to find life more satisfying. Husbands and wives who support their spouse's pursuit of signature strengths will find their partner happier and more engaging. Additionally, a father who is actively using and developing his strengths can also help his partner and children do the same. A key is for fathers to support spouses or children in finding and developing their unique strengths rather than forcing them toward his own preferences or strengths.

Seligman's third level of happiness involves using signature strengths in service of a cause, which might be building a strong family or serving in the community. When one of a person's major purposes in life is to support and strengthen family members, life is better for both the giver and the whole family. No man will ever do any more important work than his participation in his family. The psychologist Erik Erikson has suggested that we don't reach our full potential and contribution to the world unless we give our family the best we have to offer.

Family members can talk about shared and separate interests. They can celebrate and cultivate shared interests while encouraging individual development. These practices will allow for growth within relationships that will also make them more satisfying over time.

Marital Principle 3: Understand

It is common for individuals to comment that they just wish to be understood. Understanding is not mind reading or imposing our interpretations on others' behavior. It is closer to "walking in their moccasins." Compassionate understanding is a vital prelude to a healthy relationship and effective negotiation. Essentially, understanding is coming to know and appreciate another person through his or her worldview and being willing to accept and value differences.

Stephen R. Covey, in his well-known book *The 7 Habits of Highly Effective People*, offers this recommendation: "Seek first to understand, then to be understood."[18] A key practice, then, in understanding is to focus on understanding a person through his or her worldview. Covey tells the story of his wife's irrational attachment to Frigidaire appliances.[19] He could never understand it, and he could not dissuade his wife, Sandra, from buying only Frigidaire appliances. It was not until he was willing to let her explore her feelings about Frigidaire that they discovered the reason for her loyalty. As a young girl, Sandra's father was a school teacher and operated an appliance store. During a time of economic difficulty, the Frigidaire company was willing to finance her father's inventory. That allowed him to stay in business. It made a big difference for her family. She was loyal to Frigidaire because the company had been loyal to her family, but only understanding this from her point of view allowed her husband to truly accept this deep-seated loyalty.

Two related practices that facilitate understanding in relationships are to allow for continuing differences and to accept and value existing differences. In marriage, men and women differ. As parents, fathers and their children will deal with differing thoughts, personalities, and feelings. Very often in relationships we "ritualize" our differences; that is, we turn our fights and problems into habits. You may act in a certain way. I interpret it in a predictable way and accuse you based on my interpretation. You react with hurt and counteraccusation. The cycle of misunderstanding and accusation feeds on itself. If either person is willing to set aside his or her own preconceptions and listen to what the partner is saying—and why it is important to the partner—amazing relationship progress can be made.

This may be part of what marital scholar John Gottman means by accepting influence from a partner. Accepting influence means that, rather than discounting or depreciating our partner's ideas and preferences, we honor them. We listen carefully. We work to understand the importance of their ideas from their perspective. We work to incorporate their preferences into our actions. Gottman argues that, in family life, men in particular must learn to "yield in order to win" or to accept and honor feelings or suggestions from their spouse or children. Even if a spouse suggests something he does not agree with, accepting influence means to listen and be respectful rather than getting defensive or hostile. Husbands and fathers who practice accepting influence have much happier and more stable marriages.[20]

Haim Ginott, the guru of understanding in parenting, provided wonderful examples of understanding in relationships.[21] For example, rather than reacting to a person's "selfish" intentions, we can give them the benefit of the doubt. We can assume they are acting in a certain way for reasons that make sense to them—even reasons that are truly noble. As fathers practice understanding, it prepares them for the relationship skills they need to listen to children, understand a problem from the child's viewpoint, and be patient and respectful with children.

Yet another beneficial practice is to understand and appreciate a partner's pressures and needs. Because each person tends to be more aware of his or her own feelings, needs, and preferences, it is challenging to really understand another person. When people feel bad, they feel their pain is so bad that no one can really understand it. That's why a person who is hurting would probably rather have you say, "Your pain must be awful. I wish I could understand just how sad (or hurt or lonely) you feel." Sometimes the best way to show understanding is to admit you can't understand how bad a person feels. The key to understanding is to discern what the other person is feeling and be sensitive to it.

Showing understanding in marriage is difficult in part because we think we already know our partners. We may think their suffering is due to bad decisions or character flaws, so we do not respond with healthy compassion. We often feel

Tips for Understanding in Marriage and Parenting

Understanding one another and being patient and respectful will yield greater harmony in both marriage and parenting relationships. Here are some examples of ways to communicate that can either diminish or enhance understanding.

Ways of Communicating That Do Not Show Understanding

- Giving unsolicited or condescending advice.
  - "What you need to do is...."
  - "If you would stop being such a baby, you wouldn't have that trouble."
  - "Haven't you ever done that before? Let me show you how it's done."
- Talking about your own feelings and experiences instead of theirs.
  - "I understand."
  - "I've had tougher experiences than that."
  - "Something like that happened to me once. Let me tell you all about it."
- Making the person's pain seem unimportant.
  - "Everybody suffers. What makes you so special?"
  - "Why don't you grow up?"
  - "Stop that. You're driving me crazy."
  - "Come on, you can deal with that. Get with it!"

Ways of Communicating That Show Understanding

After listening (and watching) carefully, we might do one of the following:

- Acknowledge or identify our partner's or child's feeling.
  - "You feel strongly about this."
  - "You seem to feel very concerned (hurt, upset, confused)."
- Invite more discussion.
  - "I would like to understand how you are feeling. Will you tell me more?"
  - "Do you want to share what you're feeling?"
- Understand that the person's pain is special for that person.
  - "I wish I could understand better how you feel."
  - "Ouch. I don't know if I can even guess how terrible you feel."
- Use active listening.
  - "Let me see if I understand. You feel like...?"
  - "It sounds like you feel lonely (confused, sad, etc.)."

compelled to correct our partners, which causes pain and mistrust, yet once they feel understood and supported, they are more likely to solve problems and feel close to you. This applies to fathers' efforts because men who feel understood and accepted by their spouses are much more likely to engage actively with their children. Understanding in marriage facilitates active involvement in parenting.

The challenge with understanding others is that most of us have a hard time getting there when we feel attacked. The best time to cultivate understanding in marriage is when you are both feeling peaceful. Set aside your assumptions and judgments. Invite your partner to help you understand what a certain thing means to him or her. If you feel yourself getting upset and inclined to judge or lecture, call for a personal timeout and suggest: "I'd like to think about what you've said. I really want to understand. Let me think about it, and maybe we can revisit this later." Men who develop this kind of capacity for understanding in marriage will also be better able to express this kind of emotional awareness and sensitivity to the children in their lives. Compassionate partnering contributes to compassionate fathering.

Marital Principle 4: Nurture

Supporting each other and building connections are the heart of a healthy relationship, in both marriage and parenting. A variety of key practices that can nurture such relationships include developing common interests and activities, learning another person's love language, focusing on positives, and expressing kindness.

One practice that can encourage intimacy as a couple is finding and cultivating common interests and activities. Strong relationships are nurtured more by simple, regular, and satisfying activities than by grand vacations. As with a garden, steady efforts over time yield much better results than occasional and frenzied bouts of effort. Working in the yard together doing things you both enjoy, for example, may be more valuable than a trip to Hawaii. This is also true with children. Contemporary research shows that fathers and children often build connections over the "small moments" they share together.[22]

Yet another practice that contributes to nurturing a relationship is learning the other person's love language. John Gottman talks about "love maps" in his writings on marriage, which constitute awareness of the specific things that are important to your partner, such as a specific type of dessert or an activity they particularly enjoy.[23] I prefer to think in terms of love languages. How does your partner prefer to experience support and affection? Understanding and expressing love to partners in a way that is most meaningful to them is another important practice that nurtures and strengthens marriage.

For example, I have tended to buy "stuff"—flowers, knick-knacks, or clothes—for my wife, Nancy, when I want to express my love for her, but she does not care for things the way I do. She has usually given me little notes of affection, which are sweet—but I want stuff! When we express love in ways not in tune with our partners' preferences, more effort can be counterproductive. After decades of marriage, I finally discovered that Nancy would much rather have a detailed and affectionate note from me than any amount of stuff. Learning this kind of attention to the specifics of how to engage and nurture another person also pays off for fathers in their relationships with their children.

A third practice that nurtures a relationship is to contribute many more positives than negatives to it. John Gottman, in his marital research, found that being positive with each other is even more important than the type of relationship style a couple develops (volatile, avoidant, or validating). Those couples who provide five positives to their partner for each negative have the strongest relationships.[24] What does this mean? Each spouse must work at focusing on things to appreciate and doing small, positive things rather than criticizing or complaining. This principle applies equally well to parent-child relationships, which can become burdened by negative discussions or frustrations. Fathers must also work on remaining positive with their children.

According to research by Tom Lee at Utah State University, simple expressions of kindness are one of the best predictors of family happiness.[25] That is good news. All of us can cultivate kindness. We do not have to discuss every discontent. We can enjoy our partners' strengths. As we do, we are likely to have stronger couple relationships. Additionally, kindness is critical for fathers as they nurture their children and help children to feel an influence that is caring and warm from the men in their lives.

Marital Principle 5: Solve

One major problem with traditional marriage programs may be the assumption that, if we can only talk about our problems effectively, we will have a good relationship. I think that single idea may have caused more marital mischief than any other idea in the history of relationships. Such an approach can at times keep partners focused on their discontents: thinking about, worrying about, organizing, and ruminating on them. That is clearly a bad idea. Helpful practices that focus on solving rather than simply debating issues include learning to accept some differences and finding ways to soften how we approach each other about differences.

One of the more helpful practices in strengthening couple relationships and solving problems is simply to accept some differences and allow for them as a continuing part of the relationship. Gottman estimates that as many as 69 percent of our discontents in marriage are not going to go away.[26] Daniel Wile suggests that even the best relationships have unresolvable differences.[27] The key to marital happiness is not to rid the relationship of differences: we ignore some, tolerate others, laugh about our humanness, and discuss those things we can do to work better together. I can make requests instead of expressing complaints. In fact, according to Gottman, "one of the great paradoxes . . . is that people don't change unless they feel accepted as they are."[28] Accepting your partner may be more important for a healthy relationship than changing your partner.[29]

Learning to be accepting of a child, not focusing on his or her inadequacies, is a practical and powerful practice that applies to fathers. Children have different temperaments and preferences that may at times rub a parent the wrong way. Fathers, however, will find such relationships strengthened as they allow children to be different and simply accept some differences.

An additional principle that can benefit couples is to remain calm in the face of differences and be open rather than defensive about other views or ideas. In Gottman's research on marriage, he traces the very predictable pattern that couples often follow when they fight.[30] First, a spouse will become irritated and then begin a discussion by making a harsh or negative comment; second, a negative interaction will begin that often includes criticism, contempt, defensiveness, or stonewalling; third, partners become physically agitated or "flooded" with negative feelings; and fourth, spouses begin to turn away from each other and become distant or isolated by their anger or irritation. He suggests that, rather than travel down the "distance and isolation cascade," women in particular can "soften the startup"—they can find inviting ways to launch relationship discussions. For example, rather than saying, "I'm just about sick of you making messes all over the house," one might say, "I'm having a hard time keeping the house clean and would like to talk with you about how we can do a better job of keeping it clean."

Gottman also suggests that men in particular, rather than react with anxiety and defensiveness to a spouse's suggestions, can learn to soothe themselves so they can participate helpfully in the relationship discussion. For example, when a husband feels himself getting upset or defensive, he might calm himself with an inner conversation: "She cares about our relationship. If I listen attentively and patiently, I may learn things that will make our relationship even better." Learning and practicing these skills can assist couples in solving difficulties rather than making them worse. Additionally, these skills carry over into other relationships and can benefit men as they interact with their children.

Ultimately, each couple must find the process of solving problems that works for them. For example, 30 years of marriage have taught me that I should not try to discuss problems when I am tired and crabby. A few tips that can help in solving problems include:

- Do not let yourself have a conversation about an issue if you are feeling tired, sick, or irritable. Many problems disappear after a good night's rest.
- Avoid assuming that a spouse does things that bother you out of selfishness or lack of consideration—in other words, don't assume the worst.
- Focus on communicating to a spouse how much you appreciate what they do.

- Do not take a particular problem and decide it is a huge character flaw or that it applies to all parts of a relationship.
- Listen to and consider a variety of ideas or courses of action when working through solutions to an issue.
- Allow time for changes and be respectful and appreciative of efforts that a partner makes to work on an issue.

For those who are able to manage problem-solving discussions without catastrophizing, there are good guides to communication that can also be helpful.[31]

Focusing on solutions in couples' relationships also has specific benefits for fathers in their efforts. First, if couples are more accepting of differences, there is less stress in the marriage. They are then more able as parents to spend time and energy caring for their children rather than focusing on difficulties with each other. Second, fathers who feel more at peace in their relationships are able to be more responsive to the immediate needs and interests of their children. Finally, parents who focus on reaching solutions model for their children how to work through issues in their own relationships with siblings, friends, or other adults.

Marital Principle 6: Serve

A final core principle that can strengthen relationships is for couples to focus on serving a larger cause. Togetherness is cultivated by working toward such a goal. Practices that foster serving together include involvement in common purposes or projects and building the relationship on values that unite the couple.

Blaine Fowers, a unique thinker on marriage, has suggested that relationships can be strengthened by finding common projects, causes, or opportunities to serve a larger cause together.[32] For example, a couple might remodel the house, operate a business, support Habitat for Humanity, or tutor school children together. In fact, raising good children together can be a very satisfying basis for a relationship. This allows couples to unite in significant purposes and also look beyond themselves and their own needs. While this may seem stressful in a busy world, many couples report that such efforts rejuvenate them and help them remember what is most important. An additional benefit of a focus on common projects is that children can be included and tutored in service and activities that are meaningful to the couple. Such common activities provide a convenient context in which fathers can engage their children and instruct them in life's lessons.

Building the relationship on common values that unite a couple supports the principle of serving each other and others. For many couples, finding and supporting common values allows them to join together in meaningful ways. For example, spouses might share a significant belief in the value of education. They might then support one another in pursuing educational opportunities and also creating a home atmosphere that shows their children they value education.

The principle of serving suggests development of love that is mature, solid, and lasting, not immature, shifting, and transitory. Men and women both benefit from the development of such love, and children are served well by love that serves their needs for security, permanence, and trust. Fathers who learn these lessons in marriage are more able to apply them to parenting their children and providing a home of security and love. The garden of marriage will, if well cultivated, assist men in becoming better spouses and better parents to the children who are supported by the fruits of that garden.

Conclusion

The quality of a couple's relationship often has important influences on what kind of father a man is. Men become fathers in relationships. Marriage provides the opportunity for men, women, and children to grow and flourish. This chapter has furnished a brief discussion of six principles that undergird healthy relationships. I have given a few ideas about how the principles can be applied, but ultimately the quality of a relationship depends on their creative application to each person's unique relationship. To commit, grow, understand, nurture, solve, and serve—such principles will provide a sound foundation for men as both husbands and fathers.

If we want to someday have the "family life garden" of our dreams, we must be prepared to invest years of patient work. Just as a determined gardener consults experienced neighbors and professionals for solutions to problems, so a determined marriage partner seeks the counsel of wise neighbors and authors. Applying this counsel can enable individuals to cultivate relationships—as spouses or parents—that will be planted in good soil, nurtured over time, and productive of beauty and love. Mature love is not breathless discovery and fascination but rather . . . like cultivating a garden.

Endnotes

1. Grych, J.H., 2002, "Marital Relationships and Parenting," in *Handbook of Parenting, Vol. 4: Social Conditions and Applied Parenting*, 2nd ed., edited by M.H. Bornstein, Mahwah, NJ: Lawrence Erlbaum, pp. 203–225, at 222.

2. Doherty, W.J., Kouneski, E.F., and Erickson, M.F., 1998, "Responsible Fathering: An Overview and Conceptual Framework," *Journal of Marriage and the Family*, 60, 277–292, at 286.

3. Ibid., at 286.

4. Hawkins, A.J., and Dollahite, D.C. (Eds.), 1997, *Generative Fathering: Beyond Deficit Perspectives*, Thousand Oaks, CA: Sage.

5. Gottman, J.M., 1994, *Why Marriages Succeed or Fail and How You Can Make Yours Last*, New York: Simon and Schuster.

6. Gottman, J.M., Coan, J., Carrere, S., and Swanson, C., 1998, "Predicting Marital Happiness and Stability from Newlywed Interaction," *Journal of Marriage and the Family*, 60, 5–22.

7. Gottman, J.M., 1999a, *The Marriage Clinic: A Scientifically Based Marital Therapy*, New York: W.W. Norton and Co.

8. Christensen, A., and Jacobson, N.S., 2000, *Reconcilable Differences*, New York: Guilford.

9. Smith, C.A., Cudaback, D., Goddard, H.W., and Myers-Walls, J.A., 1994, National Extension Parent Education Model (NEPEM), Manhattan, KS: Kansas Cooperative Extension Service.

10. Gottman, 1999a.

11. Goddard, H.W., and Olson, C.S., 2004, "Cooperative Extension Initiatives in Marriage and Couples Education," *Family Relations*, 53, 433–439.

12. Ibid.

13. Doherty, W.J., 1999, "How Therapy Can Be Hazardous to Your Marital Health," presentation at the Annual Conference of the Coalition for Marriage, Family, and Couples Education, www.smartmarriages.com/hazardous.html.

14. Glass, S.P., 2003, *Not "Just Friends,"* New York: Free Press.

15. Gottman, 1994, at 127.

16. Ibid., at 224.

17. Seligman, M.E.P., 2002, *Authentic Happiness*, New York: Free Press.

18. Covey, S.R., 1989, *The 7 Habits of Highly Effective People*, New York: Simon and Schuster.

19. Covey, S.R., 1997, *The 7 Habits of Highly Effective Families*, New York: Golden Books, at 205.

20. Gottman, J.M., 1999b, *The Seven Principles for Making Marriage Work*, New York: Crown.

21. Ginott, H.G., Ginott, A., and Goddard, H.W., 2003, *Between Parent and Child*, New York: Three Rivers Press.

22. Brotherson, S.E., Dollahite, D.C., and Hawkins, A.J., 2005, "Generative Fathering and the Dynamics of Connection between Fathers and Their Children," *Fathering*, 3(1), 1–28.

23. Gottman, 1999b, pp. 47–60.

24. Gottman, 1999b.

25. Lee, T.R., Burr, W.R., Beutler, I., Yorgason, F., Harker, H.B., and Olsen, J.A., 1997, "The Family Profile II: A Self-Scored, Brief Family Assessment Tool," *Psychological Reports*, 81, 467–477.

26. Gottman, 1999a.

27. Wile, D.B., 1988, *After the Honeymoon*, New York: Wiley.

28. Gottman, 1994, at 184.

29. Christensen and Jacobson, 2000.

30. Gottman, 1994; Gottman, 1999b.

31. Notarius, C., and Markman, H., 1993, *We Can Work It Out*, New York: Perigee.

32. Fowers, B.J., 2000, *Beyond the Myth of Marital Happiness*, San Francisco, CA: Jossey-Bass.

Author Scott S. Hall playing a game with his three daughters

The Daddy-Daughter Dance: Insights for Father-Daughter Relationships

Scott S. Hall and J. Neil Tift

There was always a kick in my experiences with Daddy, in the things he taught me about the world. If someone were to tell me that I 'think like a woman,' I'd know it was meant as an insult, but I'd consider it a compliment. My father encouraged my interests in science and art, but he never forgot to tell me that he thought I was beautiful, too.[1]

The father described above left a lasting impression on his daughter. Her comments reflect the potential for good in a father's contributions to the life of a daughter. Such a father has much to offer a daughter. He influences many aspects of her development and identity. In return, she influences him. This process of mutual influence presents both fathers and daughters with the opportunity to engage in a dance that will shape their lives. Some schools and churches sponsor a daddy-daughter dance, a fun and enlightening evening reserved for young girls and their admired fathers. In life, a daddy-daughter dance of sorts occurs with much more at stake.[2]

As fathers of daughters, we have experienced much of this dance firsthand. Scott is the father of an eight-year-old daughter and twin five-year-old daughters who constantly challenge and reward his efforts to guide and build a lasting relationship with them. Neil is the father of two adopted daughters with special needs who are now ages 38 and eight. They have taught him many wonderful lessons in trying to be the best dad he can be. Throughout this chapter, we will discuss several main points about father-daughter relationships based on scholarly research, established theory, and our own experiences. We will explore (1) some popular portrayals of father-daughter relationships in media and history, (2) research findings that show the importance of fathers for daughters, (3) insights regarding the nature and significance of father-daughter relations ("the dance"), and (4) suggestions for fathers and daughters to help develop and enhance their relationship.

Popular Portrayals of Father-Daughter Relationships

Sadly, father-daughter relationships have been historically portrayed in a relatively negative light in many instances. For example, scholars Goulter and Minninger documented six patterns of father-daughter relationship styles depicted in various forms of fiction, drama, biographies, case histories, and myths.[3] The troubling aspect of this research is that all six styles focus on negative patterns of father-daughter interaction. Here is a brief summary of the six styles described:

- *Lost father and yearning daughter.* This pair is a distant or absent father and a daughter who feels inadequate and unable to earn a man's acceptance.
- *Abusive father and victimized daughter.* After years of abuse by a father, the daughter holds on to the victim role and plays it out in her other relationships.
- *Pampering father and spoiled daughter.* These fathers struggle to let go of the feelings of being idealized and adored they receive from a daughter, and this makes it difficult for her to learn a sense of inner control and autonomy.[4]
- *Pygmalion father with a companion daughter.* This pattern suggests a father as mentor who molds her into his perfect companion, and thus the daughter feels she would be nothing without her father's guidance and support.
- *Ruined father and rescuing daughter.* This portrayal may take the form of a distant but suddenly needy father and a daughter who takes the opportunity to win his approval at the sacrifice of her own well-being.

- *Anguished father and angry daughter.* This would be a father who regrets the enmity between him and his daughter and a daughter who punishes and rejects him in his time of need.

For the most part, these suggested patterns give little cause for optimism about the father-daughter relationship and leave the impression that most such relationships are unhealthy if not destructive.

Does this summary reflect reality? Certainly there are myriads of examples of healthy father-daughter relationships. Numerous studies, including some reviewed later in this chapter, indicate there are fathers who are present, warm, interested, and caring toward their daughters as well as daughters who appreciate their fathers and thrive in part due to their interaction with them. However, if these suggested portrayals accurately indicate commonly accepted perceptions of father-daughter relationships, might this promote a self-fulfilling prophecy? Might fathers and daughters assume these relations are doomed to failure, resulting in less commitment between them? Might others they rely on for support be less enthusiastic about helping to maintain prolonged interaction between them? If so, there is great need for more positive models and portrayals of this important relationship.

Scott recently had a conversation with a man whose wife had given birth to their first daughter a few months earlier (they already had two sons). The father believed he understood how he wanted to raise his sons and what they needed to be prepared for adulthood but had merely a vague vision of what he had to offer his daughter. He expressed his love for her but saw his role in her life as inherently peripheral relative to the one he would play in his sons' lives (he looks forward to reading this chapter as soon as it is published!). Having more positive, abundant, and visible examples of father-daughter relationships can help such fathers—before they even become fathers—appreciate the relevance they have for daughters and give them some ideas about how to have a healthy, mutually satisfying relationship.

The styles described above, however, are useful for developing an appreciation of the kinds of issues fathers and daughters may deal with in their relationships. They are also examples of patterns that generally should be avoided. A given father and daughter who mirror one of the negative patterns might not be able to see it in themselves because they are too close to the situation.[5] It would be especially important for a father to talk to others who can reflect back to him the patterns they observe between him and his daughter. It is possible that Scott's discussion with the father described above, for example, provided such enlightenment. A spouse, parent, grandparent, sibling, close friend, clergy member, or other trusted associate can approach a father with a nonthreatening tone and help him see his father-daughter relationship from a different perspective. When fathers gain a clear understanding of common relationship dynamics between fathers and daughters and realize the positive and negative consequences of their own patterns of interaction, they will better be able to support and guide their daughters. They may even learn a few new steps in the daddy-daughter dance.

The Importance of Fathers for Daughters

What do research findings tell us about father-daughter relationships? This is still an emerging area of scientific research, and much remains to be learned. However, discoveries persuade us to suggest that fathers play a critical and lasting role in the lives and well-being of their daughters.

In recent years, the presence and involvement of fathers in the lives of their children has received significant attention in many sectors of society. This spotlight on fathers and children is important, especially in light of the increasingly obvious consequences of growing up without a father.[6] A father's influence on his daughter sometimes may seem less immediate or obvious than on sons.[7] This may lead many observers and service providers to minimize the importance of the father-daughter relationship. Though a great deal more remains to be learned about a father's impact on his daughter, much has already been discovered about his important contributions to her life.

Fathers are indeed important to their daughters' development. An in-depth review of recent studies shows that daughters with warm, supportive fathers tend to also have higher self-esteem, greater life satisfaction, less depression, more social competence with peers, and more psychological maturity.[8] Compared to those who grow up without a father in the home, girls who live with their fathers and mothers tend to score higher on standardized math, science, reading, and history exams.[9] Fathers who spend time with their adolescent daughters in leisure and home activities experience closer-father daughter relationships that result in their daughters' higher levels of well-being.[10]

Another strand of research suggests that caring fathers can play an important protective role for daughters in shielding them from social and behavioral risks. For example, a 15-year-old from a single-mother household is three times as likely to lose her virginity before her 16th birthday as one who has lived with both parents.[11] Fathers, more than mothers, seem to play an especially significant role in preventing their daughters' antisocial behavior. Specifically, daughters whose fathers spend time with them, show them affection, and listen to their opinions are less likely to engage in behaviors such as substance abuse, violence, and theft.[12] For various reasons discussed later, daughters with loving, involved fathers may feel less need to prove or validate themselves through negative or destructive behavior.

The active role of a father in his daughter's life not only is critical for her well-being but also has unique qualities that are somewhat distinct from father-son relationships. For example, Dean Peterson and Shelley Kirkpatrick, a father-daughter research team, have shown through their research that father-daughter relationships are based upon mutual affection and are more relaxed, more stable, and less complex than father-son relationships.[13] In predicting a child's self-esteem, sustained contact with the father matters more for sons, but physical affection from fathers matters more for daughters.[14] Other research has shown that physical affection from a father is particularly important for adolescent daughters' self-esteem but not as important for sons' self-esteem.[15] Similarly, spending time with their fathers was strongly related to school-aged girls' feelings of closeness with them, whereas for boys other factors were more important for creating such feelings.[16] In short, what a father does to benefit his son may not be identically beneficial for his daughter.

It is important for fathers, particularly those with experience raising a son, to recognize and react to the unique aspects of their father-daughter relationship. This is not to suggest that a father should simply treat a daughter differently because of the mistaken assumption that she is in some way less competent, willing, or durable than a son. However, a father needs to realize things might be different between him and his daughter than between him and his son for a variety of reasons described below. Fathers who are sensitive to their daughters' needs and requests that may originate from the unique qualities of the father-daughter relationship will be better able to respond in a helpful and meaningful way.

Insights into the Father-Daughter Relationship Dance

The daddy-daughter dance can be quite complex and unique. Various aspects of both fathers' and daughters' experiences and expectations come together to create numerous twists, turns, and dips. Some key issues that emerge from examining this relationship dance include taking advantage of opportunities to learn from each other's diverse perspectives, promoting healthy individual development, creating a template for close relationships, and influencing a positive female identity.

Learning from Each Other's Diverse Experiences

What is it about the father-daughter relationship that makes it particularly important and sometimes unique? Gender is perhaps one of the more obvious factors. The nature of a cross-gender relationship is sure to create some circumstances that differ from same-sex parent/child combinations. To the extent that males and females experience life differently, fathers and daughters may struggle at times relating to one another, which may pose a barrier to the quality of their relationship. For example, some fathers feel threatened and even betrayed when their daughters experience the changes associated with puberty.[17] Having grown up seeing the world through the eyes of a male, some fathers simply find it difficult to relate to their maturing daughters.[18]

Scott (who has all daughters) describes his opportunity to learn from his daughters:

> In addition to having three daughters and no sons, I grew up without sisters. Our pets were even male! It is something new for me to observe dance classes, learn about tights and dresses, and discover the never-ending hairstyle possibilities of decorative bows and barrettes. Despite my efforts thus far, my daughters have shown little interest in participating in some of my favorite leisure activities, like watching or playing sports. Thus, finding things to relate to with them hasn't come as easily as it might have with sons, but I have looked for meaningful ways to spend time together. I know that if I don't take the time to appreciate their interests and experiences I will miss out on building a strong relationship with them.

Though finding ways to bond with their daughters may take special efforts for some fathers, having diverse experiences due to their gender differences is also an opportunity for fathers to broaden their own horizons. Learning to see things from a daughter's perspective (one to which fathers may feel quite unaccustomed) can help them appreciate different aspects of life. At the same time, fathers have an opportunity to help their daughters understand some of the commonly shared experiences and perceptions of boys. This can lead to daughters' greater appreciation of some of the unique aspects of growing up male in a given social context and better equip them to interact with boys and men. For example, Neil and his eight-year-old daughter were once stuck in a motel room on a road trip. Hannah found a Three Stooges movie marathon on TV and invited her dad to join her. After watching their antics for a while, Neil explained that the violence was not real. Hannah responded that she was just watching them because she knew it would help her when she was talking to boys.

Fathers may be able to offer insightful advice on how to thrive in male-dominated contexts and how to be assertive and firm when rejecting boys' unwanted advances. The nature of experiences shaped by gender differences may make it more difficult for fathers and daughters to identify with one another at times. However, it can also be a strength in their relationship because of what they have to offer each other.

Healthy Individual Development

The connection a father makes with his daughter is also critical for influencing her healthy social, physical, and psychological development as an individual. Simple daily interactions, such as when Daddy plays the growling monster and she has to decide when to run and hide and when to confront the monster, promote decision-making skills at a young age. He can also encourage her sense of competitiveness with games like racing to the bedroom or trying to outlast one another in a staring contest. Scott and his daughters have developed all sorts of engaging bedtime rituals (that tend to energize them before bed, but he can't resist). Sometimes his daughters race him, often they see how far they can walk on their hands toward their rooms while he holds and tickles their feet, and most typically they request in what fashion they want to be carried to bed (on his shoulders while twisting and running into walls is an unfortunate favorite). Some fathers shy away from rough-and-tumble play with their daughters even though it would help foster their physical development.[19]

Because of his male perspective, a father can provide especially credible guidance while his daughter learns to portray socially her femininity, sexuality, and personhood to other males. He may have many opportunities to help a daughter recognize situations in which she is discounted for being a female by paying attention to the music she listens to, the television shows and movies she watches, or the posters and pictures that collects and displays. Neil describes such an experience with his daughter:

> Ophelia wanted to start wearing makeup around the age of 12. She came home one day and asked if she could purchase and start wearing eye shadow, lipstick, and blush at school. I tried to explain to her the derivation of the concept of makeup and the message behind it. When she was applying her makeup, she was attempting to "make up" for a flaw in her natural beauty or did not think she was pretty enough without the application of this powder and paint. I was not opposed to my daughter's desire to wear it but just wanted her to understand the implications of her actions and society's messages to which she was responding.

Daughters who miss out on the emotional and psychological security of a loving, accepting father are also at risk for trying to prove their worth to males in self-destructive ways. When fathers are absent or distant, daughters may learn to idealize them (children tend to romanticize what they don't have as being better than what they have) and obsess about what they are missing.[20] If the father is present but there are problems in the relationship, some (especially insecure) daughters have a tendency to blame themselves for those problems.[21] Thus, as a young woman matures, she may find herself in overly dependent and/or abusive relationships with men, trying to adjust her behavior and values in ways that will win a male's approval, leaving her open to further suffering and insecurities.[22] In the extreme, the absence of a father who can defend his daughter's safety and honor may lead girls toward "perverse alternatives," such as pursuing intimacy with older, predatory men.[23] A father's affirming behavior can go a long way in promoting healthy psychological development that helps her feel inherently worthy of respect and mutuality from others, especially males.

Relationship Template

The father-daughter relationship can influence girls' future relationships with men, romantic or otherwise. A father is typically the first man a young girl loves, which helps her form a template for male-female relations.[24] The way this man that she looks up to treats another important person in her life—her mother—can set a profound example of what such interactions should entail. Similarly, the way he treats his daughter models to her what she will likely assume to be appropriate cross-gender behavior. What will she think if he is too angry and rough with her? How will she feel if he insults and demeans her? Will she begin to associate love with abrasiveness? Will she learn to tolerate abuse from a future partner who professes to love her? Recognizing such possibilities—that they are constant role models for future healthy relationships—can and should motivate fathers to be in control of their anger, treat family members appropriately, and grow and mature as healthy adults. Fathers tend to be especially susceptible to the motivating influence of caring for and guiding their children.[25] The daddy-daughter dance can create meaningful, lasting memories and healthy behavior patterns for both partners.

Fathers can also directly instruct their daughters about forming healthy relationships. Neil recounts another incident with his daughter:

> While I was driving Hannah to school one morning, the radio DJ made a sexist reference about a famous young movie star's body parts. I immediately turned off the car radio and had a frank discussion with her about what to do if any boys tried to judge her by the quality of her body parts. I told her that she or any girl always deserves to be treated with respect. I hope that through the art of healthy male-female communication skills, she will be able to ask for what she wants in her relationships and refuse what she does not want.

The guidance of a trusted father can help young girls critically evaluate the social messages they receive about relationships and the types of men with whom they desire to form relationships.

Developing a Positive Female Identity

Father-daughter relationships are also important for girls' identity development and gaining a personal sense of competency. Fathers can act to reinforce a daughter's sense of femininity and self-worth while at the same time she is busy identifying and bonding with her mother. She learns about gender roles by acting out complementary roles to her father and observing how he responds to stereotypically feminine or masculine behavior.[26] His views about the worth of girls and women send profound messages to girls that affect their beliefs about their value as females.[27]

Fathers need to be cautious and purposeful about the messages they give their daughters about gender. Neil recalls the following experience with his daughter:

> We were watching a children's movie involving a medical procedure. A young nurse walked in and helped save a child's life. Hannah leaned over to me and said that she wanted to be a nurse when she grew up. I whispered to her that, if she really liked medicine, she should think about becoming a doctor.

When fathers value their daughters' intellectual and athletic pursuits and engage in more physical play, adolescent girls and young women tend to be more assertive and have higher achievement orientations.[28] The opposite effects tend to occur when fathers are protective to the point that they smother and overindulge their daughters.[29] Thus, fathers who take the opportunity to read to their daughters, play chess with them, or teach them about finances and politics provide a broad exposure to flexible gender-role possibilities.

Fathers also play a major role in guiding their daughters through the developmental task of breaking away and transitioning from their tight bond with mothers toward the larger social world.[30] This is a critical part of the dance that helps prepare a daughter for multiple aspects of her future. Underinvolved fathers put their daughters at greater risk for developing personal insecurity, rigidity, and/or isolation. For daughters to develop a strong sense of competence, especially in academic skills or their femininity, a close and warm relationship with a father is a great asset and blessing.[31]

Learning to Dance—Suggestions for Fathers and Daughters

Father-daughter relationships can be very diverse and distinct, depending especially on the father's level of commitment to be intimately involved in his daughter's life. There are a number of things that fathers can do as they learn to guide the relationship dance with their daughters and build a caring relationship.

First, it is important to mention that it isn't just fathers who affect the tone of the relationship (or dance). Daughters also take part. However, the father is in a position to set the stage early for the course of the relationship and deliberately create and maintain certain relationship patterns. He must take the responsibility of doing so as his daughter gradually becomes more autonomous and asserts more control over the relationship. He should also be flexible and realize their relationship will fluctuate and evolve over time but that they can still make contributions to each other's lives regardless of how peripheral they may feel at times. Each positive example of father-daughter interaction can also help foster more encouraging and empowering social expectations of what fathers and daughters can establish and maintain in their relationship. You never know who may be watching you and learning from your example of how to treat and connect with a cherished daughter.

Fathers can do many things to positively connect with and influence their daughters. Consider the following suggestions:

- Spend time with her—amount and quality of time are both important. Be there for your daughter. No man ever says at the end of his life that he wished he spent more time at work. His regrets are typically that he did not spend enough time with his family.
- When you genuinely praise a young girl's efforts and not just her results, she can learn how a significant man in her life shows his appreciation. Help her to feel accepted for who she is and avoid sending messages of rejection.
- Encourage her curiosity and sense of exploration. Encourage her to find ways to pursue her interests in math, science, medicine, law, and related fields. Help her by building a science project together or entering an inventors' contest.
- Encourage the development of her dexterity and motor skills. Teach her to fold a paper airplane, jump on a trampoline, whistle through her teeth, eat with chopsticks, build a kite, play with a yo-yo, or walk on stilts.
- Promote academic achievement in her life. Read to her, play checkers or chess with her, show her how to pay bills, and teach her the importance of managing money and economic accountability.
- Enhance her relationship skills and values. Teach her to believe in and love herself.
- Assist her in developing meaningful and fun hobbies. Engage in sports and other types of physical activity with her such as playing catch, tossing a Frisbee, shooting baskets, hitting a tennis ball, playing tag, jumping rope, etc. Encourage appropriate opportunities for her to express her competitiveness.
- Create routines such as tickle time, cuddle time, homework time, and story time that generate opportunities to communicate as well as build trust and reliability in your interactions.
- Help her to recognize the myriad messages that can influence her personal body image. Take time to help her understand healthy eating habits.
- Celebrate rites of passage with her. Look at the minor milestones in her future and discuss them with her: her first dry night in bed without a diaper; her first sleepover; her first day of school; her first bicycle ride without training wheels; her First Communion, Bas Mitzvah, or other religious rite of passage; her first dance; her first date.

- Teach her how to protect herself. Show her how to avoid unnecessary risks and vulnerable situations.
- Model how she can be assertive, how to say "no," how to maintain her stance when she means "no." Teach her how to present a confident presence. Teach her to identify and safely exit situations where others might be trying to use or exploit her.
- Model how she should be treated and respected by men in her life by respecting her mother. You have the greatest influence on her ability to relate to boys and men.
- As she discovers the world of relationships, she will need to be able to make healthy decisions about who is compatible as a potential friend. Discuss with her the values and behaviors she should look for in friends and relationships.
- Help to guide her decisions about female role models. Take her to meet a female polar explorer, stock car racer, scientist, businesswoman, or artist. Point out exemplary women who thrive and overcome obstacles in their family relationships. Let her hear their stories, which will invite her to pursue her unique dreams and passions.
- Encourage her to engage in appropriate risk-taking behaviors: what to drink, where to go, when to dive, when and where to swim, when to accelerate, and how to brake. Teach her to take care of herself and others. Teach her skills to survive and thrive in the parts of her world that are male-dominated.
- Become her champion. Give her the security she needs growing up. Be there for her so she doesn't have to look elsewhere for a positive male influence. Don't let her feel "father hunger." Don't let your absence be a reason for your daughter to seek out alternative or unhealthy relationships with men.

Fathers can contribute significantly to a daughter's sense of self and influence her views of the world and potential impact on it. A caring father takes an active role in shaping the person his daughter becomes and the type of relationship they experience together throughout their lives.

Conclusion

The nature of the father-daughter relationship shifts and changes in step with the diverse rhythms and stages of life—like the loosely choreographed movement and interaction of an evening of dance. Dancing usually includes some awkward moments of silence and stepping on toes, yet the father of a young daughter must be willing to lead her across the entire dance floor, weaving in and out of the crowd of fellow dancers. He has to know when to pause (listen to her), when to pick up the tempo (concentrate on her needs), when to spin her (play), when to dip her (offer her guidance and support), when to let her dance by herself, and when to determine they have had enough and that the evening is over. As she grows older, Dad has to be willing to let someone cut in on their dance and share her. Overall, this dance can be very rewarding for fathers and daughters alike. However, many aspects of a maturing daughter's future rely on how well her father leads her and adjusts to the ever-changing music. What she learns about males and relationships with them, how she develops socially and psychologically into a healthy woman, and how valued she feels as a female are some of the key areas in which her father can have a significant positive or negative impact.

The issues and recommendations highlighted in this chapter can give fathers important insight into the typical opportunities and pitfalls that are essential elements of the father-daughter relationship. Ultimately, the most critical thing for a father to do is get to know his own daughter. To the extent possible, he should learn about her needs, desires, and dreams from her. She may not simply express all of them vocally or directly. A father will have to be patient and attentive, but the better he knows his daughter and the more she trusts him, the more accurately and frequently he will pick up on her clues. No two father-daughter pairs dance exactly alike, but one reality is true for all: the rhythm and pattern of the father-daughter relationship dance will have a lasting impact on who our daughters become. Listen to the music, don't be afraid to take some dance lessons, and have fun.

Endnotes

1. Fields, S., 1983, *Like Father, Like Daughter: How Father Shapes the Woman His Daughter Becomes*, Boston: Little, Brown, and Company.

2. Goulter, B., and Minninger, J., 1993, *The Father-Daughter Dance: Insight, Inspiration, and Understanding for Every Woman and Her Father*, New York: G.P. Putnam's Sons.

3. Ibid.

4. Kavaler, S.A., 1988, "The Father's Role in the Self-Development of His Daughter," in *Critical Psychophysical Passages in the Life of a Woman: A Psychodynamic Perspective*, edited by J. Offerman-Zuckerberg, New York: Plenum Medical Book Company, pp. 49–65.

5. Perkins, R.M., 2001, "The Father-Daughter Relationship: Familial Interactions That Impact a Daughter's Style of Life," *College Student Journal*, 35, 616–627.

6. Goulter and Minninger, 1993.

7. Morgan, J.V., Wilcoxon, S.A., and Satcher, J.F., 2003, "The Father-Daughter Relationship Inventory: A Validation Study," *Family Therapy*, 30, 77–93.

8. Ibid.

9. Downey, D.B., and Powell, B., 1993, "Do Children in Single-Parent Households Fare Better Living with Same-Sex Parents?" *Journal of Marriage and Family*, 55, 55–71.

10. Brotherson, S.E., Yamamoto, T., and Acock, A., 2003, "Connection and Communication in Father-Child Relationships and Adolescent Child Well-Being," *Fathering*, 1, 191–214.

11. Smith, L., 1994, "The New Wave of Illegitimacy," *Fortune*, 18, 81–94.

12. Kosterman, R., Haggerty, K.P., Spoth, R., and Redmond, C., 2004, "Unique Influences of Mothers and Fathers on Their Children's Antisocial Behavior," *Journal of Marriage and Family*, 66, 762–778.

13. Kirkpatrick, S.D., and Peterson, R.D., 1999, interview for National Institute for Healthcare Research.

14. Duncan, G.J., Hill, M., and Jeung, W.J., 1996, "Fathers' Activities and Children's Attainments," paper presented at the Conference on Father Involvement, Washington, DC, October 10–11, pp. 5–6.

15. Barber, B., and Thomas, D., 1986, "Dimensions of Fathers' and Mothers' Supportive Behavior: A Case for Physical Affection," *Journal of Marriage and the Family*, 48, 783–794.

16. Crouter, A.C., and Crowley, M.S., 1990, "School-Aged Children's Time Alone with Fathers in Single- and Dual-Earner Families: Implications for the Father-Child Relationship," *Journal of Early Adolescence*, 10, 296–312.

17. Endres, T.G., 1997, "Father-Daughter Dramas: A Q-Investigation of Rhetorical Visions," *Journal of Applied Communication Research*, 25, 317–340.

18. Perkins, 2001.

19. Power, R.G., 1985, "Mother- and Father-Infant Play: A Developmental Analysis," *Child Development*, 56, 1514–1524.

20. Morgan et al., 2003.

21. Goulter and Minninger, 1993.

22. Contratto, S., 1987, "Father Presence in Women's Psychological Development," in *Advances in Psychoanalytic Sociology*, edited by J. Rabow, G.M. Platt, and M.S. Goldman, Malabar, FL: Robert E Krieger Publishing Company, pp. 138–157.

23. Hsu, G.S., 1996, "Leaving the Vulnerable Open to Abuse," *Perspective*, (September 9), 32–37.

24. Perkins, 2001.

25. McAdams, D.P., de St Aubin, E., and Logan, R.L., 1993, "Generativity among Young, Midlife, and Older Adults," *Psychology and Aging*, 8, 221–230.

26. Russel, A., and Saebel, J., 1997, "Mother-Son, Mother-Daughter, Father-Son, Father-Daughter: Are They Distinct Relationships?" *Developmental Review*, 17, 111–147.

27. Goulter and Minninger, 1993.

28. Morgan et al., 2003.

29. Snarey, J., 1993, *How Fathers Care for the Next Generation: A Four-Decade Study*, Cambridge, MA: Harvard University Press.

30. Ibid.

31. Coley, R.L., 1998, "Children's Socialization Experiences and Functioning in Single-Mother Households: The Importance of Fathers and Other Men," *Child Development*, 69, 219–230.

Pictured clockwise are author Alan C. Taylor (top, center) with his grandfather, Wallace; son, Bronson; and father, Robert

Grandfathers:
Rediscovering America's Forgotten Resource

Alan C. Taylor

Many of us have wonderful memories, past or present, of times spent with our grandfathers. Whether it was at family reunions, celebrations, dinners, or just hanging out together, shared times with my grandparents were positive and worthwhile. I vividly remember my grandfather teaching me to play pool and telling me stories of his childhood growing up on a cattle ranch in southern Idaho. He recounted tales of his life as a young man, rounding up wild horses in Nevada to earn enough money to purchase his own cattle ranch.

Often parents don't realize the important contribution a grandparent can play in children's lives. Research has shown that grandfathers can be a positive resource for grandchildren in many ways. They can actually influence fundamental aspects of their grandchildren's lives, including helping them form their own individual identities and conveying to them family values, ideals, and beliefs. The idea that grandfathers are influential in their grandchildren's development has been noted in scholarly research over the past 20 years.[1] Grandfathers can be a bridge across time to care for and nurture a new and rising generation. Wendell Berry, a farmer and author, once suggested that an image of the best and most responsible kind of agriculture was that of "an old man caring for a young tree."[2] Grandfathers can represent such an image of linking families together over generations and nurturing their growth.

Grandfathers in Family Life—What Do We Know?

Grandfathers have been referred to for many years as the silent and distant grandparent, often sitting in the background and supporting grandmothers as intergenerational families interact with one another. Past social science research has indicated that, based on gender differences among grandparents, grandfathers have predominantly been viewed as less nurturing and less involved in the lives of their grandchildren. Ideas that focus on traditional gender differences have too often been interpreted to support an emphasis on the negatives of grandfathering. These negative portrayals end up promoting caricatures of grandfathers as distant figures or "grumpy old men" rather than the larger reality of grandfathers who are warm and interested in their grandchildren. Too often such images imply that grandfathers simply do not live up to the expectations we have of a quality grandparent, ultimately devaluing grandfather-grandchild relationships.

Unfortunately, most of what we know about grandparenthood through social science research is based on grandmothers' experiences, attitudes, and behaviors. Though there has not been much research on grandparenting, a greater problem lies in the fact that grandfathers are largely underrepresented in studies of grandparents of both genders. In other words, although an article may report "grandparenting" statistics, often many of the people interviewed are grandmothers. However, we can paint a portrait of grandparents today.

In the United States, currently about 70 million adults are grandparents (or one in three adults). The average age of a first-time grandparent in the United States is 47, which means that many adults will be grandparents for 25 to 30 years or longer.[3] Additionally, both grandmothers and grandfathers tend to be quite actively involved in the lives of their grandchildren. A national survey of grandparents by the AARP in 2001, for example, indicated that 78 percent of grandparents have seen or talked by phone with a grandchild in the past month, 65 percent have talked with grandchildren at least once a week, and 85 percent have eaten a meal together in the past six months.[4] Grandfathers who were asked about the importance of different roles in their lives considered only the roles of parent and spouse as more important than their role as grandparent.[5] The role of grandparents is increasingly critical for grandchildren. The number of grandparents raising grandchildren in the United States has reached 2.4 million, and nearly one in 10 adults over the age of 30 live with grandchildren in black, Native American, Pacific Islander, and Hispanic populations.[6]

Influences of Grandfathers on Their Grandchildren

The impact and influence that grandparents, and in particular grandfathers, can have on the lives of their grandchildren is significant. Grandfathers tend to exert their influence in a variety of ways that include shaping a child's sense of identity, transmitting family values, and serving as an example of caring and respect.

One area in which grandfathers can affect their grandchildren's lives is by influencing their sense of identity.[7] A better understanding of who we are and where we came from can be developed through relationships with those of previous generations. Research regarding adolescents and young adults has shown that sharing knowledge about cultural and familial roots may be the most important and influential way grandparents can influence an adolescent's search for identity. A lack of bonds, especially at the intergenerational level, may contribute largely to a less developed sense of identity and to a greater struggle in resolving the identity crisis that is common in adolescence and young adulthood.

For example, when an individual does not have positive intergenerational family relationships, a lack of cultural and historical "sense of self" may result. A few years ago I worked at the Utah State prison, teaching a life skills class for inmates preparing for their release. I also conducted research and, as a result, interviewed prison inmates about their grandparental relationships. Those who had strong bonds and support, from not only parents but grandparents, had a much better sense of what they would do to "stay clean" after release. Those without strong ties to their family and extended family seemed more indecisive and, I predicted, were probably more likely to return to their old way of life after leaving prison. This illustrates how a link with grandparents can help younger generations understand who they are and who they want to become.

Grandfathers play a unique and crucial role in this process of developing a sense of identity by serving as arbitrators between parents and children concerning values that are central to family continuity and individual identity. Children gain more abstract concepts of kinship and family heritage through the informal family stories and accounts that grandfathers may tell of earlier generations. One of our family's most precious possessions is the personal scrapbook my father compiled for his grandchildren when he fell ill with cancer. In it he wrote extensive letters to his grandchildren expressing what he hoped for them in this life. In the details of these letters, there was a general feeling of encouragement and advice that has endeared him to the grandchildren he knew before his death and those that were yet to be born. He stressed the importance of family, encouraging us to stay close as family members amidst life's trials and turmoil. He also encouraged his grandchildren to be educated through formal college and university degrees and lifelong learning.

My father's objective to bond with current and future grandchildren taught me a lesson I hope to replicate one day. Writing letters to future grandchildren and great-grandchildren can be done immediately and may help one focus on the type of grandfather one wants to be. It also provides grandchildren with a tangible sense of family heritage that serves as a model for them in developing their own identity within the family context.

In addition to contributing to a sense of identity, grandparents are also influential in the transmission of values, ideals, and beliefs to their grandchildren.[8] The transfer of values from one generation to another is both an aspect of socialization and a fundamental task for families. Historically, socialization of children has been described as a linear process in which values flowed from parents to children. However, today family units are being viewed more as a system of interaction between generations. Grandfathers have significant potential to influence developing children and adolescents by modeling values for younger generations. With the increased longevity among older adults, it is more likely than ever before that we will spend significant time with our grandparents. In addition, more grandparents are raising their grandchildren today than ever before due to divorce, incarceration, or work circumstances of parents.[9]

Grandparental teaching is unique. Sometimes grandparents teach actively, at other times they set an example of what they are trying to convey, and sometimes they simply establish a quiet presence. They are able to serve as living encyclopedias of knowledge by transmitting lessons that can be learned nowhere else. These lessons have lifelong consequences: giving grandchildren a heritage, setting standards for ethics and values, and even providing guidance on religious matters that may not be readily available through other sources.

My own grandfather was a great teacher regarding how to save money and spend wisely. Throughout his life, he saved his hard-earned money as a ranch hand to buy portions of land, piece by piece, in order to establish his own functional cattle ranch. He rarely went into debt or borrowed money as he spent 40-plus years piecing together the necessary components for a successful ranch lifestyle. He showed me how he started from scratch to become a successful businessman with only an eighth-grade education and a lot of determination.

Growing up, I remember that he and my grandmother sent us grandchildren yearly birthday cards with money enclosed. However, there were always specific instructions on how the money was to be spent—for example, $10 for whatever I would like and the other $20 to be put into a savings account for college. These simple instructions helped me to understand the concept and importance of establishing a savings plan.

Many grandfathers hope their grandchildren will learn moral or religious values from them. Current grandfathering research has shown that many men believe in teaching their grandchildren to love their country, serve God, attend church, or develop integrity. In turn, grandchildren perceive their grandfathers as influential in setting standards. Previous social science research studies have reported that grandmothers have a greater influence than grandfathers in almost every value domain and have suggested that grandmothers play a more active role than grandfathers with their grandchildren. However, recent intergenerational research has found that grandfathers have a significant but more subtle influence.[10]

Specifically, respect and consideration for the needs of others are values often transmitted by grandfathers to grandchildren. Respect can be taught regarding the importance of caring for humanity and the environment. Children who observe grandfathers treating others with altruistic values such as kindness, respect, and openness have a template for generating these qualities in their own relationships.

The Roles Grandfathers Play in the Lives of Children

Grandfathers also have the potential and ability to influence their grandchildren through the various roles they play in their lives. In his book, *Contemporary Grandparenting*, grandparenting expert Arthur Kornhaber, M.D., outlined a number of roles assumed by grandparents that include family historian (or link to the past), mentor or teacher, nurturer of emotional and physical well-being, role model for the family and society, and playmate.[11] Grandfathers fill each of these roles in unique ways and help to shape their grandchildren's lives.

Family Historians
Grandfathers acting as family historians teach current generations about the experiences of their ancestors and the origins of their family lineage. Grandfathers are often very knowledgeable about family history and able to provide continuity regarding family traditions and practices. Grandchildren cannot listen to enough stories about when their grandparents were young and the activities they participated in while growing up. These stories also provide valuable insights regarding the lives their parents lived as children.

Sometimes grandfathers are eager to share their life stories. They have one tale after another to tell their family members. Other grandfathers may need a little encouragement. Perhaps taking your grandfather back to the neighborhood he grew up in might trigger some interesting memories of when he was younger.

Another idea is to take a walk with your grandfather through a family cemetery. My wife, Kelly, did this with her father and grandfather a few summers ago.

She found them both to be a wealth of information about relatives who had passed away. They seemed grateful for the opportunity to reminisce about childhood memories featuring their own parents and grandparents who are no longer with us. My wife values that afternoon spent with her father and grandfather as particularly special. Grandfathers who pass on their knowledge of family stories and share their insights allow this information to be passed on to the next generation.

Mentors and Teachers

Just as being a family historian is an important grandparenting role, the role of mentor and teacher is significant to family well-being. Children need caring teachers. Grandfathers, who are mentors or teachers to their grandchildren, often take time to teach a moral principle, share a skill, or instruct in some meaningful way. Through teaching, grandparents may also be sharing their personal or family histories. For example, a grandfather who teaches a grandchild how to tie fishing flies may also be sharing a favorite hobby or pastime from his childhood. Grandparents who prioritize reading with their grandchildren and tell them stories often fall under this category.

If grandfathers seem reticent to share what they know, grandchildren can take a turn initiating this type of conversation. After observing their grandfathers, they can ask them to share something they are good at or something they enjoy doing. For example, if your grandfather is a gardener, take a stroll through his garden with him. Ask him what tips he has for growing certain plants successfully. Engage him in a conversation about why gardening interests him.

People often cannot resist sharing information about their favorite pastimes. As a child, my wife remembers her grandfather as a skilled artist. His letters always included little caricatures of certain family members. He was also talented at drawing and painting landscapes. Kelly remembers asking her grandfather how he painted trees so realistically. He became animated as he explained sponging techniques and the importance of blending different colors of greens and yellows into the leaves. To this day, when my wife sees a painting of trees, she recalls that moment of teaching shared with her grandfather.

Through mentoring, children can obtain a perspective on life that is not only rewarding but can bring them security, peace, and strength. In addition, grandchildren may emulate their grandparents' examples observed through one-on-one interactions. Another aspect of mentoring by grandparents involves demonstrating leadership skills and assuming paternal and maternal responsibilities within the extended family unit. Grandfathers become mentors when they teach everyday skills and values, such as the importance of completing an education and working hard. A mentoring grandfather takes a grandchild under his wing and fosters the child's ambition and imagination.

Nurturers of Emotional and Physical Well-Being

Another role grandparents play is that of nurturers for grandchildren's emotional and physical well-being. Even though a small percentage of grandparents find themselves having primary responsibility for their underage grandchildren, a much larger portion will occasionally assume a nurturing role in the lives of their grandchildren. Many grandfathers consider the physical and emotional well-being of their posterity a top priority, which makes this role a vital one in many families.

I recall a time when my son was no more than four or five years old. He was sent to spend time in his room as a disciplinary measure. During this time he tip-toed to the master bedroom, absconded with the telephone, and very quietly called my mother and father-in-law long distance. He subsequently told them he was in "time out" and proceeded to try to elicit their sympathy on his behalf. He obtained it, and together with a large dose of love, also gained the strength to endure the last five minutes of "serving his time." Children who feel nurtured by their grandparents will even reach out to receive that support from a distance. Grandfathers can provide a respite from the storms of life for their grandchildren, serving to remind them that it is possible to get through challenges and helping to strengthen their emotional and physical well-being.

Role Models

Children growing up in today's society are provided with a variety of role models, many of which seem less than desirable. Grandfathers may fill the need many children express for positive role models. Children, adolescents, and young adults are continually searching for people to emulate. Grandfathers can serve this function for families and society simply by living honorable and respectable lives. They can be the heroes many children seek to pattern their lives after.

Most grandchildren are observant and will strive to emulate specific qualities they find admirable in the adults with whom they associate—especially their parents and grandparents. Related to this, in my own study of religious grandfathers and their adult grandchildren, I found that many participants respected and acknowledged their grandfathers as the responsible leader of their families. Consequently, many of these grandchildren felt they wanted to emulate the ways in which their grandfathers fulfilled this role.

Playmates

Finally, grandfathers can serve as playmates in the lives of their grandchildren. Parents are often preoccupied with jobs and the responsibilities of caring for other children. However, most grandparents are less burdened with such obligations. Often they have more unscheduled time they can devote to recreation and play with their grandchildren. For example, I also found in my research of grandfathers that recreational activities were a dominant theme discussed by adult grandchildren as a source of bonding between grandfathers and their grandchildren.

In my own life, my grandfather was a hard-working rancher, routinely starting at dawn and working until dusk. However, when my family spent time visiting my grandparents, he took time off to play with us. He was not one to roll around and wrestle with us on the floor, but he played with us in his own manner. He would take us fishing at a small creek where he had fished as a young child. He and my father would show us how to approach the small fishing holes so that our shadows would not scare the fish away. Fishing was a way my grandfather would play with us grandchildren. He also spent time teaching us how to shoot pool and throw horseshoes. He was fun to be with, even though his competitive nature would often come out during close games. This made our playtime enjoyable and memorable.

Activities That Strengthen Intergenerational Family Ties

Most people acknowledge that strengthening relationships between grandparents and grandchildren is important to family well-being. But what is the best means of building these intergenerational ties?

Activities Grandfathers Can Share with Grandchildren to Strengthen Intergenerational Ties

Grandfathers and their adult grandchildren have identified a variety of activities that have been helpful to them in developing and maintaining strong relationships. Families may wish to try some of the following activities:

- Family get-togethers (reunions, birthday and holiday celebrations)
- Working and doing chores together (running errands, community service, paid employment)
- Recreational activities (board games, puzzles, playing catch, hunting and fishing, shopping, taking walks and drives)
- Religious activities (attending church services and socials together, participating in religious ceremonies)
- Family-oriented activities (writing and sharing personal histories, visiting extended family, visiting cemeteries, and discussing one's childhood and ancestors)
- Conversation and phone calls
- Offers of advice and counsel when requested

Activities between grandparents and grandchildren often provide the setting for meaningful interactions. In my research talking with grandfathers and their older grandchildren, I identified several categories of activities that proved effective in strengthening intergenerational bonds, including family gatherings, working and doing chores together, recreational activities, phone calls and conversations, and family and church-oriented activities. In addition, grandparents were sought out as sources of advice by their grandchildren. These activities are identified and discussed in brief detail in the sidebar below.[12]

For my research, I spent countless hours interviewing grandfathers concerning their relationships with their grandchildren. I also interviewed a granddaughter and a grandson of each of the interviewed grandfathers to get a perspective on grandfathering and the impact of activities on intergenerational ties besides that of the grandfathers themselves. After several interviews, I discovered that, while not all of the relationships were strong, four themes encompassed the strongest intergenerational families. Below, I briefly explore each of these themes and discuss ways in which grandfathers can incorporate them into their own intergenerational familial relationships.

Table 1: Themes of Strongly Connected Grandfather-Grandchild Relationships

Theme	Relationship Practices
Frequent Contact	■ Visits ■ E-mail, telephone calls, letters ■ Spending time together
Serving One Another	■ Caring ■ Chores ■ Errands ■ Monetary gifts for education and weddings
Conversational Family	■ Talking ■ Sharing feelings, stories, and experiences
Shared Religious Beliefs and Activities	■ Being a good example ■ Attending church meetings and socials together ■ Sharing religious beliefs openly

Frequent Contact with Each Other

The theme I found most influential in developing a strongly connected relationship between grandchildren and grandfathers is frequent contact. This is not an extraordinary, earth-shattering piece of insight but rather common sense. However, unfortunately many people assume their relationships can be maintained at a high level of closeness with minimal contact or effort. Frequent contact is essential to maintaining strong intergenerational relationships, and a lack of this feature makes such relationships less beneficial and meaningful. I found that grandfathers were the major initiators of but not the sole contributors to this frequent contact.

Grandfathers typically use a variety of methods to stay in touch and have meaningful interaction with their grandchildren. Grandfathers who are involved in various activities with their grandchildren, such as traveling, visiting and talking with them, writing letters, calling on the phone, and offering assistance, are helping to build strong relationships. Even from a distance, grandfathers can maintain frequent contact with their grandchildren by creative methods such as e-mail, phone calls, letters, and frequent visits in order to develop lasting and influential relationships. Grandfathers must put forth a significant amount of time and effort to maintain consistent contact with their grandchildren.

Serving One Another

The second important theme in building strong relationships between generations involves the idea of service and serving one another. The strongest grandfather-grandchild relationships also have a strong nurturing aspect. These relationships were characterized by grandfathers who exhibited great amounts of caring, nurturing, and watching over their extended family members. They expressed a strong desire to serve one another, which surfaced as a central priority in their intergenerational relationships. The grandfathers were very involved in offering service. It does not always require money to serve a grandchild but usually some time and energy.

The types of service a grandfather may provide are varied and include:

- helping grandchildren move;
- giving advice and guidance;
- giving monetary gifts for travel, weddings, and college;
- teaching a skill; and
- babysitting grandchildren or great-grandchildren.

Such hands-on, practical efforts to nurture or serve their grandchildren were instrumental in helping grandfathers feel they were remaining connected across generations.

The Conversational Family

Another important theme related to strong relationships between grandfathers and grandchildren was that of being a conversational family. What does this mean? Family members not only gather together and interact frequently but also spend much time talking with one another. It is only through communication that thoughts and feelings are shared among individuals. I talked with some grandfathers and grandchildren who mentioned that the lack of conversations in their families greatly hindered the strength of the relationships.

One particular grandson explained that he and his grandfather spent a lot of time conversing, which was a primary reason for their closeness. He said:

> I am glad to see him every time he comes through the door—he's always got something interesting to talk about, something he has done, something he's seen, something he's bought. It's good to see him and my grandmother walk through the door.

Conversely, some of the grandfathers and grandchildren I interviewed were able to recognize that a lack of conversational skills greatly affected their relationships. It was not uncommon for these family members to admit that an area within their relationships that needed improvement was communication. One particular grandson explained how the lack of conversation between him and his grandfather influenced their relationship. He stated:

> You know, Grandpa and I never really did very many things alone together. Our family get-togethers were when we would all go to the house and just kind of hang out. There would be conversations here and there. But Grandpa and Grandma just kind of sit there and listen to everybody. They don't really get deeply involved in conversations. I think they just kind of like to have their family there. That is just kind of their style . . . . We talk a lot about how he doesn't talk a lot, but I've grown up knowing that is just the way he is. I guess I might change . . . I would like to know more about what he thinks. Maybe when he passes away . . . maybe at that point I will think, "Wow! I wish we would have talked more. I wish I knew more of what he was thinking."

Although this does not happen in all families, situations in which grandfathers converse and share their ideas and feelings seem to have a positive and beneficial effect on improving the quality of relationships across generations.

Shared Religious Beliefs and Activities

A final and major theme I discovered in sound, healthy grandfather-grandchild relationships was sharing religious beliefs and activities. Although this finding relates to the fact that I primarily interviewed religious individuals, it also suggests one strong mechanism for linking generations. In general, the grandfathers and grandchildren of strongly connected intergenerational families not only seemed to be close emotionally but also tended to apply many religious principles personally and within their relationships. The influence of shared religious beliefs and activities was evident in a number of ways.

First, the grandfathers viewed themselves and were viewed by their grandchildren as being the spiritual leaders in their intergenerational families, or the person that children and grandchildren could go to for advice and counsel. Several grandchildren, especially granddaughters, mentioned this seeking of advice and guidance regarding life choices. Another principle evident in the lives of these families was that of attending church as well as church meetings and socials together. Shared religious beliefs and activities thus seemed to provide a common structure in which grandfathers could be looked to for counsel while also participating in meaningful activities with their families.

Finally, grandfathers and grandchildren both mentioned how important it was for a grandfather to be a good example. The grandfathers in this study frequently referred to always feeling the need to be a good example to their grandchildren. This idea involved being honest and truthful, attending church and fulfilling responsibilities, living according to religious principles, and being a good parent and grandparent. This finding relates to the strong role grandfathers play as a model in the lives of their grandchildren in addition to their roles as custodian of family heritage, nurturer of well-being, mentor, and teacher. For grandfathers and their grandchildren, the benefits extend down through all generations of family life when grandfathers furnish a caring and admirable example.

Conclusion

"It takes a village to raise a child." This statement is frequently used in today's society when referring to family life. Young people are exposed to a host of adults throughout the day: parents, teachers, neighbors, coaches, etc. However, grandfathers are an often overlooked resource in their lives. Grandfathers are perhaps America's greatest forgotten resource, and yet they will become increasingly available as the Baby Boom generation ages and enters grandparenthood.

Research has shown that grandfathers are typically capable, caring adults who can influence their grandchildren in a number of positive ways and affect their growth and development. Men care about the role of being a grandfather and rate it highly among the roles in life they consider most important. My own research has shown that both grandfathers and grandchildren value and benefit from a caring, quality relationship between generations. In the future, I hope not only that research will acknowledge but that society will continue to celebrate and enhance the positive impacts grandfathers have on their grandchildren's lives.

Endnotes

1. Roberto, K.A., and Skogland, R.R., 1996, "Interactions with Grandparents and Great-Grandparents: A Comparison of Activities, Influences, and Relationships," *International Journal of Aging and Human Development*, 43(2), 107–117.

2. Berry, W., 1986, *The Unsettling of America: Culture and Agriculture*, San Francisco: Sierra Club Books, at 129.

3. Paul, P., 2002, "Make Room for Granddaddy," *American Demographics*, Media Central Inc., pp. 40–45.

4. Davies, C., and Williams, D., 2002, *The Grandparent Study 2002 Report*, Washington, DC: AARP.

5. Reitzes, D.C., and Mutran, E.J., 2002, "Self Concept as the Organization of Roles: Importance, Centrality, and Balance," *Sociological Quarterly*, 43, 647–667.

6. Simmons, T., and Dye, J.L., 2003, *Grandparents Living with Grandchildren: 2000*, Washington, DC: U.S. Census Bureau.

7. Boon, S.D., and Brussoni, M.J., 1996, "Young Adults' Relationships with Their 'Closest' Grandparents: Examining Emotional Closeness," *Journal of Social Behavior and Personality*, 11, 439–458.

8. Cherlin, A.J., and Furstenberg, F.F., 1986, *The New American Grandparent: A Place in the Family, a Life Apart*, New York: Basic.

9. Hirshorn, B.A., 1998, "Grandparents as Caregivers," in *Handbook on Grandparenthood*, edited by M.E. Szinovacz, Westport, CT: Greenwood Press, pp. 184–199.

10. Waldrop, D.P., Weber, J.A., Herald, S.L., Pruett, J. Cooper, K., and Juozapavicius, K., 1999, "Wisdom and Life Experiences: How Grandfathers Mentor Their Grandchildren," *Journal of Aging and Identity*, 4(1), 33–46.

11. Kornhaber, A., 1996, *Contemporary Grandparenting*, Thousand Oaks, CA: Sage.

12. Taylor, A.C., 1999, "Perceptions of Intergenerational Bonding: A Comparison between Grandfathers and Their Adult Grandchildren," paper presented at the Annual Conference of the National Council on Family Relations, Washington, DC, November 1999.

Fathers and Family Interactions

The four chapters in this section provide a window into how fathers associate with children and contribute to their well-being through key family interactions. In this section we seek to focus on specific contexts of interaction that are concrete and important to child well-being, including activities and connectedness, play, reading, and love and nurturance.

In Chapter 7, "Bonds of Connection: How Fathers Connect with Children and Why It Matters," Sean Brotherson shares the significance of connectedness between fathers and children as a primary factor in positive outcomes for children. He outlines specific practices that research suggests are powerful in facilitating connectedness between fathers and children, including recreation, working together, spiritual activities, consistent family traditions, and sharing memories and stories.

George Williams addresses the topic of "Fathers, Play, and the World of Children" in Chapter 8, noting how important it is for fathers to be "bilingual" in the language of their child's world—play. He discusses the important role of fathers in aiding their children's development through interaction and play and connecting with their children through the language of play to communicate, help them cope with life, comprehend the world around them, and assist them in achieving success in their pursuits. The benefits associated with play for children are significant and central to fathers' contribution to their children's well-being.

In Chapter 9, "Exploring New Worlds Together: Reading, Relationships, and Father Involvement," Stephen Green of Texas A&M University documents the relationship between fathers, reading, and children's well-being. He identifies specific benefits of joint book reading for fathers and their children and offers practical suggestions on how fathers can use reading to strengthen their children's literacy skills and the overall quality of the father-child relationship. He shares unique insights from the Fathers Reading Every Day (FRED) program he developed and its impact on fathers and their children.

In Chapter 10, "A Father's Love: Impacts of Sacrifice and Care on Fathers and Their Children," Shawn Christiansen and Jeffrey Stueve present a compelling portrait of the impact fathers and father figures have on children's lives through their sacrifice and care. They discuss examples of sacrifice by fathers for children during daily routines or times of extreme hardship. Further, they offer ideas on fathers' nurturing abilities and the impact of fathers' nurturance on children. The authors explain key characteristics of fathers' love, including focusing on the child and his or her well-being, accepting the child, sharing life, and enduring in their efforts.

This section of the book introduces the centrality of family interactions in which fathers can connect with, care for, and contribute to their children's well-being. These specific family interactions reflect practical, concrete elements of parenting that most fathers can and do experience in raising their children. Whether playing outside, reading a book together, or expressing love and support, fathers make a difference through the daily family interactions that shape their lives with children and give meaning to their efforts to care.

Author Sean E. Brotherson reading with his children, Ethan, Bryn, and Mason

Bonds of Connection:
How Fathers Connect with Children
and Why It Matters

Sean E. Brotherson

A few years ago, when my youngest son was about six years old, we had developed an established bedtime routine each night. I would tuck him into bed, give him a hug and a kiss, then turn off the light and say, "Good night, boys." One night after giving him a kiss, my little boy asked me how they kiss in other places in the world. I thought wildly for a minute and then suggested the old idea that the Eskimo people rub noses as a sign of affection. He thought about this and then insisted, after our regular routine of a hug and a kiss, that I put my head down and rub noses with him. This pattern continued for a few nights until one evening he asked again how they show affection in other places in the world. I thought about it and said that in Italy they kiss each other on both cheeks, so kissing each other on both cheeks after the nose rub was also added to our nightly routine.

Now, a couple of years later, it is impossible for me to tuck my son into bed at night without giving him a hug, rubbing noses, kissing him on both cheeks, giving him a peck on the forehead, and then finishing with a last hug. He insists on it. I had thought it would become tiresome, but now I look forward to it as a personal moment when we can connect with each other each day. No matter how our interaction has been during the day, he and I know there will be a moment for us to feel and express a connection to each other, as father and son, that involves closeness, affection, and love. It is a great connecting moment.

Recently I met a colleague in the hall at work, and he had his two little boys with him. As they started down the hall, a preschool teacher of theirs from the previous year appeared out of a doorway. Those two little boys responded with instant recognition, yells of delight, and running. They sprinted the length of the hall and threw themselves into the arms of their teacher and let her know how much they missed her. It was obvious they felt a powerful sense of connection to her.

How important is the sense of connection a parent feels with a child and vice versa? How vital are those moments of understanding and feeling understood, of sharing a laugh together or wrestling on the floor in a moment of play? I am persuaded by research and experience that connectedness between children and parents, particularly fathers, has a vital and lasting influence on the well-being of children. This chapter will explore the concept of connection between fathers and their children, cite examples of its influence from contemporary research, and illustrate some of the key strategies fathers can use in forging strong connections with their children.

What is Parent-Child Connectedness?

It is important to understand what factors influence father-child relationships because research has shown their quality directly affects children's well-being in a variety of areas.[1] Contemporary research generally shows that children deprived of a positive relationship with their father may be at increased risk for problems such as drug abuse, delinquency, and depression.[2] Children in their school-age and adolescent years tend to exhibit better academic achievement and adjustment to school, social relationships with peers, and self-esteem when their relationships with their fathers are positive.[3] What is a key factor that affects the quality of relationships between fathers and children? The short answer: connectedness.

Connecting with one's son or daughter involves the sense of feeling emotionally linked with the child as well as one's tangible efforts to create and maintain healthy bonds between the child, oneself, and others in the child's family or environment.[4] Basically, this process of feeling connected involves both a parent's efforts to be close to and involved with a child and the child's feelings of closeness to the parent. When children are born, they must depend on parents for their food, safety, protection, and nurturance. The link that a child develops to a caring parent or caregiver is often called "attachment." Fathers who respond to a child's need for care can also establish a relationship bond or sense of connectedness that will benefit both the father and the child over time.

What is important to understand about connectedness is that it does not simply mean a father's sense of love for his son or daughter; it is more than that. It is also the degree to which a child perceives a parent's love, warmth, and acceptance. Dr. Robert Blum, a nationally recognized researcher on parent-child relationships, summarized it this way:

> We actually went out and asked groups of kids, "What is this sense of connectedness?" There was this clear understanding on their part of what it is. It isn't that "my mother or father is always there, is always available, is sitting at home," but it's that "she or he is available when I need them." It's that "my mother remembers that I had a test last Thursday and asks, 'How did it go?'" It's that "my father remembers that I had a date, not only that I had a date, but it was with Johnny, and not Sam or Harry or Larry, and asks how my date with Johnny was." It's that "my mother has a message on the refrigerator door: 'I'll be home at 6 o'clock, but there's a snack in the refrigerator for you.'" It's concrete things that say, "You matter; I care, even when I'm not home." It's the neighbor who stops by and says, "Your mom asked me to come by after school and see how things are going." Connectedness.[5]

The essence of connectedness between a parent and child is developed in the details of loving another person and the trust and closeness that develops in that relationship. It is a child trusting that you will be there to read a book each night. It is a teenage son knowing that you will listen and say, "I know it can be tough." It is a daughter appreciating the fact that you remembered her favorite kind of candy treat from the store was red licorice.

The Influence of Connectedness between Fathers and Children

My personal and scientific interest in the power of connectedness between parents and children began more than a decade ago. I was conducting some research as a graduate student with fathers about their relationships with both a special needs child and another child in their family. I wanted to understand what truly made father-child relationships work. During the research that emerged from this effort, it became clear that connectedness between fathers and children was a powerful influence on children and their well-being. This concept was being explored by other researchers in different ways as well. I would like to highlight a number of examples from scientific research and other contexts that illustrate the influence of connection between fathers and their children.

Dr. Brian Barber, a family studies scholar at the University of Tennessee, has focused his research on the most important factors in parent-child relationships in cultures around the world. He has worked to identify influences that are vital for parents and children across diverse cultures and situations and has studied parents and children in the United States, New Zealand, South Africa, the Middle East, India, China, and Europe. Speaking about his research findings in 1999, he made the following observation about parent-child connectedness and its importance:

> Extensive scientific research has been conducted on the parent-child relationship over the past 60 years. This research literature is voluminous, complex, redundant, fragmented, and at times confusing and/or contradictory. My aim has been to integrate it based on the belief that there are a limited number of essential aspects to the parent-child relationship that matter to child development. . . . The important scientific work that has been produced over the decades . . . can be integrated and synthesized into three central conditions of parenting that have been shown to be important to healthy child development. We refer to the first condition as connection, or the positive, stable, emotional bond between parent and child.[6]

The strength of parent-child connectedness has thus been found to be important, particularly for parents and teenagers, in cultures on every inhabited continent in the world. Specifically, the findings from this international study suggest that the more connection a child experiences with his parents, the more likely he or she is to trust others and seek out stable relationships with peers and adults outside the home. The stable, positive connection between a parent and child seems to give children a pattern to repeat in their relationships with other friends or adults they know and trust. Also, Dr. Barber's research indicates that children who experience a strong parental connection are much less likely to experience anxiety or depression, so such a connection also balances a child's emotional well-being.[7]

Additional research findings that support the power of connection between parents and children have emerged in recent years from the National Longitudinal Study on Adolescent Health (known as the "Add Health study"). This research study is the most comprehensive and complex ever conducted on youths, their behavior, and how they are affected by parents, peers, and other influences. It is a gold mine of information and understanding. Conducted in the United States, it is a nationally representative study of 90,000 adolescents who answered survey questions that also includes information from 20,000 parent-teen interviews. One major finding that stands out from this study is that common factors protect children and adolescents from different challenges such as depression, suicide, or drug use. Perhaps the most potent and repeatedly highlighted factor is the power of parent and family connectedness.

In 1999, at a briefing in Washington, D.C., some of the Add Health study's leading researchers shared their findings. Dr. Michael Resnick of the University of Minnesota discussed what protects kids from the risk of suicide or violence toward others and summarized, "It is connectedness to parents and family, a strong sense of connection to other adults."[8] Further, Dr. Robert Blum summarized factors that protect teenagers from early sexual behavior or pregnancy thus: "Independent of most of the factors—whether you're poor or not, regardless of your ethnicity, independent of what your geography or family structure is—*parent and family connectedness is powerfully protective*" [emphasis added].[9] So again, in a national study, concrete evidence appears repeatedly across various contexts that connectedness between parents and children is protective to children. It assists them in feeling the emotional stability they need to say no to dangerous propositions while also providing them with the capacity to be secure and close in their relationships with others.

I have been interested specifically in how this phenomenon of parent-child connection might be reflected in the relationships between fathers and their children. Could such findings be repeated with fathers specifically? I chose to work with a friend, Takashi Yamamoto, and Dr. Alan Acock at Oregon State University to try to assess the influence of connection in fathers' relationships with their adolescent children. We decided to analyze survey data from interviews with 362 married fathers from the National Survey of Families and Households who had at least one adolescent child at home. One of the main concepts we analyzed was the specific influence of connection between fathers and their teenagers on the quality of their relationship and the well-being of these teenagers.

Did we learn anything? Again we found that the connection between a father and an adolescent child profoundly affects the quality of their relationship and also the child's well-being. Fathers who regularly connect with their children through recreational activities, games, play, working on a project, helping with reading or homework, or other types of involvement have relationships of much higher quality with their children. Additionally, the stronger this connection is, the better the children's emotional stability and relationships are. We summarized our findings in this way: "We have shown that it is not a father's mere presence but his connection to his children that is pivotal. It is important to recognize that strong connections can have beneficial effects, but the opposite is also true: poor connections can have adverse effects. Fathers, it seems, really do matter."[10]

These brief summaries of research findings from an international study and two national studies of parents and children all point toward the significance of connectedness between parents and children. Parental connections provide a pathway for fathers to influence and protect their children in meaningful ways.

Strengthening Connections between Fathers and Children

While research has established connectedness as one of the most powerful factors fathers can pursue in their interactions with children, its importance naturally leads to the next critical question: What is it fathers do that establishes a strong connection with their children? In this section, eight practical strategies that facilitate such connections, based on findings from research interviews with fathers and children, are briefly discussed.

Shared Activities with Children: Recreation

Fathers tend to connect with their children primarily through personal involvement in activities they can do together. For men, recreational activities are mentioned most frequently as a context for spending time with and connecting to their children, so a key strategy for fathers is connecting with children through spending meaningful time together in activities involving recreation.[11]

A number of years ago, a study of how parents and adolescents spend time together showed that a great deal of the time fathers in the United States spent with their teenagers was "recreation" time: watching television, camping, fishing, or participating in other leisure activities.[12] Ross Parke, a scholar and the author of *Fatherhood*, has indicated that "the style of fathers' involvement as a play or recreational partner appears to be consistent from infancy through adolescence."[13] Recreational activities offer fathers and children an opportunity for time together that combines companionship and enjoyment of the time shared. Recreational activities, such as picnicking or watching a baseball game, allow fathers to see how children enjoyed the time they shared. One father recounted his time with a young son:

> [My son] and I would have a lot of fun together. One of the enjoyable experiences I remember is that we would play hide-and-go-seek. He couldn't talk, and he couldn't walk, but he would crawl. I would go hide and say, "Okay, Ben, come and find me," and he would come and find me. When he'd find me he would laugh, and we had a really fun time doing that. I think about that a lot.

This father suggested this memory is "so vivid" because of the happiness he saw in his son's face as they shared this activity. Fathers who spend time in recreational activities with children can witness a child's positive reaction, and this may be one reason they prefer such activities in connecting with children.

Shared Activities with Children: Play and Learning

Another practical strategy fathers tend to utilize is connecting with children through togetherness in activities involving play and learning. Fathers are natural teachers, and children tend to learn through play. As fathers describe connecting with children in this context, they tend to emphasize a focus on teaching and learning that occurs through play or other types of involvement. Fathers may connect with children by helping them learn to play chess or ride a bike. A number of studies have shown that, in time spent with children, fathers are quite a bit more involved in play than mothers, on average. Also, fathers tend to be more physical, active, and highly engaging in their play activities with children.[14] Play is children's work. Fathers seem to understand this pattern and use play and other types of involvement as a way to both connect with children and teach them so they learn and grow.

Shared Activities with Children: Work and Important Events

A third context of shared activities fathers engage in is connecting with children through working together or attending a child's important events. Such activities let fathers observe their children as they grow and mature and symbolically suggest that fathers are supporting a child's gradual steps toward adulthood. One man I interviewed spoke of connecting with his father in this way:

> My family is in the newspaper publishing business, and my father would cover our hometown football team, so we would go to those football games. Generally, I would be out there on the sidelines with him, and he would keep the football statistics while I would do the photography. This was for our own newspaper, and so we always used the photographs. . . . We were doing something that we both enjoyed and in which we related; we could talk about the football game and about our chances for the next game, whereas typically we didn't have a whole lot to talk about.

This account reflects a son's recollection that working with his father gave them a common activity that allowed them to talk and connect. I have interviewed many adult men who recalled moments from childhood when they had an important event, such as a school performance, and a father was not there to watch them. Fathers' involvement through working together or attending important events seems to provide children with a memorable experience that helps them grow toward maturity. Such experiences let children feel their fathers value them.

Expressions of Support to Children in Need

Children are typically dependent on parents for many of their needs, and children of any age are particularly vulnerable when in need due to anxiety, fear, illness, stress, or other concerns. Another important approach for fathers in building strong connections occurs through connecting with children by giving support and care at times when they are ill, anxious, or otherwise in need of comfort or attention.

Times of stress or challenge are likely to highlight a child's dependence on parents and initiate a need for support, comfort, or help. Moments of difficulty for a child often become powerful moments of connection when a father slows down, listens, gives support, soothes anxious feelings, and responds to a child's needs or concerns. Fathers should not let these moments pass by without giving their support and attention. One father I interviewed explained how his teenage stepdaughter had wanted to be adopted, so he and his wife initiated the paperwork. Her biological father had little contact with her for many years and agreed to the adoption but then withdrew his consent. The stepfather commented, "It was very difficult for her to handle that. It was when she and I connected the closest emotionally, but it was also the most painful." This stepfather realized the emotional challenges associated with this experience for his daughter and was supportive of her, and through that experience they became closer. Through being sensitive at such times of need for children, fathers can strengthen bonds with the children in their lives.

Spiritual Activities with Children

Yet another meaningful approach for many fathers is connecting with children through participation in specific spiritual activities (prayer, etc.). For men, spiritual activities can provide a context for interacting with children that allows them to share moral and spiritual lessons. Dr. David Dollahite, a scholar on religion and family, notes religious or spiritual motivation can furnish a "powerful, meaningful, and sustained influence for encouraging men to be fully involved in children's lives."[15] Fathers often describe a powerful connection with their children when involved in spiritual activities.

The activities fathers might share with children in this context include such things as attending worship services, giving service to others, engaging in prayer, or being involved in spiritual practices. Spiritual activities can provide a context that allows fathers and children to connect in deeply personal ways. For example, serving others together by cleaning a local park through community service or visiting an elderly neighbor can be a meaningful avenue for personal connection. Some fathers and children find themselves involved in such activities through participating in a particular faith community, while others simply learn to appreciate the spiritual dimensions of life and share their thoughts and feelings with each other.

Expressions of Love and Affection

Many fathers find their lives enriched by connecting with children through frequent expressions of love and affection. Laughter and expressions of love between fathers and children are the basis for feeling close. The sense of connection encouraged by such expressions of love and affection seems to focus on feelings of warmth and mutual appreciation. One father who was interviewed said:

The most enjoyable experience [with my daughter] is when she comes up and snuggles with me on the couch. She'll just come up and sit by me and put her head on my shoulder. She won't do anything else; she just wants to snuggle and be close. I think that's the most enjoyable time I have. It happens quite regularly. . . . I just feel closer to her, and I know that she feels close to me.

Some fathers may need to slow down and take the time needed to communicate these small expressions of love or affection. Other fathers may need to become more comfortable with giving their child a hug or saying "I love you" or "It was great spending time with you today." Children thirst for positive messages from their parents, and fathers can strengthen their connections with children by providing such messages on a regular basis.

Consistent and Enjoyable Family Traditions

Another useful strategy helpful to many fathers is connecting with children through involvement in consistent and enjoyable family traditions, generally activities that are significant and meaningful for family members and coordinated and repeated over time. For example, a divorced father may cook a pancake breakfast for his children each time they come to stay with him over a weekend, which becomes a tradition.

What are your important family traditions? What others would you like to develop? Family traditions establish built-in opportunities for parent-child connection and do not have to be elaborate. As noted, such traditions that facilitate connection can be as simple as cooking pancakes together every Saturday morning or reading nightly for twenty minutes. Some family traditions that naturally promote regular opportunities for connection between fathers and their children tend to include meals, morning and bedtime routines, outings, and vacations.[16] As a boy, my father would take my brothers and me out on the opening morning of fishing season each June, and we would go fishing together. We always looked forward to it with excitement, and we still remember it to this day as a time of enjoyment and connection. Traditions, big and small, make connection much easier and richer.

Sharing Memories and Stories

A final, important strategy that is beneficial for many fathers is connecting with children through sharing memories and telling stories. Children not only enjoy time spent together in activities but appreciate recalling past activities and experiences with their father that they enjoyed. In particular, younger children will often ask their fathers to retell a memorable story or talk about experiences from his own childhood. Children naturally seek a connection with fathers through this pattern of sharing memories and stories. In addition, children may enjoy going through pictures or watching videos of themselves from the past. Taking out the photo album, watching a home video, or sharing family stories can be positive ways to build connections. Memorable parent-child moments from the past can help to strengthen and reinforce parent-child connections in the present. A father I interviewed about his experiences with his own father recalled:

> One time that stands out with my father was when I stayed with him for a few days before I went back to school, and I just remember sitting up with him at night and talking a lot about my mother. I'd never heard him do that. I had never talked to him about my mother before at any great length. He talked to me for a long time about her and what she was like, how they met, what their life was like, and how he expected me to live to be true to her. . . . It gave me a connection to her and to him in understanding what his life had been like and why he had done the things that he'd done.

For this man, an evening of sharing memories with his father had deepened his feelings of connection to both his father and his deceased mother in a powerful way. Fathers can become closer to their children through sharing such memories and responding to their children's desires for such stories and recollections.

Conclusion

Most fathers want the best for their children and hope to have caring and positive relationships with them. They want their children to be protected from harm and to learn skills that will help them to make decisions and have good relationships with others. Building and maintaining strong bonds of connection with their children may be the most powerful thing fathers can do to realize such hopes for their children.

Research with fathers and children across the world has shown connectedness is a vital and lasting influence in father-child relationships. It consists of children feeling close to their fathers, accepted by their fathers, and valued by them, and it includes the positive feelings and efforts of fathers to be close to their children. Connectedness between fathers and children contributes significantly to a child's well-being, and its absence puts children at higher risk for a variety of negative outcomes in life. An important finding is that fathers generally express connection to children when participating in shared activities of one kind or another. If you want to search for common factors that protect children and adolescents from different challenges, such as depression, suicide, or drug use, you come back repeatedly to this same finding: the power of parent and family connectedness.

The importance of building such connections with children challenges us as parents. It forces fathers to ask themselves questions such as the following. Do I smile often at my children? Do I express my love and affection to them consistently? Do I make it easy for my children to talk with me and feel close to me? Do I make my children feel better and not worse when they are upset? Do I make my children feel that they are the most important people in the world when they are with me? As I tuck my young son into bed each night, I know the chance will come to do the "hug/kiss on the forehead/rub noses/kiss on both cheeks/hug one more time" routine. We will laugh and hug and feel close to each other. That is how fathers connect with children, and that is what matters.

Endnotes

1. Lamb, M.E. (Ed.), 1997, *The Role of the Father in Child Development*, 3rd ed., New York: Wiley.

2. Blankenhorn, D., 1995, *Fatherless America: Confronting Our Most Urgent Social Problem*, New York: Basic Books; Hetherington, E.M., and Stanley-Hagan, M.M., 1997, "The Effects of Divorce on Fathers and Their Children," in *The Role of the Father in Child Development*, 3rd ed., edited by M.E. Lamb, New York: Wiley, pp. 191–211.

3. Biller, H.B., and Kimpton, J.L., 1997, "The Father and the School-Aged Child," in *The Role of the Father in Child Development*, 3rd ed., edited by M.E. Lamb, New York: Wiley, pp. 143–161.

4. Brotherson, S.E., Dollahite, D.C., and Hawkins, A.J., 2005, "Generative Fathering and the Dynamics of Connection between Fathers and Their Children," *Fathering: A Journal of Theory, Research, and Practice about Men as Fathers*, 3(1), 1-28.

5. Blum, R.W., June 1999, "Briefing Summary," in *Protecting Adolescents from Risk: Transcript of a Capitol Hill Briefing on New Findings from the National Longitudinal Study of Adolescent Health*, Washington, DC: Institute for Youth Development, at 43–45.

6. Barber, B., July 1999, "Hear Me, Understand Me, Love Me": Pleas to Parents from Adolescents around the World," *Proceedings of the First Annual World Family Policy Forum*, Provo, UT: Brigham Young University, pp. 22–26.

7. Ibid.

8. Resnick, M.D., July 1999, "New Research on Violence: What Predicts? What Protects?" in *Protecting Adolescents from Risk: Transcript of a Capitol Hill Briefing on New Findings from the National Longitudinal Study of Adolescent Health*, Washington, DC: Institute for Youth Development, pp. 5–13, at 11.

9. Blum, R.W., July 1999, "Reducing the Risk: Recent Lessons from Add Health on Adolescent Sexuality," in *Protecting Adolescents from Risk: Transcript*

of a Capitol Hill Briefing on New Findings from the National Longitudinal Study of Adolescent Health, Washington, DC: Institute for Youth Development, pp. 15–23, at 22.

10. Brotherson, S.E., Yamamoto, T., and Acock, A.C., 2003, "Connection and Communication in Father-Child Relationships and Adolescent Child Well-Being," *Fathering: A Journal of Theory, Research, and Practice about Men as Fathers*, 1(3), 191–214, at 211.

11. Brotherson et al., 2005.

12. Larson, R., and Richards, M.H., 1994, *Divergent Realities: The Emotional Lives of Mothers, Fathers, and Adolescents*, New York: Basic Books.

13. Parke, R., 1996, *Fatherhood*, Cambridge, MA: Harvard University Press, at 67.

14. Ibid.

15. Dollahite, D.C., 1998, "Fathering, Faith, and Spirituality," *The Journal of Men's Studies*, 7(1), 3–15.

16. Doherty, W.J., 1997, *The Intentional Family*, Reading, MA: HarperCollins.

Author George Williams with his son Geordy Paul and daughter, Sydney Grace

Fathers, Play, and the World of Children

George R. Williams

Imagine traveling to a foreign country where you cannot speak or understand the language and the flood of feelings you would experience from not being able to communicate. How would you feel? Perhaps frustrated from not being able to understand or be understood by those around you about your wants and needs. Maybe helpless, disconnected, or alone and isolated. You might even feel ignorant or like less of a person than those around you. What you quickly learn is that there is an intense need to understand and communicate in a language that makes sense to the people you wish to connect with. This is how fathers often feel in the world of children.

As adults, fathers have a different language than their children have, and children have a language that differs from that of their parents. These two languages often separate the world of fathers from the world of children. When children cannot speak their father's adult language, they are prone to experience the flood of feelings described above. Fathers can prevent that experience and strengthen their bond with children if they learn their child's language.

The language spoken in the world of children is play. A baby doll, a bouncing ball, a dress-up hat—these are the tools of play for children. They represent the language younger children use to engage each other, their parents, and the world around them. Play is critically important to a child's healthy development and provides opportunities for mastering physical tasks, engaging in social interaction, and thinking creatively. Play provides endless opportunities for learning and growth. It has been said that play is a child's work. However, it is even more. Play is a child's world, and fathers must understand and engage in play if they wish to understand and engage their children. Fortunately, fathers typically enjoy play and tend to perform very well in this particular area of parent-child interaction.

Much of my work involves outreach to low-income, urban fathers who often face significant challenges in their efforts to be the involved fathers their children need. My work as executive director of the Urban Father-Child Partnership at the National Center for Fathering in Kansas City brings me into regular contact with fathers from all walks of life. Our programming efforts attempt to meet dads where they are, and we find there is no quicker way for a man to reach his child's heart than through the shared language of play. Learning a child's language of play and engaging with children through play is a key aspect of how we help fathers connect with their children. Fathers and father figures don't need to move into their child's world, but they do need to visit it through play. The doorway to a child's world is small, and it requires getting down on a child's level and engaging in play.

The focus of this chapter is primarily on preschool and school-age play of children and its important role in a child's development. It also addresses specifically the powerful role of fathers in aiding their children's development through interaction and play. It discusses the purpose of children's language of play and how dads can connect with their children through play to communicate and help them cope with life, comprehend the world around them, and achieve success in their pursuits.

Dads at Play with Children

Someone has said, "Man is more childlike than woman." It seems men of any maturity level are often more predisposed than women to enter the world of play. Perhaps the excuse to play again is one of the benefits of being a dad.

For example, talk to children about what they've done recently with their parents, and you're probably more likely to hear about snowball fights and wrestling matches with dad than with mom. I can personally relate to this benefit. My wife and I have three sons and a daughter. It is as if my children have awakened something in me to play. I purchase toys more often than my wife does to engage in play inside or outside with my children. And when it is time to throw ourselves into play, my wife would usually rather be a spectator than a playmate. Does this mean mothers and other caregivers cannot play with children like fathers do? Of course not. It simply means fathers seem to bring a willingness to engage in play to their involvement with children, and this capacity should be recognized and built on as a strength in their parenting.

One area of play in which fathers are recognized as experts is rough-and-tumble, interactive play with children. I believe my sons, Timothy, Jeremy, and Geordy, would testify to my expertise, and if they won't, then let my scars speak for themselves. The play of fathers is typically more physical and exciting than that of mothers—it is play with a turbocharger! Fathers' play with their children usually is noisier, involves exaggerated movement, and is more likely to include the element of surprise.[1] This type of interaction between fathers and children is evident even in the first months of a baby's life. Fathers are more likely to play by moving the baby's legs and arms in imitation of walking or kicking, by lifting the baby through the air, or by tapping or tickling the baby's stomach.[2] The result is that these infants are more likely to laugh and cry in episodes of play with daddy. Children learn from early ages that fathers typically offer excitement and a chance to explore the world around them.

Although many fathers care for their infants, typically fathers are just as likely to focus on playing with their infants as on caring for them. A majority of exchanges between fathers and their babies, for example, are brief play episodes that come at a specific period of the day.[3] As the infants grow older, fathers generally increase the time they spend with them and are more likely to engage in physical play. When my children were toddlers, I crawled after them in chase, swung them around, wrestled with them on the floor, and carried them on my back and shoulders. I remember a time I carried my son Geordy on my back and ran half a mile to his school. I paid for that ride in pain for the next week. At times fathers have been criticized for being the "playmate" parent and avoiding the hard work of being the caregiving parent. However, play is a key component of a healthy caregiving environment, and it is probably the most important interaction facilitating a child's healthy development during the first few years of life. This means that fathers and father figures who play actively with their children provide tremendous benefits to their child's growth and learning.

Play is a hands-on, practical approach to involving fathers with their children. Many fathers may be unenthusiastic about attending a parenting class but interested in participating in activities in which they can interact and play with their children. For example, asking parents to help children make a holiday treat or gift for family members at school is more likely to draw fathers than a lecture on children's language development. One especially well attended father-involvement activity was a "water fun" day at a local park where fathers and kids could throw water balloons and slide on a wet sheet of plastic. Programs that utilize play as the basis for fathers' interaction with their children focus on this strength and provide a means for fathers and children to connect with each other in positive ways.

The unique approach of fathers to play can benefit their children in a variety of specific and practical ways. Consider the following:

- *Dads at play help their children further develop physical abilities.* Lev Vygotsky called a child's developing physical skills a "zone of proximal development," which means that a father or other parent supports a child in a physical action that he or she will later learn to accomplish independently.[4] For example, a father may help a small child learn to walk, climb, wave, bounce a ball, or jump up and down.
- *Dads at play can help a child cope with emotional issues.* An important role of a father is being aware of his children's feelings and what hurts, challenges, or brings joy to them. Through play, a father can learn his child's questions and concerns or notice some danger sign that leads him to seek out appropriate help. Play is a meaningful pathway to getting in touch with a child's emotions and helping him or her cope with feelings of frustration, sadness, or boredom.
- *Dads at play help their children develop social skills and moral character.* Even in rough-and-tumble play, fathers can teach children about limits and love; after all, dads get hurt, too. Fathers interacting with children in play can soothe emotions and guide behavior so kids learn appropriate boundaries for their actions. As children grow older, they begin to play rule-based games, such as chess or soccer, which provide opportunities to learn about fairness and making choices in a safe environment.
- *Dads at play help their children develop cognitively.* As children develop intellectually, dads learn to adjust play activities accordingly. This not only helps a child's ongoing development but is also a great way for dads to shape their children's long-term educational destiny. Fathers are able to help children extend their cognitive abilities and think creatively, which will help them succeed in school and other areas.

Many of the benefits associated with such play between fathers and children are unexpected bonuses. However, if fathers and father figures understood the significance of play to a child's well-being and development, they would likely engage in more frequent and longer periods of play.

It is not accurate to suggest that fathers are falling down on the job when they "just play" with their children. Play is fun, relaxing, and a vital part of a child's world, learning, and development. Fathers are great play companions for children because they like to tickle, make faces, play games, wrestle, and engage kids in all kinds of adventures. This is what children need as they encounter the world around them.

Why a Child's Play Matters and How Fathers Help

Jean Piaget, a renowned scholar of child development, sought to understand how children come to know the world and act effectively within it. In Piaget's view, knowledge is acquired (or in his words, "constructed") through action.[5] This particular perspective maintains that nature and nurture are equally necessary for development—both the child's play environment and those whom the child engages in play assist that child in his or her development. Most children engage in play because it is fun, but play also has purpose. Through the power of play (action), children acquire (construct) knowledge to:

- communicate their thoughts and feelings;
- cope with life's stresses and emotional distress;
- connect with those around them in their family, school, or neighborhood; and
- comprehend the world around them through imagination, exploration, and learning.[6]

With my daughter, Sydney, who is eight years younger than her brother Geordy, I have another opportunity to introduce the world to one of my children through play. I have to admit that she makes it easy with her natural curiosity and assertiveness. Children's play matters because it facilitates so much of their interaction with the world and others. Fathers can shape this world and give it greater meaning as they play with children.

Communicating Thoughts and Feelings

Children experience feelings and form thoughts long before they can express them clearly in verbal language. The interactions of a baby with the world are physical, interactive, and social. For example, a baby will see a person's face and reach up to touch it. A toddler will climb onto a couch and begin jumping on it. This is the language of play. From early infancy, before children learn the language used by adults, they learn the language of play.

Through that play, children communicate what they think and feel with those around them. The language of play is universal in the world of children. They do not have to be taught to play, because it is not just what they do but an expression of their identity. If a father bounces a one-year-old on his knee and then stops before the child wants him to, the child will likely begin moving in a bouncing fashion to encourage more fun. This action communicates several things: the child is feeling happiness and enjoyment, wants more fun activity, and connects play with the involvement of a parent. This single small example of play between a child and father communicates thought, feelings, and social awareness.

The vocabulary of the language of play includes at least four different types of play. *Active play* is described primarily by the gross motor skills of running, jumping, climbing, or throwing. Fathers engage in this type of play as they roll a ball to a child or race to see who can run faster around the house. *Object play* is exploration of the senses that may employ fine motor skills through actions such as picking up, observing, smelling, shaking, and tasting. Fathers facilitate this kind of play by doing things like giving a child a rattle to shake or letting the child play in the sand at the beach. *Social play* involves an exchange with another person that may or may not include physical contact. Peek-a-boo games or wrestling are examples of social play. *Pretend play* typically involves make-believe or use of the imagination with objects and acting. A father might facilitate or encourage such play by letting his kids take his temperature with a play thermometer or watching their made-up skit. All of these varieties of play are opportunities for children to form thoughts, express themselves, and communicate with others.[7]

Coping with Stresses and Challenges

Through the course of a child's life, he or she may experience injuries, personal stresses, or insults. A child's healthy development requires that children receive physical and emotional healing from these hurts. Play is a powerful approach children often use to cope with the stresses of life and emotional distress. Play gives a child an outlet to explore emotions without the threat of shutting down emotionally or being out of control. For example, after 9/11, it was not uncommon for parents and preschool or kindergarten teachers to see young children focusing on play involving firefighters and emergency response personnel or drawing pictures of planes and buildings. Children were using different forms of play to explore their fears, thoughts, and feelings about the events. Fathers can help to facilitate such play and guide it in positive, caring ways.

A child can sometimes be hurt or insulted as part of a domino effect within the hierarchy of the family, as in this example: the dad yells at the mom, the mom yells at the child, the child yells at the dog, and the dog whimpers in the corner. Such a sequence of events can leave a child feeling powerless and out of control. However, play can serve as a natural outlet for a child to express feelings of frustration and learn to deal with them in healthy ways. Play is a natural stress-reducer for kids. As they engage in play, their bodies and minds become more active and produce hormones that help to diminish feelings of stress.

The sheer fun of play can help children to forget minor issues that upset them. Play is absorbing, and small emotional distresses typically fade as children engage in play that engages their minds and energy. Also, friendship concerns can be overcome as children bond with each other through play. More serious issues can be resolved by giving children a place where they have the power and control to act out some of their hurts, questions, and feelings through pretend play. Coping with stresses becomes more manageable as children engage in play, express their feelings, and learn different ways to approach their world.

Connecting with Family and Others

Who does a child feel close to, and why? Shared, enjoyable experiences help a child build close connections with others.

Attachment theory examines the topic of connection. Forming connections with others starts at an early age and continues through adulthood. When the primary caregiver (often the mom, but can also be or include the dad) responds to an infant's needs, the child develops trust, a sense of worth, and security in that relationship. This usually translates to being secure in relationships with others. Play is a key pathway fathers can use to build children's sense of connection to the world and trust in parents, family, and others as they grow older.[8]

A father whose son became involved in a community soccer league decided to spend some time playing soccer at a local park with his son. They spent a couple of hours kicking the soccer ball around and working on skills and laughing together. As they left the park, the son said, "Dad, this was the greatest day!" What had seemed like an hour or two of fun to the father became more important in his mind as he listened to his son talk about the time they had spent together and what a great day it was for him. He realized that the simple activity of playing soccer together was a powerful message of love to his son and a way for them to connect.

This concept of play as a pathway for children to connect with family and others is covered in the National Center for Fathering's urban program, "Quenching the Father Thirst." We compare children to a cup: when they are empty, they are lonely or bored and need to be heard and loved and to learn. The cup is refilled when significant others interact in a positive way, take time to listen and talk, affirm the child verbally and physically, teach the child a skill, or play together in fun. Play refills the cup by connecting children with those who play with them. Fathers are great candidates for playing with children and meeting a child's needs for connection through time shared in play.[9]

Comprehending the World

As children encounter the world, they are immersed in opportunities for growth and learning. They must learn to comprehend the world around them. During a child's preschool years in particular (ages birth to five), his or her brain is developing and forming learning connections. The mind of a child is "wired" for learning. For example, an infant reaches curiously to grasp a ball on the floor, or a toddler repeatedly sings a song he or she has learned. As a child interacts with others and his or her environment, connections between brain cells are formed that become "highways" for processing information and provide the foundation for learning.[10]

Although it is never too late to encourage learning, these early years of a child's life are a key period of development. Most of a young child's learning involves one or more of these three techniques: seeing (visual memory), hearing (auditory memory) and doing (kinesthetic memory). The interactive experiences of play involve all of these patterns and help to establish these important neural connections in a child's brain. Children *learn through play.*[11]

Ross Parke has summarized research on fathers and children and notes that a number of studies consistently indicate that fathers across cultural backgrounds are more likely than mothers to engage in play with children.[12] Parke further notes that playing games with a child has a direct connection to their cognitive development. For example, he suggests that games in which fathers get children to reach for objects, such as catching a rolling ball, help young children learn how to interact with their environment. A game like peek-a-boo engages a young child in social interaction and learning how to take turns. These examples link fathers' involvement through play with cognitive development in children and suggest that play is very important for helping children to comprehend the world around them.

All children are unique and express different types of intelligence. However, various kinds of play can help a child learn, regardless of his or her learning style. Fathers tend to bring variety, energy, and enthusiasm to their play and involvement with children, which allows them to influence their children's development of different types of intelligence. Following is a list of specific types of intelligence and how fathers can use play to assist in developing them:

- *Linguistic intelligence* involves a love for words and using language, learned by seeing, hearing, and saying words, as in reading or practicing the alphabet.
- *Spatial intelligence* is visual learning, learned by using pictures, diagrams, and films.
- *Bodily kinesthetic intelligence* is learning through movement, as in role-playing, drama, dance, sports participation, or other active experiences.
- *Musical intelligence* is learned with rhythm and melody, as in singing, tapping the beat, or using an instrument.
- *Logical-mathematical intelligence* is based on patterns and relationships involving numbers or problems, developed by solving puzzles, playing games of logic, or learning and using numbers.
- *Interpersonal intelligence* involves ability to relate to and cooperate with others, facilitated by group play activities, cooperation, and interactive games.
- *Intrapersonal intelligence* is expressed in children who learn most effectively individually or in a solitary environment, for example by doing chores or practicing and mastering a skill.[13]

The many different ways fathers can play with their children are fundamental in developing the neural wiring of different parts of a child's brain, which aids in developing a child's multiple types of intelligence. Conversely, a child's natural, unique strengths in terms of types of intelligence may be expressed through his or her play preferences. Whatever children's unique capacities might be, those who are encouraged to play and develop their skills in multiple areas are much more likely to enjoy learning for a lifetime.

Entering a Child's World through Play

Fathers as well as children benefit from play. Whether a father is running around in sports-related activities like soccer, teaching board games, or dressing dolls or action figures, he is connecting with his child. Moments of connection with a little boy or girl through play can bring great satisfaction.

Why don't fathers play more frequently with their children and for longer periods of time? Often, fathers' early experiences playing with their own dads can shed light on this question.

Take a trip down memory lane. With whom did you play during childhood? You remember these people because they had a significant influence on your life. What were your favorite toys or games? Whether they were wind-up, battery-operated, or electronic, the memories of these toys and games are etched in your mind. This kind of reflection—recalling your childhood play—may bring up fond memories and make you smile: play is fun!

Now let's relate these memories back to your role as a father or to fathers in general. Did your dad ever play with you? Chances are, if he did, you can remember it even if the play was only brief, because the enjoyment of the time together is embedded with the memories. Although my father was the picture of health and fitness, he did not engage me or my three brothers and two sisters in play. There were only a handful of times that he played with me, but they were glorious, and I still emotionally remember them today. Play with dad is forever!

Fathers need to consistently set aside time to play with their children in order to enter their children's world, connect in a deeper way, and exchange thoughts and feelings. The father and child can help each other release life's stresses and get to the bottom of other challenging issues. Finally, through play fathers can help their children develop in other domains of their life—physical, emotional, social, cognitive, and moral. Some dads relish the idea of playing with their children; others find it difficult. Lawrence Cohen, author of *Playful Parenting*, reminds us that the goal is to *visit* the world of children through play, not to "move into their world." Dads are required to step down from their adult language and concrete thinking to speak the sometimes abstract language of play to their children.

How can we help fathers reenter the world they were once so familiar with? How can they be retaught the childhood language they spoke so fluently? The answer lies in the parts of the language they have retained over the years. Sports, hobbies, and possessions are often a continuation of men's playfulness, carrying over from games or toys that were meaningful to them in childhood.

My daughter, Sydney, invites me into her world through play almost every day, asking "Daddy, will you play with me?" or "Don't you want to play?" or suggesting "Let's play after you eat." And if that doesn't get my attention, she will say it louder, look me in the eye with her hands on my cheeks, or pull my arm. My sons were never that assertive. Perhaps your children aren't, either. The message is simple: don't wait to be invited into your child's world to play; invite yourself. To enter a child's world through play, here are a few important points for dads to remember:

- *It isn't about you.* Entering your child's world of play is about your child— not you. Children are not looking for someone to tell them how to play but to play with them. Dads need to ask children what they want to do and allow them to lead—and if they want to play the same thing over and over, do it!
- *Be childlike.* The doorway to your child's world of play is small. It requires one to become childlike and get on the child's level (sometimes on hands and knees). There is no room for machismo or embarrassment. You may have to play with dolls or sing silly songs. Do it; it will mean the world to your child.
- *Make play a priority.* The adult world is busy. We have important things to do, people to see, and little time in which to do it all. Unfortunately, those most important to us (family) often get the least of our time. Employ the sanity principle: Do things creatively and intentionally *differently* if you want different results. Schedule playtime with your child, and guard it like a watchdog!
- *Play hard.* You can con a con, and you can fool a fool—but you can't kid a kid. Children know when you are are only half-hearted and not fully engaged in play. You have to be completely, actively involved.
- *Have fun.* Laughter is a good gauge for how well play is going with a child. Sometimes a dad can initiate laughter through tickling. Remember, it is not about how well your children do something but the fact that you are playing together. Steer clear of the adult role unless the play becomes dangerous. Keep encouraging your child.[14]

Entering a child's world is a gift. You have the opportunity to send and receive love, share warmth and laughter, and build self-esteem. Communicating in a child's language may mean throwing a ball or building a tower of blocks. "I love you" can be said in so many ways through play.

Conclusion

One of the greatest strengths a father can bring to his involvement with children is play. Remember that the language spoken in a child's world is play. Play is much more than fun; it has a powerful influence on children and their development in many areas of life.

Taking time to play with children assists them in developing physical abilities and learning to manage emotions. It also enables them to become more skilled in social interactions and understand their environment. Play is not only a language children understand but a primary way in which they encounter and explore the world around them. Growth through meaningful play allows children to communicate feelings, cope with life's stresses, connect with others, and comprehend the world.

Play speaks powerfully to a child. The giggles and shrieks of joy, along with the smiles, gestures and other nonverbal signals, convey contentment more deeply than words and language can. Playing with Dad confirms some important truths to a child: that he is highly valued by a very important person in his life, that he is gaining competence in skills and wisdom, and that he belongs and is at home.

Endnotes

1. Brazelton, T.B., Yogman, M., Als, H., and Tronick, E., 1979, "The Infant as a Focus for Family Reciprocity," in *The Child and His Family*, edited by M. Lewis and L. Rosenblum, New York: Plenum, pp. 29–43.

2. Parke, R.D., and Tinsley, B.R., 1981, "The Father's Role in Infancy: Determinants of Involvement in Caregiving and Play," in *The Role of the Father in Child Development*, 2nd ed., edited by M.E. Lamb, New York: Wiley, pp. 429–457.

3. Lamb, M.E., Pleck, J.H., Charnov, E.L., and Levine, J.A., 1987, "A Biosocial Perspective on Paternal Behavior and Involvement," in *Parenting across the Lifespan: Biosocial Perspectives*, edited by J.B. Lancaster, J. Altmann, A.S. Rossi, and L.R. Sherrod, Hawthorne, NY: Aldine de Gruyter; Roopnarine, J.L., Talukder, E., Jain, D., Joshi, P., and Srivastave, P., 1990, "Characteristics of Holding, Patterns of Play, and Social Behaviors between Parents and Infants," *Developmental Psychology*, 26, 667–673.

4. Vygotsky, L.S., 1978, *Mind in Society*, Cambridge, MA: Harvard University Press.

5. Piaget, J., and Inhelder, B., 1969, *The Psychology of the Child*, New York: Basic Books.

6. Cohen, L. J., 2001, *Playful Parenting*, New York, NY: Random House, Inc.

7. Smith, P.K., 1982, "Does Play Matter? Functional and Evolutionary Aspects of Animal and Human Play," *Behavioral and Brain Sciences*, 5, 129–184; Smith, P.K., 1990, "Rough-and-Tumble Play, Aggression and Dominance: Perception and Behavior in Children's Encounters," *Human Development*, 33, 271–282.

8. Brotherson, S.E., Yamamoto, T., and Acock, A.C., 2003, "Connection and Communication in Father-Child Relationships and Adolescent Child Well-Being," *Fathering: A Journal of Theory, Research, and Practice about Men as Fathers,* 1(3), 191–214.

9. Williams, G., 2002, *Quenching the Father Thirst*, Kansas City, MO: National Center for Fathering.

10. Shore, R., 1997, *Rethinking the Brain: New Insights into Early Development,* New York: Families and Work Institute.

11. Conklin, W., 2001, *Smart-Wiring Your Baby's Brain*, New York: HarperCollins.

12. Parke, R.D., 1996, *Fatherhood*, Cambridge, MA: Harvard University Press.

13. Gardner, H., 1999, *Intelligence Reframed: Multiple Intelligences for the Twenty-First Century,* New York: Basic Books.

14. Williams, G., 2004, *Coach Dads: Playbook*, Kansas City, MO: National Center for Fathering.

Author Stephen D. Green with his daughters, Autumn and Sydney

Exploring New Worlds Together: Reading, Relationships, and Father Involvement

Stephen D. Green

O ne of the joys of reading aloud is being able to rediscover books that you enjoyed as a kid, even as you uncover new treasures with your own child.[1]

In households all across the nation, reading is an activity enjoyed by parents and children alike. Some of our fondest childhood memories revolve around stories read to us by our parents. From the unique characters in E.B. White's classic *Charlotte's Web* to the clever rhymes in Dr. Seuss's *Green Eggs and Ham*, generations of readers have been entertained and inspired by the lessons found in children's literature.

Reading is an activity that has the power to transform minds, both young and old. Well-written stories are capable of bringing out the full range of emotions in readers and listeners. Some stories provoke us to laughter, others to tears. There are stories that inspire us to action and stories that cause us to reflect on our priorities. Reading is a magical endeavor in the sense that it opens doors to discovery. It enables parents and children to travel together to the remotest parts of the world and explore new horizons without leaving the security and comforts of home.

As I reflect back on my own childhood, I vividly recall sitting on the edge of my bed with my brother and sister just before bedtime as my father read Franklin W. Dixon's *The House on the Cliff*, an adventure novel from the Hardy Boys series. Night after night, we were carried away to a world of mystery and intrigue as we joined my father on an adventure to unravel the secret behind the house on the cliff. I don't recall exactly how long it took my father to read the book, but I remember how disappointed we were when we reached the end of a chapter. It meant we would have to wait a whole 24 hours for my father to lead us on another adventure! Today, I too have the privilege of joining my children on exciting adventures as we read books together each evening. The fact that I can pass this experience on to them is due in large part to the example my parents set for me and my siblings, especially my father's commitment to spending time with us in such a meaningful and rewarding activity. It is with these experiences in mind that I encourage fathers from all walks of life to begin a regular routine of reading aloud to their children.

The purpose of this chapter is to explore the subject of reading in the context of father-child relationships. I have divided the chapter into two sections. First, I will address the relationship between fathers, reading, and children's well-being. Second, I will identify specific benefits of reading books together for fathers and their children. As I describe the various benefits, I will offer practical suggestions on how fathers can utilize reading as a mechanism for strengthening their children's literacy skills and the overall quality of the father-child relationship. Interspersed throughout the text are quotations from actual fathers who read to their children daily for four weeks in a program designed to encourage father involvement in children's early literacy development.

Fathers, Reading, and Children's Well-Being

Recognizing the inherent value in reading, millions of parents in the United States set aside a special time each day to read to their children. According to recent statistics, 58 percent of children ages three to five have a family member who reads to them daily.[2] This is a five-percentage-point increase from 1999; however, more than 40 percent of children in this age range still do not experience the joys and benefits of daily shared book reading with their parents. Reading may be one of the simplest, most practical things that parents—especially fathers—can do to contribute to their children's future.

The famous author Mark Twain once said, "The man who does not read good books has no advantage over the man who *can't* read them." Children are naturally curious. They like to explore their surroundings, discover new and exciting things, and use their imaginations to travel to faraway places. Good books can help children satisfy their innate desire to learn, but younger children especially are dependent on their parents and other adults in their lives to introduce them to the world of reading. When parents fail to take on this important task, children lose the opportunity to be transported by a parent's voice into realms of imagination and learning.

Whatever obstacles exist—whether illiteracy, poverty, inexperience, competing interests (e.g., television), limited access to print materials, divorce, or parental indifference—parents and children who do not spend regular time in joint reading activities are missing out on a meaningful form of interaction. This may be especially true for fathers, who are just as capable as mothers but appear less inclined to read to their children. In a random survey conducted with 894 men and women across the nation, researchers discovered that 42.5 percent of fathers never read to their children.[3] In addition to the factors mentioned above, one possible explanation for this troubling finding is the common belief, held by both men and women, that mothers alone should be primarily responsible for the early care and education of their children.[4] The reality is that reading with children may be one of the best opportunities available for fathers to care for and connect with them.

Shortly after the birth of my oldest daughter, with a little push from my wife, who happened to be a reading teacher at the time, I made a conscious decision to read to my daughter on a regular basis. It was a decision I will never regret. Holding my infant daughter in my arms while I read to her allowed me to connect with her in a unique way. I was able to witness firsthand how quickly children learn to recognize and respond positively to their parents' voices. My daughter's developmental advances became quite apparent as we read simple but entertaining children's books such as *Brown Bear, Brown Bear, What Do You See?* by Bill Martin Jr. or *Goodnight Moon* by Margaret Wise Brown. As my daughter began to grow, so did our selection of children's books. We made frequent trips to our local library and bookstore during her early years. When my second child was born, I had the opportunity to begin the process all over again. Today, one of our favorite family outings remains a trip to the library or bookstore, where we can search for exciting new books to share with each other.

While many individuals are unaware of the important contributions fathers make to their lives, mounting research points to the fact that fathers play a critical role in their children's cognitive, social, emotional, physical, and moral development. Children whose fathers are consistently and positively involved in their daily routines are more likely to be self-confident, get along well with their peers, and perform well academically than children who grow up without a positive father presence in their lives.[5] Many fathers, custodial and non-custodial, want to be more involved in the daily routines of their children but are uncertain how to do this. Joint book reading, a rather simple, fun, inexpensive, and cognitively enriching activity, provides fathers with a tool that can be utilized to promote daily interactions with their children.

When fathers are actively involved in their children's education, children benefit in profound ways. In a landmark study, researchers at the U.S. Department of Education analyzed data on father involvement in children's schooling from the 1996 National Household Education Survey (NHES).[6] These researchers discovered that when fathers were actively involved in their children's education, children were more likely to receive A's, enjoy school, and participate in extracurricular activities. The same children were also less likely to drop out of school if their fathers were involved.

Reading aloud to and with children is a powerful tool for enhancing the quality of father-child relationships. At the same time it will equip the next generation with the language and literacy skills needed to succeed academically and socially.[7] According to a joint position statement issued by the International Reading Association (IRA) and the National Association for the Education of Young Children (NAEYC), "One of the best predictors of whether a child will function competently in school and go on to contribute actively in our increasingly literate society is the level to which the child progresses in reading and writing."[8] But what can parents and other adults do to help children progress in these critical areas? According to many experts, the single most important thing parents can do to help their children acquire essential literacy skills is to read aloud to them.[9] Joint book reading has been shown to improve children's literacy development across a variety of domains, including vocabulary growth, print awareness, enjoyment of reading, and writing abilities.[10]

Benefits of Joint Book Reading for Fathers and Children

Although I've always been fascinated with children's literature, my interest in fathers and reading on a professional level didn't take shape until after the birth of my first child more than eight years ago. It's amazing how the birth of a child can open one's eyes to a whole new world of inquiry! Shortly after accepting my current position with Texas Cooperative Extension at Texas A&M University, I discovered that one of my colleagues also shared an interest in fathers and reading. Dr. Lynn White, a family economic specialist with Texas Cooperative Extension, revealed to me that she had developed a concept known as "FRED," or *Fathers Reading Every Day,* as a tribute to her father, Fred Bourland. Lynn recalls the unique influence her father had on her and her sisters, particularly in the area of reading. Mr. Bourland firmly believed that reading opened the door of opportunity for himself and his children and that reading can do the same for others. After hearing of Lynn's vision, I was able to team up with some of my colleagues at Texas Cooperative Extension to develop the content for the FRED program, which seeks to involve fathers in daily reading activities with their children.[11]

For four weeks, 15 minutes a day for the first two weeks and 30 minutes a day for the last two, fathers and their children select and read books together at a time and location of their choosing. Participating fathers are given a set of materials including tips on reading aloud to their children, lists suggesting age-appropriate children's books, and a reading log to document their reading activities. During the course of the program, fathers document the amount of time spent reading to their children and the number of books read. Since the program's inception, more than 5,000 fathers and children have participated in approximately 60 Texas counties. FRED is catching on; eight other states had plans underway to implement FRED in 2005. The purpose of the program is to encourage fathers to take an active role in their children's early literacy development through daily reading activities, but FRED was never intended to be simply an intellectual exercise. The program was designed from the very beginning to serve as a road to meaningful father involvement by which fathers and children can come together to learn and grow in their relationship.

For the purposes of this chapter, I have classified the benefits of joint book reading for fathers and children into the following five categories: (1) father involvement in the development of children's emergent literacy skills; (2) expanded opportunities for father involvement in children's formal and informal education; (3) father-child quality and quantity time; (4) opportunities for father-child communication; and (5) father-child bonding. To illustrate the benefits that fathers and children enjoy as a result of reading together, I also share quotes and examples from surveys of fathers who participated in the reading program with their children.

Father Involvement in the Development of Children's Emergent Literacy Skills

The cognitive (or intellectual) benefits associated with reading aloud to children are well established. Reading stimulates children's imaginations, expands their vocabularies, enhances print awareness, introduces them to components of stories (e.g., characters, plot, action, sequence), and teaches them valuable information about the world that surrounds them.[12] Children who are read to frequently by their parents tend to become better readers and perform better in school than children who are read to infrequently.[13] Beyond these documented benefits, fathers or mothers who read to their children also help to establish the core foundations of learning and literacy.

For years, it was thought that learning to read was something that occurred when children entered kindergarten or first grade. Today, however, there appears to be broad consensus among researchers and educators that the process of learning to read is initiated much earlier in life. It now seems clear that children develop "emergent" literacy skills (i.e., the precursors of formal reading) during the early stages of infancy.[14] While multiple strategies exist to promote children's literacy development, recent studies indicate that reading aloud to them in an interactive style is the most effective strategy for promoting the language and literacy skills of children from birth to age five.[15]

It is important for fathers to establish a habit of reading to a child early in the child's life. Children as young as six weeks enjoy being read to by their parents. Fathers who read to their children from an early age will make valuable contributions to their language and literacy development. This is especially true when fathers engage their children as active participants in the process. Fathers can help promote their children's early literacy skills by:

- setting aside a special time each day to read to their children,
- reading books that focus on the three R's (rhythm, rhyme, and repetition),
- reading and re-reading a variety of books (e.g., storybooks, informational books, alphabet books),
- helping their children identify letters of the alphabet and their corresponding sounds,
- pointing out the differences between upper- and lower-case letters,
- teaching children that print runs from left to right and from top to bottom on a page (in the English language),
- teaching children to recognize various features of books (e.g., title, author, illustrator, front and back cover),
- assisting their children in distinguishing between colors, shapes, and sizes of objects found in a children's book, and
- asking analytical questions (e.g., "What is the child doing on this page?").

The strategies identified above can all be accomplished during joint book reading and have been shown to improve preschool-age children's emergent literacy skills.

Research suggests that fathers themselves tend to prefer interactive styles of involvement with children, and reading provides a great format for this type of interaction. One father who reads frequently to his daughter noted, "I do a number of things to help her become an active participant in the reading experience. I read, and she turns the pages. I ask her what's going to happen next, and she gives her best guess. I stop in the middle of a sentence, and she fills in the blanks." Engaging children in these simple reading exercises makes reading not only an enjoyable experience but also one that helps children acquire the skills they will need during their formal schooling years.

Reading Expands Opportunities for Father Involvement in Children's Formal and Informal Education

The few studies conducted to date indicate that fathers play an instrumental role in their children's education. In the U.S. Department of Education study mentioned earlier, researchers examined father involvement in the school activities of kindergarten to 12th-grade students. Fathers (married and nonresident) who were moderately or highly involved in certain activities (e.g., participating in parent-teacher conferences, attending general school meetings, or volunteering at school) positively influenced their children's academic performance.[16] The study, however, did not examine father involvement in educational activities at home, which can be just as or even more important than involvement outside the home.

Fathers all across America use reading as a tool to become more involved in their children's formal and informal education. By reading aloud to and with children on a regular basis, fathers gain a better understanding of their children's capacity to read as well as their children's ability to comprehend what they are reading. Illustrating this point, a father who completed the FRED program with his son stated, "I better understand my son's education, how well he reads and understands what he is reading." Another father noted that reading aloud together "helped me understand what areas my child needs to work on."

Reading is a great way for fathers to acquire information about their children's educational progress; however, it also opens up opportunities for further learning and involvement. Reading can be used by fathers to explore and follow up on a child's unique interests. For example, if a father discovers his child is especially interested in dinosaurs, he can arrange a visit to the local library with his child to check out books on the subject. In another instance, a teacher may give a school-age child a homework assignment to find out more about Egyptian artifacts or Renaissance art. Fathers can help their children learn more about these subjects and others by taking their children to local museums or searching the Internet together for reliable information.

Reading in specific ways to promote children's emergent literacy skills is an effective way for fathers to be involved at an early stage of a child's life. Fathers have an additional set of opportunities to be involved in the education of older children who are reading independently. Fathers can use reading as a tool to:

- expand their children's vocabularies by helping them understand the meaning of more complex words and phrases,
- explore books together that deal with historical events, famous personalities, and other subject matter areas,

- follow up on subjects that children are learning in school (e.g., science, art, history, current events) through additional learning opportunities (e.g., reading books and magazine articles or visiting local museums),
- bridge the gap between what is learned in school and the home environment, and
- encourage more frequent outings to the library or bookstore.

Reading not only provides fathers with an avenue to expand their involvement in their children's education but also an opportunity to carve out time during a busy day to spend with their children.

Quality and Quantity of Father-Child Time

One of the scarcely mentioned benefits of joint book reading between parents and children is simply spending time together in a meaningful and enjoyable activity. Fathers who make a conscious decision to read to their children on a regular basis make a conscious choice to spend time with their children, which many children claim is one of the best gifts their father can give them. In surveys conducted in the United States and abroad, children frequently rate time with parents above most other activities.[17] A recent, large-scale study conducted with British school-age children found that, instead of wanting expensive toys, computers, and bikes from their dads, children much preferred spending time with their dads in ordinary activities.[18] Reading, for the most part, tends to fit into the category of "ordinary."

While there is not a perfect time or place to read to children, establishing a consistent routine (e.g., reading to a child for 15-30 minutes before bedtime) accomplishes a number of important objectives: (1) it ensures father-child time together, (2) it creates excitement and anticipation on the part of the child who looks forward to reading together, and (3) it sends a strong message that a father cares for his child and values their time together. Children who learn to expect this routine will encourage it and feel the excitement that waits around the next corner of a tale like *Encyclopedia Brown* or *Harry Potter*.

Sentiments shared by several fathers who participated in the FRED program illustrate the essence of how reading together facilitates genuine quality time between fathers and children. When asked what they took away from reading daily to their children, one father wrote:

Although we spend a lot of time together, it sometimes revolves around my schedule. "FRED" time was all for them. No matter what was going on at 8 p.m., it was reading time. It brought us closer together because I would always have to stop what I was doing just for them.

Another father noted that the thing he liked most about reading daily to his child was "the excitement my child had in anticipation of the reading time." A third father stated, "A busy day didn't allow me to skip spending some quality time with my son. This time became a priority." Reading together provides opportunities for both quality and quantity of time, but in some cases time is in short supply.

Circumstances prevent some fathers from being able to spend regular time in reading activities with their children. This is particularly true for noncustodial fathers, fathers who are deployed in the military, incarcerated fathers, and fathers who travel frequently in their jobs. Cases such as these require greater creativity on the part of fathers and their children. Fathers who face these challenging circumstances can:

- read books and other print materials to their children over the phone,
- record themselves reading on audio or video cassette and mail the tapes to their children,
- designate a certain day of the week as a special "reading night" with dad, and
- write stories for or with children that can be read from a distance (e.g., by mail or e-mail).

Fathers that make a special effort to spend time together in reading activities, even if at a distance, will learn more about their children and strengthen the overall quality of the relationship.

Opportunities for Father-Child Communication

Communication plays an integral role in building strong father-child relationships. It is through communication processes that fathers and children verbally and nonverbally express their needs, wants, and concerns as well as their love and admiration for one another. As parents, fathers have a unique opportunity to influence the lives of their children, including the important decisions they make that affect their futures. Much of the influence fathers have on their children comes from their daily interactions with them, and communication processes lie at the heart of these interactions.

Due to its interactive nature, joint book reading provides fathers and their children with an open forum for communication. Before, during, and after the actual experience of reading together, a number of processes take place that enhance opportunities for father-child communication. Through shared reading experiences, fathers can learn more about their children's unique interests, share their own interests, discuss sensitive topics, respond to children's questions about various issues that arise during the reading times, pass along important family traditions, and instill moral values in their children. I recall from my own childhood how my mother and father set aside a special time each day to read the Bible to my siblings and me. I also remember the discussions that followed and how those shaped my character.

Suggestions for promoting father-child communication around reading include:

- discussing topics of interest to the child and selecting books to read that are educational and enjoyable,
- making a trip to the library, bookstore, or bookshelves at home to explore available books to read,
- discussing the significance of certain events as well as the different character traits of the story's protagonists and antagonists,
- posing questions to children that cause them to reflect on the meaning of the stories they read and how it applies to their lives (e.g., "What would you do if you found yourself in a similar situation?"), and
- asking or responding to questions of an ethical or moral nature that arise during or after reading times (e.g., "How do you think the boy felt when his brother made fun of him, and how could he have responded differently?").

The opportunities for father-child communication before, during, and after reading times are plentiful, and it is through these interactive experiences that fathers and their children have great potential for relationship growth.

Father-Child Bonding

Fathers contribute to their children's early literacy development in a variety of ways, but the interactive nature of the reading experience itself holds the greatest promise for enhancing father-child relationships. When parents read to their young children, they tend to do so by holding them in their lap or sitting with them in bed just before bedtime. The physical closeness, the time together, and the enjoyable experience of reading a good book all combine to create an environment conducive to relationship growth. Joint book reading provides fathers with an opportunity to interact with their children across multiple domains of development: physical, intellectual, social, and emotional.

Fathers can bond with their children by:

- allowing young children to turn the pages as they sit in their father's lap,
- establishing a routine of daily reading with their children just before bedtime,
- selecting humorous books that allow fathers and their children a chance to laugh together,
- sharing personal thoughts and feelings about books as they read them, and
- processing feelings of sadness and disappointment when reading books for older children (e.g., Wilson Rawls's *Where the Red Fern Grows*).

Reading can allow fathers and children to laugh, learn, and draw close together as they appreciate shared time and experiences. Good books are not easily forgotten. A father and child who spend weeks together reading an adventurous book such as Robert Louis Stevenson's *Treasure Island* have, in a sense, traveled on a journey together. The experiences are theirs to share, reflect on, and recall months or even years later. The power of reading to enhance the quality of father-child relationships is captured in the following quote from a father. He wrote of daily reading with his child:

> [Reading together] challenged me to be more involved. It provided us with time alone, during which we grew closer through reading a variety of stories/books that allowed us both to travel, explore, and go on adventures that expanded my child's vocabulary, imagination, and horizons.

Reading with children can truly cement the bonds between fathers and children and pass on a special kind of magic that enriches the lives of children for years to come.

Conclusion

Years of research have demonstrated the value of reading aloud to children. Reading stimulates children's imaginations, enhances their vocabularies, and lays a foundation for future learning. Fathers who read to and with their children on a regular basis are contributing to their children's intellectual development in important ways. However, the benefits that emerge are not limited to children's intellectual development. By its very nature, joint book reading is an activity that encourages meaningful father-child interaction.

Whether learning valuable life lessons from *Charlotte's Web* or laughing out loud while reading *Green Eggs and Ham*, fathers and their children quickly realize that reading together can be enjoyable, exciting, and educational, all at the same time. My father made a commitment to read to me, and I have made that same commitment to my children. I encourage fathers everywhere to pass this wonderful tradition on to their children, knowing it will make a difference for generations to come. Reading truly is a magical endeavor. In the words of Dr. Seuss, "The more that you read, the more things you will know. The more that you learn, the more places you'll go."

Endnotes

1. Nelson, K., 1998, *The Daddy Guide: Real-Life Advice and Tips from Over 250 Dads and Other Experts,* Lincolnwood (Chicago), IL: Contemporary Books.

2. Federal Interagency Forum on Child and Family Statistics, 2004, *America's Children in Brief: Key National Indicators of Well-Being, 2004*, www.childstats.gov.

3. National Center for Fathering, 1999, *Fathers' Involvement in Their Children's Learning*, www.fathers.com/research/involvement.html.

4. Levine, J.A., Murphy, D.T., and Wilson, S., 1998, *Getting Men Involved: Strategies for Early Childhood Programs*, New York: Families and Work Institute.

5. See the following: Grolnick, W., and Slowiaczek, M., 1994, "Parents' Involvement in Children's Schooling: A Multidimensional Conceptualization and Motivational Model," *Child Development, 65*, 237–252; Lamb, M., 1997, "The Development of Father-Infant Relationships," in *The Role of the Father in Child Development*, edited by M.E. Lamb, New York: Wiley, pp. 104–120; Parke, R.D., 1996, *Fatherhood*, Cambridge, MA: Harvard University Press; Radin, N., 1986, "The Influence of Fathers upon Sons and Daughters and Implications for School Social Work," *Social Work in Education*, 8, 77–91; Radin, N., 1994, "Primary-Caregiving Fathers in Intact Families," in *Redefining Families: Implications for Children's Development*, edited by A.E. Gottfried and A.W. Gottfried, New York: Plenum, pp. 55–97; Snarey, J., 1993, *How Fathers Care for the Next Generation: A Four-Decade Study*, Cambridge, MA: Harvard University Press; Yogman, M.W., Kindlon, D., and Earls, F.J., 1995, "Father Involvement and Cognitive Behavioral Outcomes of Preterm Infants," *Journal of the American Academy of Child and Adolescent Psychiatry, 34*, 58–66.

6. Nord, C.W., Brimhall, D., and West, J., 1997, *Fathers' Involvement in Their Children's Schools*, U.S. Department of Education, Office of Educational Research and Improvement, Washington, DC.

7. Snow, C.E., Burns, M.S., and Griffin, P. (Eds.), 1998, *Preventing Reading Difficulties in Young Children*, Washington, DC: National Academy Press.

8. International Reading Association and National Association for the Education of Young Children, 1998, "Learning to Read and Write: Developmentally Appropriate Practices for Young Children," *Young Children*, 53, 30–46.

9. Ibid.

10. Halle, T., Calkins, J., Berry, D., and Johnson, R., 2003, "Promoting Language and Literacy in Early Childhood Care and Education Settings," Child Care and Early Education Research Connections (CCEERC), www.childcare research.org.

11. See Green, S.D., 2002, "Involving Fathers in Children's Literacy Development: An Introduction to the Fathers Reading Every Day (FRED) program," *Journal of Extension, 40(5)*, www.joe.org/joe/2002october/iw4.shtml; Green, S.D., 2003, "Involving Fathers in Family Literacy: Outcomes and Insights

from the Fathers Reading Every Day (FRED) Program," *Family Literacy Forum*, 2, 34–40.

12. Bus, A.G., van Ijzendoorn, M.H., and Pellegrini, A.D., 1995, "Joint Book Reading Makes for Success in Learning to Read: A Meta-Analysis on Intergenerational Transmission of Literacy," *Review of Educational Research*, 65, 1–21.

13. Snow et al. (Eds.), 1998.

14. Whitehurst, G.J., and Lonigan, C.J., 2001, "Emergent Literacy: Development from Prereaders to Readers," in *Handbook of Early Literacy Research*, edited by S.B. Neuman and D.K. Dickinson, New York: The Guilford Press, pp. 11–29.

15. Halle et al., 2003.

16. Nord et al., 1997.

17. See Taylor, B., 2003, *What Kids Really Want That Money Can't Buy*, New York: Time Warner; Galinsky, E., 1999, *Ask the Children: What America's Children Really Think about Working Parents*, New York: William Morrow & Co.

18. For a press release on the British survey, see www.fathersdirect.com.

Four generations of the Stueve family: Jeff, T.J., Bernard (Cappy), Will, and Jim

A Father's Love:
Impacts of Sacrifice and Care on Fathers and Their Children

Shawn L. Christiansen and Jeffrey L. Stueve

I remember when my son was in preschool and he was in a class of *about 20 girls and only three boys. Unfortunately, my son was the odd boy out. I often volunteered at the preschool and saw him playing with some of the girls or engaged in solitary activities at the center. He did not appear distressed about his relationships with the two boys. However, one night, with a quivering lip and teary eyes, he told me how it hurt that the boys would not let him play with them. In response to his emotional pain, I did the only thing I could think of: I held him and wept. My tears distilled my concern, empathy, and love for a little boy struggling to fit in and be accepted. The act of holding him filled us both with the warmth of love. Sometimes in the relationships with my children, love has been less poignant and more difficult to give. Well-known psychiatrist M. Scott Peck, in his classic book,* The Road Less Traveled,[1] *states that*

love is an act of giving attention. I have been guilty of being less atten-
tive to the needs of my children than situations have required. But it is in
the struggle to be attentive to our children that we grow as fathers and
learn to love and act according to our children's needs. In reflecting back
on the moment when I held my son and comforted him, the feelings of
love and compassion affirmed that I had given genuine attention and care
in the embrace we shared.

—Shawn, the first author

For years, I have played a nightly bedtime game with my sons, now 10
and eight. When the lights are going out and the "I love you's" are
exchanged, often one of us will say, "I love you more than you love me!"
or boast, "Well, I love you to the end of the universe and back!" or "I love
you more than all the money in the world!" Since becoming interested in
the concept of paternal love, I've come to ask myself questions about what
it means to my children and me when I tell them I love them and about
how I can more fully live out the simple statement "I love you."

—Jeff, the second author

As scholars and fathers, we have both conceptual ideas about the love fathers share with their children and personal experiences that validate these ideas. Children naturally desire and respond to being loved. As scholars it is sometimes difficult to adequately describe, label, and measure what most fathers take for granted in their daily interactions and feelings toward their children. Despite the current lack of specific research and conceptualization of paternal love, social science research supports the belief that children and fathers are more likely to thrive when love is present and practiced and struggle when it is not. This chapter will discuss how fathers love and nurture their children and how these actions benefit fathers and their children.

Love and Nurturance in Parenting

Most parents relate to the idea of loving and nurturing their children. Fathers and mothers understand that children need and respond to the gift of love. Love bonds parents and children and defines their relationships. In many ways, parents across the world have a much better handle on this reality than the scientific community.

The majority of social science scholarship does not represent the common-sense understanding that parents have in loving and caring for their children. For example, Howard and Kathleen Bahr,[2] a husband-wife research team at Brigham Young University, have documented that family love seems to have little place in contemporary family theories. Not only is there little mention of love in family theory and research, but many family theories are built on ideas that are in opposition to principles of love, care, altruism, and sacrifice. Instead, many contemporary theories focus on the self-interest of the individual. Love, however, encourages us to think about the interests of others.

What is the role of love and nurturance in the context of fathering? Love is a concept that involves concern, attention, devotion, and sacrifice for another. While most people seem to understand and accept the importance of love in family relationships, there is not a clear definition of love in the social sciences. Perhaps love is a concept that defies easy definition. It has been discussed by poets, philosophers, religious leaders, and scientists, yet no single definition has emerged. Love and nurturance, however, lie at the heart of family relationships.

M. Scott Peck defined love as "the will to extend one's self for the purpose of nurturing one's own or another's spiritual growth."[3] Thus, love might include (1) the active choices we make (our will), (2) the effort we put forth (extending ourselves), (3) both our own and the other person's well-being, and (4) the purpose of growth. Howard and Kathleen Bahr state that family love involves "the sacrifice of self or extensions of self, in the interest of priorities or persons whose needs we see as more pressing than our own."[4] This statement is consistent with the common definition of love found in the Merriam-Webster Online Dictionary: "unselfish, loyal, and benevolent concern for the good of another."[5] Nurturance, as described by fathering scholar Henry Biller, includes physical affection, verbal declarations of love, and "positive attention and support for [a] child's interest and competence."[6] Biller's definition is also consistent with Merriam-Webster, which defines nurturance as "affectionate care and attention."[7] These conceptions of love give insight into what it means and how it can influence the relationship fathers share with their children.

Fathers, Sacrifice, and Love for Children

Sacrifice as a dimension of a father's love and care for his children occurs in a variety of settings. It is a timeless aspect of loving another person. Fathers have exhibited love by sacrificing for children in times of great societal stress, during periods of family difficulty, and especially every day in the mundane choices of family life.

There are many historical and contemporary examples of fathers making sacrifices for their children, often during times of difficulty or social crisis. In his analysis of fathers in colonial America, social historian John Demos gives an example of one prominent New England merchant who stayed up all night with his children whenever they became seriously ill. Demos also describes a village craftsman who recalled that "when his child was sick, and like to die, he ran barefoot and barelegged, and with tears" all night to find help.[8] These examples contrast with the notion that historically fathers were more concerned with the labor the child provided than the relationship they shared as father and child.

Additional examples of paternal sacrifice are provided from a scholar, Mirra Komarovsky, who studied families during the Great Depression. Komarovsky records the sentiment of a wife: "This depression proves to me how courageous and devoted my husband is to the family. He will go without food for the sake of the children."[9] The practice of sacrifice by a father may lead him to serve his children at the expense of his own health or well-being. Examples of such sacrifice come from the annals of war and disaster. Tzvetan Todorov documents the love shown by family members living in the deprivation, abuse, and horror of Nazi concentration camps. In the camps of death, those individuals who were no longer able to work were often the next to be killed. Todorov recorded the story of a father who is still capable of work and yet lies next to his son, who is too weak to work, "so that they might await death together."[10] To sacrifice as a father is truly to put the needs of those you love ahead of your own personal interests or desires.

There are also many contemporary examples of fathers who sacrifice for their children during trying times individually or within the family. Sean Brotherson and David Dollahite, in their research on fathering children with special needs, cite the example of a father who sacrifices his time, sleep, personal needs, and work hours to care for his sick child. The father recounted:

> Last night I stayed up till about 4 a.m. because Lee was having a high fever, etc. When kids get sick, you really reach out to them.... The first thing I did this morning was to call the doctor and make an appointment for him. It wasn't an emergency, but the high fever was very bad. I would use two towels, putting water on them and helping him to cool down. Then today I went to work and called the doctor's office again. They told me that the doctor would be in by 9 o'clock, so I took about two and a half hours off work today and missed lunch. I took him to the doctor because I feel that this is what fathers are for—to stand up and take responsibility when your children need you.[11]

The significance of this story is the attention given to the sick child rather than the sacrifices of the father. This father could have easily pointed out how the sick child interfered with his sleep, his work productivity, or his personal time, but the father's concern was on the needs of his child. Love involves self-sacrifice, or forgetting self, in the service and care of others. This is especially true in the case of parenting, in which children are totally dependent on their parents for survival. For fathers, love through sacrifice involves coming to see the needs of children as more pressing and significant than their own personal needs or wants.

With Wesley, It's about the Soul

When someone tells you your son can't talk and will always have the mind of a two-year-old . . . it really shattered a lot of dreams I had about the relationship I was going to have with him. And, yeah, it hurts. It felt like a part of me was dying.

And sometimes I catch myself just driving in silence. Just sitting there driving, and you start really thinking about what's important in life. I've got a kid back there that can't talk. You know, what kind of relationship are you having with your son?

Instead of walking with you, I will crawl with you. Instead of focusing on what you cannot do, I will reward you with love for what you can do. Instead of isolating you, I will create adventures for you. Instead of feeling sorry for you, I will respect you. And so, I know someday I'm going to have my special moment with him, in a different way. And nobody can take it away from me. And that's what I'm looking forward to. With Wesley I've begun to realize that the father-child relationship is about the soul.[12]

—Wesley's father, *The Story of Fathers and Sons*

Many of the acts of sacrifice shared thus far have occurred during extreme trials or serious crisis. However, fathers also make sacrifices for their children in the mundane acts and choices of everyday life. Some fathers fail to take responsibility and care for their children. However, many more take responsibility by partnering with the mother in raising their child, providing financial support, and working to furnish food, shelter, clothing, and opportunities for education, growth, and development. Daily sacrifices are made by fathers who are caring for and meeting the needs of their children. Most fathers love their children and want to be able to demonstrate it. These daily sacrifices are perhaps the most common efforts fathers make for their children and the best evidence of the love they wish to give them.

Fathers, Nurturance, and Raising Children

Another critical aspect of love involved in raising children is nurturance, which can involve hugging a child, verbally expressing affection, showing support, and acknowledging children's success.[13] Such behaviors, once thought to be primarily practiced by mothers, are increasingly common and important in fathers' interactions with their children. Fathers can practice nurturing and develop skills necessary to meet the changing needs of their growing children.

Much of the research literature demonstrating the nurturing abilities of fathers deals primarily with father-infant interaction. For example, parenting scholars Douglas Sawin and Ross Parke have observed both mothers and fathers interacting with their babies in the hospital.[14] What did they learn about fathers and their nurturing abilities? Fathers were found to be just as involved and nurturant with their infants as mothers. Areas of interaction observed included fathers holding, kissing, and talking to their infants. Also, fathers were observed to be as sensitive as mothers to an infant's feeding cues and just as successful at bottle-feeding the child. Feeding cues noticed by parents included sucking, coughing, and burping, and success in feeding the infant was determined by the amount of milk consumed. Fathers were just as competent at demonstrating nurturant behaviors with their children when the mother was present as when she was absent. Other studies on fathers and nurturing behavior have shown similar results.

Sawin and Parke's research highlights fathers' abilities to be sensitive and responsive to their children's needs and developmental opportunities in caring for them. Such findings illustrate the intricacy of the development and nurturance of love in a relationship through small behaviors like noticing a child's desire to be fed. A father's attention to the details of such needs assists him in both loving the child and developing the capacity for love. As a new father, Shawn remembers his anxiety when bathing his son for the first time and fear that he might hurt such a tiny newborn. As time passed he recalls the feelings of connection, concern, and confidence that developed through these interactions. While writing this paper, Jeff met with staff members who work with young incarcerated fathers. They noted that even the toughest men, some with seriously violent backgrounds, are capable of showing affection by hugging and kissing their young children. In fact, most value and enjoy doing so.

Researcher Scott Coltrane, in his study of 20 dual-earner couples with school-aged children, further demonstrated the nurturant capabilities fathers develop as they participate actively in parenting their children.[15] Fathers in this study shared their experiences of having to learn how to care for and nurture their children. These fathers were usually described as being transformed by the parenting experience and developing sensitivity to the needs of their children. Mothers reported that their husbands began to notice subtle cues from their children as the fathers increased their involvement in childcare. Parents who equally shared childcare reported that their children were emotionally close to both parents. A child who was hurt or upset would typically go to the parent who was nearest or had most recently been with them. Coltrane summarized his findings by stating that fathers needed active participation in childcare to further develop parenting skills. Fathers not only have the capacity to nurture their children at all ages but also more fully discover and develop the capacity for love and nurturance as they care for their children's needs.

As fathers and children mature in their relationship, there is a continuing need for care and nurturance. While much of the research on nurturant fathering has focused on fathers of younger children, in discussions with numerous university students, we have found they still greatly appreciate being told they are loved, or even hugged and kissed, by their fathers. Many who have not received such affection say they miss it. Even such simple expressions of love can make a meaningful difference in the relationships between fathers and their adolescent or adult children.

Implications of Fathers' Love for Relationships and Development

Accomplished family researcher Michael Lamb points out that "contrary to the notion of maternal instinct, parenting skills are usually acquired on the job by

---

In the Middle of the Night, in China

She had come from an orphanage, and we put her to bed. We had gone to bed, and in the middle of the night she woke up and was crying. I went over to comfort her, and I picked her up and put her in my arms. I was standing in front of this window in this hotel in China. It was about three in the morning, and I started to rock her by doing what I would refer to as the "daddy two-step." You sort of move from your right foot to your left foot, and you have this light little bounce that takes place . . . that you don't ever do until you have a child in your arms.

It's like this genetic program kicks in where you learn how to do this little hopping thing, and you rock back and forth, and I was doing that with her. I started to talk to her to soothe her, and I remember distinctly telling her that I was there for her now. She would no longer be alone. She wouldn't have to worry about being hungry. She wouldn't have to worry about being loved. She was now a part of our family.

I was talking to her about these things and expressing my heart to her, and when I got finished talking to her, she had stopped crying. She looked up to me and made a motion with her hand, as if toward my chest. And it was as if she just reached out and grabbed hold of my heart and just tugged on my heart, and since that moment I have never worried about the idea of whether I'd bond with her. I mean, it was just taken care of at that moment.[16]

(A narrative an adoptive father told of the night his daughter joined his family)

both mothers and fathers."[17] In other words, parenting actually stimulates growth of the skills, including love and nurturance, needed in raising children. Fathers can not only be nurturant and sensitive to their children's needs but also develop individually through their experiences. In addition, their children benefit in concrete ways from such efforts.

Development of Men as Fathers

Fathering requires men to be loving in their interactions if they are to be good fathers. The impact of fathers' involvement in child rearing on the fathers' own development has been discussed and studied.[18] For example, feminist writer Dorothy Dinnerstein notes, "The process of nurturing life is the most profoundly transforming experience in the range of human possibilities. Because women have this experience and men generally don't, we live and think and love across a great gap of understanding."[19] Two interesting ideas may be drawn from this quote. First, this statement highlights how nurturing can be transforming. Second, the statement assumes men generally don't have the experience or opportunity to nurture life. Another way of saying this is that fathering has been generally more optional for fathers than mothering has been for mothers. From the point of conception, a mother carries the child within her womb, goes through the pains of labor, and in most cases takes primary care and custody of the child. In contrast, fathers must show their love and commitment through establishing paternity, providing material aid, supporting the mother and child, and loving and caring for their child. While some men never become fathers beyond the biological sphere, many fathers make the most of their opportunities to care for and nurture their children, and through the relationships fathers and children share, both are changed.

Well-known lifespan psychologist Erik Erikson originated the concept of *generativity*—defined as concern and care for the next generation.[20] Erikson argued that parenting is the prime opportunity to develop this sense of care and regard for the next generation. This may be especially true for fathers. Emory University researcher John Snarey conducted a longitudinal study of involved fathering over several decades.[21] He found that fathers who were involved in their younger and teenage children's social-emotional development were more likely to extend care beyond family to others and the community in their own middle years.

In Shawn's research with Japanese fathers, there was a strong relationship between involvement in child rearing and generativity, particularly among fathers who rated themselves highly in showing their children praise and affection.[22] Though not part of the study, Shawn's Japanese friend the late Kiyotake Okada exemplified generativity in care to his wife, children, students, and friends. In Japan, where involved fathering is often the exception rather than the rule, Kiyotake supported, encouraged, and nurtured his two children, Kiyoaki and Izumi, while he also cared for his sick wife. Kiyotake was a high school teacher in a school for troubled youth. He mentored many of these students and influenced them to make choices to better their lives. In one case, a family came in distress to him about their family relationship, especially the relationship with their high school son. Through Kiyotake's influence, their family and parent-child relationships were strengthened, and the son's behavior improved. Kiyotake's optimism and concern for others continued even as he battled cancer, which eventually took his life. He passed on the gift of his life in a book about his experiences that was published shortly before he died. His generativity and legacy of love continues in the lives of his wife, children, grandchildren, students, and friends.

Being a father generates opportunities for men to become more loving individuals. The featured speaker at a state fatherhood conference Jeff attended went so far as to say he didn't truly know what love was until he became a father. Some research shows the impact of father involvement in child rearing on several aspects of adult development. Fatherhood scholar Rob Palkovitz found that involved fathering produced changes in fathers' perceptions of personal well-being, family relationships, and career development.[23] Probably one of his most important findings was that active fathering produced many positive emotions. Often these positive emotions were reciprocal between the child and the father. One father in his study, Leo (pseudonym), stated his experience in this way:

> The relationship I've gained as a father has been very fascinating to me. I don't think I ever understood or could imagine how close and beautiful the relationship would become, how the love and respect would grow and develop between my kids and myself. It's been pretty incredible.[24]

As this father suggests, probably the greatest benefit of loving and caring for children occurs in the transformation of the father-child relationship itself. Early involvement of fathers typically leads to later positive interactions with their children. In one study, 74 percent of fathers and 66 percent of mothers felt that sharing childcare had helped fathers become closer to their children and develop a stronger parent-child bond.[25]

Love and the Development of Children
In a 2001 article on the importance of father love, Ronald Rohner and Robert Veneziano found strong support for the assertion that paternal love plays an important role in children's lives.[26] In the more than 90 studies they reviewed, they found a range of psychological and behavioral outcomes linked to levels of paternal love, as defined as parental acceptance or warmth. Evidence suggests that fathers' love can matter as much as, and in some specific contexts even more than, mothers' love. A few selected examples that highlight the importance of fathers' love and nurturance for their children's development follow:

- One benefit of paternal nurturance is higher cognitive competence and academic performance in children. A child's intellectual development is stimulated by the father's support, encouragement, and example.[27]
- Positive, supportive, encouraging paternal involvement is strongly related to children showing more empathy for others.[28]
- Children with warm and affectionate fathers are more likely to have long, happy marriages and closer relationships with friends as adults.[29]
- Children have fewer behavior problems when their fathers are actively involved, supportive, and affectionate.[30]
- Nurturance and moderate availability of fathers is related to a more positive self-concept and better adjustment in adulthood.[31]
- Children of highly involved and nurturant fathers have less stereotyped perceptions about the roles of mothers and fathers.[32]
- Sons with nurturant fathers have a model they can emulate, and girls with nurturant fathers feel supported and accepted as females. Gender identity in girls and boys is influenced by fathers who are warm, emotionally expressive, and active in childcare.[33]

These and many additional findings indicate that fathers who are nurturant and loving with their children contribute in positive ways to their children's emotional, social, and behavioral development and competence.

Ways for Men to Provide Love and Nurturance to Children: The FASE of Father Love

In interviewing and working with fathers and university students, four themes have emerged that capture characteristics of a father's love.[34] These can be conceptualized as the FASE ("face") of father love: *f*ocusing on the child and the child's well-being, *a*ccepting the child, *s*haring life, and *e*nduring. The specific ways love is demonstrated may vary according to such factors as the child's age, gender, and temperament, whether or not the father lives in the same residence with the child, and the family's cultural heritage, but these four factors capture much of the essence of paternal love. The four FASE father love components overlap, work together, and provide a guide for fathering with love across different contexts.

Focusing on a Child's Needs and Well-Being
A father's love is demonstrated by focusing on a child's physical, emotional, social, cognitive, and spiritual needs. The foundation for this is a father's commitment to meeting his child's needs. Possible ways for deepening this commitment include making explicit commitments to self, child, others (the child's mother, other fathers, etc.), or prayer.

Since needs vary according to child, a father needs to know his child as a unique and special individual. Many fathers say that the primary way they meet their children's needs is providing for and protecting them, but fathers can meet their children's needs in many ways. Many older children say knowing their fathers care about their well-being is a key need. How can a father better know what his children need? By talking to them and asking them (be aware that there can be a big difference between needs and wants!), asking the child's mother or others who know the child (teachers, grandparents, or other relatives may have important insight into the personality or needs of a specific child), and carefully observing the child (what does he or she respond to, what causes frustration, what are his or her talents and strengths?).

It can also be useful to know more about the general developmental needs of children as they grow. There are many resources for learning about these aspects of child development, including libraries, schools and childcare centers, and healthcare providers.

Accepting One's Child

Many students and fathers said a father's love is *unconditional* in nature. This does not mean all behavior is acceptable. In fact, some fathers pointed out that if a father loves a child, sometimes tough discipline is necessary. But no matter what, the child is loved and accepted for who he or she is. Here is one father's extreme example:

> I mean they could go out and kill someone, and they would know that they would STILL be loved. They know there is not something they could do to make their parents not love them. Although we may be (expletive), or we may, you know, lash out irrationally, we know that, no matter what he does, we'll still love him so.[35]

A central aspect of father love is acceptance of the child. (For example, Ronald Rohner and colleagues' work focuses on parental acceptance. See Rohner's website for more information and support for the importance of parental acceptance: http://vm.uconn.edu/~rohner.)

Sharing Life with One's Child

Sharing includes physical involvement but can incorporate other levels of sharing oneself with the child. One participant in a study by Stueve and Pleck said a father's love meant he was willing to give all of himself for his children.[36] Both students and fathers mentioned the importance of a father's communication of his love to his child. Some said this did not have to be done verbally, but others noted how important saying or hearing it was to them.

The theme of sharing life with children was perhaps the most poignantly expressed by some fathers interviewed. Their explanations or descriptions of paternal love included comments like these:

- "You spend time with them, just be with them, and do things they enjoy together."
- "I can watch. I know that my son plays by himself, but, you know, sometimes he's just so happy when I join him."

These comments embrace a father's recognition that love to a child means being together and sharing life's moments. In summary, sharing life with a child means sharing time, activities, conversation, and self.

Enduring

Paternal love and its influence are enduring. Words like "always" or "whenever needed" appeared regularly in interviews and conversations with fathers and students. The first FASE component of father love is focusing on a child's needs, but the needs of children must be met across time. A father's love cannot be subject to the whims of the world but must be enduring as a meaningful and constant source of support.

Jeff gave talks about fatherhood as a guest speaker to two different university classes one semester. Afterward, a student from each class approached him, and both told him a bit about their deceased fathers. These students described in moving ways the enduring nature of their fathers' love and how important it was to them still. What a legacy these fathers left. One father interviewed about paternal love perhaps captured this theme best. He defined love as "being there till . . . till the end, you know, till the end."

Conclusion

We benefit from the examples of fathers who sacrifice, nurture, and care for their children. One limitation of our discussion and the fathering literature in general may be the lack of a clear definition of father love. Then again, maybe the power of a father's love is that it cannot be easily defined because it is expressed and experienced individually by each father and child. Perhaps father love cannot be found in a scholar's theory but only in the personal stories and lives of individual children and their fathers. For example, the father serving in Iraq who writes a letter home to his son (next page), telling him of the love and joy he felt in being his father—not knowing the letter would be his last.[37] Or the American father standing in a hotel in China holding his newly adopted daughter and comforting her as she cries.[38] Or the father with the disabled son who has to rethink his dreams and learn to accept and love his son as he is, not for who he hoped he would be.[39] These images of fathers' love for their children may not fit neatly into one definition, but they inspire and encourage us to better love and honor the gift of fatherhood.

To His Son, Cecil, Age 8

Email from Marine Staff Sergeant James W. Cawley, 41, Layton, Utah

Just a quick note preface before I start in earnest. When I wrote this you were eight, still a little boy. In 2002, I was called to active duty in the Marine Corps in the War on Terrorism. On the 11th of September, 2001, when America was attacked, I knew that I would eventually have to go, and I was filled with a deep sense of sadness.

That night as you and Keiko were asleep, I looked at your little faces and couldn't help but fight the tears. I knew it would be hard for you because I had a similar experience. When I was a little boy aged six, my dad, your Grandpa Cawley, was sent to Vietnam during the war there. I remember how much I missed him, too. But now unfortunately I have come to realize just how rough it must have been for Grandpa to be away from his children for a year. Thinking about this, I wanted to put my thoughts and feelings down for you and your sister.

I am so sorry that I had to leave for such a long time. There is no place I would rather be than with you and Keiko. You two are the lights of my life. I have known no greater joy than in the few years since you two were born. I hope to have many more years with you. If this doesn't happen, then know that I love you more than words can express. If for some reason I don't make it home, I will need you to take care of your little sister and your Mom. You will be the man of the Cawley family. Be good, my son, and God will watch over you as he has me. I will be waiting impatiently for the time when we can all be together again.[40]

All my love, Dad

(Staff Sergeant Cawley was killed during a firefight on March 29, 2003).

Endnotes

1. Peck, M.S., 1978, *The Road Less Traveled: A New Psychology of Love, Traditional Values and Spiritual Growth,* New York: Simon and Schuster, Inc.

2. Bahr, H.M., and Bahr, K.S., 2001, "Families and Self-Sacrifice: Alternative Models and Meanings for Family Theory," *Social Forces*, 79, 1231–1258.

3. M. Scott Peck, at 81.

4. Bahr, H.M., and Bahr, K.S., 2001, at 1232.

5. Merriam-Webster Online Dictionary, www.m-w.com/dictionary/love.

6. Biller, H.B., 1993, *Fathers and Families: Paternal Factors in Child Development*, Westport, CT: Auburn House, at 75.

7. Merriam-Webster Online Dictionary, www.m-w.com/dictionary/nurturance.

8. Demos, J., 1986, *Past, Present, Personal: The Family and the Life Course in American History,* New York: Oxford University Press, at 48.

9. Komarovsky, M., 1940, *The Unemployed Man and His Family*, New York: Dryden Press, at 55.

10. Todorov, T., 1996, *Facing the Extreme: Moral Life in the Concentration Camps*, New York: Metropolitan Books, at 71.

11. Brotherson, S.E., and Dollahite, D.C., 1997, "Generative Ingenuity in Fatherwork with Young Children with Special Needs," in *Generative Fathering: Beyond Deficit Perspectives*, edited by A.J. Hawkins and D.C. Dollahite, Sage Publications, Inc., pp. 89–104, at 97.

12. Weimberg, G., Ryan, C., and Leonard, J. (Producers), 1999, *The Story of Fathers and Sons*, ABC television documentary, Princeton, NJ: Films for the Humanities and Sciences.

13. Biller, 1993.

14. Parke, R., 1979, "Perspectives on Father-Infant Interaction," in *Handbook of Infant Development*, edited by J. Osofosky, New York: Wiley, pp. 549–590; Sawin, D., and Parke, R., 1979, "Fathers' Affectionate Stimulation and Caregiving Behavior with Newborn Infants," *Family Coordinator*, 28, 509–513.

15. Coltrane, S., 1989, "Household Labor and the Routine Production of Gender," *Social Problems, 36,* 473–491.

16. Stueve, J.L., and Pleck, J.H., November 2004, "What's Love Got to Do with Fathering? Exploring Paternal Love," presented at the Theory Construction and Research Methodology Workshop of the National Council on Family Relations, Orlando, FL, at 17–18.

17. Lamb, M., 1987, "Introduction: The Emergent American Father," in *The Father's Role: Cross-Cultural Perspectives*, edited by M.E. Lamb, Hillsdale, NJ: Lawrence Erlbaum, at 11.

18. Christiansen, S.L., and Palkovitz, R., 1998, "Exploring Erikson's Psychosocial Theory of Development: Generativity and Its Relationship to Paternal Identity, Intimacy, and Involvement in Childcare," *The Journal of Men's Studies*, 7(1), 133–156; Hawkins, A.J., Christiansen, S.L., Sargent, K.P., and Hill, E.J., 1993, "Rethinking Fathers' Involvement in Childcare: A Developmental Perspective," *Journal of Family Issues*, 14, 531–549; Hawkins, A.J., and Dollahite, D.C., 1997, *Generative Fathering: Beyond Deficit Perspectives,* Sage Publications, Inc.; Snarey, J., 1993, *How Fathers Care for the Next Generation:*

A Four-Decade Study, Cambridge, MA: Harvard University Press; Palkovitz, R., 1996, "Parenting as a Generator of Adult Development: Conceptual Issues and Implications," *Journal of Social and Personal Relationships*, 13, 571–592; Palkovitz, R., 2002, *Involved Fathering and Men's Adult Development*, Mahwah, NJ: Lawrence Erlbaum, Inc.

19. Blakely, M.K., August 1983, "Executive Mothers: A Cautionary Tale," *Working Mother*, 70–73.

20. Erikson, E., 1950, *Childhood and Society*, New York: Norton.

21. Snarey, 1993.

22. Christiansen, S.L., November 1999, "Understanding Predictors of Generativity in a Sample of American and Japanese Fathers," presented at the National Council on Family Relations Annual Conference, Irvine, CA.

23. Palkovitz, 2002.

24. Palkovitz, 2002, at 95.

25. Russell, G., 1982, "Shared-Caregiving Families: An Australian Study," in *Nontraditional Families: Parenting and Child Development*, edited by M.E. Lamb, Hillsdale, NJ: Lawrence Erlbaum, Inc., pp. 139-172.

26. Rohner, R.P., and Veneziano, R.A., 2001, "The Importance of Father Love: History and Contemporary Evidence," *Review of General Psychology*, 5, 382–405.

27. Biller, 1993; Snarey, 1993.

28. Koestner, R., Franz, C., and Weinberger, J., 1990, "The Family Origin of Empathic Concern: A 26-Year Longitudinal Study," *Journal of Personality and Social Psychology*, 58(4), 709-717.

29. Franz, C.E., McClelland, D.C., and Weinberger, J., 1991, "Childhood Antecedents of Conventional Social Accomplishment in Midlife Adults: A 36-Year Prospective Study," *Journal of Personality and Social Psychology*, 60(4), 586–596.

30. Amato, P.R., and Rivera, F., 1999, "Paternal Involvement and Children's Behavior Problems," *Journal of Marriage and the Family*, 61(2), 375–385.

31. Biller, 1993.

32. Radin, N., 1982, "Primary Caregiving and Role-Sharing Fathers," in *Nontraditional Families: Parenting and Child Development*, edited by M.E. Lamb, Hillsdale, NJ: Lawrence Erlbaum Associates, Inc., pp. 173-204.

33. Biller, 1993.

34. Stueve and Pleck, 2004.

35. Ibid, at 15.

36. Stueve and Pleck, 2004.

37. "Last Letters Home," February 1, 2004, *Esquire*, 41(2), retrieved online at www.esquire.com/features/articles/2004/060518–mfe_February_04_Letters_1 .html.

38. Stueve and Pleck, 2004.
39. Weimberg et al. (Producers), 1999.
40. *Esquire*, 2004.

II

Fathers and Domains of Development

Four chapters in this section introduce a developmental perspective and explore fathers' influence on varying aspects of a child's development. Domains of development addressed in this section include fathers' influence on a child's developmental journey, psychological development of a child, fathers and moral development, and fathers and spiritual development.

Chapter 11, "The Developmental Journey: Fathers and Children Growing Together," highlights the developing father-child relationship and fathers' influence in guiding their children from infancy through adolescence. Glen Palm, accomplished fathering scholar, addresses how fathers and children share "intertwined developmental journeys" and how the developmental context sets the stage for growth in both fathers and children. He discusses how the developmental journey needs to focus on the changing needs of children as they grow and suggests some new and old ways that fathers might approach each stage to strengthen their relationship with their child and build their parenting skills through meaningful involvement.

In Chapter 12, "The Influence of Fathers and Children's Psychological Well-Being," Vicky Phares and David Clay focus on a central aspect of development in children and youth. Psychological well-being is associated with a host of positive and negative outcomes for children. Phares and Clay describe persuasively how fathers count in their influence on a child's mental health and well-being—in both positive and negative ways. The authors' treatment of the topic includes discussion of parenting styles, involvement, emotional engagement with children, levels of conflict, and fathers' mental health as key factors associated with children's mental health and well-being.

Terrance Olson and James Marshall explore the territory of fathering and moral development in Chapter 13, "Fathering and the Moral Development of Children." The authors consider aspects of fathers' moral influence with their children including the tie between who we are and the quality of our relationships, how fathers can be advocates for their children, what it means to meet children's needs, helping children connect principles with practices, and the idea of citizenship as a moral act. The extended discussion and examples furnish insight into an often mentioned but seldom thoroughly explored domain of fathers' influence on development.

The final chapter in this section, "Fathers as Spiritual Guides: Making the Transcendent Pragmatic," shares findings from research by Loren Marks and Rob

Palkovitz. These fathering scholars present ideas concerning the role of fathers in children's spiritual development and the meaning of spirituality to some fathers. They discuss several themes that highlight the work of fathers as spiritual guides to their children, including role modeling, parenting with humility, "being there" for their children, and viewing fatherhood as a spiritual calling. The chapter includes a number of narratives from fathers that suggest the influence of spiritual beliefs and behaviors on fathers and their interactions with children.

This section presents the importance of a developmental perspective in father-child relationships and suggests several areas of development where fathers make a difference in children's lives. Although not exhaustive, the chapters in this section make a compelling case for the value of fathers in shaping the development of children in multiple domains of life. Fathers can influence not only a child's physical and language development but other key areas such as cognitive and moral development. As they assist children's growth, fathers themselves grow and change as well.

Author Glen Palm and his youngest daughter, Allison

© Glen Palm

The Developmental Journey:
Fathers and Children Growing Together

Glen Palm

Fatherhood is a developmental journey. It is a journey that follows our children as they move through rapid growth in infancy into the active preschool period, the development of new cognitive and social skills during the school years, and finally the sometimes turbulent waters of adolescence. Fathers frequently describe their own parental development as learning through hands-on experience.

Jim, the first-time father of three-month-old Lisa, is learning different ways to comfort his daughter during her fussy period in the early evening hours by walking her around the house and talking to her. Lisa is also learning to trust that her dad will come when she begins to fuss and help her to calm down. Jarrod is learning how to set limits for two-year-old Jamila when they go to the grocery store and she demands a candy bar at the checkout line. Jamila is learning she may not always get everything she wants when she goes to the grocery store with her dad. Al is discovering new ways to help six-year-old Sam enjoy books by attending a Dads and Kids Book Club and learning tips about reading to children. Sam is learning that books are fun to share with his dad and that reading is a valued skill in his family.

The journey continues into the adolescent years as fathers learn to deal with the moodiness of puberty and the development of a new, independent identity. Fathers and children share intertwined developmental journeys and learn from each other as they weave a close relationship in the context of growth and changes in their individual pathways of development.

The main focus in this chapter will be the developing father-child relationship as fathers learn new roles for nurturing and guiding their children from infancy through adolescence. It will highlight how fathers grow through their parenting experiences and how they can facilitate a strong, caring relationship as their children progress on their own journey of growth and development. As most fathers of young adults will readily admit, this time goes by too quickly, and while the opportunities for father involvement are plentiful, they evaporate if you postpone spending time together. Involved fatherhood means growing with your children as you strive to raise responsible, capable, and loving human beings. Fathers retain some of the lessons about parenting they learned growing up, but they also create their own unique parenting style as they learn through experiences with their child.

A Framework for the Developmental Journey

As a new dad in 1978, I was excited by the opportunity to create a new fatherhood role that emphasized a close, caring, nurturing relationship with my new infant daughter. I was going to be a pioneer with other fathers of young children in the late 1970s. We were going to be different from our own distant dads and establish close, caring relationships based on greater involvement in the care and learning of our children. We were part of a changing culture that had begun to emphasize the broader opportunities for men to be involved in the lives of their children in caring ways.

Men continue to create and construct new fatherhood identities by blending traditional roles with what Jim Levine and Ed Pitt called "new expectations" for men in family life.[1] These expectations include increased responsibility for the care and support of children from infancy through adolescence. "Being there" for children has become the mantra for fathers in American society at the beginning of the 21st century.

Several stages of fatherhood are used here as a framework to explore the developmental journey of parenting for men and children. These stages are based on Ellen Galinsky's stages of parenthood, adapted to emphasize the unique styles of fathers.[2] The four stages that will be explored are (1) the nurturing/playmate stage from birth through 12–15 months, (2) the authority/emotional coach stage from 15 months through age five; (3) the interpretive/encourager stage from ages 6 through 12; and (4) the interdependent/lighthouse stage from ages 13 through 18. In each stage, the basic theme for parents is expressed in the first descriptive word, while the second word or phrase has been added to describe how fathers tend to approach the basic parenting themes.

Men bring to parenting their own memories of childhood and role models for fatherhood as they begin their experience as fathers. For example, you may carry the memories of a father who told funny stories to you at age four, took you on your first fishing trip with the men at age six, or never came to your Little League baseball games. All of these experiences and the emotional memories connected to them surface as men encounter their child in similar situations. This trip through the developmental journey will focus on the changing needs of children as they grow and some new and old ways fathers might approach each stage to strengthen their relationship with their child and build their own parenting skills through meaningful involvement.

Meaningful involvement for fathers blends new and old roles and expectations. Four major assumptions behind the developmental journey of fatherhood are:

- Children's development and changing needs are driving forces for meaningful father involvement in all family and cultural contexts.
- Fathers are influenced by cultural/ethnic backgrounds, family systems, and social and religious beliefs in selecting values to pass on and deciding which skills their children need in order to be successful in society.
- Each developmental stage builds on the father-child relationship patterns and fathering skills developed in the previous stages. Fathers who wait until their child is old enough to play catch or go fishing miss the critical early stages of building a close father-child relationship.
- Fathers are a natural resource for the care and socialization of children that has not been fully tapped.[3] Education and support for fathers can be a catalyst for unleashing the power of this resource.

I. The Nurturing Stage: Fathers as Playmates

Nurturing is a central theme of parenting during a child's first 12 to 15 months, and fathers in this stage learn to engage children both as nurturers and playmates. When a child is born, the typical father today begins his journey in the delivery room with a "hands on" experience. For some men this is a turning point as they experience the miracle and awesome responsibility of life. Fathers describe holding their infant for the first time as "unbelievable," "awesome," "frightening—they are so small and fragile," and "amazing." Martin Greenberg describes a child's birth as a time of intense new feelings, engrossment, and the place where the fatherhood journey begins.[4]

The main task for new fathers is to build a positive connection with their baby. This is not always easy for men, since male socialization often pushes them into the provider role as they face the financial responsibility of raising a child. Not all men "click" with this new relationship or grasp the importance of this change in their lives.[5] Many new fathers are overwhelmed with all of the changes in their lives a new baby brings, from sleepless nights to a changing sexual relationship with their partner and uncertainty about their ability to care for and comfort their babies. Fragile family contexts and lack of support systems can make this transition even more challenging. A strong sense of commitment and responsibility, as well as the joy and excitement of becoming a father, can help men get through this transition. It can also help to take a parenting class, read a book on child development, or find another new dad for story sharing and mutual support.

The child's needs during this time are very basic unless the baby has special needs or circumstances such as a premature birth. Infants require sensitive care to meet their basic needs of hunger, sleep, clean diapers, cuddling, and play as they come to know and trust the people in the world around them. These needs seem so basic and simple at times. However, a baby's needs may also be demanding and not always in tune with adult schedules and needs—creating new responsibilities for fathers who want to be involved. Fathers may also find that the typical nurturing tasks of caring for an infant may be unfamiliar territory. The first task for the involved father is to sort out new responsibilities with his partner. The second task is to develop a nurturing style that is sensitive to the child's needs and builds on his own strengths as a father. For example, as a new father Jim has learned that three-month-old Lisa likes to be held up against his chest looking out when she is awake and alert as he talks to her about her surroundings. He also has discovered that she likes to be held on his shoulder and gently rocked when she is feeling tired and ready to take a nap.

What do we know about fathers and infants that can help us navigate these first few months? First, we have discovered that fathers are able to form a close attachment relationship with a baby that in many ways is similar to the mother-infant attachment. Ross Parke describes the way fathers often think about and interact with their babies.[6] Fathers tend to be more tactile, more physically stimulating, and less verbal. Babies often see fathers and seem to light up and think, "It's play time!" Thus, a father's natural tendencies in parenting may lead him to value and play the role of a child's "playmate"—a fun, warm part of a growing baby's world. The classic image of the father lifting his six-month-old high into the air as the child grins and laughs depicts what continues to be a popular game among fathers and their infants. Fathers also learn to be sensitive to an infant's cues so that playtime does not become overstimulating and scary for the infant. Fathers learn to meet the baby's physical needs but may do so in a different manner than mothers. Fathers will find their own ways to comfort a crying baby or play different kinds of games to amuse their six-month-old infants. This works well when fathers and babies find a mutually engaging and satisfying interactive style.

Fathers can blend their natural tendency to play in an active, stimulating manner (the old role) with learning to be sensitive and responsive to a child's verbal and nonverbal cues (new expectations). A father can learn to share in baby care and develop his own style of play and care that meets his child's needs and individual temperament. Building a close relationship at this stage provides a strong foundation for the challenges of the next stages.

Meaningful Involvement during Infancy

What can fathers do during this first developmental stage to both meet the child's developmental needs and build a positive, trusting relationship?

- Carefully observe infants and learn about their unique cues and communication style.
- Learn to care for their basic needs like feeding, changing, bathing, and comforting.
- Talk to your baby—they know your voice and enjoy listening to you.
- Make up active games that are fun and engage and challenge your baby.
- Find 100 different ways to make your baby laugh.
- Watch your baby and learn to appreciate some of his or her basic temperamental characteristics (typical patterns of behavior, reactions to new people, intensity of reactions)
- Spend time alone with your baby to give your partner a break and build your own confidence as a competent caregiver.

II. The Authority Stage:
Fathers as Authority Figures and Emotional Coaches

Fathers know they have entered the next stage when infants turn into toddlers and begin to assert their authority, which triggers the parenting task of developing discipline and teaching styles. Children at this stage are full of energy, curiosity, and rapidly changing emotions. A two-year-old wants to be a big girl and cross the street by herself and then wants to be picked up and held as soon as she gets to the other side of the street.

Fathers often enter this stage with the tendency to assert their authority with their deep voice and physical strength. This may bring some initial positive results, but it is easy to become engaged in power struggles with two-year-olds and fall into the trap of believing that physical power is the only way to approach these struggles. Power assertion is not the best way to handle a child's growing needs for identity and independence at this time. A young child is learning to assert his or her initiative, and a father represents a figure of authority who sets and enforces rules and limits. Fathers at this time also become aware of their children's emotions and begin coaching them in the management of feelings.

Children from ages two to five display many emerging skills and needs that can challenge parents. Children are learning about family and society, and their parents have the task of socializing them to learn manners, express and control emotions, and learn basic social skills. Children at this age are also developing important attitudes about learning and literacy that require the support of their parents. During this stage, the roles of authority figure, emotional coach, and teacher are all important for fathers to add to the still-important roles of playmate and nurturer they developed during their child's infancy.

Fathers tend to engage in more rough-and-tumble play at this stage. McDonald and Parke explain this helps children learn to develop social relationships by setting physical boundaries and limits.[7] Fathers also teach their young children about sex roles; both boys and girls look to fathers as a primary example of masculinity. Kyle Pruett describes how more involved fathers are likely to raise children who exhibit fewer sex-role stereotypes.[8] Finnish researchers have documented that fathers who read to their children also have an important impact on their literacy skills and later school achievement.[9] Fathers perform these roles in their unique way to support their child's development during this stage. As fathers take on more responsibility for the day-to-day care of young children, this style difference remains, and research by Pruett suggests that this nurturing-father style has positive impacts on children's cognitive and social development.[10]

This stage for children is one of rapid and lifelong learning about people, the world, literacy, emotions, and relationships. A father can let this period slip by and play with his child only when he finds the time and energy, or he can take advantage of the rich opportunities for socializing and teaching his child in a more intentional manner. Sometimes this means monitoring his own behavior and changing some of his own habits. Young children are like a mirror, and sometimes they repeats words or actions their fathers hadn't wanted them to learn. For example, three-year-old Marissa was watching her dad repair a fence in their back yard. Dad noticed a few minutes later that Marissa was pretending to pound nails and punctuating each hammer stroke with a swear word. As he listened more closely, he noticed she was perfectly mimicking the emotional tone and expression he had used when he bent a nail. Fathers are models of how to manage emotions and challenges, and children look to them to learn how to behave and express feelings.

A primary task for fathers during this stage is to develop a parenting style based on their understanding of their child's needs and their own beliefs about parenting roles. Today there are higher expectations for fathers to be involved in the care of young children. Reading books about child behavior and development or joining parent education and support programs for fathers during this stage can be a way to enhance the basic trial-and-error learning style. Instead of rediscovering (learning from scratch) all of the lessons of fatherhood at the expense of one's children, it's possible to take some time to learn from the experiences and ideas of other parents and professionals who work with young children. A father in this stage, Jarrod, had been attending a parenting class for parents of toddlers and learned that two-year-old Jamila was typical in her demands for a candy bar in the checkout line. He also learned from the parent educator and other parents about some preventative strategies that might help to manage this situation and avoid an embarrassing public meltdown. Learning such skills can be very helpful for fathers who wish to navigate this stage of parenting successfully and confidently.

Meaningful Involvement during Early Childhood Years

The following are some ways fathers can support development at this stage:

- Introduce children to nature by taking them for a walk in the park, planting a garden, or going fishing.
- Talk to children and listen to their questions to encourage their natural sense of curiosity.
- Include children on errands so they can learn about the outside world.
- Encourage early literacy by telling stories, reading picture books, and providing opportunities to see how literacy is used in daily life.
- Give children opportunities for scribbling, drawing, and writing.
- Play games that include learning about letters, words, and sounds.
- Teach words for emotions and show ways to express them appropriately.
- Model respect for others through your manners and interactions.
- Let children watch and help as you do household cleaning and repairs.
- Monitor children's use of TV and computers to screen for unintended learning about sex roles and aggression.
- Take children on trips to the library, zoo, and children's museums.
- Model problem solving and negotiation with your partner.

III. The Interpretive Stage: Fathers as Encouragers

My oldest child at age six was looking at a stamp book I had recently bought to introduce her to one of my hobbies: stamp collecting. She was helping me mount a collection of presidential stamps and asked, "Why are all of these presidents men?" This was one of many insightful questions she posed. I had to learn how to explain gender inequality to her. Fathers have traditionally been viewed as children's connection to the outside world. Children between the ages of six and 12 seek understanding about the world, and fathers play a major role in interpreting it for them and encouraging them to learn more as they grow and question.

Fathers help to introduce their children to the world of sports, politics, and work. As they interpret and explain the world to their children, they must be clear about their own values and how these connect with the larger society their children are entering. It is also a time when children are eager to learn new physical and mental skills valued by society, and fathers can help by fulfilling the important function of encouraging the development of these new skills.

Children from ages six to 12 are learning rapidly and have many different needs. Most take a giant step outside the family and are immersed in the school system and the new world of peer culture. This is the time when they learn basic literacy skills and new physical skills as they continue to develop social skills within their peer group. What children need at this stage is encouragement and support from parents. Fathers appear to have a strong influence on a child's self-concept. Children are excited about learning and developing new skills but also concerned about failure and how others see them. Their self-concept often revolves around their physical appearance, ability to make friends, and development of athletic or cognitive skills. They view their fathers as important judges of their competence.

Research reviewed by Hennon and colleagues documents the importance of fathers' involvement in children's education during this stage.[11] If fathers are involved during the middle childhood years, children tend to be more successful in school. Children whose fathers are involved in school have higher grades. Children take school more seriously when they know it is important to their fathers. They have higher grades, better attendance, and a more positive attitude toward school. Ross Parke notes that father engagement with children during this stage also has a positive impact on social skills and relationships with peers.[12]

The middle childhood years are a time when children begin to move away from parents and spend more time with friends. This can relieve parents of some day-to-day care responsibilities of the early childhood years, but parents are still a home base where children can check in for emotional support and guidance. "Being there" takes on a whole different meaning. Children need enough time to just "hang out" with parents to open up and share their feelings, thoughts, and questions about the world. Fathers often find themselves investing more time and energy in their careers as children start to need less direct care. It is easy to slip into the automatic provider role. Fathers may be able to provide children with the "things" they "need." However, it is possible to forget that what children really need is someone to be there when they have questions or doubts and need emotional support and guidance. This is where a solid foundation built in the first two stages makes it easier for both fathers and children to expand their relationship. They can enjoy new activities and connections together as fathers interpret the world to their children and encourage their new capabilities. Al, a father described at the beginning of this chapter, found that his attendance at the book club with Sam was an effective way to encourage Sam's emerging ability to read. During this stage many fathers enjoy sharing their interests in areas like baseball or fishing with their children, and forming new connections through these shared activities.

Meaningful Involvement during Middle Childhood Years

This stage holds many new opportunities for meaningful involvement as fathers and children connect by way of new activities at new levels of sophistication. A father's memories from this age are more lucid, and many dads enjoy interaction with their children in the areas of sports, schoolwork, or hobbies. The following is a list of ideas for meaningful involvement during this stage.

- Introduce children to new skills: riding a bike, playing baseball, swimming.
- Show interest in schoolwork by asking about school, going to conferences, and helping with homework.
- Encourage new interests such as crafts and hobbies, from building forts to collecting sports cards.
- Read a book with or to your children, take them to the library, and find out what kinds of books they enjoy.
- Monitor TV and computer time as needed and provide alternatives such as playing games, playing catch, or completing a craft project together.
- Model and encourage family responsibilities by teaching and performing household tasks with children.
- Become involved as a volunteer for a sports team, scouts, 4-H, or a church youth group to observe your child in a social context outside the family.
- Get to know children's friends by volunteering to take them on outings, to the beach, to a ball game, or to a movie.
- Take children to work with you so they can see what your world is like.
- Help to create and plan family rituals and traditions as a way to pass on values: birthday celebrations, holiday traditions, etc.

IV. The Interdependent Stage: Fathers as Lighthouse and Guide

The teen years from 13 to 18 can be a whole new world for fathers. Thirteen-year-old Danae comes home from school and goes to her room with the phone to talk to a friend, barely acknowledging her father when he tries to strike up a conversation. Fifteen-year-old Dustin has been asked to clean his room all week before his grandparents arrive for a visit. He tells his dad he has to go to a friend's house to work on a school project that is due tomorrow and will get to the room later. Sixteen-year-old Denise is out with friends on a Friday evening. She is supposed to be home by 11 o'clock. She calls at 10:59 from her cell phone and asks to stay another half hour until a movie is over. Many parents dread this stage because they are faced with new uncertainties about setting limits and managing the new independence of adolescents.

Fathers know something about this stage from still-fresh memories of their own adolescence. Children begin to assert their independence and are more connected to the larger world and exposed to the temptations of drugs, sex, and consumerism. It can be an exciting time to watch children grow into adults, but it is also frightening as they confront difficult choices and sometimes make mistakes. Their changing bodies and mood swings are confusing for them as well as their parents. It is also a time for adventure, development of deeper friendships, understanding their own sexuality, understanding the world at a deeper level, and identifying their own ideals and beliefs.

Galinsky labels this stage as a time of interdependence.[13] Adolescent children seek the independence that accompanies their available choices in life and their maturing bodies and minds, yet they also need guidance and the security of a good relationship with parents. I have chosen the image of a lighthouse as a symbol of the role fathers could play during this stage. A lighthouse guides from a distance and is most visible and necessary during storms. Teens need some distance or emotional space as they try to find their place in the world, but they also need a steady force they can look to and count on for guidance.

The years from 13 to 18 are times of physical change, growing mental capabilities, and searching for identity. Self-concepts are shaped by the values of the larger culture and peer group. Puberty and changing hormones strike teens at different times and change their bodies, personalities, sexual awareness, and identity. Teens continue to grow more independent from parents and spend more time away from home with peers, at school, in extracurricular activities, or at part-time jobs. They are more introspective and need time and space away from parents, yet they depend on parents for basic needs and continued psychological support and guidance.

Father involvement during earlier stages sets the tone for the father-teen relationship. Researchers Charlie Lewis and Michael Lamb confirm that close relationships with fathers during these years continue to promote school achievement, lower the use of drugs, and inhibit early sexual behavior.[14] Kyle Pruett reports that fathers play different roles in their relationships with sons and daughters during adolescence.[15] Sons need to move away from their fathers and challenge their authority, while daughters benefit from a father's emotional support as they gain independence from their mothers. Positive father involvement is connected to self-esteem for both sons and daughters.

The father's role as a lighthouse during the adolescent years provides safety and guidance in times of stress and uncertainty. Fathers can provide a model of care, support, and responsibility. As teens push away from parents, fathers' presence and availability can be essential for safe passage through the adolescent years.

Meaningful Involvement during the Adolescent Years

Fathers can provide guidance and should continue to monitor adolescent progress in school and seek moments of connection with teens to listen to problems, concerns, feelings, and new ways of thinking about the world. Meaningful involvement during this stage might include the following activities:

- Monitor school progress by attending conferences, encouraging and supporting achievement, and discussing higher education and future careers.
- Make space for one-on-one opportunities to spend time with your teen doing something fun for both of you.
- Welcome your teen's friends into your home as a comfortable and safe place to hang out.
- Encourage and support outside activities by your attendance at sports or extracurricular activities.
- Encourage responsibility through part-time work as a way to learn how to earn and manage money.
- Continue to show affection and caring through words and actions in ways that don't embarrass your child.
- Be emotionally available so your adolescent can share feelings.

Conclusion

The developmental journey for fathers follows the child's growing capabilities and changing needs. The father-child relationship can grow in depth during this journey as fathers integrate new roles to meet needs and developmental challenges at each stage. Fathers develop their own unique parenting style as they meld new and old roles combining a playmate and nurturer role during their child's infancy, developing authority and emotional coach roles during the early childhood years, and learning interpreter and encourager roles during the middle childhood years. Finally, during the adolescent years, fathers move into a new role as a lighthouse, guiding adolescents with constancy and vigilance. Some of the lessons for fathers that emerge from this overview of the developmental journey are:

- Sensitivity to a child's changing needs and interests from infancy through adolescence is essential.
- Fathers must be clear about the values they want to pass on to their children.
- Fathers are important role models of masculinity and positive gender relationships at each stage.
- Understanding and respect for children's unique strengths and interests support the child's emerging sense of self-esteem.

The developmental journey provides multiple opportunities for fathers to grow and learn as they develop a supportive and loving relationship with their children. In addition, their children learn and develop through the natural course of growing up. Men who invest the time and effort will find this is the most important, challenging, and rewarding journey of life.

Endnotes

1. Levine, J., and Pitt, E., 1995, *New Expectations: Community Strategies for Responsible Fatherhood*, New York: Work and Family Institute.

2. See Galinsky, E., 1987, *The Six Stages of Parenthood*, Reading, PA: Addison-Wesley. Galinsky's book focuses on the basic themes and parenting tasks during each of six stages. The child's changes and needs tend to drive the adult's adaptations. Galinsky captures parenting tasks and challenges from the parents' perspectives. The adaptation in this chapter adds a descriptive phrase to capture father's tendencies for approaching parenting tasks in a unique manner based on male socialization and reflected in research literature on fathering.

3. See Pruett, K., 2001, *Fatherneed: Why Father Care is as Essential as Mother Care for Your Child,* New York: Broadway Books. Pruett uses the metaphor of fathers as an underdeveloped and underutilized natural resource for child development.

4. Greenberg, M., 1985, *Birth of a Father*, New York: Continuum.

5. Daniels, P., and Weingarten, K., 1988, "The Fatherhood Click: The Timing of Parenthood in Men's Lives," in *Fatherhood Today: Men's Changing Role in the Family,* edited by P. Bronstein and C.P. Cowan, New York: Wiley, pp. 36–52.

6. Parke, R., 1996, *Fatherhood*, Cambridge, MA: Harvard University Press.

7. McDonald, K., and Parke, R., 1984, "Bridging the Gap: Parent-Child Play Interaction and Peer Interactive Competence," *Child Development,* 55, 1256–1277.

8. Pruett, 2001.

9. Lyytinen, P., Laasko, M.L., and Poilkeus, A.M., 1998, "Parental Contributions to Child's Early Language and Interest in Books," *European Journal of Psychology of Learning,* 13, 297–308.

10. Pruett, 2001.

11. Hennon, C., Olsen, G., and Palm, G., 2003, "Fatherhood, Society and School," in *Home-School Relations,* edited by G. Olsen and M.L. Fuller, Boston, MA: Allyn & Bacon, pp. 290–323.

12. Parke, 1996.

13. Galinsky, 1987.

14. Lewis, C., and Lamb, M., 2004, "Fathers: The Research Perspective," in *Supporting Fathers: Contributions from the International Fatherhood Summit 2003*, The Hague: Bernard van Leer Foundation, pp. 45–76.

15. Pruett, 2001.

Author David Clay with his wife, Monica Watkins-Clay, and niece, Jada Watkins

© David Clay

The Influence of Fathers and Children's Psychological Well-Being

Vicky Phares and David Clay

*W*hen I was an undergraduate student at UCLA in the early 1980s, I had an opportunity to serve as a research assistant on a project that explored parent-child relationships in families with a child who had emotional or behavioral difficulties. I would meet the family in the waiting room of the psychiatric hospital and then invite them to the interviewing room to begin the data collection. Since the research protocol called for interviewing only mothers and children, I often had to explain to the father that he was not needed for the interview and that he could sit in the waiting room until we were finished. Most fathers took this information in stride, but it made me wonder why a project on "parent"-child relationships was exploring only mother-child relationships. I wrote a paper for that research class and have been writing on the topic ever since. For more than 25 years, my work has centered on a central question: Do fathers count?

The evidence can be seen throughout this book and in other sources: fathers count. They count in their relationships with their children, in their relationships with their children's mothers, and in how they live their lives as role models.

This chapter adds to the knowledge of how fathers count in their influence on a child's mental health and well-being—in both positive and negative ways. The positive ways often relate to fathers' impact on their children's psychological well-being and good mental health. The negative ways are typically related to the occurrence of fathers' and children's psychological problems. First, the good news.

—Vicky Phares

Children's and Fathers' Good Mental Health

Like mothers, fathers can have a crucial role in raising well-adjusted, psychologically healthy children. From more than three decades of intense research on fathering, we know that certain aspects of parenting are associated with well-functioning children and adolescents.[1] Factors such as appropriate parenting style, high levels of involvement, low levels of interparental conflict, and good mental health in fathers are associated with good mental health in children and adolescents.

Fathers' Parenting Styles

How does a person's particular style of relating to his or her children affect a child's well-being? Fathers (and mothers) can behave individually in a vast array of ways toward their children. However, decades of research into styles of parenting suggest three main types of parenting are displayed across many different cultural backgrounds within the United States and internationally: (1) *authoritative* or democratic parenting (showing high levels of age-appropriate structure and control paired with high levels of warmth and positive regard), (2) *authoritarian* parenting (showing high levels of structure, control, and discipline with low levels of warmth), and (3) *permissive* parenting (showing low levels of discipline and structure).[2] Of these three parenting styles, the authoritative parenting style is associated with the best outcomes for children.

Specifically, fathers (and mothers) who provide age-appropriate options for their children while also furnishing structure, discipline, and lots of love and affection are likely to have well-adjusted children and adolescents. These fathers support and reason with their children, set limits while providing the rationale for the limits, encourage independence while still providing a strong parental base, and provide logical, consistent, age-appropriate structure to children and adolescents. Overall, fathers whose parenting style is authoritative are likely to have children who feel secure with themselves and exhibit good mental health.

In your daily life, you have likely witnessed all of these parenting styles. Imagine a father's trip to the video store with his five-year-old daughter on a crowded weekend evening. When the daughter runs around and collects four movies (some rated G and some R) and collects four boxes of candy, how might fathers with differing styles react? The authoritarian father would probably chastise the daughter for running around the store and then take all of the movies and candy away from her. He might then choose one movie (not from her selection) that he felt was appropriate for her and then tell her to be quiet when she complained she was not interested in that movie. On the other extreme, the permissive father would not mention anything about the inappropriateness of some of the movies and just acquiesce to his daughter's wishes, pay for all of the movies and candy, and let her watch all of the movies while eating all of the candy late into the night.

In contrast, the authoritative father would likely discuss the movie and candy choices with the daughter and try to negotiate a compromise that met both of their needs. For example, he might explain that she had time to watch only two movies that weekend and that she could only rent movies meant for children (rated G) because she might get scared or upset by movies meant for adults. He would show her which of the movies she chose fell into the acceptable range and let her choose from those appropriate movies. He would likely go on to say that she could only have one box of candy but let her make the choice herself within certain constraints (e.g., a single-serving rather than a jumbo box). The father's demeanor would be warm and loving but firm. In general, he would respect his daughter's opinions and feelings while still providing age-appropriate choices and structure. We would expect the daughter being raised by the authoritative father would show the best mental health outcomes and feel the most secure both during childhood and later into adolescence and adulthood.

Fathers' Involvement

Fathers' involvement with their children is another important influence on children's mental well-being that can be broken down into two broad categories: the quantity and the quality of involvement. Quantity of fathers' involvement is often addressed by measuring the amount of time fathers spend with their children, which can be further broken down into three types of involvement: (1) direct engagement (e.g., playing a game, having a discussion), (2) accessibility (e.g., the child is playing a computer game, and the father is reading the paper), and (3) responsibility (e.g., the father is responsible for making sure the children do their homework and for making doctors' and dentists' appointments).[3]

What factors tend to increase fathers' involvement with their children? Fathers tend to be more active in their children's lives:

- when the fathers hold favorable attitudes toward their role as a father,
- when they are more satisfied with their marriage relationship,
- when the mother is employed,

- when they have fewer children,
- when they work fewer hours,
- when they have higher educational attainment, and
- when the children are older.[4]

All of these factors have an influence on how fathers involve themselves with their children. However, these are not the only factors that matter, and a father's commitment and choices also have much influence. It should not be assumed that a father is less involved if his spouse stays home with children, he has several children, or his children are very young. Increasing the quantity of a father's involvement with his children, at all ages, is a central element of expanding the opportunity for him to have a positive influence on their well-being.

Quality of involvement refers to what fathers and children do with their time together. One interesting aspect of the quality of involvement is the *emotional availability* of fathers.[5] Specifically, fathers who are engaged in their children's lives, supportive of them, and responsive to their emotional needs are considered emotionally available to their children.[6] Children and adolescents who feel their father is emotionally available agree to statements like:

- "My father supports me."
- "He consoles me when I am upset."
- "Dad shows he cares about me."
- "My father shows a genuine interest in me."
- "Dad remembers things that are important to me."
- "He is available to talk any time."
- "My dad asks questions in a caring manner."
- "He spends extra time with me just because he wants to."
- "Dad is willing to talk about my troubles."
- "He pursues talking with me about my interests."
- "My father values my input."
- "Dad makes me feel wanted."

In general, emotional availability is an important aspect of fathering in the healthy development of children and adolescents. In reading over those statements, did you think children would say those things about you?

Overall, both quantity and quality of involvement are important to children's well-being, but the quality of father-child interactions appears to be a bit more important than the quantity.[7] For example, a father who spends huge amounts of time with his son but argues and fights with him constantly will probably have a less positive influence than a father who spends a bit less time with his son but spends that time in mutually enjoyable conversations and activities. It is not simply spending time with children that is important but *what is done* during that time and *how fathers relate* during their time with children.

When fathers show higher amounts of both quantity and quality of involvement with their children, they appear to influence their children positively in a number of ways. Children of highly involved fathers tend to have better social skills, be more emotionally mature, excel more in school, be smarter, and have better jobs as adults than children of uninvolved fathers.[8] Similarly, fathers who are engaged in their children's lives with higher amounts of involvement and emotional availability tend to have children who experience lower levels of emotional/behavioral problems and show better mental health outcomes.[9] A multitude of outcomes that highlight children's well-being are thus affected by fathers' quantity and quality of involvement. Overall, fathers' (like mothers') positive involvement in their children's lives is associated with better mental health for the children.

Low Interparental Conflict

The frequency and intensity of conflict between parents, or *interparental* conflict, is a key influence that can affect children's well-being. Regardless of whether parents are married, fathers and mothers who show low levels of interparental conflict (low levels of arguing and fighting with each other) are more likely to have well-adjusted children.[10] It is sometimes difficult for parents, especially those separated or divorced, to deal with each other in respectful and agreeable ways. However, it is important for parents to try to limit their conflictual interactions with each other, especially in the presence of their children.

Imagine, for example, a 10-year-old boy whose parents are divorced from each other but are both very involved with him. At the child's soccer games, the parents occasionally sit together or at least converse about their son's excellent playing abilities. The parents occasionally disagree about child-related issues (especially child support, which they discuss over the phone and away from the son), but in general the parents get along well and almost never show any conflict in front of their son. In this situation, the boy can feel confident and secure without concerns of embarrassing fights between his parents. Now imagine a situation with a 10-year-old girl's divorced parents who actively and overtly despise each other. At soccer games, they often get into shouting matches about child support payments, and the girl is routinely embarrassed by her parents' behavior. In this situation, the daughter will likely feel sad, angry, and conflicted about her parents' arguments. She may feel she has to choose sides between her parents, and she is routinely mortified that her friends and their parents hear her parents' arguments. Even before reading this book, you could probably have guessed that the boy is likely to have a better level of mental health than the girl. Keeping interparental conflict at low levels can be a difficult, yet important, aspect of raising healthy children.

If arguments arise, it is important for children to know conflict can be resolved in mutually beneficial ways. Fathers who are able to limit conflict with their children's mother and deal with it successfully are more likely to have psychologically healthy children. In fact, some research suggests that keeping interparental conflict at low levels is more important than keeping the parents married to each other (assuming that the interparental conflict cannot be decreased if the parents stay together).[11] Thus, whether parents are married or divorced, children from families with low levels of interparental conflict are more likely to grow up with lower levels of psychological problems.

Key Parenting Tips for Fathers

There have been decades of research on parenting strategies and hundreds if not thousands of books about parenting. Here are a few parenting tips consistently found to improve the well-being of children as well as parents:

- Be conscious of your child's age and developmental abilities (e.g., give your two-year-old a choice of wearing the blue or the red jacket out into the snow storm, but do not ask her whether or not she wants to wear a jacket).
- Be consistent with rules and consequences as much as possible. If the consequence for not doing homework is no television at Mom's house, the consequence for not doing homework should be the same at Dad's.
- Try using praise and positive rewards for good behavior first rather than resorting immediately to punishment. Praise and positive rewards can be more effective than punishment and bring about longer-lasting behavior improvement.
- Try to develop interests in your child's activities, engage your child in activities that interest you, or try an activity that is new to both of you.
- If you want your son to talk to you about his feelings when he is 13 years old, then make sure to listen to him when he is three, four, and so on.
- Try to be a good role model of how to talk, behave, and treat others (children are more likely to do what you do than what you say, so if you say reading is important but do not spend time reading books, your child will likely learn that reading is not really important).
- Do not expect perfection from yourself in parenting, but consider seeking professional help if you are not treating your children the way you think they should be treated.

Fathers' Own Mental Health

Fathers' (like mothers') own psychological functioning is related to their children's psychological functioning. Specifically, fathers who exhibit good mental health tend to have children who also do.[12] Research suggests these connections are related to a number of factors, including genetics, environment, behavioral modeling, and parenting behaviors. Regardless of the reason, fathers who experience low levels of psychological symptoms, exhibit good self-esteem, do not drink excessively, and are happy and secure with themselves and their families tend to have well-adjusted children and adolescents. Occasionally, of course, psychological difficulties can occur in anyone's life. In these cases, fathers who can deal successfully with their own mental health challenges (e.g., by seeking help when they need it) are likely to have children who exhibit good psychological functioning. Overall, fathers' positive well-being and behavior can have positive influences on children's well-being and behavior.

Children's and Fathers' Mental Health Problems

The flip side of the positive influences fathers can extend to their children is the potential for maladaptive (or problematic) outcomes for children due to their fathers' (and mothers') characteristics and behaviors. Like good mental health, psychological problems in children and adolescents can also be related to a number of characteristics in their fathers, including harsh parenting and abuse, disengagement, interparental conflict, and fathers' own psychological problems.

Harsh Parenting and Child Abuse

Imagine a father who punishes his two-year-old for not sitting still as he wishes and who yells frequently and loses his temper with his child constantly. Such a father would be displaying harsh parenting. The opposite of healthy parenting (like authoritative parenting) is harsh parenting or even child abuse. Harsh parenting is evident when fathers are inconsistent and punitive with their children and set unrealistic expectations for their children's behavior. Although it is not realistic and is actually inconsistent with a two-year-old's development to expect him or her to constantly sit still, parents may ignore or misunderstand this fact and get upset or be too forceful and harsh. Fathers may fall into parenting patterns that are unhealthy at best and destructive at worst. At the extreme, child abuse has many different forms. Specific types of abuse include:

- physical abuse (e.g., hitting, beating, or physically harming the child),
- emotional abuse (e.g., calling the child names in a harmful manner or manipulating the child emotionally),

- sexual abuse (any sexual involvement or exposure to sexual material that is inappropriate for the child's age), and
- physical neglect (not providing food, shelter, or physical needs).

Harsh parenting and all forms of child abuse are associated with problematic outcomes for children.[13] Overall, fathers and mothers who are concerned about their parenting skills should seek professional help to see if they can find ways to improve how they deal with their children.

Disengagement from Children

Just as fathers' presence and emotional availability are important to their children, a factor that contributes to negative outcomes is fathers' *emotional disengagement*. Fathers and mothers who show emotional disengagement tend to ignore their children routinely, not become involved in their children's daily or special activities, and not have meaningful contact with their children.[14] Emotional disengagement can occur whether the father lives away from the child or in the same house. Children raised by emotionally disengaged fathers tend to have psychological problems themselves, although the effects of one emotionally disengaged parent can be lessened if children have another supportive parent or caregiver in their life.[15]

Although it can be difficult for most parents to remain emotionally engaged with their children at all times, fathers who are chronically disengaged tend to have children who experience mental health problems. Examples of emotional disengagement include the following:

- A father chronically ignores his infant son's crying.
- After a toddler completes her first successful somersault and says "ta-da" with a big grin on her face, her father merely looks away and shows no expression of joy.
- A father continues to read the paper while his six-year-old son excitedly tells him about his new friends on the baseball team.
- After repeated voice mail and e-mail messages from his adolescent daughter who lives in another state, the father continues not to respond to his daughter's attempts at communication.

These examples may occur on occasion in most families, but repeated and chronic emotional disengagement by parents is associated with low levels of self-esteem and high levels of behavioral problems in children.

Interparental Conflict

In contrast to family circumstances in which low levels of interparental conflict are a positive aspect of children's lives, higher levels of interparental conflict are associated with emotional and behavioral problems for children and adolescents.[16] When parents fight and argue openly and consistently over time, children suffer. In fact, children whose parents stay married and maintain high levels of conflict tend to be worse off than children whose parents separate or divorce, if the conflict decreases significantly after the separation or divorce.[17] Although it is nearly impossible to co-parent children without some level of disagreement and conflict, parents who continue to show high levels of conflict, especially in the presence of their children, are likely to have children who develop emotional and behavioral problems.

Imagine that you work in a store and have two bosses of equal power whom you respected equally. Now imagine that one boss says you have to work the cash register all morning while the other says you have to stock the shelves all morning. When the bosses learn of these conflicting directions, they make you choose one boss's directions over the other. You might correctly feel this is a no-win situation for you and that, no matter what you choose, you will be at a disadvantage in future dealings with at least one of the bosses. You might feel conflicted, helpless, and angry. Now imagine that the two bosses are a child's parents.

Conflict in which the child is put in the middle of the parents' arguments (called "triangulation") is strongly associated with poor adjustment in children. When children are put between their parents in arguments or made to choose sides between them, they are in a no-win situation and often feel helpless, scared, confused, and potentially angry. When parents put children in the middle of their arguments, children are almost always the losers in terms of mental health. Similar to other difficulties in parenting, if parents find it difficult to manage their conflict with each other, they can seek professional help to resolve or at least decrease their interparental conflict.

Fathers' Own Mental Health Problems

Like mothers, fathers who exhibit mental health problems are more likely to have children who also experience some type of mental health problem.[18] Nearly every type of psychopathology studied in fathers is associated with increased risk that their children will have emotional and behavioral problems. For example, children of fathers who drink too much are likely to show elevated behavioral problems when compared with children whose fathers do not drink excessively.[19] Children of fathers who are depressed show more emotional and behavioral problems than children of fathers who are not depressed. Overall, if fathers believe they are experiencing psychological distress of some type, it would benefit them and their children if they would seek professional help to decrease their psychological distress.

Fathers are less likely than mothers to seek out professional help such as psychotherapy.[20] This pattern is similar to findings that men are less likely than women to seek medical help for themselves.[21] When fathers seek treatment for themselves or for their children, they can often find a great deal of comfort and help from professional therapy. In fact, there has been a recent focus on effective treatments (called evidence-based treatments).[22] This focus is to ensure that therapists are using the most effective and established techniques to help their clients.[23] Thus, if fathers

What Fathers Need to Know about Therapy

In general, men are much less likely than women to seek counseling or therapy. This pattern is true for adults who seek help for themselves or their children. Many men seem to have concerns that therapy is a lot like day-time talk shows—which feature a lot of gut-wrenching revelations followed by a lot of tears. Although that may be the case in some sessions, a wide variety of therapies are available that do not require a box of tissues. Happily, therapy can be an effective tool to address concerns about oneself or one's children and can be a father-friendly experience. Here are some things to know about therapy:

- There has been a huge revolution in therapy choices over the past 30 years, and the current focus is on evidence-based (effective) treatments.
- Effective treatments tend to use cognitive-behavioral, cognitive, or behavioral strategies. Although the strategies depend on the problem being addressed, the large majority of evidence-based treatments fall into the cognitive-behavioral realm of therapy.
- In cognitive-behavioral therapy, the therapist usually helps individuals with their cognitions (how they think) and their behavior (how they act). These strategies can be used for an individual adult, individual child, marital couple, unmarried co-parenting dyad, or family.
- Even if the child is the focus of treatment, fathers tend to appreciate a session or two to address their own concerns. If you are in that situation, it makes sense to share those thoughts with the child's therapist.
- If you are hesitant about seeking treatment but feel it is needed, you can address your concerns with the therapist or even "shop around" for a therapist who fits your needs (if you have that option). If resources are limited, you can call your local community mental health clinic to learn what options are available. Some mental health centers or schools run parenting groups to help parents learn more effective strategies in raising their children.
- It shows much courage and strength to ask for help for yourself or your child, but using evidence-based treatments is a way to increase the chances of having a happy, healthy, well-adjusted child and improve his/her world.

feel they need help or that their child needs help, they should be encouraged to know there are usually effective approaches to help resolve their distress.

Conclusion

Overall, fathers influence their children's mental health and well-being in both positive and negative ways. On the positive side, fathers with an authoritative or democratic parenting style (high levels of age-appropriate structure along with high levels of warmth and love), are involved and emotionally engaged with their children, experience low levels of conflict with the child's mother, and experience good mental health are likely to have happy, healthy, well-adjusted children. On the negative side, fathers who exhibit harsh parenting or abuse their children, are emotionally disengaged from their children, show high levels of conflict with the children's mother in front of the children, or suffer from mental health problems without seeking help tend to have children who exhibit difficulties in adjustment (such as being depressed, anxious, angry, or oppositional).

If you are part of a family that largely falls into the positive category, then keep up the good work! It can be a lifelong struggle to provide children with positive, healthy experiences that allow them to flourish psychologically, but the struggle is worth it.

If your family largely falls into the negative category, then it is time for reflection on how to change these patterns. No parent is perfect, but taking steps to improve one's parenting style, involvement with children, communication style with the child's other parent, and mental health are all ways to improve the experiences of children. If these difficulties seem beyond your capacity to resolve, then perhaps seeking professional help from a counselor or therapist is warranted. Quite often, when parents seek help for themselves and their family, they begin to realize how good life can be with happier, better-adjusted children. What better way to "count" with children than to improve your own life as well as theirs.

Endnotes

1. Lamb, M.E. (Ed.), 2004, *The Role of the Father in Child Development,* 4th ed., New York: Wiley.

2. Baumrind, D., 1971, "Current Patterns of Parental Authority," *Developmental Psychology Monographs*, 4(1, part 2).

3. Tamis-LeMonda, C.S., and Cabrera, N. (Eds.), 2002, *Handbook of Father Involvement: Multidisciplinary Perspectives,* Mahwah, NJ: Lawrence Erlbaum Associates.

4. Aldous, J., Mulligan, G.M., and Bjarnason, T., 1998, "Fathering over Time: What Makes the Difference?" *Journal of Marriage and the Family*, 60, 809–820;

McBride, B.A., and Rane, T.R., 1997, "Role Identity, Role Investments, and Paternal Involvement: Implications for Parenting Programs for Men," *Early Childhood Research Quarterly*, 12, 173–197.

5. Easterbrooks, M.A., and Biringen, Z., 2000, "Guest Editors' Introduction to the Special Issue: Mapping the Terrain of Emotional Availability and Attachment," *Attachment and Human Development*, 2, 123–129.

6. Lum, J.J., and Phares, V., 2005, "Assessing the Emotional Availability of Parents," *Journal of Psychopathology and Behavioral Assessment*, 27, 211–226.

7. Tamis-LeMonda and Cabrera (Eds.), 2002.

8. Parke, R.D., and Brott, A.A., 1999, *Throwaway Dads: The Myths and Barriers That Keep Men from Being the Fathers They Want to Be,* New York: Houghton Mifflin Company.

9. Lum and Phares, 2005.

10. Cummings, E.M., and Davies, P., 1994, *Children and Marital Conflict: The Impact of Family Dispute and Resolution,* New York: Guilford Press.

11. Ibid.

12. Phares, V., 1999, *Poppa Psychology: The Role of Fathers in Children's Mental Well-Being,* Westport, CT: Greenwood Publishing Group, Inc.

13. Phares, V., 2003, *Understanding Abnormal Child Psychology,* New York: Wiley.

14. Lum and Phares, 2005.

15. Masten, A.S., and Coatsworth, J.D., 1998, "The Development of Competence in Favorable and Unfavorable Environments: Lessons from Research on Successful Children," *American Psychologist*, 53, 205–220.

16. Cummings and Davies, 1994.

17. Amato, P.R., and Booth, A., 2000, *A Generation at Risk: Growing Up in an Era of Family Upheaval,* Cambridge, MA: Harvard University Press.

18. Connell, A.M., and Goodman, S.H., 2002, "The Association between Psychopathology in Fathers versus Mothers and Children's Internalizing and Externalizing Behavior Problems: A Meta-Analysis," *Psychological Bulletin*, 128, 746–773.

19. Phares, 1999.

20. Carr, A., 1998, "The Inclusion of Fathers in Family Therapy: A Research Based Perspective," *Contemporary Family Therapy*, 20, 371–383.

21. Addis, M.E., and Mahalik, J.R., 2003, "Men, Masculinity, and the Contexts of Help Seeking," *American Psychologist*, 58, 5–14.

22. Kazdin, A.E., and Weisz, J.R. (Eds.), 2003, *Evidence-Based Psychotherapies for Children and Adolescents,* New York: Guilford Press.

23. Nathan, P.E., and Gorman, J.M. (Eds.), 2002, *A Guide to Treatments That Work*, 2nd ed., London: Oxford University Press.

Author James P. Marshall with his wife, Kathie, and children, Kate, Jordan, Kammie, Zack, and Spencer

Fathering and the Moral Development of Children

Terrance D. Olson and James P. Marshall

Consider this possibility: *The influence of parents on their children is not primarily a matter of specific techniques or strategies or even rules or principles.* All these may be characteristics or symptoms of something more fundamental. Parents may influence children intentionally through behavioral example and the articulation of beliefs and values, but parents also affect children unintentionally, in ways not rationally thought out or explicitly demonstrated. This unintentional influence is grounded simply in who they are. By just being who they are, parents invite children, usually indirectly, to consider the meaning and value of being human. Children see value and meaning in the way parents discuss the future, read them stories, make decisions, share tasks, plan vacations, communicate with school teachers, respect grandparents, and respond to movies that illustrate compassion or revenge. Parents who wish to foster the moral dimension of their children's lives will probably do so more during the unintended, unscripted, spontaneous times with their children than during the formal, deliberate, structured "moral lessons" that might be presented at dinner table discussions or family lesson times. This does not mean that formal, structured teaching or demonstrating are not valuable but that the success of those formal times will be governed by the spirit and quality of the informal times.

We will assume in this chapter that moral development is fundamental to the quality of life, but the possibility will unfold that the moral is not first understood as lists of rules or even as specific principles, although both are probably important. The point of this chapter will be to consider how fathers, by virtue of who they are and through the compassionate, committed relationship they develop with their children, can have a moral influence on those children, with ramifications for the family and the community. We begin by considering the tie between our way of being in the world and the relationship we experience with our children. We will show the place of personal commitment and beliefs regarding how fathers can be present for their children in responsible, nurturing ways. We will examine context (the setting in which family life takes place) and what it means to meet children's needs.

We recognize that threats and challenges to moral influence, including stress, personal needs, and injustice, can undermine a father's best hopes and efforts, yet we intend to show how fathers can still make a difference with their children. We will show that reasoning with children is fundamental to their moral development and an essential feature of helping children connect principles with practices. Moral development is also a feature of a community's quality of life, so we will address the idea of citizenship as a moral act. Finally, we will acknowledge that, for many, religion is a source of support for moral influence and development.

The First Task of Moral Development

Who we are as human beings and parents is revealed in every moment. When we are not trying to teach something formally, children learn from who we are. Our wholeness—our characteristic way of being in the world—provides a foundation for children. It is what they have seen in everyday life, in everyday interaction, that children draw upon to make sense out of formal teaching, when some topic of moral relevance is made explicit. This suggests that *our first task in fostering moral being in our children is to examine our own way of being.* Essentially, our way of interacting with life sets the pattern for our children as they develop a sense of moral awareness regarding themselves and their world.

The quality of a father's moral influence is influenced by the quality of the father-child relationship itself.

In an informal survey by teachers in public schools as part of a character education curriculum, adolescents were asked: If you were to be born tomorrow, what would you want the circumstances to be, and what setting or context would you most like to become a part of? The vast majority of the answers from these 15-to-17-year-old students addressed the characteristics of the relationship they wanted with their parents: to be loved, supported, and nurtured and to experience patience, care, concern, commitment to their well-being, and so on. More practical realities, such as the availability of food and clothing, were rarely mentioned.[1] The majority of answers clearly indicate that *adolescents sought a quality relationship with parents as the foundation of a home they would choose to be a part of upon being born*. The fact that student answers were predominantly concerned with family relationships suggests how important those relationships are to adolescents. Whatever the actual material circumstances of the students who answered these questions—they were very economically and geographically diverse—it is significant that so many of their responses focused on the quality of the parent-child relationship. (The students were from 16 public school districts in California, Arizona, New Mexico, and Utah). Teenagers want to know they are cared about and cared for, and these results sustain that idea.

In a subsequent class period, teachers presented a different question: If you were to become a mother or father tomorrow, what would you want the circumstances to be? The answers took an unexpected turn toward logical, practical concerns. This question differs from the first in at least one important way. It asks students to place themselves in a situation where *they are responsible* for the well-being of someone else. The first question asked them to imagine a situation where *their* well-being would be served. The first question didn't even mention the idea of relationships, yet the largest number of answers addressed that issue. Their answers to the second question, however, focused primarily on how they could provide *materially* for a child. Their answers addressed the temporal realities of parenting rather than the more abstract qualities of a parent-child relationship or home setting. The students noted they would need a home, food, a job, financial resources, and perhaps an education. Some responses could be called immature. Occasionally, a student would express this idea: "My child is going to go to school well dressed. Ain't nobody goin' to make fun of my child!" Nevertheless, their sensibilities were that the practical and realistic demands of caring for a child would require them to be in a financial and educational position to furnish such care.

An interesting feature of student responses to the question about becoming a mother or father was that nobody said, "What that child needs isn't my problem." They took it for granted that, if they were a mother or father, they would feel it essential to "do right by that child." Their moral sense surfaced in response to a question about a possibility, not a current reality, and was equal to the imagined task. Their answers addressed their own responsibility and the needs of others. In fact, moral maturity was evident in the answers. Students' answers to both questions reveal they were addressing what choices would be right or good for themselves as well as for others. Their answers qualify as moral, for they focused on both the consequences of their actions and the idea that doing right by someone else is inherently correct. Both consequences and the nature of an act itself qualify as criteria of moral judgment. Moreover, the answers provided by these students were practical and could be applied to a situation, task, relationship, or need that might appear as early as tomorrow.

There is a simple but weighty significance in such answers regarding moral development, for the first task of fathers regarding how to have a moral influence on their children is grounded in how to foster a quality relationship with them, which children recognize as being critical to them from the beginnings of life. The quality of that father-child relationship may begin in a simple commitment and desire to "do right by the child."

Fathers and Moral Influence

To do right by a child is to be "for" the child. It is to honor one's personally held moral sense of how to foster a child's best interests, a term that implies a moral judgment regarding what would benefit a child the most. Making that judgment is not the same as seeking to serve a child's self-interests. For example, a father may have moral influence when he nurtures a relationship by demonstrating his committed interest to the everyday life of a child.

Imagine that Jack, a pharmaceutical salesman, promised his 10-year-old son Chad that, upon returning from his three-day sales trip, he would play ball with him. Jack returns and is using the last daylight hours at home to prepare and file the report to his company. Chad appears in the doorway with two baseball gloves and says, "Look, Dad!" Jack looks around, and before Chad can even invite him to play, Jack says, "Look, I've got to get this report in." Chad looks at the floor and says, "But, Dad, it's going to be dark, and you—." Jack interrupts: "I said I'm BUSY!" Chad turns around and mumbles something as he retreats down the hall. Jack turns back to his report as he tunes in to the last syllable of Chad's mumbling he had heard—it had sounded like "missed." Oops. Jack's conscience brings the whole word to him: "promised." The whole issue with Chad enters center stage in Jack's mind. He thinks, "Oh, yeah. I promised him I'd play ball when I got back, but I am really bushed, and . . . if I don't do this report now, then . . . and besides, I got back later than I thought, and . . . boys just have to learn that sometimes life gets in the way." However, no excuses or rationalizations can bring Jack peace of mind. The truth is he made the promise. The truth is that reports can be done when it is dark outside, but baseball cannot. Jack puts the pen down and wanders down the hall searching for his baseball partner. It is not that 45 minutes later Chad has learned some great moral lesson. All he has learned is that Dad is at his best when he honors his promises. And, more meaningful to a 10-year-old baseball nut, he has experienced a dad who is committed to him. Jack has demonstrated a moral truth without abstract words. He has considered his boy a real person, someone who matters.

Similarly, best interests can be communicated when certain boundaries are respected. Dad and four-year-old Kevin are in the grocery store. Kevin grabs a bag of red licorice from the shelf and protests when dad puts it back and says, "No, we aren't buying that today." Kevin protests again and then yells whimperingly, "I want it!" If Dad yells back and threatens Kevin, it is not only impractical—if anything, Dad is now "teaching" Kevin that yelling is a legitimate response to not getting your way—but also immoral. It would be wrong to yield to Kevin's temper tantrum and try to shut him up by offering the licorice: it would teach a four-year-old how to be self-centered, demanding, and manipulative. Being firm without exhibiting an adult version of a temper tantrum communicates, "I care about you, but this is a time when we will not buy treats." Dad does this by ignoring the whimpering, quietly saying no, going to another aisle, or—in extreme circumstances—suspending the shopping trip and going out to the car. Dad can explain that yelling is not acceptable grocery-store behavior and ask whether Kevin wants to go back in and continue to help Dad shop or go home and stay while Dad returns to shop alone. Here the father is treating Kevin as a real person who matters to him but not as someone who can dictate outcomes. The issue here is not that Dad is playing a particular parental role but that he is living responsibly as a parent by teaching and demonstrating which behaviors are acceptable and which are not.

Sara Ruddick agrees that fathering is much more than a set of roles dictated by cultural demands (e.g., provider, protector, and disciplinarian).[2] She believes fathering is a kind work that ought to be shaped and determined by children's needs. Fathers, then, exert moral influence by means of the work of kindness they perform in response to children's needs and concerns.

Another way of expressing this idea appears in the work of Dollahite, Hawkins, and Brotherson, who have offered a definition of generative fathering or "fatherwork" as: "fathering that meets the needs of children by working to create and maintain a developing ethical relationship with them."[3] It is probably the quality of the relationship that governs how influential a father really is with any given child. The work of fathering is in response to an ethical call to labor for and meet the needs of their children and is based on the assumption that men have both the obligation and the ability within them to be good fathers. This generative fathering approach offers a realistic starting point for everyday practice in parenting and suggests that moral influence is at the heart of the relationship between fathers and their children.

For example, one father called his 16-year-old son in to speak with him shortly after his birthday to offer him the use of the family car. He also described the conditions under which the car would be available. The rules were that his son's use of the car could not compete with the demands of Mom and Dad for the vehicle. However, when parents didn't have need of the car, it would be available to him. Another condition was that the son was always to bring the car back with a full tank of gas. The son also had to pay a monthly "oil and wear and tear" fee. One warning from the father was that if his son were ever to get a speeding ticket, he would be grounded from using the car for two weeks.

At first, the son took the car to school several days a week. Then the costs of gasoline prompted his reduction in its use to just special occasions. All went well for nearly two years. He made his payments as agreed and, to keep costs down, used the car minimally. One Friday afternoon, he approached his father in the den and silently laid a speeding ticket on his father's desk. The son was asked to explain the circumstances of the citation. The conversation continued:

> His father paused, then asked, "Do you know what the consequences of this are?"
>
> The son replied, "Yes, sir. I am grounded for two weeks."
>
> The father continued, "Isn't the junior prom tonight? And aren't you responsible to drive two other couples to the dance?"
>
> "Yes, sir, that's right."
>
> "O.K., then," replied the father, "you are hereby grounded for two weeks, starting tomorrow morning."[4]

Such a response by the father to this circumstance suggests a trust between father and son that might be envied, but is the father's response a moral one? Did the father honor the consequences of the boy's transgression or not? Can a case be made that the father was indulging his son in the face of a wrongdoing rather than holding him to the agreed-upon consequences of an irresponsible act? What will be the impact on the boy? What will he "get away with" next?

Perhaps answers to some of these questions could be drawn from the greater context and history of this particular father-son relationship. We must acknowledge that the father was both generous and demanding. He was nurturing as he outlined how his son could have access to the car and bold in setting the boundaries governing responsible use. The moral question may focus on the way the father implemented the consequences. The lengthy use of the car without incident surely is relevant to the father's response. The son's immediate presentation of the ticket to his father suggests a straightforwardness (rather than "forgetting" about the ticket until the next day). Some might say the boy knew he wouldn't get away with anything and so deserves no moral points for coming clean immediately. These are plausible guesses about the moral meaning of this incident.

An interview with the son regarding his father's approach, and specifically matters of moral understanding, would be a great capstone to this story, but it is unavailable. We can take from this story, however, the importance of understanding the total context of the relationship and how that context is fundamental to understanding the moral meaning of specific behaviors. This affirms the claims in the introduction to this chapter: namely that who we are in our informal moments with each other and in the way we treat each other is inextricably bound up in the formal rules and boundaries we use to teach our children moral responsibility. The factors related to the moral response of the son to having gotten a ticket are founded in his personal moral way of being and in the quality of the relationship with his father. His father's response is evidence of having confidence that his son is capable of being more cautious in the future and that the son will benefit from paying the consequence after the big school event.

Alternate versions of this story could be told. The boy hides the ticket. He lies about how he got it. The father flies into a rage. He complains about what this will do to his image or his auto insurance costs. Perhaps the father threatens greater punishments and withdraws auto privileges indefinitely. To imagine the practical consequences of such a scenario, we each need individually to ask, "What would be my response to that?" When we are willing to place ourselves in a situation where we know we are morally culpable regarding some lapse in judgment or betrayal of trust and imagine our frustration, sorrow, disappointment, resentment, or hostility, we can begin to ask the more fundamental question: "What do I believe is right to do, and why do I believe it is right to do it?" Such a question sidesteps the potential moral destructiveness (specifically, the end of moral influence) that is frequently the case when adolescents lie and fathers rant and rave.

This case is, to us, a prime illustration of what Ruddick and others mean when they suggest that both kindness and the quality of the relationship itself are relevant to the latitude parents have in setting boundaries, implementing consequences, explaining principles, and even understanding children's hopes, dreams, and fears.

As demonstrated in the actual version of the speeding story, it is possible to enforce boundaries and consequences without being an ogre. It is possible to live responsibly without being defensive. It is possible to require justice while showing mercy. This incident is a snapshot of the quality of an ongoing relationship of moral influence. The son and the father wordlessly acknowledge that who they are with each other is what makes the father's decision a moral one. Had the boy been consistently dishonest, manipulative, and self-centered, the options open to the father would be different.

This incident supports research findings that fathers transmit their attitudes, beliefs, and values to their children by the example of their own behavior, direct teaching, and acceptance or rejection of their children's behavior.[5] It is in these patterns of living that fathers generate and sustain the moral influence they have with their children. This father had transmitted his beliefs and values regarding the use of the car specifically. He likely was an example of a responsible car owner who attended to regular maintenance. The father gave direct instruction. He also accepted the son's honesty regarding the traffic ticket and did not excuse him without consequences.

This story is additionally illustrative of how children also influence their father's attitudes, beliefs, and values. Fathers frequently point out that the birth of their first child gives them an entirely new perspective on life. Palkovitz and Palm noted that fatherhood was related to some major shifts in values and worldview for most men, including less selfishness and a greater emphasis on the value of life, time, family, education, modeling, and the environment.[6] These researchers point out that fatherhood prompts a seemingly universal generative spark that creates an opportunity for change, or a sensitive period, for fathers. Being sensitive to children, both when they are morally honorable and when they are out of bounds, is essential to being a moral influence. Being sensitive does not mean excusing or indulging a child in wrongdoing. It means being respectful of the person and of the inescapable link between moral responsibility, quality of life, and family relationships.

Fathers who are respectful and humane with their children enjoy a certain freedom that fathers who are harsh and inhumane do not. The latter group always feels the need to defend themselves, guard against being manipulated, assert their authority and rights, and win any argument, confrontation, or disciplinary moment. Thus, they are trapped by their own view of the world into living the life of a dictator who is in fear every moment of being toppled by a superior power.

In contrast, humane fathers—living true to the best moral interests of their children—are free in every moment to reason, reflect, listen, seek to understand, and most important, be persons who, by their very way of being, draw children and adolescents to them. Inviting and enticing children to do good is more likely to succeed than threatening or cajoling. The influence is in the relationship before it is in the skills of the father. What would otherwise be skills and talents in a father living compassionately become, in the experience of harsh fathers, weapons of relationship warfare.

Challenges and Threats to Moral Influence

Research done by Phil Cowan found that new fatherhood can be a time of disequilibrium, stress, and crisis as well as a time of joy and a developmental oppor-

Jared, Jonesy, and the Runaway Tractor

Jared did morning chores on the farm because football practice kept him after school. The school bus picked him up at 8 a.m. One morning after the chores and shower and breakfast, he was heading out the door when his dad said, "Oh, Jared, Jonesy (the neighboring farmer) needs to borrow one of our tractors to haul things today. Please take one over there before you go to school." Jared looked at the clock and protested, "Dad, it is five minutes to 8, and I can't miss the bus!" His father responded, "Then you'll have to hurry, won't you?"

Jared burst out of the house and saw that the tractor used for hauling milk was the most accessible. He leapt on it, noticing that the spindles in the middle of the rear wheels were horizontal, in preparation to haul the milk wagon. He didn't have time to move them into the vertical position. Each stuck out about four inches, but he fired up the tractor and popped it into gear.

He gathered speed as he neared the lazy curve toward Jonesy's farm. He was flying now and wasn't prepared for what came into view around the curve. He was expecting the horizontally cut stump that protruded slightly out onto the road from the right side. The stump had been there for generations and had seen many a chicken prepared for Sunday dinners. The rusting axe was firmly planted in the middle of the stump. But on the left side was Jonesy's car sticking out into the road, and Jonesy was busy filling it with gasoline from the farm pump.

In a flash, Jared realized he was going too fast to stop and that, with the spindles down, it was going to be "touch and go" to get through the narrowed opening between the car and the stump. It was touch. He had hoped to clear both the stump and the car as he struggled to slow the tractor. He missed the stump. The left spindle caught the left headlight and peeled the panel over the wheel well so that it flipped up and shattered the driver's-side window. It moved the car about six inches. Jonesy moved with the car, keeping the gasoline hose in the tank.

Jared, flushed with the meaning of the disaster he had just created, kept slowing the tractor to make the necessary U-turn and, red-faced, returned to the scene of the crime. He parked the tractor in the farmyard and slowly approached Jonesy, who was still filling the car with gasoline. Jonesy said, "Hi, Jared, what can I do you for?" Jared stammered. He had hardly expected such a greeting after his destructive pass between the stump and the car. "Mr. Jones, I—I—I—I—," stammered Jared.

Jonesy put the gas cap back on the tank and wordlessly walked to the driver's window and peered in. He brushed a few pieces of glass off the seat.

He pulled the light switch on and went to the front of the car and said, "Hmmm . . . took out that headlight, sure enough." While he was surveying the body damage, Jared said, "Mr. Jones, I'll—we'll fix it—my dad will talk to you." Jonesy nodded, "That's fine, son. I'll be here all day. Thanks for bringing the tractor over."

Jared was mystified so far by Jonesy's response. But then he began imagining his father's response when he found out what had happened. He walked into the house, picked up his books, and paused. He hesitated by the window that gave him a view of the road toward Jonesy's place. He waited until the school bus appeared around the corner and then said, "Dad, I took the tractor over to Jonesy, but he's got to talk to you today." He raced to the school bus.

On the way home after football practice, Jared told the parents in the car pool not to drive all the way to his farm. He would get out of the car and hike over the one hill that brought him into the farm from the "blind side" away from the road. He trudged across the field wondering what he was going to say, when he was startled to see his dad leaning against the back fence, watching him. So much for coming in on the blind side.

When he got close enough to talk, Jared began with, "Dad, I forgot I was on the milk tractor, and the spindles. . . ." His dad interrupted. "Now, Jared, you have had more experience on both tractors than anyone else in the family except me. You can't tell me you didn't see the spindles. Jonesy said you were really moving when you came into view around that curve." Jared was silent. His dad continued, "Jonesy and I have talked, and we don't have a final estimate yet, of course, but here's the deal I want you to consider. I'm thinking you were going too fast and you know better than to leave those spindles down in the first place. Except when we are hauling milk, they can catch on the barn, the fence posts, even scrape the car—as is painfully clear. I figure about 60 percent of the responsibility to reimburse Jonesy comes from you. That's because you ignored your own knowledge and skill about how to drive, how fast to go, and to do the right thing with those spindles. I figure I am responsible for about 40 percent of the damage because I gave you a job when there wasn't the necessary time to do it right. Does that sound fair to you?"

Jared stood unbelieving. No matter what script he had reviewed in his mind about what to say or about what the outcome of this disaster might be, what his dad was actually telling him sounded like science fiction. He paid off his 60 percent—it took five months of his share of the milk money—and his dad covered the rest. That was 15 years ago. Jared has never forgotten it.

Questions to Ponder

- What points strike you as the important moral features of this story?
- What was Jared thinking and feeling as he pondered what excuses he would give?
- How do you explain that Jonesy did not become upset and hostile?
- What would the outcome of this event have been had Jonesy been resentful?
- What do you think Jared's dad was trying to teach with the solution he came up with?
- If Jared were to teach anyone else what he learned from this whole thing, what do you think he would say?

---

tunity for personal and marital maturation and growth.[7] This is because fatherhood invites men to expand their horizons to become less self-centered and more other-centered. Cowan's work also reveals that if fathers of preschool-age children display more warmth and less anger, the children have higher academic achievement scores when they enter first grade. Impatience, anger, stress, or personal wants can challenge our willingness to be available to our children, but making moral choices in the midst of such challenges changes the equation of moral influence.

A friend of ours with young children at home was concerned about the heavy load his wife carried as a mother. He was typically at work and occasionally on the road. Although his wife didn't complain—she thrived on the demands of motherhood—he noticed the children would respond to and obey her but either ignore or retreat from him. His own father suggested that, any night he was home, he should be the one to bathe the children, get them ready for bed, read to them, and so on. At first this father saw such a request as unfair. He would have preferred to make bedtime an efficient use of time that would guarantee his "freedom" after the children were in bed, but he decided not only to follow his dad's advice but to put his whole heart into it. At first, it seemed exhausting. After three months it dawned on him that his children were paying attention to him. They were asking him questions. They were telling him about the muskrat they had chased to the fenced canal. He quit watching the clock at bedtime and found he enjoyed the evening tasks better than the freedom he was trying to guarantee himself. Of course he had his own moments of self-centeredness and even impatience, but he became a different person when he put his children first. A surprising byproduct of this was almost immediate. His wife, who had heretofore been quietly exhausted at the end of the day, was more resilient. She was an amateur writer who rose early to put pen to paper but never seemed to have enough time to get as much done as she wished. His bedtime routine with the children gave her additional time to write and revise.

In fact, his single act of taking over evening time with the children began to affect the marriage relationship positively. Meaningful father involvement in a child's life is beneficial not only to the parent-child relationship but to the marital relationship as well. In the "Becoming a Family Project," men who were more involved in caring for and nurturing their children also experienced more satisfaction with their marriage.[8] It seems that, by honoring our feelings of moral commitment to the well-being of the children, our sensitivities and sensibilities toward all family members are transformed. The starting point for all this seems to include a fundamental forgetfulness about our own assumed needs or wants. At the very least, a moral way of being with others seems available to us, even in times of stress and situational complications. It is as if our moral choice seems to be whether to continue to do right by others in times of challenge, disappointment, injustice, or stress or to use such contexts to justify abandoning our own beliefs and conscience regarding how to treat others.

Thus, a father in the home who is involved in the life of his children is generally a positive influence on their moral development. Fathers are most effective in fostering moral development in their children when they are present in their children's lives. Similarly, a father's absence in the life of his child limits his influence and may even have a negative impact on moral development.[9] More specifically, Daum and Bieliauskas found that adolescent males whose fathers were present in the home attained higher moral maturity scores on the *Moral Judgment Interview* than those whose fathers were not present.[10]

Obviously, father presence or absence is crucial to the nature of influence, but once fathers are present, the key to their moral influence in times of stress or challenge may not be the intensity of the threat but their response to it. The father's response is a major factor in how children respond as well. Humane responses that express a father's commitment to and concern for the others in the family serve as the best examples a child or adolescent could be exposed to in learning moral awareness and judgment.

Reasoning and Moral Development

We have already hinted at another significant act of influence that has an impact on moral development: a father's willingness to reason with a child or an adolescent regarding *why* the family has rules and boundaries and *why* it operates the way it does. Reasoning and being reasonable go hand in hand. If a father feels a sense of obligation to explain the principles, beliefs, or commitments guiding his decisions, then youths have a chance to ponder, ask questions, and even challenge family ideas, philosophies, and directions. The process of such discussions becomes as valuable as the content of the issue being discussed, because it is through reason and being reasonable that relationships are built.

As a practical example, let's take the idea of sex education for children. Professionals and practitioners are almost unanimous in the belief that parents ought to be their children's primary sex educators. Many parents seem to agree in theory but hesitate in practice. Some parents feel uncomfortable or feel they are not knowledgeable enough. What if the most important basis for sex education were in the quality of the parent-child relationship? That is, what if a father said to his child or adolescent, "I want to try to explain to you what I discovered being a father meant to me the first time I saw you"? What we are suggesting here is that a father would do well to go to the heart of what it means to be a father as a prelude to talking about the meaning of human sexuality.

Whether a child is welcomed to a family by giving birth or adoption, being a father has meaning that is fundamental to the meaning of the power to create and nurture life and why children matter to parents. For most fathers, children are not a casual consequence of a physical act but are evidence of commitment and care across time, even across generations. When children know their presence in a family is meaningful to their parents, the environment is conducive to discussing either how babies come to be or under what circumstances and in what context sexual feelings are expressed and acted upon.

Perhaps the most common question preschoolers ask as parents introduce them to the meaning of human experience is "why?" When fathers respond with reasons, personal beliefs, and everyday examples, the child is invited to see how theory is linked to practice, ideas are tied to behaviors, and beliefs are related to decisions and outcomes. Reasonable fathers make such discussions and understanding possible.

The Moral Relationship and Citizenship

Communities that support and surround family life are relevant to the success of fathers who are seeking to nurture moral development in their children. A family seeking to teach responsible living is not helped if the neighborhood, peer group, or school football team are espousing or acting in ways that subvert the preferred parental influence. Fathers serve as bridges to the community for children and must teach children that moral living is central to living with others in a community.

A father watching a competition soccer match saw a shot from the opposing team go into the goal just inside the left pole but under the netting. The referee could not see whether the ball had gone outside the goal or inside and under the net. The referee asked the father whether he had seen where the ball actually went. The father said it was, in fact, a goal. His son's coach came up to the father and asked, "Why did you tell him?"

A third base coach in a high school tournament game tricked the opposing third baseman into tossing him the ball with the coach's runners on base. The third baseman, being respectful to an adult coach from the other team, tossed the ball as requested. The third base coach stepped out of the way and, as the ball rolled to the left sideline fence, wildly waved two runners home. When confronted by the third baseman's coach, the unjust coach said, "Just part of the game, sir, just part of the game." Well, perhaps so, if we wish to make legitimate such shenanigans inside the walls of our own homes. It is significant that the team with the sly third base coach went on to take second place in the tournament, but when the trophies were presented, no team member would look the presenter of the trophies in the eye.

To be a good citizen is pretty simple. It means, on a community level, treating others as one believes it is right to treat them. Not all communities operate under such moral norms. Hoffman describes moral norms in a community as the way one person behaves toward another, including being considerate of others' feelings, telling the truth, keeping promises, and not deceiving, lying, stealing, betraying a trust, or inflicting physical harm. Moral norms are considered internalized when people act in accordance with them, regardless of the circumstance or potential outcome. Hoffman found that fathers are instrumental in the development of overt moral behaviors (e.g., the importance of laws, rules, and sanctions against violating them) in their children as well as using moral standards to evaluate the actions of others.[11] This confirms that the father's relationship to his children and the example he sets interact to create an understanding of what constitutes moral behavior and good citizenship, increasing the likelihood that his children will perceive and act on what they see.

A wise person once said, "Actions speak louder than words." The reality is that fathers speak to their children in a multitude of ways. For example, it would not be surprising to hear a three-year-old yell "Stupid lady!" about the driver of another car who has cut in front of the family car if she has heard her parents respond to other drivers that way in the past. It should be no surprise if children speak unkindly to others, lie, or are dishonest in their dealings if that is the example their parents have set for them. Of course, young children are typically great imitators but lousy interpreters. The moral meaning of a child yelling offensive words at a neighbor is much different than if the words were being yelled by a dad. A single act is not so much a sign of what that child is as a signal that the child is immature in judgment, development, and interpretation of the examples he or she has witnessed.

However, fathers can help. In those moments when a father has been caught in actions that counter his words, his response must be to humbly admit, in actions and words, his previous inappropriate behavior. To admit he is wrong models moral responsibility and invites children to consider that a parent need not portray a perfect image to be of moral influence. Actions of parental regret about their treatment of others also speak loudly. The way a father treats others is a laboratory of learning for children who watch him. Their observations of his actions toward others become a template for understanding citizenship as a moral way of being that contributes to the cohesion of a community.

Fathers help children develop moral character when they seek to foster their becoming productive citizens. Let us accept the premise that, as human beings, we have a moral sensibility about how to treat others (as revealed previously in the answers of high school students to hypothetical questions about being born or becoming a parent tomorrow). In the act of caring for, nurturing, and reasoning with their children, fathers demonstrate good citizenship. When fathers enact publicly what they have reasoned with their children about, it shows children the practicality of the principles they have been taught.

A strict family dimension of citizenship is demonstrated when fathers, at their moral best, act in behalf of the next generation. In so doing, they inescapably become moral educators who define and simultaneously demonstrate those ways of living in the community that can enhance their child's future. They also declare what styles of living are associated with self-destruction.

Fathers are educating for citizenship when they discuss with their children what constitutes a life of moral character and invite their children to promote the well-being of fellow family members and others outside their family. How a father treats a neighbor or a relative demonstrates the morality of citizenship. Wrapped up in the treatment of others are perceived ethical obligations, personal qualities of character, moral meaning, and moral action. Thus, fatherhood is more than merely providing and demonstrating relevant knowledge or skills: it is helping children link who they are to their relationships with others in ways that promote cohesion of relationships in a community.

To foster moral development, then, more is required of fathers than teaching a rule (e.g., do not hit others) or fostering a skill (e.g., cooking for family members). To borrow language from Neal Maxwell, a prominent educator and churchman, if moral ways of being were grounded only in knowledge and skills, there would be no moral anchor (grounded starting point) or moral compass (responsible direction) regarding how to use such knowledge and skills.[12] In other words, knowledge and skills are most effective in promoting citizenship when grounded in the moral treatment of others outside as well as inside the home.

Religiosity and Moral Development

When discussing moral development and a father's sense of moral awareness, it is appropriate to consider the relevance of religious communities and the religiosity of men as fathers. The responsibilities and obligations of fathers are clearly defined in moral terms in many religious traditions.

In the Bible, for example, the moral influence of fathers is boldly asserted. In the Old Testament, Proverbs 22:6 teaches that if fathers train their children in the

---

How Fathers Can Have a Moral Influence on Their Children

Your attitude and actions communicate morality to your children. The following items represent a few ideas concerning how fathers can be a moral influence:

- Be present in the home and involved in the lives of your children.
- Communicate that you care *about* as well as *for* them by being respectful and humane.
- Remember it is the quality of the relationship that governs how influential you really are with any given child.
- Teach through behavioral example and articulation of beliefs and values.
- Be willing to reason with them regarding *why* the family has rules and boundaries and *why* it operates the way it does.
- Accept that you influence children at least as much during the unintended, unscripted, spontaneous times with them as during any formal, deliberate, structured "moral lessons."
- Be compassionate with children, both when they are morally honorable and when they are out of bounds.
- Respond with kindness and reason to children's needs and concerns.
- Discuss the future, read them stories, help them make decisions, share tasks, plan vacations, communicate with schoolteachers, and respect their grandparents.
- Watch movies together and discuss whether the outcomes illustrate compassion or revenge.
- Remember that both kindness and the quality of the relationship itself are relevant to the latitude you have in setting boundaries, implementing consequences, explaining principles, and even understanding children's hopes, dreams, and fears.
- Assess the quality of the communities outside the family that will affect your children.
- Provide knowledge and skills grounded in the moral treatment of others outside as well as inside the home.
- Help children become productive citizens.
- Acknowledge that your religious beliefs generally support you in your goal to foster the development of moral character in your children.

way they should go, when they are older they will not depart from it. Religious traditions may assert that fathers often know much of what their children need simply due to their nature as moral and spiritual beings. For example, in the New Testament, the following questions are posed to a group of fathers: "What man is there of you, whom if his son ask bread, will he give him a stone? Or if he ask a fish, will he give him a serpent?" (Matthew 7:9–10). The answers to these questions are clear: fathers are to do right by their children and not be stumbling blocks to their moral progress.

Religious involvement is an important and typically positive influence in the lives of fathers that is often overlooked. Bollinger and Palkovitz found that fathers who were active members of a church, regardless of their religious affiliation, were more involved in their children's lives than inactive church members or nonmembers.[13] David Dollahite, in a review of research on fathering and spirituality, found that religion supports responsible father involvement in the lives of children, including the development of moral character. As a result of his study, he also suggests that religion is the most powerful, meaningful, and sustained influence encouraging men to be fully involved in their children's lives.[14] In fact, many men in the United States and other countries realize that religious practice provides them with a sense of meaning, direction, and solace as well as the support of a caring, faith-based community, all of which can contribute significantly to effective fathering.

Historically, religious groups—and, more recently, social movements such as Promise Keepers, the National Center for Fathering, and the National Fatherhood Initiative—have emphasized fathers' roles in contributing to their children's moral development. During the 18th and 19th centuries, many fathers took the lead and were very involved in teaching and maintaining moral conduct in their homes.[15] During the past century, it seems that mothers have taken more of a lead in teaching and maintaining moral standards in the home[16] and encouraging religious activity.[17] Fathers, however, continue to play a pivotal role in the moral development of their children. In fact, as noted previously, becoming a father is often a powerful influence prompting men to make changes in their own lives. Half of the men in the Palkovitz and Palm study "saw fatherhood as not only an opportunity to change but as an imperative to change for the sake of their children." For many of the fathers in their study, that change included decisions about becoming more active in church and stopping destructive behavior so they would be "better models of positive moral behavior for their children." These fathers wanted to be good examples for their children and wanted to provide them with "an anchor or starting place for the cultivation of their own moral development."[18]

It is likely that the influence of a father's religiosity on his child's moral development is most evident when it is an expression of an internal commitment rather than a bow to some external expectations. This may be a final reminder that the wholeness of how fathers live in relationships with family members is understood by children. They discern between being genuine and shallow, real and phony, in the moral words and examples presented to them.

Conclusion: A Father's Moral Opportunities

What is moral is probably not first *defined* for children as much as it is *demonstrated*. Moral influence begins with how fathers treat spouses and children in the laboratory of family relationships. Children seem to thrive—socially, emotionally, spiritually—according to how they are treated. The degree of moral influence a father has is likely mediated by the depth and quality of family relationships. Thus, moral influence is a matter of whether a father supports his children's well-being, future, and quality of character.

Recall the story of the boy and the speeding ticket on the day of the junior prom. What possible influence for good could the father have had if he had become blustery, harsh, arrogant, or dictatorial about the ticket? If the quality of the father-child relationship is the springboard for long-term influence, this father was a perfect example, in that moment, of how to exercise influence. It is likely the son will continue to be influenced by the father not only when his dad is not physically present but even after the son has left home for school, the military, or whatever opportunities he chooses to pursue after high school. Too often, fathers mistake the ability to control the present moment with long-term influence. A father can experience both but not if the present moment is full of harshness and resentment. If a father is sincere in his commitment to foster moral conduct in his children, his knowledge and skills in teaching, demonstrating, and articulating the meaning of being moral will enhance his influence. The father then becomes both an anchor and a compass for children as they make their moral way toward a quality future.

Endnotes

1. Olson, T.D., and Wallace, C.M., 1984, "AANCHOR: An Alternative National Curriculum on Responsibility," curriculum approved by the Department of Health and Human Services for use in a Title XX prevention grant.

2. Ruddick, S., 1989, *Maternal Thinking: Toward a Politics of Peace*, Boston: Beacon.

3. Dollahite, D.C., Hawkins, A.J., and Brotherson, S., 1997, "Fatherwork: A Conceptual Ethic of Fathering as Generative Work," in *Generative Fathering: Beyond Deficit Perspectives*, edited by A.J. Hawkins and D.C. Dollahite, Newbury Park, CA: Sage, pp. 17–35, at 18.

4. Personal anonymous communication in possession of the authors.

5. Ambert, A.M., 2001, *The Effect of Children on Parents*, 2nd ed., New York: The Haworth Press.

6. Palkovitz, R., and Palm, G., 1998, "Fatherhood and Faith in Formation: The Developmental Effects of Fathering on Religiosity, Morals, and Values," *Journal of Men's Studies*, 7(1), 33–51.

7. Cowan, P., 1988, "Becoming a Father: A Time of Change, an Opportunity for Development," in *Fatherhood Today: Men's Changing Role in the Family*, edited by P. Bronstein and C. Cowan, New York: Wiley, pp. 13–35.

8. Derogatis, L.R., Lipman, R.S., and Covi, L., 1973, "SCL-90: An Outpatient Psychiatric Rating Scale—Preliminary Report," *Psychopharmacology Bulletin*, 9, 13–28.

9. Hoffman, M.L., 1981, "The Role of the Father in Moral Internalization," in *The Role of the Father in Child Development*, 2nd ed., edited by M.E. Lamb, New York: Wiley, pp. 359–378; Lamb, M.E., 1981, "Fathers and Child Development: An Integrative Overview," in *The Role of the Father in Child Development*, edited by M.E. Lamb, 2nd ed., New York: Wiley, pp. 1–70.

10. Daum, J.M., and Bieliauskas, V.J., 1983, "Father Absence and Moral Development of Male Delinquents," *Psychological Reports*, 53, 223–228.

11. Hoffman, 1981.

12. Maxwell, N.A., 1999, "C.S. Lewis: Insights on Discipleship," in *C.S. Lewis: The Man and His Message*, edited by A. Skinner and R. Millet, Salt Lake City: Bookcraft, pp. 8–19.

13. Bollinger, B., and Palkovitz, R., 2003, "The Relationship between Expressions of Spiritual Faith and Parental Involvement in Three Groups of Fathers," *Journal of Men's Studies*, 11, 117–129.

14. Dollahite, D.C., 1998, "Fathering, Faith, and Spirituality," *Journal of Men's Studies*, 7, 3–15.

15. Rotundo, E.A., 1985, "American Fatherhood: A Historical Perspective," *American Behavioral Scientist*, 29, 7–25.

16. Hoffman, 1981.

17. Bohannon, J.R., 1991, "Religiosity Related to Grief Levels of Bereaved Mothers and Fathers," *Omega*, 23, 153–159.

18. Palkovitz and Palm, 1998.

Author Loren Marks with his children, clockwise from top, Haley Renee, Logan, Denton, and Mishonne

Fathers as Spiritual Guides: Making the Transcendent Pragmatic

Loren D. Marks and Rob Palkovitz

*F atherhood is the greatest thing I could attain. If I were president of the United States, if I were CEO of a major corporation—that would end. The time would come that I would be voted out of office or I would resign and retire. Yet I will **always** be the father of my children.*
— Martin, a father of six

Fathering is at the center of life for many men. Over the past decade in our work as teachers and researchers on family life, we have had the opportunity to interview more than 100 men from a variety of racial, economic, and educational backgrounds. We asked them how fathering changed and challenged them. We asked them what having and raising children *means* to them.[1] The fathers we talked with ranged from men who were very religious to those who were highly skeptical of organized religion. Despite the differences, however, these fathers shared the commonality of being involved in their children's lives and often referred to their fathering in spiritual terms.

This chapter will explore fathering and spirituality through examples and themes drawn from our qualitative research with fathers and their children over the past decade. Spirituality is a broad concept, and its borders are larger than those of organized religion; hence, most of the examples we share address sacred relationships and beliefs but may not be explicitly religious. In the chapter, we first briefly explore the father's role in the spiritual development of children and what spirituality means for some fathers. We then discuss four themes that highlight the work of fathers in being spiritual guides to their children, including being a role model, parenting with humility, "being there" for their children, and viewing fatherhood as a spiritual calling. An overriding theme of this chapter is that *father spirituality* is both transcendent and pragmatic. Our hope is that the narratives fathers have shared with us will illuminate spiritual beliefs, spiritual behaviors, and the connection between the two for the reader in a way that will be transformative.

Children, Spirituality, and a Father's Teaching

A majority of adults hold the belief that there is a spiritual reality.[2] In addition, a recent review of research findings published in *American Psychologist* reports that religion and spirituality constitute "the single most important influence in [life]" for "a substantial minority."[3] Spiritual meaning or religious ideals can be a powerful motivating force in the lives of adults with such convictions. For example, John expressed in an interview the influence of spiritual beliefs on his fathering:[4]

> Either you believe this stuff or you don't, and if you do and if you have
> a faith that is meaningful and alive, then faith is the most important thing
> that exists. If it's not true, it's the most important lie that exists. I am bas-
> ing my life and my future and eternity on the fact that this is true.

Although many fathers are not as committed to spirituality as this father, the majority want their children to have some kind of spiritual guidance and education. Surveys of average Americans conducted by the Barna Institute indicate that 85 percent of parents with children under the age of 13 believe they are primarily responsible for teaching their children about religious beliefs and spiritual matters. Only 11 percent of parents said their church or faith community was primarily responsible.[5] In addition, nearly all parents (96 percent) of children under the age of 13 contend they have the primary responsibility for teaching their children values. Thus, according to parents themselves, parents are the gateway to children's spiritual education and development.

Although the data above refer to parents, historically the role of spiritual and moral guide in family life rested primarily upon fathers. Historian John Demos has shown that the father's responsibilities before the Industrial Revolution included *pedagogue, guidance counselor, benefactor, moral overseer, psychologist,* and [role] *model.*[6] We have argued elsewhere that "new, highly involved" fathering is not necessarily new but is in some ways a resurgence of previous patterns of father-child connection, including instruction and modeling in the spiritual and moral realms.[7] The long-held historical tradition of fathers acting as spiritual guides to their children provides a template for how fathers today can attend to this need in family life.

Defining Spirituality for Fathers

At this point, we offer a general definition of spirituality to lay the groundwork for several points we will offer regarding *father spirituality* specifically. For many people, religion has an institutional connotation, while spirituality is more personal and relational. In harmony with this personal view of spirituality, White and colleagues define spirituality as "an internal search for meaning and purpose that ultimately enhances the person's relationship with God or a Higher Power."[8] We would like to add that this personal spirituality and relationship with a Higher Power should affect the way one behaves, particularly toward others. Dollahite and Hawkins have identified *spiritual work* as a cornerstone of father-child interaction in their perspective on generative fathering and suggest this involves both believing in and guiding one's children.[9]

Spirituality can bring meaning to men's lives and also enhance the way they understand and interact with others. Seth, a father we interviewed, said:

> I don't always treat people well, but that is the target I aim for to feel spiritual, or if I were trying to explain to someone how they should go about being spiritual, [I would suggest] everyone you meet all day, everyday— treat them well. Going to church or synagogue on the weekends seems rather small and insignificant by comparison.

According to Seth, spirituality is not only a search for meaning and a relationship with the divine but also involves a pragmatic application: being spiritual through treating people well. Our definition of *father spirituality* is *care, connection, and guidance between a father and child that is moral, emotional, behav-*

ioral, and often rooted in a connection with a Higher Power. In sum, spirituality ultimately involves treating others well. Father spirituality involves cultivating spiritual awareness, treating one's child well, and making an active effort to promote his or her spiritual development.

Among the fathers' narratives we have read, one father's reflection on his feelings relating to his newborn daughter captured this spiritual sense:

> I learned that I would die for this person. I learned that, from this moment on, we will be linked forever. This child is my responsibility forever, to guide, to direct, and to nurture.[10]

As sensed by this father, father spirituality is not just a sense of meaning or connection with the divine but the ongoing effort "to guide, to direct, and to nurture" in ways that reflect meaning and connection. A father may act as a spiritual guide and foster the spiritual development of his child and himself in a number of ways. We highlight four themes with accompanying narratives that illustrate how fathers spiritually guide their children through (a) being role models, (b) making spiritual commitments to "be there," (c) showing humility in fathering, and (d) accepting fatherhood as a spiritual calling.

Fathers as Role Models in Spiritual Development

In a 1993 television ad, NBA basketball legend Charles Barkley solemnly warned the audience, "I am not a role model. Parents should be role models."[11] We believe his first statement was incorrect. Every adult (especially those with high visibility and public stature) unavoidably becomes a role model for children and youth. The question is not *whether* an adult is a role model to youth but rather what *type* of role model he is. Even so, Barkley's second point is well made: parents *are* the primary role models and should strive to be positive, involved ones.

Most of the fathers we interviewed were keenly aware of their influence as role models, and many underscored the importance of their example to their children in all areas of life, with a particular emphasis on spirituality. Rashaad, a father of three, passionately asserted:

> It's not what you do in the [church] building; it's what you do outside the building. When everyday struggles challenge you, are you able to overcome adversity, are you able to withstand the things that are being thrown at you? Not when you're in the church. Because we can clap the right "hallelujah" and say the right words and everybody sees, but when no one that's in your church sees you, how are you acting then? Hmmm? Are

you living the walk of faith, or are you living like the world's living? I can't say it any plainer than that. Are you practicing what you preach?

Oui, an immigrant father from Korea, said, "I can't really 'teach' my son through talking; we have to show him by what we do during our life. If we do very well for God and other people, then he will know what he has to do." Both Rashaad and Oui suggest clearly that the lives they live as role models have a more significant impact than lecturing on their children's spiritual development.

Other fathers also attest to the validity of the practicing-over-preaching approach to spiritual guidance. Joseph, a father of four who discussed his own upbringing, recalled, "I could see from my parents' behavior over time that faith was something that matters. This is something that is real. This is something you invest in. My parents were very formative in providing a foundation for my faith." Notice that Joseph refers, first and foremost, to his parents' *behavior*. Teaching and instruction may have been influential as well, but he did not mention them. Joseph again referred to the power of example in connection with his own fathering:

Kids just want to know the truth, and you have to represent that in a way that's meaningful and in a way that's real. Your kids live with you; they see you. They see if this is a Sunday morning thing or a 24/7 thing. When Dad slams his thumb in the car door, what does he do? When something goes wrong, does he freak out, or does he have faith?

Fathers who seek to influence their child's spiritual development in meaningful ways not only realize that they are role models but take steps to be examples that are positive and healthy. These examples illuminate a central element of a father's influence as a role model on spiritual development, which is that *fathers who accept the role as a spiritual guide practice what they preach.*

There are also other dimensions of how a father's role modeling influences his children. While the preceding examples directly reference God or faith, spiritual references may also be less direct. Speaking first of his own father and then of his efforts to be a good father to his son with severe developmental delays, Ray shared the following thoughts:

One of the things that I remember [from my childhood] is when we were working on the yard [at our] cabin in Minnesota. We children would get tired and leave and go play, but my father would always stay until the job was done. It would always impress me that I would be playing with my friends, and then I would still see my dad working on the same job until the job was done. It always impressed me and has carried throughout my life that that's what men do. They accomplish the job.

I think the feeling that I have is, "Yeah, [having a child with severe disabilities] is tough; it is a disappointment. This is not fair." But I think that this is what you are dealt and this is what you play with. You don't just sit and whine and moan about it. You just get up and go to work and do the things that you need to do and deal with it. As far as spiritual things go, I see from my father through his example that this is my job (to be a good father). I am to finish the job, so no matter what it takes or how long it is, you just stick to it and go to work until the job is done. It is the father's responsibility—you are responsible; you are the support.

For Ray, daily commitment to his family and the work needed to care for his son with special needs was the path of choice. We further see that his own father's positive example affected him greatly through providing him with the model he needed to understand how to make his own positive choices and commitment as a father when he faced challenges in his adult life.

Another father, Martin, did *not* experience life with such a father. In his experience, the lack of such a role model made him realize the importance of being a good father himself. He commented:

In my youth, one catalytic experience in helping me realize the importance of a father and wanting to be as good a father as I could was my experience in being generally disappointed in my own father. I think around fifth grade I began keeping a secret list (it totaled about 111 things) that I would do differently than my father. Being a good father was important to me.

Martin offers a living illustration of the possibility of choosing to commit to be a generative father even when this course of action was not chosen by one's own father. We mentioned at the outset of this theme that adults do not get to choose whether to be role models but only what quality of role model they will be. The examples shared by Ray and Martin highlight this point: children observe their fathers' behavior, good and bad. *Fathers who choose to be spiritual guides model commitment to principles, promises, and people.*

Spiritual Choices and the Commitment to "Be There"

Our second theme centers on the commitment by fathers to "be there" for their children. Much of the recent scholarly and public discourse about men as fathers has focused on the need to encourage responsible fathering.[12] Conversely, American pop culture frequently contrasts the liberty of nonattachment with the heavy chains of familial responsibility. The masculine "good life" is portrayed as one free of strings and commitments. Indeed, recent years have seen a rise in the number of men who do not want to be fathers—a trend we have referred to as "the rise of paternity-free manhood."[13] However, neither media images nor trends that lead men away from involved fatherhood capture the genuine reality that many men experience great meaning in choosing and fulfilling family responsibilities.[14] Fatherhood can certainly bind a man to certain choices, but often it binds not with burdensome chains but with what philosopher C. Terry Warner refers to as "the bonds of love."[15] Many men viewed the choices they described to us as outward expressions of their inner spiritual understanding, part of which involves the simple but lasting commitment to "be there" for their children.

In our interviews with fathers, we found that their decision to commit to a child's care was not a one-time choice. Instead, such commitments and choices often involved an ongoing challenge. For example, many fathers discussed occasionally working too long or "blowing it" in a variety of other ways. One father, Ollie, recalled refusing to read a story to his daughter because he wanted to relax and watch TV after a day at work. However, he also related an instance when he did "capture the moment":

> One of the kids was out trying to ride a bicycle, and I came home. She asked me to come out and help her learn to ride. I thought, "I don't know why I'm doing this," but something forced me to go out there. She learned to ride a bike that day. I just held her up for a second and ran along by her, and the next thing I knew she was riding the bike. You do learn things almost instantaneously, and if you miss that moment, then you've missed the moment. There is nothing else you can say. I was there at that one experience, and if you want to let them continue to happen, then you've got to catch them.

Moments of life with a child are precious. They represent, in a sense, spiritual opportunities to forge a connection between father and child. At times, children themselves provide the best reminders of this truth.

Ethan, another father who had missed important moments, shared the following experience that jolted him into reality and prompted his choice to make some significant changes in his fathering. He recalled:

> [My son] Bryce jerks me back to reality, to what's really important. When he was eight years old, he ran away from home, and when I found him, I just knelt down and hugged him. We got out to the car and drove around for a little bit. I was just trying to think of what to say. I'd never dealt with something like this. We ended up parking over by Green Hill Park. I just sat there thinking, and I said, "Bryce, what's going on?" And he said,

"Dad, I don't know you. You're never home." You know, at that moment, I was a leader in my church. I had a wonderful wife; I had wonderful children. I was getting research awards. I mean, by every measure I was on top of the world, and in one instant he put it all into focus.

This singular moment led Ethan to become much more serious about being responsive to his children's needs and their input. It demonstrates the significance of missed moments. In contrast, the shared moments with a child can be spiritual moments—moments of connection when fathers feel part of something larger and more important than themselves. This second theme and the accompanying examples indicate another primary element of a father's spiritual work: *fathers recognize their daily choices to "be there" for their children are spiritual choices that enhance or diminish the quality of their influence and relationship with a child.*

Most dads want to be good fathers and feel they should provide some kind of spiritual guidance in a child's life. However, many fathers also find themselves trying to be good fathers in situations that are not what they had envisioned. Their challenges may range from being divorced to working long hours to parenting a special needs child. However, faced with disappointment, adjustment, and challenge, fathers who embrace a spiritual role commit to their children's care anyway.

Research data indicate the top three goals of American parents for their children are, in order, (1) happiness, (2) career success, and (3) educational attainment.[16] Yet circumstances may challenge these goals. For example, the odds may be slim, at best, that some fathers of special needs children will see their children achieve significant career success or educational attainment. Are there things that matter more to them in such circumstances? Nathan, a father of a two-year-old son with severe developmental delays, reflected:

I ask myself, "Are you going to be resentful or angry or somehow punish your handicapped son for being a burden?" It is better to be Christ-like than it is to be resentful. It is better to express love and mercy to your child than it is to harbor frustration or disappointment that he is not going to live up to your expectations or do the things that you want him to do. Our boy is never going to go into soccer or play baseball—the things that you dream of your son doing. But he will be a joy to our hearts. I will have wonderful, loving feelings toward this child.

Fathers who see their relationships through the lens of spirituality often rely on that spiritual understanding to shape their perspective in such circumstances. For example, David, a father of a seven-year-old daughter with autism, said, "There is always hope. . . . I am convinced that there is a plan for my daughter, and we are a part of that plan, and I don't want to thwart the purposes of God by denying her ability to achieve all that she can achieve and being all that I can be as her father." These examples suggest another important principle of father spirituality: *fathers who commit to "be there" for a child often rely on a spiritual focus to help them maintain perspective despite circumstances that challenge their parenting.*

The choice to commit time and energy to a child is inherently a spiritual one that involves the giving of self. For a few of the interviewed fathers, whose children's lives had hung in the balance for a period of time, this commitment seemed particularly vital. Ethan, whose son Bryce eventually received a heart transplant that saved his life, recalled this challenging incident:

> When Bryce had his fifth open heart surgery, he really had a hard time keeping his heart beating. Bryce just wouldn't settle down to keep his neck still, and so they were essentially going to have to put him back on the ventilator, which is an awful experience. Bryce hates it. Well, they called me. It was about midnight. We had been at the hospital all day, and they said, "Bryce's gonna have to settle down, or we're going to have to put him out." And I said, "You can't do that. It would just destroy him emotionally." He was really kind of at his limit. So I jumped in the car and rushed up there and said, "What do I have to do to prevent you from putting him under again?" They said, "He has got to hold his head still." So I held his head; I held his head all night. It was one of the hardest things because he was just groaning. He would go in and out of sleep. It was a long night, but it was a great experience.

Megan, daughter of Tom, died of leukemia at age five after unsuccessful treatment and lengthy hospitalization. Tom recounted his thoughts about being there for her with considerable emotion:

> I was always there for her. Megan got my time. She had leukemia, and I was going to make sure that I spent time with her when I wasn't at work. Maybe the hospital is the part we'd like to forget but can't. When her pain got to the point that she couldn't go to the bathroom, I was the one that did her bedpans for her. She would only let me do it; I was the one that did that. It wasn't a thing for Mom, and she didn't want anybody else in the room. She kicked everybody out of the room—nurses, Mom (Mom had to be outside the door)—and I would get the bedpan as best I could under her bottom without hurting her. Moving the sheets hurt her. It was not a good thing. But she let me do that for her, and I was able to take care of her needs, and it helped me that I was the only one she'd let do it. You wouldn't expect bedpan shuffling to be a wonderful memory, but it

was. She trusted me to do my best job not to hurt her, and that was special to me that she let me do that.

Referring back to the goals that American parents tend to target for their children (educational attainment and career success), we can envision the contrast for fathers parenting children under trying circumstances. From the description of the circumstances of Ethan, Tom, and their children, it seems clear that these children were not on the path of educational attainment or career success. Yet we find these fathers commenting that being there for their children in these most critical moments was, in retrospect, a great experience or a wonderful memory. What did these fathers find in these situations? A child who needed them. Spiritual meaning and purpose. The opportunity to give of themselves. From these and other fathers, we learn that *fathers who choose to be spiritual guides for their children strive to "be there," especially when life is tough, because that is when fathers are needed the most.*

Fathering, Humility, and a Child's Leadership

Our third theme centers on humility, often considered among the most important spiritual virtues. In parenting, it is common for fathers to offer guidance and provide correction when needed. Fathers are looked to for leadership, yet humility suggests that fathers may also allow themselves to be led. This theme of humility and its importance as a dimension of father spirituality was common in our interviews with fathers.

Although a father's role in providing guidance and correction is vital, our research suggests that for a humble father correction is not a one-way street. A willingness and openness to accept correction, acknowledge error, make changes, and learn was evident in our interviews with many fathers. Some fathers specifically discussed experiences in which their children had taught them or provided a corrective lesson. One father, Gerald, noted, "One of my sons the other day said, 'Dad, you never play catch with me.' That's when you know you're spending too much time at work. If parents would only listen, they've got warning signals out there in their kids." The cultivation of humility as a spiritual virtue seems to help fathers be responsive to such "warning signals." Another father, Ty, was talking about his young daughter and explained:

I drove a truck for a while, and I think that has contributed to our being distant. She felt like she didn't have a daddy. I came home and told her to clean something up, and she said, "You can't tell me what to do. You're not my daddy." That ripped me apart . . . I stopped driving a truck really fast and brought myself back home. She was more or less saying, "You should be home [more]."

For fathers, cultivating humility that allows responsiveness to such suggestions from a child may beneficially change their parenting. It involves letting spiritual virtues such as kindness and patience become genuine characteristics of living and not just ideals. One father noted an active effort to do this in his fathering:

I have an interesting relationship with my children in that I invite them to help correct me when I demonstrate that I'm not being patient or long-suffering or kind. My oldest daughter is really quite good at it, and my son is becoming good at it. They'll be very candid with me, saying, "Dad, I feel uncomfortable with the way you're handling this."

These examples generate another important principle of fathering and spirituality: *fathers who are spiritual guides are not hypocritical (or beyond criticism); they accept due criticism or suggestion and are willing to improve their efforts or behavior.*

Another aspect of humility that can affect fathers is their willingness to learn lessons for life from their children. Children, especially young children, are constantly told by parents to do things such as get dressed, eat their vegetables, do their homework, brush their teeth, get ready for bed, and other such necessities. Humility is a dimension of spirituality that also helps fathers be receptive to how their children might guide them. Mark was the father of a special needs child, Andrew, who had been born with spinal deformities, severely shortened forearms, and only two fingers. He recalled:

One time Andrew and I were alone in the kitchen, and he just looked up at me and said, "You know Dad, if I were born again, I would like to have hands like Kate and Ben" (his older sister and brother, who had 10 fingers). And I didn't say anything for a moment, and then he said, "But this is just the challenge that God has given me for this life." And he paused again, and he said, "So it's okay." You know, it wasn't a mournful okay; it was a "this is all right," like a little bit of spunk and possibly even enthusiasm in the tone—"this is all right; this is just my challenge."

In another example Tom, whose daughter died of leukemia, explained what she had taught him:

We went to give blood at a church blood drive. I was happy because I'd just gotten a penicillin shot and they wouldn't take my blood. Sandra, my wife, had given her blood, and our friend Clyde was there giving blood. Megan went over and held his hand while he had that blood drawn because she knew what it was like to have needles poked in your skin and she felt for him. She couldn't do much, but she could hold his hand, and she did that. The impact that had on me just tells me that a little bit of loving concern for others goes a long way, not just in the life of either person in the interaction, but in the people who see that. It makes you want to go forth and do likewise.

Children, who so often perhaps are more attuned to the spiritual aspects of living, have many things to teach that adults can learn. From these fathers and their children, we see that *fathers who seek to be spiritual guides are humble, teachable, and not so busy "leading" that they do not learn from the leadership and example of others, including their children.*

Fatherhood as a Spiritual Calling

Our final theme addresses fatherhood as a spiritual calling. Our research with fathers has covered a variety of topics, including spirituality, but one in particular has been fathers of children with special needs. In light of the significant challenges and higher divorce rates among such fathers, we have been interested in what motivates some men in these trying situations to remain committed to their families and children. An important and central finding has been that fathers who make such commitments view fathering as a *spiritual* responsibility or commitment.

A recurring theme in many of our interviews with fathers was the notion that children are gifts from God and therefore fathering is a spiritual calling. Trent, a father of four, including two sons with special needs, commented:

I felt like I had a special calling when they were born. When they first come out, that is when I feel like my calling has begun. I don't think that calling ends when they turn 30. I think a father's calling is always a father's calling. So whether you're fathering a 45-year-old man or a two-year-old son, it's a very special calling. It means God has entrusted me with these four spirits to help them grow and to teach them the things that He thinks I need to teach them. So I think if I don't teach them I'll be accountable. It means that God has entrusted me and called me, and He wants me to be a father.

Another father of four, Stan, said:

My role as a father is the single most important role that I will ever perform in my lifetime here. Whatever I do in terms of anything else in my
life will be secondary in terms of importance to me and ultimately what
I achieve in this life. My marriage and our relationship as a couple to God
is the most treasured thing that I have in my heart, and these children that
we have were sent to us by God to richly bless our lives.

Trent's and Stan's visions of fatherhood clearly extend beyond the biological
and social roles into the spiritual realm. A spiritual perspective on their roles as
fathers underlies the meaning of fatherhood for them.

Many of our fathers not only viewed fatherhood as a sacred calling or spiritual responsibility but believed they were ultimately answerable to God for their
efforts as fathers. Perhaps no one captured this idea more vividly than Luke,
whose son had profound disabilities. He shared this hope and belief:

After this life is over, we will meet the Savior, and my son, Robert, will
be there, and he will be perfectly normal and alert and the child of God
that I hoped he would be. He will look at me and say, "Thank you for taking care of me, for doing the things that you did." I think about the long-
term perspective after this life when we meet the Savior, and he looks at
you and says, "You did a good job as a father," and when Robert will say
to me that I did good.

Luke's son, Robert, could not speak coherently at the time of his father's
interview and may never do so in this life, yet hope, faith, and spiritual belief provide a sacred motivation in the present for Luke to be a caring and committed
father to Robert. Indeed, *fathers who choose to be spiritual guides exemplify hope,
faith, and love.*

Conclusion

Many of the fathers we have interviewed over the years have viewed their
connections to their children as sacred. They have actively sought to serve as spiritual guides for their children. As with most parents, they have felt a primary
responsibility to care for their children and teach them about spiritual matters.
Their insights and experiences have helped us to understand *father spirituality,*
which we assert involves *care, connection, and guidance between a father and a
child that is moral, emotional, behavioral, and often rooted in a connection with
a Higher Power.* In summary, we offer these key themes from fathers we have
learned from. Fathers who strive to spiritually guide their children:

- practice what they preach;
- model commitment to principles, promises, and people;
- recognize their daily choices to "be there" for their children as spiritual choices that enhance or diminish the quality of their influence and relationship with a child;
- rely on a spiritual focus to help them maintain perspective despite circumstances that challenge their parenting;
- strive to be there, especially when life is tough, because that is when they are needed the most;
- are not hypocritical (or beyond criticism) but accept due criticism or suggestion and are willing to improve their efforts or behavior;
- are humble, teachable, and not so busy leading that they do not learn from the example of others, including their children; and
- exemplify faith, hope, and love.

This is not meant to be an exhaustive list of themes regarding fathers and spirituality. However, it provides a useful set of related themes in considering fathers' efforts to be spiritual guides and assist spiritual development in their children.

In conclusion, father spirituality is both transcendent and pragmatic. These fathers and children provide inspiring examples of how families can draw closer to each other when fathers strive to spiritually guide and respond to their children. Fathers who are guided by spirituality view their responsibilities to their children, wives, and spiritual values as more important and meaningful than their desire for personal freedom or escape from life's difficulties. Indeed, heeding the call of liberty alone is not a guarantee for a life rich in meaning and spiritual purpose. We believe the examples of these fathers are of great worth, not only because they inform but because the efforts, commitment, and behaviors of these fathers (and their children) provide an implicit invitation to us—like the one Tom described from his daughter Megan to "go forth and do likewise."

Endnotes

1. Marks, L.D., 2004, "Sacred Practices in Highly Religious Families: Christian, Jewish, Mormon, and Muslim Perspectives," *Family Process*, 43, 217–231; Palkovitz, R., 2002, *Involved Fathering and Men's Adult Development: Provisional Balances,* Hillsdale, NJ: Erlbaum.

2. James, W., 1904/1997, *The Varieties of Religious Experience*, New York: Touchstone.

3. Miller, W.R., and Thoresen, C.E., 2003, "Spirituality, Religion, and Health: An Emerging Research Field," *American Psychologist*, 58, 24–35.

4. All names have been replaced by pseudonyms except for Megan's (at her father's request that her real name be used).

5. Barna, G., 2003, *Transforming Children into Spiritual Champions*, Ventura, CA: Regal.

6. Demos, J., 1982, "The Changing Faces of Fatherhood," in *Father and Child: Developmental and Clinical Perspectives*, edited by S. Cath, A. Gurwitt, and J.M. Ross, Boston: Little Brown, pp. 425–445.

7. Marks, L.D., and Palkovitz, R., 2004, "American Fatherhood Types: The Good, the Bad, and the Uninterested," *Fathering*, 2, 113–129; Palkovitz, R., and Marks, L., 2002, "Refining Fatherhood and Motherhood: An Analysis of Cultural Trends in American Parenting," in *Mutterschaft, Vaterschaft*, edited by W.E. Fthenakis and M.R. Trextor, Weinheim and Basel: Beltz Verlag, pp. 156–169.

8. White, J.M., Wampler, R.S., and Fischer, J.L., 2001, "Indicators of Spiritual Development in Recovery from Alcohol and Other Drug Problems," *Alcoholism Treatment Quarterly*, 19(1), 19–36.

9. Dollahite, D.C., and Hawkins, A.J., 1998, "A Conceptual Ethic of Generative Fathering," *The Journal of Men's Studies*, 7, 109–132.

10. Brotherson, S.E., and Dollahite, D.C., 1997, "Generative Ingenuity in Fatherwork with Young Children with Special Needs," in *Generative Fathering: Beyond Deficit Perspectives*, edited by A.J. Hawkins and D.C. Dollahite, Thousand Oaks, CA: Sage, pp. 89–104.

11. www.hickoksports.com/biograph/barkleyc.shtml, retrieved August 10, 2006.

12. Doherty, W.J., Kouneski, E.F., and Erickson, M.F., 1998, "Responsible Fathering: An Overview and Conceptual Framework," *Journal of Marriage and the Family*, 60, 277–292.

13. Marks and Palkovitz, 2004.

14. Hawkins, A.J., and Dollahite, D.C., 1997, *Generative Fathering: Beyond Deficit Perspectives*, Thousand Oaks, CA: Sage; Palkovitz, 2002.

15. Warner, C.T., 2001, *Bonds That Make Us Free: Healing Our Relationships, Coming to Ourselves*, Salt Lake City, UT: Shadow Mountain.

16. Kail, R.V., and Cavanaugh, J., 2000, *Human Development: A Lifespan View*, 2nd ed., Belmont, CA: Wadsworth.

Fathers and Contexts of Influence

T he three chapters in this section give insight into particular contexts that may influence a father's experience and involvement with his children in powerful ways, including race and ethnicity, separation and divorce, and incarceration.

In Chapter 15, "Beating the Odds: How Ethnically Diverse Fathers Matter," Andrew Behnke and William Allen outline the influence of race and ethnicity as a factor for fathers of color. Both authors have significant scholarly and practical experience in studying and working with fathers of varying ethnic and racial backgrounds. They explore some of the issues affecting fathers of color in America today, delineate contributions of Latino and African American fathers in the lives of their children, and identify potential hurdles some fathers of color may face in being involved fathers. Further, they present a number of ideas to help others understand and appreciate the contributions made by fathers of color.

The influence of separation and divorce on fathers' involvement with their children is dealt with in Chapter 16, "'I Am Still Your Dad!': Father Involvement in Children's Lives after Divorce." Nate Cottle and Paul Dixon provide information on how nonresidential fathers may remain involved in their children's lives after a divorce. They identify a number of issues related to the effects of divorce on children and make a special case for the importance of father involvement in such a context. The authors then address obstacles to quality interaction with children in circumstances surrounding divorce, including custody arrangements and other factors, and offer a number of ideas that may help nonresidential fathers find ways to overcome these obstacles and fulfill their parental roles.

In Chapter 17, "From Behind Prison Walls: Incarcerated Fathers and Their Children," Randell Turner focuses attention on a significant and emerging social issue in America: incarcerated fathers and their children. As the developer of a program intended to assist incarcerated fathers, Turner shares hands-on, practical examples and stories that illuminate their world. He explores the context of men in prison and shares an inside view of what can happen with support for fathers in prison settings. He discusses the impact of fatherhood support efforts on incarcerated fathers, their families, and the prison system and examines key elements of programs intended to provide support to incarcerated parents.

This section presents an exploration of key contexts that may influence how some men encounter the experience of fathering. Fathers' growth and experiences are certainly shaped by ethnic heritage, separation or divorce from a child's mother, or incarceration in prison. These contexts of influence need to be understood and examined so that potential and existing barriers to father involvement can be better managed. Fathers, families, and community members who understand these influences will be better able to facilitate effective parenting opportunities for men shaped by such contexts.

Author Andrew O. Behnke (third from left) shown working with Latino fathers

Beating the Odds:
How Ethnically Diverse Fathers Matter

Andrew O. Behnke and William D. Allen

*M*y dad's my biggest hero, because I'm important to him, I can trust him and he trusts me, and it's like I can . . . I can talk to him about personal things and all that, like when I have a problem."[1]

These are the words of the 16-year-old daughter of Jorge, a father of four, who has spent the past three years as a single father of two teenage girls while working to obtain visas for his wife and two children who remain in Mexico. Jorge works the second shift, but he doesn't let that keep him from spending time with his daughters. The girls have mentioned they often wait up for him, and when he's not at work they're never apart. Additionally, Jorge enjoys showing the detailed painting and decorating he did to make his home warm and *bonita* (attractive) as a surprise for his daughters when they first came over from Mexico.

Jorge exemplifies the critical efforts many ethnic minority fathers are making to show love to their children and be involved in their lives despite sometimes challenging circumstances.

A discussion of why fathers count would be incomplete without a better understanding of how ethnic minority fathers matter to their children and families. We believe this is true in part because of their increasing presence in the United States. For example, Latino, African American, and Asian American families have higher fertility rates than most European American families and are expected to account for as many as 90 percent of all births in the next 50 years.[2] In fact, ethnic minorities are expected to account for more than 50 percent of the U.S. population by 2050, with Latinos becoming the largest ethnic minority group in the United States.[3] Although much energy has gone into the study of fatherhood in the past two decades, research on the experiences of fathers of color has received relatively less focus.[4] Men in these ethnic families may differ in the cultural values or backgrounds they bring to parenting, and this deserves greater understanding. Additionally, fathers of color face many of the same issues and challenges all fathers face and need to be included in discussions of fathering.

Fathers of color typically include men born or raised in families of diverse ethnic heritages. There is a great diversity of ethnic and immigrant experiences in the United States. Fathers of color may include men of varying ethnic backgrounds, including Japanese, Native American, Greek, Russian, or other family origins. Despite this diversity, Latino and African American fathers account for the largest number of fathers of color in the U.S. Our discussion will thus focus somewhat on men from these two groups, but we also believe that much of what we present is equally applicable to fathers from other ethnic groups as well as fathers who are recent immigrants. In this chapter, we explore some similarities and differences among fathers of color, demonstrate the contributions of Latino and African American fathers in the lives of their families, and discuss some of the hurdles many of these men face in being involved fathers. We also propose practical ideas to help others understand and appreciate the contributions of these fathers.

Understanding the Lives of Ethnic Minority Fathers

How would you stay involved in your children's lives if they lived thousands of miles away in Mexico and you lived in the United States? How would you manage things if your ex-wife and her parents wouldn't let you be around your kids? Many ethnic minority fathers have had to develop alternative ways of being meaningfully involved in their children's lives. Such extenuating circumstances and trying situations may seem insurmountable to some, yet we don't have to look far to find positive examples of fathers who nurture and provide for their children under even the most difficult conditions. In addition, many ethnic minority fathers have unique yet valid perspectives that may shape the ways they father and define their family life. Thus, in order to provide the best future for the growing numbers of ethnic minority children in this country, we ought to be sensitive, understanding, and supportive of these fathers in diverse contexts. We briefly explore five key points that are useful in understanding ethnically diverse fathers and appreciating some of the factors influencing their efforts.[5]

Availability of Material Resources

Some ethnic minority fathers may lack material (economic and other physical) resources to facilitate greater physical involvement with their children. These fathers often find themselves with limited economic assets and limited access to other material resources such as housing, time, computers, or community institutions (recreation centers, parks, and libraries).[6] For example, African American and Latino fathers are similarly represented in poor urban neighborhoods, with their related challenges of social deprivation, criminal dangers, and lack of opportunity.[7] Ross Parke and his colleagues have shown that these poor neighborhoods can influence the ways parents interact with their children and have adverse effects on child outcomes.[8]

Poverty is also a real concern for families in African American and Latino communities. In 2000, 24 percent of African Americans and 23 percent of Latinos lived below the poverty line, but only 8 percent of Caucasians lived in poverty.[9] Also, studies have consistently confirmed that economic hardship is associated with reduced levels of family functioning (e.g., negative interactions).[10] For example, Simons and colleagues have shown economic hardship is related to heightened family conflict, negative parent-child interactions, and overall unhealthy family interactions.[11] Stresses related to working long hours for inadequate pay can at times spill over into parenting behaviors and other interactions (e.g., irritability or aggression) in the home.[12] Certainly, however, many fathers find ways to successfully navigate these outside pressures while raising their children, yet we would like to emphasize that some ethnic minority fathers are in real need of economic or material support beyond what is currently available. It is important that we be mindful of the contexts and the day-to-day hassles some of these fathers experience, so that we can be part of the solution in helping them succeed.

Development of Human Capital

Some ethnic minority fathers lack the human capital (e.g., education, skills, abilities) that would assist them in being more actively involved in the lives of their families. Some have come from situations that may have made it more difficult to acquire education and other skills, which in turn may complicate their paternal roles. For example, some fathers struggle to help their children with their school assignments. Illustrating this point, some Latino fathers have reported they feel less able to be involved in their children's education than they would like to be due to their own limited English abilities or (in some cases) limited formal education. Recent data indicate on average only 57 percent of Latino fathers are high school graduates, and the number may be even lower in economically depressed, urban areas.[13] In addition to these academic issues, many immigrant fathers struggle in their roles as advocates for their children in institutions that are often dominated by teachers and administrators of other ethnic groups (generally European American). Cultural differences in gender roles also play a critical role in determining how comfortable these fathers feel as they try to understand and negotiate various educational systems.

The fact that many ethnic minority fathers have a more limited grasp of the English language than their children can exacerbate the "disconnect" most fathers experience as their children reach the teenage years. For instance, limited English abilities can make it harder for these fathers to know where their children are and what they are doing on a daily basis. Moreover, limited language abilities may make it difficult to share interests or at least be involved in the interests of their children.

On a different note, some ethnic minority fathers may not have grown up with positive paternal role models and may at times have difficulty feeling successful as fathers. Though this may be the case for fathers of any ethnic group, family structure and socioeconomic features often make father absence more prevalent among ethnic minority families.[14] On the other hand, some ethnic minority fathers struggle to realize the expectations others hold for them in terms of the way they should be as fathers. In fact, fathers struggling to surmount these issues have increased and prolonged stress in their lives and are at particular risk for physical and emotional problems (i.e., depression).[15] We would like to emphasize that ethnic minority fathers are not less resourceful or less able; they are just more likely to have struggled with poverty, poor options for education, and the lack of employment opportunities, which may have made gaining certain skills and education more difficult.

Support and Social Capital

The amount of "social capital" that ethnically diverse fathers can count on varies over time and according to certain contexts and circumstances. *Social capital* refers to support fathers receive from family members, friends, neighbors, and other members of their communities.[16] Social support can influence the means by which a father interacts with his children in various ways. First, family and friends can have both positive and negative influences on fathers. For example, a father may receive a good deal of informal support from other fathers with whom he plays basketball, yet at the same time these same individuals may give bad advice or become such a distraction that they detract from the time a father spends with his child. The same thing can happen in any number of social support groups, from the poker table or bar to the Rotary club, country club, or religious group. Positive messages can be mixed with less healthy messages, which can lead to ambiguities in terms of the expected ways a father should interact with his family.

Second, family members can act as "gatekeepers" in disallowing fathers from being involved in their children's lives.[17] Especially common among nonresident fathers, gatekeeping by a child's mother or other family members is often related to inadequate economic support on the part of the father or to other factors that lead to relationship conflict. In this way, adverse economic conditions or heated relationships can have unpleasant effects on fathers' abilities to be involved in their children's lives.[18] Similarly, contextual factors such as imprisonment or migration may also reduce social capital and make it more difficult for fathers to maintain relationships with their children.

Due to other contextual factors such as economic conditions, cultural charac-teristics, and family structure differences, some fathers grow up with few positive fathering role models. For instance, many Asian American fathers have grown up in homes where they felt very distant from their fathers, and as a result some of these fathers indicate they have difficulty navigating a nurturing and warm rela-tionship with their children. Alternatively, many ethnic minorities have grown up in single-parent homes with few reliable models of how to be involved dads. We realize that parenting is a challenging prospect regardless of ethnicity or cultural heritage, and we acknowledge that support groups of all types can be helpful. We suggest, however, that fathers balance the time and energy expended participating in outside social activities with those required for healthy involvement in the home.

Diversity among Ethnic Minority Fathers

Great diversity is found among ethnic minority fathers in terms of their values, cultural characteristics, and socioeconomic status.[19] This diversity exists both within and between various ethnic and cultural groups. By culture we mean the shared behaviors, beliefs, and institutions (e.g., religions) of a particular group of individuals, and by values we refer to the specific beliefs and standards held by an individual or group of individuals. Many fathers from similar ethnic minority groups share specific cultural attributes, yet some fathers exhibit an even greater range of differences in terms of their values and actual ways they father within these ethnic groups. For instance, while we may more easily think of differences between Latino and Asian American fathers, in practice we may find more differences within and across specific subgroups of Latino fathers (e.g., Mexican American versus Salvadoran) than we might expect. Considering the diversity within ethnic groups suggests that even fathers within a specific ethnic group may have different needs. We must consider the diversity of fathers of color as well as their ethnic identity.

Finding Balance

We suggest that recognizing a balance between similarities and differences in fathers of different ethnic backgrounds is the hallmark of effective practice with and policy for fathers and their families. Generally, when ethnic fatherhood is discussed, conversations revolve around the differences that minority fathers at times exemplify from their mainstream counterparts. And though these differences are significant and crucial to understanding fathers in their appropriate contexts, there are equally important similarities between fathers regardless of their ethnic background. In fact, these similarities seem to dominate over differences. Men from diverse ethnic and cultural backgrounds often share common understandings of what fatherhood means to them. Some examples include fathers' adoration and love for their children, their aspirations for their children's success, and their desire to teach and nurture their children. Similarities also include a father's focus on the financial well-being and emotional needs of his partner and children.[20]

Observed similarities in fathers from differing ethnic backgrounds may arise from similar experiences. Adaptations to similar experiences, for example, may translate into greater similarities between recent immigrant fathers from Mexico and Croatia than between first- and third-generation Mexican American fathers from the same town. Experiences related to immigration, work, language difficulties, discrimination, and shared socioeconomic situations can manifest in the ways fathers interact with their children. Furthermore, similarities resulting from shared experiences in fathers' lives at times contrast with differences caused by unique situations and backgrounds.

On the other hand, differences in parenting may be rooted in culture. What may be considered involved fathering by one culture may not be viewed similarly across or even within ethnic boundaries. In other words, what passes for involvement in one cultural context may not constitute involvement in another culture. For example, one culture might hold that reading to a child is an indicator of involved fatherhood, whereas in another culture reading may be replaced by storytelling or playing basketball. In this case, in spite of shared context, a father's culture and values may still play out as important factors in determining his parenting style. For instance, Puerto Rican and African American fathers in New York at times may share various fathering characteristics (e.g., types of interactions and actual time with children) that may be related to shared family structures and socioeconomic situations. Yet these men may father in quite different ways because of their values (e.g., *marianismo, respeto*), their roots (e.g., immigration history), and their culture (e.g., games they play with the children, *quinceñeras*, religious beliefs).[21] The key point is that observers need to balance apparent differences with greater understanding of the commonalities among fathers regardless of their ethic or cultural backgrounds.

A Strengths-Based View of Ethnic Minority Fathers

In this section, pulling from our experience with African American and Latino fathers, we explore some personal strengths common among many ethnic minority fathers. Ethnic minority fathers are often viewed through a lens of deficiency, and yet they exhibit many strengths. There is great resiliency among them, and the contributions they make to families, communities, and future generations should be acknowledged and appreciated.

Personal Strengths of African American Fathers

Much of the current scholarship on fatherhood among ethnic minority groups has come from the study of African American fathers. Several writers, including Robert Staples (writing about African American men)[22] and the late John McAdoo (writing specifically about black fathers),[23] were pioneers in expanding our understanding of the roles African American males play in black family life across the lifespan. Specific strengths that tend to be seen among African American fathers include high levels of physical and emotional involvement.

A recent study of ethnically diverse fathers countered the generally negative portrayal of African American fathers, showing that they provided more physical care for their children than Asian American, European American, and Latino fathers.[24] In other words, African American fathers more commonly reported that they bathed their children, disciplined them, took them to activities, changed diapers, and made appointments. Many of these fathers know what it is like to be raised without an involved father and have taken it upon themselves to be the involved father they want for their children.

However, such direct and physical involvement is more difficult for fathers in limited-income or nonresidential situations. For example, present-day researchers as well as early pioneers who studied the family lives of African Americans have found that African American fathers are more likely to be physically involved when they have higher income and education levels.[25] Researchers have also established that involved fathers typically are married longer, have better communication skills, and enjoy more support from outside their primary relationships. Such findings suggest the value of a supportive context for involvement for African American fathers, which benefits both them and their children.

Allen and Connor theorized that there were ethnic differences in the way African American fathers approached their paternal work in families.[26] They described an "afrocentric" conceptualization of generative fathering that included economic support, workplace challenges, transmission of cultural values, and bicultural socialization. Identifying the concepts that give meaning and motivation to father involvement for ethnic minority fathers can be helpful in using cultural values to sustain and renew healthy family relationships.

In addition to physical care, emotional involvement and feelings of paternal responsibility are also important to African American fathers. Ahmeduzzaman and Roopnarine have shown that African American fathers are generally quite emotionally involved and take responsibility for their children.[27] Researchers have also pointed out that, although relationship and economic obstacles prevent some African American fathers from living with or spending time with their children, these deprivations often lead to heightened feelings of responsibility toward the children.[28] Continuing research needs to be done to examine the many ways African American fathers are involved with and valued by their children.

Personal Strengths of Latino Fathers

Most Latino fathers express a number of personal and family-related strengths that set them apart as real family men. Various authors have expressed new typologies of generative Latino fatherhood such as the loving husband, the consumed father, and the family man.[29] This nondeficit or resilience perspective is becoming a new way to approach Latino men in research, the media, and other venues. Some of the specific strengths typically expressed among Latino fathers include emotional involvement, family involvement, and physical involvement.

Research has demonstrated that Latino fathers are generally affectionate and emotionally involved in their children's lives.[30] In fact, in some domains Latinos have been shown to do better than fathers of other ethnicities. For example, one study found Latino dads were more engaged, warmer, and less controlling than African American, Asian American, and European American fathers and more responsible for their children's needs than Asian American and European American fathers.[31] Other research studies have found that Latino fathers are often more nurturing, concerned, and emotionally supportive than their European American counterparts.[32] Such findings confirm the caring and competent attitudes many Latino fathers bring to family life.

Many Latino fathers are known for the emphasis they put on cooperation, family unity, and child rearing—or, in other words, *familismo*.[33] This term refers to Latinos' cultural emphasis on family cohesiveness, interdependence, loyalty, and responsibility to care for one another.[34] To many Latinos, *familismo* means placing the family before one's personal needs and assuring that all family members are emotionally supported.[35] In fact, some have asserted *familismo* is the most constant and fundamental dimension of Latino family life.[36] Latino fathers are expected to bring the family together, and once it is together, the fathers are expected to limit the potential disarray that could be expected when multiple generations and many children get together.

Machismo is a different term often used to emphasize Latino men's role as head of household in place of their roles as father and husband. It has generally been defined with negative connotations, such as "exaggerated masculinity, physical prowess, and male chauvinism."[37] Others have come to think of machismo in a more positive light, defining it with terms like "true bravery or valor, courage, generosity, stoicism, heroism, and ferocity."[38] Latino fathers may at times equate machismo with feeling masculine but feel conflicting pressure in the U.S. to be more nurturing and family oriented.[39] These conflicting cultural expectations and values may lead to increased ambiguity over the appropriate role of fathers in families and how they should interact with their children.

Latino fathers are also known for being physically present in the lives of their children. For example, various researchers have found that Latino fathers are more physically involved, monitor their children more, and provide more consistent discipline than their European American counterparts.[40] Other researchers have described Latino dads as engaging in contemporary fathering roles such as playmate, participant, and emotional supporter.[41] Francisco, a Latino father of three, exemplifies this idea. He wakes up for work early in the morning and is there to pick up his kids up from school and daycare in the afternoon. He then spends most of his time in the afternoons and evenings doing things with his kids. He models the reality that Latino fathers are often nurturing, concerned, and physically involved in the lives of their children.

Common Barriers Experienced by Ethnic Minority Fathers

As discussed previously, ethnic minority fathers often struggle against barriers that inhibit their involvement or diminish their influence in their children's lives. Typically, obstacles in fathers' environments or lives that limit involvement may be beyond their control. The barriers discussed here include nonmarital births and nonresidential fatherhood, difficulty in providing for the family, lack of English language abilities, and discrimination. By understanding these barriers, it is possible to work toward reducing them and assisting fathers to overcome them.

Nonmarital Births and Nonresidential Fatherhood

One barrier commonly faced by Latino and African American men in family life is the high rate of nonmarital births and the implications for fatherhood in these ethnic populations. In 1994, 38 percent of Latino and 74 percent of African American births occurred out of wedlock.[42] While residential fatherhood is preferable in situations of nonmarital births, in some cases couples split up because of financial problems, relationship difficulties, or multiple or extended household responsibilities.[43] This type of fatherhood—called nonresident fatherhood—is prevalent among some ethnic minority groups. For example, in 2003, 30 percent of Latino children and 59 percent of African American children lived in households without their fathers.[44] Due to concern for children in poverty and children with nonresident fathers, various studies have focused exclusively on fathers in these circumstances.[45] They have found that many nonresidential fathers make significant efforts to be involved in their children's lives, and many are successful. Although such circumstances are not desirable for fathers and children, it should be acknowledged that healthy father-child relationships can still exist under such conditions.

The key structural barrier in these circumstances is that fathers often do not actually live with their children, and the distance or separation from their children becomes a distinct challenge. Some studies have shown, however, that nonresident (especially ethnic minority) dads are more involved than characteristically believed.[46] Contrasting with traditional views of nonresidential fatherhood, large-scale studies have shown that many nonresident fathers are very involved and that greater involvement on the part of fathers is related to positive child outcomes.[47] For instance, Dunn and colleagues have shown child adjustment is consistently related to the quality of the father-child relationship.[48] Thus, it appears that encouraging father involvement even of nonresidential fathers benefits children. These and other studies suggest that at least some ethnic minority fathers overcome the barriers common to nonresident father status and are able to be involved and make a difference in the lives of their children. A quote from a never-married, noncustodial African American father named Devon shares this sentiment: "Some would look down on me because I don't live with my kid, but I see my son nearly every night. He comes over to my mother's house, and we play basketball or whatever."[49]

Challenges with the Provider Role

Another common barrier that hinders some African American and Latino fathers is the challenge associated with fulfilling the provider role as parents. Given the relatively high rates of unemployment in both African American (9 percent) and Latino (7 percent) populations, we should expect that unemployed fathers' ability to be successfully involved fathers would be diminished. Being able to fulfill their obligations to financially provide for their children is a powerful expectation for most men. When fathers cannot contribute fully to the financial and material well-being of their families, they can become demoralized and isolated from family life. Fathers may become estranged from their family relationships through processes such as partner conflict, separation or divorce, long hours at work, or physical distance from their children.[50]

Unemployment and underemployment are serious barriers to success in the provider role for fathers of color.[51] Nonresidential fathers often have difficulty providing adequately for their children because of employment problems. Rather than "deadbeat dads," these fathers are more often "dead broke dads" or fathers who do not have the financial means to allow them free entry into their child's lives.[52] Socioeconomic differences are often mistaken for ethnic differences in studies of ethnic minority fatherhood.[53] Countering accepted thinking, some researchers have found that African American and Latino fathers with low incomes may in fact be more involved as caregivers than their counterparts who are better off financially.[54] This demonstrates resiliency in the face of economic and cultural pressures. A good example is furnished in a recent study of Latino immigrant fathers, which showed that fathers continued to be actively involved in their children's lives even as they struggled with acculturation and fought to acquire work and a new language.[55] These immigrant fathers have more difficulty than their wives finding and keeping work, which counters cultural expectations of the father as a provider. Studies like this indicate that some of the problems ethnic minorities face are rooted in economic disparity, yet other barriers are structural (e.g., institutional racism) or cultural (e.g., customs).

Some scholars suggest that existing welfare and child support legislation still tends to discourage father involvement (especially in relation to nonresident fathers) among ethnic minority fathers.[56] They also find that many "fragile families" are normatively still in romantic relationships at the time of the child's birth and could benefit from specific support. Thus, a rethinking of current public policy regarding fathers and families may be in order. Some of the remedies to this barrier that have been suggested include increased assistance funding for two-parent households (regardless of marital status) in poverty, the reduction of child support orders for cohabiting fathers, and reconsideration of child support enforcement procedures that take into account fathers' circumstances and income.[57]

English Abilities

The acquisition of English language skills is a barrier faced particularly by immigrant ethnic fathers who have come to the United States. Latino fathers constitute the largest group of these immigrant fathers, and more than two-fifths of them do not speak English.[58] Language barriers isolate men from public resources such as public assistance and better employment and at times also from their children. During one of our studies with Latino fathers, Pedro stated that he cannot talk to his teenagers because his "kids live in a different world," one where English and American culture prevail.[59] Limited English abilities make it difficult for these fathers to access this world and really communicate with their children. Language difficulties can also limit fathers' abilities to be involved in their children's schooling. For instance, Latino dads might want to help their children with homework but be constrained by a lack of English fluency or the fact that the schoolwork is too advanced. One Latino father reported that he used to spend hours with his kids working on their homework until one day they stopped asking for help because he was getting their answers wrong. Such barriers can discourage fathers in their involvement and thus deserve attention. Increased attention would help local communities and programs mobilize themselves to reduce such challenges and help fathers of color to be meaningfully involved.

Discrimination and Prejudice

The barriers ethnic minority fathers may encounter in their efforts to be good parents can also include social forces such as ethnic bias (e.g., institutional racism) and class bias. Though these forms of prejudice and discrimination may not be seen as directly influencing the ways men father per se, these two forms of bias have been shown to contaminate family relationships by adding stress and additional concerns that make life especially difficult for ethnic minority families.[60] Additionally, problems that flow indirectly from these barriers, such as poverty, poor options for education, and the lack of employment opportunities, lead to further stresses. Researchers have shown that fathers struggling with racial prejudice and the economic hardships that go along with it are at particular risk for physical and emotional problems (i.e., depression).[61]

Core Elements of Positive Involvement for Ethnic Minority Fathers

Understanding the complexity of family experiences faced by ethnic minority fathers helps us to recognize the core elements that demonstrate how these fathers make a difference. What does good fathering mean to fathers of color and their families? This section will elaborate on four core elements of positive involvement that we have identified with minority fathers.

Multiple Pathways of Father Involvement

Fathers can be involved in many healthy ways. They can be emotionally, cognitively (e.g., thinking or worrying about their children), and physically involved.[62] They may also be indirectly involved through such means as providing income or being supportive of the mother. For instance, as in our first example of Jorge and his teenage daughters, a father can be very involved in his children's lives but not spend huge amounts of time with them on a daily basis. However, these ethnic minority fathers have reported that to make this work they need to focus on their children or find an emotional connection with them. Similarly, many nonresidential fathers find ways to be very involved, even though it may prove more difficult for them at times. In fact, most of the children we have interviewed are proud of their dads, and though most of these children long for more time with their dads (as most kids do), they feel that their dads really care and make a difference.

Emotionally Involved and Supportive Fathers

A second core element of positive involvement among fathers of color is their level of emotional engagement, or their positive and lasting feelings for their children. Research and our experience has typically shown that African American and Latino fathers are emotionally involved in the lives of their children. A high level of emotional engagement, common among both African American and Latino fathers, benefits both the fathers and their children.[63] Though at times these fathers may have fewer opportunities to be involved fathers, this emotional bond may help them to make up for these lost opportunities.[64] For instance, Devon (nonresidential African American father) told us he made special efforts to be emotionally involved in his son's life even though he could not live with him. He said he loves to just talk and connect with his son while they play basketball, hang out on the porch, or go out to eat.[65] Such efforts to be emotionally engaged bode well for ethnic minority fathers and their children.

Willingness to Sacrifice for Children

A willingness to make sacrifices in providing for and supporting their children is a common attitude of many ethnic minority fathers. Pablo, a Latino father of three kids who worked 10-hour days at a local meat-packing plant, noted:

> See, I tell them, "You see how hard your mom and I work so that ya'll have what you need. We are making a sacrifice so that you can live well." It's always been a sacrifice.[66]

Pablo speaks for many ethnic minority fathers who see their willingness to sacrifice for the good of their children as a number-one priority. This theme of sacrificing regularly for one's family has come up time and time again in interviews with fathers of color. These sacrifices may bring fathers closer to their children, particularly as both fathers and their children achieve a deeper realization of why the sacrifices are being made. A low-income African American father, for example, reported he often uses most of his paycheck to take nice things to his daughter and take her out when he's given a chance to visit. The loss of some of his paycheck is a sacrifice, yet he finds it worthwhile because he knows they both really enjoy these special times together. Sacrificing regularly for children is a strength championed by fathers of color, who often have a heritage of hardship and sacrifice.

Traversing Multiple Meanings of Fatherhood

To be successful in their role as fathers, many ethnic minority fathers must manage conflicting notions of their fathering role. For example, fathers from Mexico may immigrate with one set of expectations about their roles as fathers and be confronted with new expectations for fathering after arriving in the United States. One father, Ruben, said, "The culture is different. Over there [meaning Mexico], the men are more machismo. They don't spend their time with the family, they spend more time with their friends. Here, it's more family-oriented and about family unity." Thus, immigrant fathers and other fathers of color must learn to balance the conflicting expectations of two cultures and parent the way they feel is best for their children. Similarly, African American fathers often must battle various negative stereotypes and balance differing expectations in their attempts to be nurturing and involved fathers.[68] Fathers who find they are able to

---

Steps toward Positive Contributions for Ethnic Minority Fathers

Ethnic minority dads should:

- believe in their ability to be a positive role model in their children's lives,
- decide how involved they wish to be in their children's lives and commit themselves to doing what they hope to do,
- be strong and counteract negative stereotypes by being the type of father they think their children need,
- work with their child's mother to create rules and reach common ground regarding parenting and remember that raising a child takes teamwork,
- keep a positive outlook even though economic and other factors may get in the way of being actively involved in children's lives, and
- find creative ways to be involved and make consistent efforts to overcome barriers (e.g., validate and repair hurt feelings, look for job opportunities).

Community professionals, programs, and organizations should:

- actively seek out ethnic minority fathers as clientele and participants,
- be aware of the strengths these fathers possess and barriers they face,
- create coalitions with local organizations to serve ethnic minority fathers,
- advocate for ethnic minority men and encourage their involvement as fathers,
- play more visible roles within ethnically diverse communities and work to overcome the hesitancy families may have about receiving parenting help,
- be sensitive in understanding and supporting the unique perspectives ethnic minority fathers may have,
- help fathers negotiate conflicting pressures and expectations that may interfere with their paternal role, and
- provide social support (informal mentoring, informal support groups, etc.).

Public policymakers should:

- increase funding for two-parent households (regardless of marital status) in poverty,
- reduce or modify child support orders for cohabiting fathers, and
- reconsider child support enforcement procedures to take into account fathers' circumstances and income.[67]

negotiate a comfortable place for themselves between two contrasting sets of expectations appear to do better in the long run and to be able to provide more consistent discipline and nurturance to their children.

Conclusion

Understanding that ethnic minorities are expected to account for more than 50 percent of the U.S. population by 2050,[69] it is imperative that we learn to appreciate how ethnic minority fathers matter to their children and families. Research shows that effective father involvement promotes healthy childhood development, regardless of ethnic background.[70] In this chapter, we have explored important structural and individual barriers that make involved fathering difficult for some ethnic minority fathers, and we recognize that these differences are significant and crucial to understanding fathers in their appropriate contexts. More important, however, we have identified important similarities (i.e., emotional and physical involvement) between fathers of various ethnic backgrounds. These similarities are often in the form of strengths fathers bring to parenting their children.

Greater focus on fathers' strengths by the media and the general public is one of the key factors needed to overcome the challenges many of these fathers face. Supporting and encouraging these ethnic minority men in their role as fathers will help the positive impact they have in the lives of their children to continue to grow. We suggest that fathers in all circumstances, including fathers of color, need to value their own potential importance to a child's well-being and take steps to strengthen their contributions and commitment to their children's lives.

Endnotes

1. Behnke, A.O., 2002, "The Educational and Occupational Aspirations of Latino Youth and Their Parents," master's thesis, Utah State University.

2. U.S. Bureau of the Census, 2002, *Statistical Abstract of the US*, 120th ed., Washington, DC: Government Printing Office.

3. U.S. Bureau of the Census, 2004, *U.S. Interim Projections by Age, Sex, Race, and Hispanic Origin*, Washington, DC: Government Printing Office, retrieved on March 10, 2005, at www.census.gov/ipc/www/usinterimproj.

4. Cabrera, N., and Garcia-Coll, C., 2004, "Latino Fathers: Uncharted Territory in Need of Much Exploration," in *The Role of the Father in Child Development*, 4th ed., edited by M.E. Lamb, New York: Wiley, pp. 98–120; McAdoo, J.L., 1988, "The Roles of Black Fathers in the Socialization of Black Children," in *Black Families*, 2nd ed., edited by H.P. McAdoo, Thousand Oaks, CA: Sage, pp. 257–269.

5. Some of the theoretical basis for this section is based on the work of Cabrera, N., and Garcia-Coll, C., 2004.

6. Coltrane, S., 1995, "The Future of Fatherhood: Social, Demographic, and Economic Influences on Men's Family Involvements," in *Fatherhood: Contemporary Theory, Research, and Social Policy*, edited by W. Marsiglio, Thousand Oaks, CA: Sage, pp. 119–147; Vélez-Ibáñez, C.G., 1996, *Border Visions: Mexican Cultures of the Southwest United States*, Tucson: University of Arizona Press; Jarrett, R.L., Jefferson, S., and Roach, A., June 2000, "Family and Parenting Strategies in High Risk African American Neighborhoods," paper presented at the National Head Start Association annual meeting, Washington, DC.

7. Gephart, M.A., 1997, "Neighborhoods and Communities as Context for Development," in *Neighborhood Poverty, Vol. 1: Context and Consequences for Children*, edited by J. Brooks-Gunn, G.J. Duncan, and J.L. Aber, New York: Sage, pp. 1–43; Gephart, M.A., and Brooks-Gunn, J., 1997, "Introduction," in *Neighborhood Poverty, Vol. 2: Policy Implications in Studying Neighborhoods*, edited by J. Brooks-Gunn, G. J. Duncan, and J. L. Aber, New York: Sage, pp. xiii-xxii; Vélez-Ibáñez, C.G., 1996.

8. O'Neil, R., Parke, R.D., and McDowell, D.J., 2001, "Objective and Subjective Features of Children's Neighborhoods: Relations to Parental Regulatory Strategies and Children's Social Competence," *Journal of Applied Developmental Psychology*, 22, 135–155.

9. U.S. Bureau of the Census, 2000, *Our Diverse Population: Race, and Hispanic Origin, 2000*, Washington, DC: Government Printing Office, retrieved on March 10, 2005, at www.census.gov/population/pop-profile/2000/chap16.pdf.

10. Gomel, J. N., Tinsley, B. J., Parke, R.D. and Clark, K., 1998, "The Effects of Economic Hardship on Family Functioning: A Multi-Ethnic Perspective," *Journal of Family Issues*, 19, 436–467; McLoyd, V.C., 1990, "The Impact of Economic Hardship on Black Families and Children: Psychological Distress, Parenting, and Socioemotional Development," *Child Development*, 61, 311–346; Peterson, J., and Hawley, D., 1998, "Effects of Stressors on Parenting Attitudes and Family Functioning in a Primary Prevention Program," *Family Relations*, 47(3), 221–227.

11. Simons, R., and Johnson, C., 1996, "Mother's Parenting," in *Understanding the Differences between Divorced and Intact Families: Stress, Interaction, and Child Outcome*, edited by B. Adams and D. Klein, Thousand Oaks, CA: Sage Publications; Simons, R., Whitbeck, L., Conger, R., and Melby, J., 1990, "Husband and Wife Differences in Determinants of Parenting: A Social Learning Model of Parental Behavior," *Journal of Marriage and the Family*, 52, 375–392.

12. Conger, R.D., Conger, K.J., Elder, G.H., Lorenz, F.O., Simons, R.L., and Whitbeck, L.B., 1992, "A Family Process Model of Economic Hardship and Adjustment of Early Adolescent Boys," *Child Development*, 63, 526–541;

Conger, R.D., Conger, K.J., Elder, G.H., Lorenz, F.O., Simons, R.L., and Whitbeck, L.B., 1993, "Family Economic Stress and Adjustment of Early Adolescent Girls," *Developmental Psychology*, 29, 206–219; Lempers, J.D., Clark-Lempers, D., and Simons, R.L., 1989, "Economic Hardship, Parenting, and Distress in Adolescence," *Child Development*, 60, 25–39; Simons et al., 1990.

13. Therrien, M., and Ramirez, R.R., 2000, *The Hispanic Population in the United States: March 2000*, Current Population Reports, Washington, DC: Government Printing Office, pp. 20–535.

14. McAdoo, H.P., 2002, *Black Children: Social, Educational, and Parental Environments*, 2nd ed., Thousand Oaks, CA: Sage; McAdoo, J.L., 1988.

15. Hoard, L.R., and Anderson, E.A., 2004, "Factors Related to Depression in Rural and Urban Noncustodial, Low-Income Fathers," *Journal of Community Psychology*, 32(1), 103–119.

16. Cabrera and Garcia-Coll, 2004.

17. Allen, S.M., and Hawkins, A.J., 1999, "Maternal Gatekeeping: Mothers' Beliefs and Behaviors That Inhibit Greater Father Involvement in Family Work," *Journal of Marriage and the Family*, 61(1), 199–212.

18. Mincy, R., and Sorensen, E., 1998, "Deadbeats and Turnips in Child Support Reform," *Journal of Policy Analysis and Management*, 71, 44–51.

19. Umaña-Taylor, A.J., and Fine, M.A., 2001, "Methodological Implications of Grouping Latino Adolescents into One Collective Ethnic Group," *Hispanic Journal of Behavioral Sciences*, 23, 347–362.

20. Hawkins, A.J., and Palkovitz, R., 1999, "Beyond Ticks and Clicks: The Need for More Diverse and Broader Conceptualizations and Measures of Father Involvement," *The Journal of Men's Studies*, 8, 11–32; Lamb, M.E., 1999, "The History of Research on Father Involvement: An Overview," in *Fatherhood: Research, Interventions, and Policies*, edited by E. Peters and R.D. Day, Binghamton, NY: Haworth, pp. 23–41.

21. Cabrera and Garcia-Coll, 2004.

22. Staples, R., 1982, *Black Masculinity: The Black Male's Role in American Society*, San Francisco, CA : Black Scholar Press.

23. McAdoo, J.L., 1988; McAdoo, H.P., and McAdoo, J.L., 2002, "The Dynamics of African American Fathers' Family Roles," in *Black Children: Social, Educational, and Parental Environments*, 2nd ed., edited by H.P. McAdoo, Thousand Oaks, CA: Sage, pp. 3–12.

24. Hofferth, S.L., 2003, "Race/Ethnic Differences in Father Involvement in Two-Parent Families: Culture, Context, or Economy?" *Journal of Family Issues*, 24(2), 185–216.

25. Ahmeduzzaman, M., and Roopnarine, J., 1992, "Sociodemographic Factors, Functioning Style, Social Support and Fathers' Involvement with Preschoolers in African American Families," *Journal of Marriage and the Family*, 54, 699–707.

26. Allen, W., and Connor, M., 1997, "An African American Perspective on Generative Fathering," in *Generative Fathering: Beyond Deficit Perspectives*, edited by A. Hawkins and D. Dollahite, Thousand Oaks, CA: Sage, pp. 52–70.

27. Ahmeduzzaman and Roopnarine, 1992.

28. Allen and Connor, 1997.

29. Coltrane, S., Parke, R.D., and Adams, M., April 2001, "Shared Parenting in Mexican-American and European-American Families," paper presented at the biennial meeting of the Society for Research in Child Development, Minneapolis, Minnesota; Gutmann, M., 1996, *The Meanings of Macho: Being a Man in Mexico City*, Berkeley: University of California Press; Gutmann, M., 2003, *Changing Men and Masculinities in Latin America*, Durham, NC: Duke University Press; Mirandé, A., 1997, *Hombres y machos: Masculinity and Latino Culture*, Boulder, CO: Westview Press.

30. Gutmann, 2003.

31. Hofferth, 2003.

32. Coltrane, S., Parke, R.D., and Adams, M., 2004, "Complexity of Father Involvement in Low-Income Mexican American Families," *Family Relations*, 53, 179–189; Mirandé, A., 1997; Toth, J.F., Jr., and Xu, X., 1999, "Ethnic and Cultural Diversity in Fathers' Involvement: A Racial/Ethnic Comparison of African American, Hispanic, and White Fathers, *Youth and Society*, 31, 76–77.

33. Vega, W.A., 1990, "Hispanic Families in the 1980s: A Decade of Research," *Journal of Marriage and the Family*, 52, 1015–1024; Vega, W.A., Patterson, T., Sallis, J., Nader, P., Atkins, C., and Abramson, I., 1986, "Cohesion and Adaptability in Mexican American and Anglo Families," *Journal of Marriage and the Family*, 48, 857–867.

34. Baca-Zinn, M., 1982/83, "Familism among Chicanos: A Theoretical Review," *Humboldt Journal of Social Relations*, 10, 224–238; Baca-Zinn, M., and Wells, B., 2000, "Diversity within Latino Families: New Lessons for Family Social Science," in *Handbook of Family Diversity*, edited by D.H. Demo, K.R. Allen, and M.F. Fine, New York: Oxford University Press, pp. 252–273.

35. Cuellar, I., Arnold, B., and Gonzalez, G., 1995, "Cognitive Referents of Acculturation: Assessment of Cultural Constructs in Mexican Americans," *Journal of Community Psychology*, 23, 339–355.

36. Sabogal, F., Marín, G., Otero-Sabogal, R., VanOss Marín, B., and Perez-Stable, E.J., 1987, "Hispanic Familism and Acculturation: What Changes and What Doesn't?" *Hispanic Journal of Behavioral Sciences*, 9, 397–412.

37. Baca-Zinn, M., 1994, "Adaptation and Continuity in Mexican-Origin Families," in *Minority Families in the United States: Comparative Perspectives*, edited by R.L. Taylor, Englewood Cliffs, NJ: Prentice Hall, at 74.

38. Mirandé, 1997.

39. Taylor, B., and Behnke, A.O., 2005, "Fathering across the Border: Latino Fathers in Mexico and the United States," *Fathering: A Journal of Theory, Research, and Practice about Men as Fathers*, 3(2), 99–120.

40. Hofferth, 2003; Mirandé, 1997.

41. Fitzpatrick, J., Caldera, Y.M., Pursley, M., and Wampler, K., 1999, "Hispanic Mother and Father Perceptions of Fathering: A Qualitative Analysis," *Family and Consumer Sciences Research Journal*, 28, 133–166.

42. Bachu, A., 1999, *Trends in Premarital Childbearing: 1930 to 1994*, Current *Population Reports*, Washington, DC: Government Printing Office, pp. 23–197, retrieved on March 10, 2005, at www.census.gov/prod/99pubs/p23-197.pdf.

43. Danziger, S., and Radin, N., 1990, "Absent Does Not Equal Uninvolved: Predictors of Fathering in Teen Mother Families," *Journal of Marriage and the Family*, 52, 636–641.

44. U.S. Bureau of the Census, 2004, *2003 Annual Social and Economic Supplement U.S. Interim Projections by Age, Sex, Race, and Hispanic Origin*, Washington, DC: Government Printing Office, retrieved on March 10, 2005, at www.census.gov/population/www/socdemo/hh-fam/cps2003.html.

45. Danziger and Radin, 1990; Mincy and Sorensen, 1998.

46. Ibid.

47. Amato, P., and Gilbreth, J., 1999, "Nonresident Fathers and Children's Well-being: A Meta-Analysis," *Journal of Marriage and the Family*, 61, 557–573; Dunn, J., Cheng, H., O'Connor, T.G., and Bridges, L., 2004, "Children's Perspectives on Their Relationships with Their Nonresident Fathers: Influences, Outcomes and Implications," *Journal of Child Psychology and Psychiatry*, 45(3), 553–566; Mosley, J., and Thomson, E., 1995, "Fathering Behavior and Child Outcomes: The Role of Race and Poverty," in *Fatherhood: Contemporary Theory, Research and Social Policy*, edited by W. Marsiglio, Thousand Oaks, CA: Sage, pp. 148–165.

48. Dunn et al., 2004.

49. Roy, K., 2006, "Father Stories: A Life Course Examination of Paternal Identity among Low-Income African American Men," *Journal of Family Issues*, 27, 31–54.

50. McLoyd, V.C., 1989, "Socialization and Development in a Changing Economy: The Effects of Paternal Job and Income Loss on Children," *American Psychologist*, 44, 293–302.

51. McLoyd, V.C., 1990; Taylor, R.J., Leashore, B.R., and Toliver, S., 1988, "An Assessment of the Provider Role as Perceived by Black Males," *Family Relations*, 27, 426–431.

52. Mincy and Sorensen, 1998.

53. Coltrane, 1995.

54. Marsiglio, W., 1991, "Paternal Engagement Activities with Minor Children," *Journal of Marriage and the Family*, 53, 973–986; Mosley, J., and

Thomson, E., 1995; Stier, H., and Tienda, M., 1993, "Are Men Marginal to the Family? Insights from Chicago's Inner City," in *Men, Work and Family*, edited by J. Hood, Thousand Oaks, CA: Sage, pp. 23–44.

55. Shimoni, R., Este, D., Clark, D., 2003, "Paternal Engagement in Immigrant and Refugee Families," *Journal of Comparative Family Studies*, 34(4), 555–568.

56. Carlson, M.J., and McLanahan, S.S., 2002, "Fragile Families, Father Involvement, and Public Policy," in *Handbook of Father Involvement: Multidisciplinary Perspectives*, edited by C. Tamis-LeMonda and N. Cabrera, Mahwah, NJ: Lawrence Erlbaum Associates, pp. 461–488.

57. Ibid.

58. del Pinal, J., and Singer, A., 1997, "Generations of Diversity: Latinos in the United States," *Population Bulletin*, 52, Washington, DC: Population Reference Bureau, pp. 1–48.

59. Taylor and Behnke, 2005.

60. Owusu-Bempah, K., 2001, "Racism: An Important Factor in Practice with Ethnic Minority Children and Families," in *Children in Society: Contemporary Theory, Policy and Practice*, edited by P. Foley, and J. Roche, Buckingham, England: Open University Press, pp. 42–51; Santisteban, D.A., Muir-Malcolm, J. A., Mitrani, V.B., and Szapocznik, J., 2002, "Integrating the Study of Ethnic Culture and Family Psychology Intervention Science," in *Family Psychology: Science-Based Interventions*, edited by H.A. Liddle, D.A. Santisteban, et al., Washington, DC: American Psychological Association, pp. 331–351.

61. Hoard and Anderson, 2004.

62. Hawkins and Palkovitz, 1999; Lamb, 1999.

63. Allen and Connor, 1997; Mosley and Thomson, 1995.

64. Coltrane, 1995; Mosley and Thomson, 1995.

65. Roy, 2006.

66. Behnke, 2002.

67. Carlson and McLanahan, 2002.

68. Franklin, A.J., 1998, "Treating Anger in African American Men," in *New Psychotherapy for Men*, edited by W.S. Pollack and R.F. Levant, New York: John Wiley and Sons, pp. 239–258; Franklin, A.J., and Boyd-Franklin, N., 2000, "Invisibility Syndrome: A Clinical Model of the Effects of Racism on African-American Males," *American Journal of Orthopsychiatry*, 70, 33–41; Majors, R., and Billson, J., 1992, *Cool Pose*, New York: Touchstone Publishers.

69. U.S. Bureau of the Census, 2004.

70. Amato, P., and Gilbreth, J., 1999; Amato, P., and Rivera, F., 1999, "Paternal Involvement and Children's Behavior Problems," *Journal of Marriage and the Family*, 61, 375–384.

Author Paul N. Dixon and his children, from left, Lily, Olivia, and Graham

"I Am Still Your Dad!":
Father Involvement in Children's Lives
after Divorce

Nate R. Cottle and Paul N. Dixon

It is not so hard to find nonresidential dads. There are many—some may be among your coworkers. In our case, several professors were sitting around a table working on a grant application, ironically, to evaluate a program aimed at teaching nurturing parenting skills to nonresidential fathers. We were working together by virtue of our skills in various disciplines from areas across a large campus. We did not really know each other professionally and certainly not personally. We discussed how many of these fathers felt distanced from their children as a result of divorce and subsequent living arrangements. As the group began to express grief for these fathers, two men broke away from the group into a personal conversation. Each had been divorced and found it difficult to remain close to his children. As they discussed the similarities in their experiences, their emotions were very close to the surface. It was easy to see the love they had for their children.

Going home to one's children has special meaning after feeling that universal sense of loss. Holding a daughter or son in one's arms and spending the evening playing dollies, trucks, or dress up becomes a more precious time. Giving a child a bath and reading to her until she falls asleep takes on new meaning as one recalls the conversation of those fathers. How fortunate a father is to have his children there to parent day to day.

And then consider the two fathers who were sitting in that same meeting with colleagues they knew only professionally, listening to the conversation move to strategies for fathers to remain close to their children when they are not the residential parent, caught in that moment of painful memories of all those precious times lost with their children. There is a special empathy, a special sense of relationship among those sharing a common loss. One sees it in combat veterans and widows and widowers of particular age groups. One also sees it among fathers who for many different reasons lost time—forever lost—with their children. A look down the table and eye contact tell all. They share sadness. So many important moments with their children have slipped away.

Nonresidential fathers may face the prospect of a distant relationship with their children. Today, however, there is good news. With knowledge of new ways of co-parenting, desire, and some hard work, fathers can be more involved in their children's lives than they have been in the past. In this chapter we examine how nonresidential fathers may remain involved in their children's lives after a divorce. We first explore the effects of divorce on children. Next we make a case for the importance of father involvement. We then address obstacles to quality interaction, such as custody arrangements and other factors. Finally, we offer some ideas that may help nonresidential fathers find ways to overcome these obstacles and fulfill their roles as dads.

When Divorce Occurs

A member of a family may fill numerous roles simultaneously, such as husband, father, son, and brother. When an individual makes a decision in one of these roles, it may have profound and important implications for his other roles within the family setting. Among the most challenging decisions an individual may make or be forced to accept in family life is divorce. The decision to divorce may be a welcome relief to a frustrated husband. However, the choice may be much more difficult for the same person who is also a father. No one likely enters a marriage expecting it to end in divorce; however, recent estimates suggest that between 40% and 45% of all first marriages may eventually do so.[1] The likelihood of divorce varies widely based on factors such as personality differences, religiosity, parental divorce, abuse, age at marriage, level of education, and other influences. It is a reality, however, that many fathers will be faced with the difficult decision of whether or not to end their marriage and likely decrease their interaction with their children. Although no label may sufficiently describe him, a father who does not live with his children on a day-to-day basis will be referred to in this chapter as a nonresidential father.

What Are the Effects of Divorce?

When a divorce occurs, each father is likely concerned for his children's well-being and may feel that his divorce could have a negative impact on them. Although several longitudinal studies have been conducted to investigate both the short- and long-term effects of divorce, results from these studies have been somewhat mixed. The current portrait of divorce and its effects leaves a somewhat muddled picture for a divorcing father to consider. But there are a number of features that can be discussed to further illuminate what happens when children experience the divorce of their parents. The reality is that some children will suffer lasting, negative effects from a divorce, whereas others may experience only moderately adverse effects or may be resilient and remain relatively unaffected. How can a father know beforehand whether his children will be greatly affected or unscathed by his divorce?

Take, for example, the case of Daniel Hillard, a newly divorced father who tried everything possible to remain involved with his children for their well-being. His flexible work schedule allowed him to pick up the kids each day from school until he lost joint custody of them. He agonized over his separation from his children until he resorted to desperate measures. Most know Daniel by the name Mrs. Euphegenia Doubtfire from the movie *Mrs. Doubtfire,* which portrays the saga of a divorced father who wishes to be a good and involved father to his children. He wishes to see them, enjoy their company, and be attentive to their needs. In the film, he resorts to masquerading as an older woman so he can be a caregiver to his children. Although we do not suggest that any father take such drastic actions, we hope each nonresidential father feels a personalized concern for his children and a strong desire to be close to them.

Fathers and others, however, need to be careful about accepting some of the "gloom-and-doom" scenarios given about divorce and children. Parents may, through their actions, compensate for or reduce some of these negative effects. Some key issues affecting children and fathers during divorce are the level of conflict between spouses, economic and behavioral effects of the divorce, and physical separation from one's children.

Issues of Parental Conflict

The frequency and intensity of conflict between spouses has an important influence on a child's well-being. Some research has shown that, although there may be fewer direct, long-term effects of divorce than previously thought, children tended to do better if the divorce removed them from a conflictual family situation.[2] In other words, divorce may at times be a better option if the continuing conflict between parents is reduced as a result. Thus, a father who is considering divorce must contemplate whether the divorce will end the conflict that may be detrimental to his children's well-being. One of the difficulties in forecasting the end of the conflict between spouses is that post-divorce interaction with the ex-spouse is ripe with opportunities for continued conflict in which the child may be stuck in the middle (e.g., child support payments, custody/visitation issues, and new romantic relationships for the divorced parents).

Economic and Social Consequences of Divorce for Children

Additional research on the effects of divorce has also focused on other factors that may be associated with children's well-being. Children's economic well-being, for example, may be greatly decreased as a result of divorce, even when financial support is ordered and paid. Children may also feel alienated from their father or mother due to the negative behavior of one parent toward the other. Additionally, due to the loss of a spouse, a mother or father may rely emotionally on a child for support or to fill the role of the ex-spouse. Each of these patterns may greatly affect the well-being of children. Fathers who wish to minimize potential negative effects need to learn as much as possible and take steps to counteract economic or relationship problems that could be harmful to children.

Physical Separation between Fathers and Children

Divorce also affects father-child relationships due to the physical separation between fathers and their children. A divorce often results in a father's physical separation from his children, as he may be forced to find a new place to live. This situation can create challenges because fathers are less able to connect with children on a regular basis, may miss out on daily interactions with children, and must negotiate with a former spouse in parenting their children. A father who is divorced and does not live with his children has often been referred to either as a *noncustodial* or *nonresidential* father. These terms, however, are not interchangeable; a nonresidential father may share custody of his children, yet he may not live with them. The term nonresidential father often provides a more accurate portrayal of the plight of the divorced father. Since five out of six custodial parents are mothers,[3] we focus primarily on the situation in which a father is separated from his children as a result of divorce and on the importance of his continued involvement with his children.

Continuing Involvement with Children Following Divorce

One research finding that constantly astonishes students in our parenting classes is the relationship between father involvement and onset of sexual activity and risks of teenaged pregnancy for their children. Various research studies report that children, especially girls, who have a connected relationship to their fathers are more likely to delay participation in sexual interactions until they are older.[4] Our students eventually see the logic behind this finding, but many fail to realize how pervasive a father's influence can be.

Clearly, a father's involvement is very important in his child's life. This continues to be true following divorce unless there are exceptional or problematic circumstances (such as abuse, etc.). Children need their fathers. However, there is no simple answer to the question of how much contact a nonresidential father should have with his children. Some may think more is better, but the research suggests that *better is better*. In other words, the amount of contact is important, but more important is the quality of the contact, especially the closeness of the relationship between father and child.

When fathers ask what a close relationship entails, they are often amazed that all their children need is to feel loved, cared for, and accepted. Although the formula appears to be simple, these feelings require that a father invest time, emotion, and, most important, himself. They must pay attention to their children and look for opportunities to get beyond the normal chitchat. Fathers and children also benefit as fathers practice authoritative parenting, which involves being both warm (through responsiveness) and structured (by setting and enforcing limits).[5] Unfortunately, many nonresidential fathers may be prone to display either less warmth when they are controlling (authoritarian parenting) or less control when they are responsive (permissive parenting).

Given the diversity in family circumstances, a father must adapt his desire for involvement to best meet the needs of his children in any given situation. A number of factors may help a father determine how much and what quality of interaction he may have with his children.[6] These factors may include parental issues (e.g., psychological adjustment, parental conflict, addiction/abuse, or parenting skills), child issues (e.g., temperament, gender, siblings, or special needs), and situational issues (e.g., visit length, proximity, or economic or housing conditions). A father may not be able to modify all of these factors, but they may have a great impact on his involvement. Structural obstacles, such as custody arrangements, relationships with ex-spouses, and efforts to begin new relationships, may require a father to put forth a considerable effort to remain involved. At times, unfortunately, such situations may entirely deny his access to his children for a time. Based on these factors and individual situations, a father may choose or be forced into varying options to increase, maintain, or limit the amount of his involvement. Ideally, however, fathers will maintain significant and regular involvement with their children after divorce and work to overcome possible barriers.

Does continuing involvement really make a difference? Existing research on the close involvement of a father with his children appears to be consistent regardless of the residential situation. A number of studies on child outcomes have demonstrated the positive relationship between quality father involvement and well-being of the child in a number of domains. A nonresidential father may serve as a teacher, supporter, and challenger for his children, perhaps even at a greater level of influence than many resident fathers provide.[7] A variety of studies exploring the associations between children's *healthy* relationships with their nonresidential fathers and their eventual outcomes suggest that children who have these close relationships appear typically to do better than those who do not in the following areas:

- psychological well-being (e.g., higher self-confidence, avoidance of depression, drug use, early sexual intercourse, externalizing and internalizing behaviors);
- social well-being (e.g., more positive peer relationships and popularity); and
- academic performance (improved grades and academic functioning).[8]

In fact, one study found that nonresidential father involvement predicted success in these areas more so than closeness in any other relationship in a divorced family.[9] Clearly, the nonresidential father has a critical role in his children's lives. As evidence mounts regarding the importance of fathering, whether fully residential or on a visitation basis, fathers must seek to find the best ways to overcome the many obstacles standing between them and their children.

Custody, Visitation, Support, and Beyond

The very terms *custody* and *visitation* conjure visions of prison life and loss of freedom. The names given to these very important parenting components affect the ways individuals interact with their children. If fathers have visitation, they are more likely to feel and act only as visitors in their children's lives. When fathers have custody, they feel a kind of ownership, and children may feel as though they are nothing more than possessions. While custody may remain the legal terminology, the best practice for parents to adopt is *shared parenting* or *cooperative parenting*. Visitation popularly describes the nonresidential father's time with his children, but *parent time* is a useful alternative phrase that helps a father visualize a better time with his children (kids aren't prisoners that parents "get to visit"). Also, the term *visitation schedule* is better replaced by a *parenting plan*, which suggests that divorced parents think more carefully and proactively about how to adjust and work together for the welfare of their children.

One of the biggest obstacles the nonresidential father may face in his involvement with his children is the parenting arrangement. Although the data suggest that mothers are five times as likely to be awarded sole custody of their children, many fathers do not contest and often agree willingly to these arrangements.

Practical Strategies for Nonresidential Father Involvement after Divorce

Divorced fathers face an uphill battle in remaining involved. Researchers have found less than one-third of boys and one-fourth of girls reported having a close relationship with nonresidential fathers compared to more than two-thirds of children from intact families.[10] Although these numbers seem staggering, many fathers overcome obstacles and remain a part of their children's lives. In many studies, closeness or a father's love is measured by children's perceptions of a father's acceptance and affection,[11] an important investment that can have significant consequences. We suggest the following tips to help fathers stay involved. We encourage fathers to determine what works for them and continually strive to improve their relationships with their children.

- **Sacrifice for the children.** Although it is important for a father to be sure his own needs are met, it is paramount for him to meet his children's needs. He can show them he cares by giving them his greatest asset, himself—his time, talents, and resources. He may have to alter his schedule at times, but his children will notice his efforts.
- **Mothers as gatekeepers.** Regardless of the divorce declaration, whether or not a father has access to his children often comes down to the relationship he has with his former spouse. A father must take the high road and avoid conflict to ensure future contact with his children. Also, mothers may serve as a key source of information on the daily happenings that are so vital to being part of the children's lives.
- **Follow-through.** A father can win over his children, and to a lesser extent his ex-spouse, when he shows he will follow through on his commitments. It is important for him to do what he says—whether a promise to do something with his child or a claim that his child support payment will be on time.
- **Gathering information.** A father may talk with his children's mother, teachers, doctors, or friends' parents to learn more about their lives. Persistence is the key. Many will notice his efforts and help look out for him and his children. It is important for a father to learn as much as possible about being a good parent through books, groups, and the Internet.
- **Don't take "fine" for an answer.** A father should actively seek to find out what is happening with his children. When they notice his sincerity, they will open up, if only a little, and let him into their lives. Additionally, a father should ask questions that do not allow a one-word answer. Instead of "How was school?" a father may say, "Tell me one experience you had today."

Additionally, in almost half of the cases in which mothers are not awarded custody, someone other than the father gets custody.[12] Many states have adopted a joint custody framework in which parents are intended to share custody and work out their co-parenting efforts. These arrangements may differ from sole custody in name only, as a father may see his child on a weekday night and every other weekend. In these circumstances, fathers are encouraged to communicate with the children's mother regarding the limitations placed on them as effective parents by the custody arrangements. With time and good intentions, shared parenting in the truest sense may be achieved.

Another significant element of fathers' lives following divorce is the responsibility of financially providing for their children via child support. Courts typically assess a specific amount that most nonresidential fathers must pay monthly for the financial support of their children. Unfortunately, too often the role of fathering for nonresidential fathers has been reduced to making a child support payment. Although child support cannot replace a father in any way, such economic support is important for children's well-being. Research findings imply an association between custody or visitation and payment of child support. Recent analysis shows a 77 percent rate of compliance with child support obligations for those nonresidential fathers with a regular schedule for seeing and caring for their children.[13] By contrast, there is only a 56 percent rate of compliance with child support obligations for those who are not able to regularly see their children. It is unclear, though, whether being more engaged through custody and visitation causes increased payment of child support or vice versa. Perhaps those who pay their child support feel a greater desire to visit their children simply because they pay the support, or, conversely, those who visit their children feel a greater willingness to pay support because of their interactions with their children. In either case, a father should pay child support in an effort to promote his children's economic and psychological well-being and to stay involved in their lives by avoiding a refusal of custody or visitation.

More Than "Disneyland Dads"

A divorced father seeking involvement with his children may find himself falling into the "Disneyland dad" approach to nonresidential parenting. Despite its negative connotation, this "let's go play" style of father involvement occurs frequently, and it might be helpful to explore it briefly. The term *Disneyland dad* is widely recognized as a pattern of parenting interactions characterized mainly by entertaining one's children apparently without most traditional parenting responsibilities. There are many reasons why a father may end up *hosting* rather than parenting a child. A father who does not live close to his children has few practical choices other than recreation for places to go and things to do.[14] Further,

Lessons Learned from Students of Divorced Families

Having taught an undergraduate parenting course requiring students to observe four to six hours of divorce and custody cases in county court, we have many sad tales to tell from students' own personal experiences—often about abuse, neglect, disappointment, or hurt. Many (average age 18–20) are products of divorce and have just left home for school. It is their first chance to distance themselves emotionally from their parents. Some have good stories:

- "My mom never has said anything bad about my dad."
- "They kept the house. We stayed there, and they took turns being with us every month. We stayed at the same school and everything."
- "Since I've grown up, I've gotten to know my dad, and we are a lot closer."
- "They have always been pretty nice to each other."
- "I lived with Dad, but I felt okay about being with Mom any time I wanted."

Unfortunately, they say fewer positive things when it comes to the divorce and its aftermath. What they say about nonresident fathers says a lot:

- "My father always tells me how bad my mother is. It gets old."
- "My father never sees me. I've gotten to where I don't care any more."
- "My dad was never around."
- "I wanted to be with my dad, but 'they' wouldn't let me."
- "I always felt guilty—like I needed to apologize to my dad when I was with my mom and like I needed to apologize to Mom when I was with Dad."
- "I don't know why I am taking parenting. I'm not going to have kids. I don't want them to go through what I did."
- "You say we tend to parent as we were parented. Are you sure? I know I will do it differently. I don't want my children to grow up like I did."
- "My sister and I were just used by them to get back at each other."

The theme of all the tales is the same: children are hurt; they are the ammunition and the target in many divorces. Our students' stories reflect what they see in court: children being pulled apart, a parent on each arm screaming "he's mine," or parents arguing over who has to take the child. No stories are as dramatic as the students' facial expressions. We know the statistics but are always struck by how widespread and deep the hurt of divorce and its aftermath can be. We fathers can and must do better—by putting our children first and finding creative ways to be the best parents possible.

because visits are often short and made shorter by the physical and psychological transition of a child from Mom to Dad and place to place, time alone is a limiting factor in building a constructive parental interaction.

Because a nonresidential father is not often party to the day-to-day happenings of his children's lives, he does not usually know about that bullying incident after school or a child's confusion over long division in math class. It takes time and often happenstance to learn the little things affecting children. Asking a child "How's school going?" during that Wednesday visitation usually gets a response of "fine" and little more. Fathers can become discouraged and may disengage or simply fall back on pizza, movies, and, yes, Disneyland. It is not easy for a nonresidential father to monitor children's behavior.[15]

The Disneyland dad may also be the parent this disparaging term usually brings to mind: a father who is uninvolved as a nonresidential parent because he was uninvolved before he was separated from his children by divorce. This is a stereotypical image of dad, and it is one reality. There are fathers who did not attend to their children in marriage and do not attend to their children in separation or following divorce. This disengagement can take the form of abandonment at its extreme or, congruent with the stereotype of fathers as the less involved parent, it may simply represent much of society's expectation of fathers.[16] Low expectations lead to meager results. In a study of nonresidential parents, researchers found that nonresidential fathers, as the Disneyland Dad stereotype would predict, spent much of their visitation time with children in leisure activities.[17] However, it is important to note researchers also found that nonresidential mothers typically expressed a similar pattern of behavior. Perhaps the term Disneyland dad would be better expressed as Disneyland parent (although it doesn't sound as cute). It appears that many times, of necessity, nonresidential parents of either sex are led to a "fun and run" means of spending time with their children.

Is there a way out? Does a nonresidential dad have opportunities to be the father his children need? There are ways to improve the quality of a father's relationship to his children in a nonresidential relationship. The belief that a father can have a quality relationship with his children is the first, and perhaps most important, step.

Steps toward Meaningful Involvement in Divorce Situations

Nonresidential fathers need to become more informed of their children's lives outside of their limited time spent together during visitation. This information is paramount to effectively using the fathering skills discussed elsewhere in this book. Fathers can take a number of steps to strengthen their meaningful involvement with their kids despite having experienced divorce. Key steps include trying to develop a productive, working relationship with the children's mother, pursuing normal family activities with children, getting more involved in understanding and tracking children's needs, and seeking out information and ideas to assist with parenting from books, classes, or support programs for divorced parents.

Steps toward Cooperative Parenting

Trying to develop a nonhostile, mutually respectful relationship for cooperative parenting with a child's mother is an important step toward meaningful involvement. A father's contact with a child's mother is an important source of helpful information and predictor of a father's involvement with his children.[18] Regular and meaningful contact and communication is obviously confounded by the stresses of divorce and parents' differing perceptions of custody arrangements. Generally, each parent overestimates the degree of the other's parenting satisfaction. Often neither parent is as happy with the situation as the other thinks.[19] Sadly, there are often two distressed and disappointed parents both wanting the best for their children and trying their best in isolation. Again, communication is key to cooperation, and cooperation is key to successful co-parenting. Efforts must be made to encourage the kind of relationship with the child's mother that will help fathers integrate normal, everyday family activities and not just recreation into their time with children. Whether the nonresidential father and the residential mother can get along or not, a father has work to do to have a fruitful relationship with his children.

Normal Family Activities

No one ever said parenting was easy. It certainly does not get any easier when children's routines are physically and psychologically disrupted. It should also be noted that fathers also disrupt their normal activities for time together. A nonresidential father usually yearns for opportunities to just be a parent, an everyday parent—no eating out, no Disneyland. While time constraints limit the chances for visitation to center around everyday life, *fathers should make every effort to keep time together as normal as possible.* Depending on the children's ages, it is entirely reasonable and healthy for the children for fathers to share time during the visit interacting with other adults or performing and requiring the children to perform the tasks of running a household—simply making some effort to carry on "business as usual." However, even Disneyland dad interaction can be good parenting if the activity itself does not become the central focus of the visitation relationship. Time spent in fun, recreational interaction is a healthy aspect of how fathers engage with their children. Leisure activities that encourage father-child interaction serve the important purpose of presenting a positive male role that will endure beyond the time spent together.

What is Parental Alienation Syndrome?

Successfully developing and maintaining a constructive relationship with a former spouse may be particularly difficult given differing perceptions and the continuing emotional, legal, and economic stresses of divorce. However, the need for a constructive relationship is enormous: the children's welfare is at stake. The ways children may be victimized in divorce and the tumultuous years that follow are legend. Often, they become the "weapons" of warring ex-spouses. Attempts to turn children against the other parent are common. At its extreme, this pattern is described as Parental Alienation Syndrome.[20]

This syndrome is described as a steadfast effort on the part of a residential parent, usually the mother, to "program" her children to reject the nonresidential parent. Children may resist efforts on the part of the mother to alienate them from the nonresidential father, but their resistance eventually may be overcome. Additionally, assertive efforts, in and out of court, by the father may only lead to further stress for his children. Unfortunately, children's well-being suffers the most in custodial arrangements where the mother is most dissatisfied with the amount of father involvement (either too much or too little).[21] In the most extreme cases, a father may have little choice but to wait for his children to reach a level of maturity that allows them a clear understanding of the situation.

Facing what may be a hopeless situation, a nonresidential father can, at least, make the worst of circumstances a shade better for his children. Sometimes selfless efforts to meet the children's needs ultimately promote mutually constructive behavior among the parents, and everyone, particularly the children, will win. Parental alienation syndrome represents the worst of outcomes for parents following divorce, and families and children suffer when spouses cannot learn to work together.

Responding to Children's Needs

A third meaningful step toward positive involvement is for nonresidential fathers to focus on getting more involved in understanding and tracking their children's needs. If a father has not been involved in his children's lives, now is the time to start. If the relationship with the mother is reasonable, it is time to ask questions. A mother may not always be there to take care of a fever or tell a neighbor whether a child is allowed to play on the trampoline. Information is the key. Even if the nonresidential father has no productive communication with the mother, many custodial agreements allow fathers the right to access health and school records. When a father meets with school officials concerning his children, he needs to leave a clear message of interest in his children's education and a desire for substantive information and feedback. Fathers can request that schools send him all information from his child's classroom and the school so he can stay engaged with what is happening. School counselors may serve as important mediators between former spouses in the interest of the children and as sources of information about school-related issues for nonresidential and residential parents.[22] School administrators and medical personnel, including mental health service providers counseling children, are also able to help keep a nonresidential father informed if he has been given legal access to children's records. A father should remember that the stereotypical nonresidential father is thought by many to have no interest and no right to such records. Such requests, therefore, may be considered unusual and met with suspicion. A nonresidential father should understand his legal rights and have a copy of the divorce agreement handy when requesting information about his children. In most cases, a nonresidential father can and should become better informed about the lives of his children and ways to best support them.

Seek Parenting Knowledge and Support

While the nonresidential father faces special parenting challenges, some things remain constant among all fathers. *A fourth step that can be productive is for fathers to seek out information and ideas to assist with parenting from books, classes, or support programs for divorced parents.* Some basic parenting skills have been found to improve the lives of children and, in turn, their parents. All fathers should work at this tough job by reading and attending programs about good parenting. Plenty of self-help books, Internet resources, workshops, support groups, and classes promote good parenting. As a nonresident father faces unique challenges, like any good parent he can always strive to do better and improve his efforts.

Conclusion

We believe good fathering is important to children's welfare. The charge to residential and nonresidential fathers alike may be best summed up in the old slogan of the U.S. Army: *Be all you can be.* A nonresidential father may face additional obstacles in achieving this goal. Whether that means he can only make his child support payment faithfully or that he can care for his child completely on a day-to-day basis, he should do so to the best of his ability. Each father should explore how best to be involved in his given situation.

Fathers who have divorced and do not live with their children face both obstacles to and opportunities for involvement. In summary, a father can do several critical things to maintain and strengthen his involvement:

- be active in the decision-making process of the custody arrangement to secure what is best for the child and his involvement,
- structure his interaction with his children to include more normal parenting and perhaps fewer leisure activities,
- improve the quality of his involvement and relationships with his children by limiting the amount of conflict with his ex-spouse,
- seek out as much information, including school and medical issues, as possible to help him parent more effectively, and
- try to improve his skills as a parent through accessing information from sources such as classes, books, and support groups.

Although there is no simple formula or recipe to fit every situation, both the residential and nonresidential father can do many of these things to increase the amount and quality of interaction with his children.

The bottom line is the children's well-being. Fathers and mothers must think first of their children, and both need to be involved in their children's lives regardless of the residential situation. It's not easy when still sitting on the battlefield of a divorce, but then nobody said parenting was easy. It is parents' responsibility to overcome petty jealousy, "prize" fights (who gets that lamp—or that child), and the blame game to protect their children from the anguish and anger of divorce, no matter what ill effects the adults may suffer. In short, we must do our best.

Endnotes

1. Schoen, R., and Standish, N., 2001, "The Retrenchment of Marriage in the U.S.," *Population and Development Review*, 27, 553–563.

2. Amato, P.R., Loomis, L.S., and Booth, A., 1995, "Parental Divorce, Marital Conflict, and Offspring Well-Being during Early Adulthood," *Social Forces*, 73, 895–915.

3. U.S. Bureau of the Census, 2003, *Custodial Mothers and Fathers and Their Child Support: 2001,* Current Population Reports, Series P60, No. 225, Washington, DC: U.S. Government Printing Office.

4. Ellis, B.J., Bates, J.E., Dodge, K.A., Fergusson, D.M., Horwood, L.J., Pettit, G.S., and Woodward, L., 2003, "Does Father Absence Place Daughters at Special Risk for Early Sexual Activity and Teenage Pregnancy?" *Child Development*, 74, 801–821.

5. Amato, P.R., and Gilbreth, J.G., 1999, "Nonresident Fathers and Children's Well-Being: A Meta-Analysis," *Journal of Marriage and the Family*, 61, 557–573.

6. Curtner-Smith, M.E., 1995, "Assessing Children's Visitation Needs with Divorced Noncustodial Fathers," *Families in Society*, 76, 341–349.

7. Munsch, J., Woodward, J., and Darling, D., 1995, "Children's Perceptions of Their Relationships with Coresiding and Noncustodial Fathers," *Journal of Divorce and Remarriage*, 23, 39–54.

8. Amato, P.R., and Gilbreth, J.G., 1999; Bronstein, P., Stoll, M.F., Clauson, J., Abrams, C.L., and Briones, M., 1994, "Fathering after Separation of Divorce: Factors Predicting Child Adjustment," *Family Relations*, 43, 463–479; Guttmann, J., and Rosenberg, M., 2003, "Emotional Intimacy and Children's Adjustment: A Comparison between Single-Parent Divorced and Intact Families," *Educational Psychology*, 23, 457–472.

9. Guttmann and Rosenberg, 2003.

10. Hetherington, E.M., and Kelly, J., 2002, *For Better or For Worse: Divorce Reconsidered,* New York: W.W. Norton and Company.

11. Rohner, R.P., and Veneziano, R.A., 2001, "The Importance of Father Love: History and Contemporary Evidence," *Review of General Psychology*, 5, 382–405.

12. Stewart, S.D., 1999, "Disneyland Dads, Disneyland Moms?" *Journal of Family Issues*, 20, 539–556.

13. U.S. Bureau of the Census, 2003.

14. Greif, G.L., and Pabst, M.S., 1988, *Mothers without Custody,* Lexington, MA: Lexington Books.

15. Maccoby, E., and Mnookin, R., 1992, *Dividing the Child: Social and Legal Dilemmas of Custody,* Cambridge, MA: Harvard Press.

16. Arditti, J.A., 1995, "Noncustodial Parents: Emergent Issues of Diversity and Process," *Marriage and Family Review*, 1–2, 283–304.

17. Stewart, 1999.

18. McKenry, P.C., Price, S.J., Fine, M.A., and Serovich, J., 1992, "Predictors of Single, Noncustodial Fathers' Physical Involvement with Their Children," *Journal of Genetic Psychology*, 153, 305–319.

19. Madden-Derdich, D.A., and Leonard, S.A., 2002, "Shared Experiences, Unique Realities: Formerly Married Mothers' and Fathers' Perceptions of Parenting and Custody after Divorce," *Family Relations*, 51, 37–45.

20. Stewart, 1999.

21. King, V., and Heard, H.E., 1999, "Nonresident Father Visitation, Parental Conflict, and Mother's Satisfaction: What's Best for Child Well-Being?" *Journal of Marriage and the Family*, 61, 385–396.

22. Friedman, B.B., 1994, "Children of Divorced Parents: Action Steps for the Counselor to Involve Fathers," *Elementary School Guidance and Counseling*, 28, 197–205.

Author Randell D. Turner with his wife, Robin, director of the Father's Workshop of York County

From Behind Prison Walls: Incarcerated Fathers and Their Children

Randell D. Turner

" **A** man will never change his behavior until he changes the way he views himself!" This profound statement came from Robert, a 32-year-old incarcerated father of four serving a prison sentence of life without parole in Pennsylvania. If you had the opportunity to meet and get to know Robert as I have, you would find a very loving and gentle man. He is a man who, despite the harsh barriers of prison, has managed to stay intimately involved in the lives of his children. As a matter of fact, as I have traveled around the country working with fathers from all walks of life, I have found that some of the most remarkable fathers have been incarcerated. That may be surprising to some. However, anyone who has worked with incarcerated fathers has found this to be true.

I first met Robert in 1996 when I went to the State Correctional Institution (SCI) at Albion, Pennsylvania, to conduct a workshop for incarcerated fathers. He became one of the initial peer leaders who worked with me to develop Long Distance Dads, an educational curriculum for incarcerated fathers. For 18 months we worked with more than a dozen incarcerated fathers who became the heart of the Long Distance Dads Program at SCI–Albion. As a result of the success of the Long Distance Dads curriculum, for almost a decade I have been directing staff training at more than 300 federal, state, and county prisons nationwide. In 2002 a Hispanic edition of Long Distance Dads was completed, which added much-needed resources for Hispanic incarcerated fathers. For the past three years, I have been working to develop programs to aid incarcerated parents in the transition from prison to home. This was the original vision of Long Distance Dads, to connect incarcerated fathers with their children and help prepare them to return to their families.

Prison is just one of a number of settings in which men can be found, and it is important that we not forget that *many men in prison are also fathers.* In this chapter I wish to explore some of what we know about fathers in prison, share an inside view of what can happen with support for fathers in prison settings, and discuss the impact of fatherhood support efforts on fathers, families, and prisons. Finally, I will discuss key elements for developing a successful program and my vision for incarcerated parents.

What Do We Know about Fathers in Prison?

In 2003, for the first time in U.S. history, according to the Department of Justice, more than 2,085,620 individuals were incarcerated in local jails or state and federal prisons—two *million*![1] Throughout the country, policymakers, law enforcement, and local communities are seeking to learn why the incarceration rate is so high. Scientific research is showing the breakdown of family ties along with its resulting effects is a leading contributor to "at risk" behavior. "At risk" behavior includes delinquency, drug use, and other activities that can lead to criminal behavior and incarceration. In fact, children raised without strong, positive family relationships are much more likely to become incarcerated than those raised with strong, positive family relationships.[2]

Tens of thousands of those incarcerated in the United States are also parents, and the majority of those are fathers. Research has been lacking on the topic of incarceration and its effects on families in the United States. A special report released in August 2000 from the U.S. Bureau of Justice Statistics on incarcerated parents and their children contributes perhaps the most comprehensive information about fathers in prison, including the following points:

■   In 1999 an estimated 721,500 state and federal prisoners were parents to 1,498,800 children under the age of 18.

- Prior to admission, less than half of the parents in state prisons reported having lived with their children (44 percent of fathers, 64 percent of mothers).
- Fifty-five percent of men in state prisons and 63 percent of men in federal prisons reported being the parent of at least one minor child. The majority of the minor children (58 percent) reported were less than 10 years old.
- Nearly two in three state prisoners reported at least monthly contact with their children by phone, mail, or personal visits. However, a majority of fathers (57 percent) in state prison reported never having a personal visit with their children since admission but rather contact by phone or mail.
- Nearly half of all imprisoned parents were black; about a quarter were white.
- Half of the parents in state prison had never married.
- A majority of parents in prison were violent offenders or drug traffickers.
- A majority of parents in state prison used drugs in the month before their offense.
- On average, parents expected to serve 80 months in state prison and 103 months in federal prison.
- More than 75 percent of parents in state prison reported a prior conviction; 56 percent had been incarcerated previously.[3]

As some of these numbers show, fathers who are incarcerated face significant challenges in maintaining any kind of consistent and meaningful relationship with their minor children. An emphasis on their roles and responsibilities as fathers, however, may be one of the strongest motivations to make needed changes in their lives.

The United States incarcerates more adult males per capita than any other nation in the world. By the middle of 2002, more than 1.8 million men were incarcerated in state and federal prisons and local jails.[4] Yet with all of these men being incarcerated, when I began working with incarcerated fathers in 1996, there were only 10 identifiable incarcerated fatherhood programs nationwide.[5] Three were being facilitated off and on in a county prison, and only two had any history of working within state prison systems. Nearly a decade later, incarcerated fatherhood programs are commonplace in many state prisons and becoming more prevalent in local and county prisons, too.

Why work with incarcerated fathers? What can we offer them? Are such men teachable? And how much of an impact do fathers really have on their children from behind bars? In the pages that follow, I hope to answer these questions and shed further light on the world of incarcerated fathers.

An Inside View of Support for Incarcerated Fathers

It's 8:30 a.m. Inmates have been given the "call out" to go to their work assignments or classes for the day. About 55 incarcerated fathers have gathered in the main lobby of the education building, waiting for the correction officer (CO) to let them into the classroom where the Long Distance Dads program is held every Wednesday morning. None is required to be here. They don't get any credit on their file, and some have asked to be excused from their work duties in order to attend the 12-week program.

Twelve inmate peer leaders, the program director, and a prison staff member are setting things up in the classroom. Chairs are placed into five small group circles, and discussion handouts are distributed to each peer leader. At 8:55, the CO lets the men enter the classroom. The room comes alive with conversation and greetings. At 9:00, the program director calls roll and turns the morning over to the small-group peer leaders. For the next 90 minutes, inmate fathers from all walks of life will discuss the topic for today: "Learning How to Nurture our Children."

Joe's group starts talking about last week's assignment. They had been given a "My Child's Information" inventory sheet to send home, asking their child's mother or guardian to fill it out and mail it back. One of the guys reports to the group he's already received the information sheet back from his child's mother. He is totally surprised; he didn't think she would take the time. One of the other fathers in the group expresses the hope that his ex-wife will do the same for him. He hasn't had much contact with his four children since coming to prison. The discussion continues and focuses on how many of us make assumptions about our children, our ex-wives, or the mothers of our children.

All the groups abide by the following rules: (1) what is said here stays here, (2) don't dominate the group, and (3) if you violate rules one or two, you will be asked to leave the group. It is interesting to note that Joe's group has added an additional rule: no discussions about politics, religion, or NASCAR! I guess the two fathers from West Virginia have some strong opinions not necessarily shared by the others.

In the back of the room, Michael's group is answering questions on a worksheet that is one of the discussion tools for today's topic. Once they are finished, Michael will open up the floor to discuss what they have written. He likes to have them fill out their answers first because it makes them accountable for their way of thinking and responding as fathers. If a father writes something down, he may learn through the group discussion that his thinking is flawed or needs to be re-evaluated. His own handwriting reveals this flaw in thinking and holds him accountable to do something about it. He has learned from the group that his children will suffer because of his unwillingness to change.

That is an example of what incarcerated fathers learn in prison programs to support fathers and families. They learn that *change is possible* but difficult.

They also learn they were never supposed to learn how to be a father all by themselves. We were supposed to have a grandfather who mentored our father, who then mentored us, and so on. Along the way we should have had a close relationship with both and watched how they lived the lessons they taught us.

Unfortunately, for most of the fathers in the room, that never happened. The typical male inmate was raised in a single-parent home and has at least one other family member who has been incarcerated; one in seven male inmates was raised by a relative; 17 percent of male inmates spent time in out-of-home care.[6] The reality for many incarcerated men was the experience of growing up without a father or with one who never stayed very long. For those who had a grandfather or father in their lives, quite often the intimate or close relationship wasn't there.

This background of insufficient family mentoring is one reason incarcerated fatherhood programs are having such an impact. Each week fathers gather in small groups to develop relationships and have an opportunity to learn from each other. This is the first time some of the men have ever had this kind of discussion with another man. Being held accountable and taught what it means to be a good parent is powerful for men. Scripture refers to it this way: "Iron sharpens iron."

Many fathers in correctional settings have learned the hard way that the myth of the "self-made man" has led too many to lives of solitude. At the same time, most men are dying just to have someone to talk to about being a man and a father. This is why the fatherhood programs behind bars are growing so much. Many of these men have yearned for a safe and honest place to talk about their hopes, fears, frustrations, and dreams as fathers.

What do incarcerated men talk about in these small groups? Here are just a few of the topics from a typical program:

- developing healthy adult relationships,
- encouraging your children,
- overcoming guilt and shame,
- expressing your anger in a healthy manner,
- preparing for reentry into the community, and
- extending your heritage through generations.

A setting in which incarcerated men can learn about their children's needs, identify the significance of their lives as fathers, and gain practical support for building better relationships can have a transformative influence on these men, their families, and the prisons in which they live.

Impact of Support on Fathers, Their Families, and the Prisons

What impact do incarcerated fatherhood programs have on the fathers, their families, and the prisons that have these programs? Evidence is emerging from both research and personal experience that highlights the influence of efforts to support incarcerated fathers and families.

Penn State University, through its Center for Organizational Research, completed an evaluation on Long Distance Dads. The incarcerated fatherhood program, started in Pennsylvania, has been used in Pennsylvania by the Department of Corrections in a number of correctional institutions. The study authors reported in their 2001 executive summary one of the reasons the program works:

> The peer-led group therapy style of the Long Distance Dads Program fosters a high degree of intra-group empathy, problem solving, and support. This allowed them to draw from the experiences of others as they related to themselves. This approach actually led to the problem solving, getting in touch with emotions and interpersonal bonding with inmates—which inmates expressed as their favorite things in the group process. It is rare in an institutional setting that inmates drop their guards and allow for personal interaction, which may be taken as a sign of weakness or vulnerability. The Long Distance Dads Program helps inmates break through those walls.[7]

Breaking down the walls that may separate a father from his child emotionally can occur even when fathers are separated physically from their children due to incarceration. According to a 2001 report by the Urban Institute Justice Policy Center entitled "From Prison to Home," a 15-year study of offenders in Virginia revealed that recidivism rates were 59 percent lower for those inmates who had participated in and completed prison educational programs than those who had not.[8]

These findings provide some insight into the potential for such programs and how they can benefit incarcerated fathers. But what about the fathers and their families? What impact do such programs have on them personally?

For Robert, the program for incarcerated dads he participated in strengthened his resolve never to lose touch with his children. He was determined to do whatever it took to reestablish and improve his relationship with them. He began writing a story with his youngest daughter. He asked her to choose the main characters; she chose a princess and a good dragon. Then he asked her what she thought the story should include, and from her input he wrote a short story using the princess and the dragon as the main characters. Once he completed it, he sent her a copy; once she received it, they read it together over the phone. That first story was more than five years ago. Since then Robert and his daughter have written several chapters together, enough to make a book, as they have allowed the adventure to strengthen their relationship.

More recently, an unexpected event occurred in Robert's life. His 16-year-old daughter, whom he hadn't heard from in more than 10 years, came to visit him. He had kept writing and sending cards to her even though she never wrote back. He wasn't sure her mother was letting her get the mail. After 10 years of silence, she reached out to him, and now they are in the process of rebuilding their relationship.

One additional note: Robert is currently serving a life sentence without parole, so his efforts take on even more significance. Though he may never get to see any of his children on the outside, from within the walls of prison he is strengthening his relationships with his children and having an influence on their lives.

Simply increasing the contact incarcerated fathers have with their children is a beginning. About 58 percent of fathers in federal prison and 40 percent of fathers in state prison report some type of weekly contact with their children, usually by telephone or mail. Fatherhood programs seem to be effective in increasing such contact. For example, an outcome evaluation of the Long Distance Dads program showed an average increase in both phone calls and letters per month by fathers to their children after participation.[9] Only as fathers in prison learn the importance of such contact and develop opportunities to reach out can they better fulfill their hopes of being better parents.

Michael is a Native American father of two beautiful daughters. Because of his incarceration, he lost contact with one daughter. After participating in the Long Distance Dads program, Michael began trying to reach out to her again while also working to improve his relationship with his other daughter. His mother and father brought her for visits when they could, and their relationship has grown. Michael also volunteered to become a peer leader in the program and began working with other fathers. Through Michael's efforts many fathers also began reaching out to their children, some of them for the first time in years.

After he had been participating in the program as a peer leader for about a year, I asked Michael how the Long Distance Dads program had affected his life. What he said amazed me: "The program taught me how important it is to obey the 'white man's laws,' for my kids' sake. If I don't, I not only hurt myself, but I really hurt my kids!"

Michael is now out of prison. He is engaged to be married and is still working on rebuilding his relationships with his children. He still faces challenges with his oldest daughter but refuses to give up. That's what being a father is all about—perseverance!

One mother whose husband is in prison in Washington State reported that, when she married, her daughter was flunking out of grade school. She commented, "She was a mess, and nothing I did seemed to help her. Then she got a new dad." Even though he's been incarcerated for most of their marriage, this father has worked with his new daughter, loving her and giving her confidence in her ability to learn. The mother continued, "She's an 'A' student now. That's what his love has done for her. And now during visits I get to watch them interact like real dads and kids. You have no idea what it means to me."

Incarcerated Fatherhood Program Model

The McNeil Island Corrections Center (MICC) in Washington State has an outstanding model of support for incarcerated fathers. It includes:

Offender Accountability

- *Responsible Fatherhood.* One of the basic principles of the MICC Family and Fathering Program is offender accountability, consistent with the Offender Accountability Act passed by the state legislature a couple of years ago. Emphasis is on offenders being responsible for their actions, including responsible fatherhood. Since more than half of all inmates have children under the age of 18, offenders need to recognize that responsibility for their children doesn't end because of incarceration. If incarcerated fathers develop responsible attitudes for their children, it is believed they will feel obligated to be actively involved with their children, including staying out of prison when they are released, taking an interest, and providing financial support.

- *Children's needs.* Children need and deserve responsible, active, involved fathers—even incarcerated fathers. While not all children should have contact with their incarcerated fathers, especially those who were victimized by their fathers, in many cases children will benefit from having a positive relationship with their incarcerated father. It is often overlooked that children of incarcerated parents are also victims because they live with issues associated with having a parent in prison. MICC is providing not only opportunities for offenders to learn how to father from a distance but also programs focused on the family and children to help meet their needs.

Education

- *Long Distance Dads.* This character-based educational and support program to assist incarcerated men in developing skills to become more involved and supportive fathers, designed to be facilitated by trained peer leaders in 12 weekly sessions in a small group format, is being used in more than 300 correctional facilities in the United States, Canada, and Great Britain. The family advocate volunteers teach this class.

- *Family Dynamics.* This broad-based educational program deals with family relationships and responsibility. Participants examine their roots and childhood in order to learn how to deal with family members in a positive manner. A violence prevention element is also included in this program to help participants learn to utilize other techniques and skills in dealing with stressful situations. The curriculum is "Strengthening Multi-Ethnic Families and Communities: A Violence Prevention Parent Training Program."

■ *Marriage Encounter.* The Marriage Encounter weekend workshop is designed to strengthen relationships and improve communication between couples, including learning to trust, listening, taking risks, and placing confidence in your partner. In addition to the two yearly workshops, four reunions are conducted each year to help encourage and support the communication skills learned in the weekend workshop.

Child and Family Focus

■ *Father/Child Gift Exchange.* This event, which takes place around the winter holidays, gives incarcerated fathers and their children an opportunity to spend a fun-filled day together doing child-oriented activities (e.g., cookie decorating, craft making, exchanging gifts, etc.).

■ *Fathers' and Children's Day Program.* This event is held around Father's Day and gives incarcerated fathers an opportunity to spend a day in the recreation yard with their children. For many, this is the first time these fathers and their children can fly a kite together, throw a Frisbee, play catch, kick a soccer ball around, put together a picture frame, fly a paper airplane, plant a flower, or make a strawberry shortcake.

■ *Read to Me, Daddy.* This program is offered in conjunction with the Tacoma Confederated Women's Club, which provides children's books, cassette tapes, mailing envelopes, and postage. Participating offenders record themselves reading a book onto a tape; the tape and book are then mailed to their children so they can hear their father's voice and follow along in the book.

■ *Family Worship and Activity Time.* Offenders and their family members have the opportunity to attend a worship service together each Sunday in the chapel. Additionally, a family activity time allows incarcerated fathers to spend time with their family members in a nondenominational activity.

■ *Visiting.* Visitation serves an important role in preserving the relationship between offenders and their family and friends, which can make a positive and powerful difference to the incarcerated loved one. Visiting is offered Friday through Tuesday in the Main Institution and weekends at the North Complex.

■ *Extended Family Visits.* The department realizes the importance of maintaining strong family ties and thus provides the opportunity for Extended

Family Visits (EFV). The EFV is a visit between an offender and his or her immediate family member(s) that occurs in a private housing unit. The visits are for up to 48 hours. There must be a gap of at least 30 days between extended family visits.

Advocacy

■ *Offender Family Advocacy.* MICC was chosen as an Offender Family Advocacy Program pilot site. Family members are given a voice in addressing issues that face them or their loved one. Family advocate volunteers, who have institution business cards, a telephone, and office space, are responsible for representing offender family issues to administration.

Financial Support

■ *A Partnership for Child Support.* The Department of Corrections has partnered with the Department of Social and Health Services, Division of Child Support, and the Employment Security Department to apply for a federal grant to expand a pilot project to identify all offenders with child support issues and include child support obligations in the Offender Accountability Plan. Offenders would be screened and referred to work or employment programs upon release to enable increased payment of child support.

Community Partnership

■ *MICC Community Advisory Council.* This committee consists of representatives from local community governments, faith-based groups, Head Start, Boys and Girls Club, Steilacoom Historical School District, Safe Streets, family advocates, the Partnership for Child Support, business leaders, and interested citizens. This group advises MICC on family and fathering issues and looks for ways to partner with the community to provide services that will benefit incarcerated fathers and their families.

■ *Families Matter.* This 501(c) (3) organization includes some of the members of the MICC Community Advisory Council. The purposes of Families Matter are to encourage, equip, and provide resources and training to offenders at MICC, utilizing active community partnerships to create and sustain healthy and productive citizens.

■ *Volunteers.* Volunteers provide mentorship to offenders. They demonstrate, by example, how to be adjusted, balanced, and positive individuals.

These are just a few examples from among the hundreds of small yet significant success stories I hear from inmates, program volunteers, and prison staff members around the county. A few unique prisons have gone the extra mile and taken their incarcerated fatherhood programs to the next level.

In Pennsylvania, several state correctional institutions (SCI) have expanded from the weekly peer-led groups to developing packets of games and activities for fathers and their children to do together through the mail. At SCI–Albion, the peer leaders developed promotional spots for the institution's television that inspired fathers to write home each month and included sample starter letters, highlighting new and interesting topics for fathers to discuss with their children.[10]

The Missouri Department of Corrections partnered with the University of Missouri at Kansas City and the Office of Child Support to develop a pilot program for two state prisons. The program included weekly peer-led Long Distance Dads groups, couples' counseling, mediation services, and home visits for mothers and their children. In addition, the United Methodist Church volunteered to provide free transportation for mothers and children to visit fathers in prison.[11] Such partnership efforts reflect the realization that a culture that values family life must also value fathers and their contributions to it.

Helping incarcerated parents successfully transition back to the community is another effort that several states have undertaken in recent years. Pennsylvania's Department of Community Corrections, working with the Father's Workshop of York County, worked to implement a transition program for incarcerated parents called *Helping Offenders Parent Effectively* (HOPE) in 2002. The focus of the two-year program was to assist fathers and mothers released from state prison to reenter society and become involved in the lives of their children. Implemented in 13 community correction centers statewide, the program helped parents gain education, maintain accountability, establish custody and visitation with their children, maintain child support, and find affordable, safe housing and good jobs.[12]

These examples represent some of the progress incarcerated fatherhood programs have made thus far. Because work with incarcerated fathers is quite new, there isn't yet a lot of research data on the success of these programs. However, it is expected that better information will be forthcoming in the near future as such programs expand and mature.

Keys for Assisting Incarcerated Fathers and Their Families

In working with incarcerated fathers and their families over the years, I have found that successful programs focus on collaborations that will assist the men in developing skills in the following areas:

- *Interpersonal Relationship Skills.* Many of these fathers have never been taught how to develop and maintain a healthy relationship. Development of parenting and personal relationship skills is a key component of programs for incarcerated fathers.
- *Academic Skills.* Too many incarcerated fathers have too little successful formal education and are in need of remediation in order to be able to enter a training program if a slot is available. Assistance with literacy skills, study habits, and other work-related abilities can be critical.
- *Vocational Skills.* Developing effective vocational skills in prison can be difficult because there are too few training slots available and too many men trying to get into the training. Therefore, effective programs collaborate with other departments to encourage the fathers to get involved in any training and education program that can help them prepare for a job upon release. Men who have felonies will have significant challenges in getting jobs and reestablishing their employment history. Thus, having marketable vocational skills is paramount for these men.
- *Spiritual/Ethical Skills.* Collaboration with the prison ministry department is critical to the success of most programs—not for spiritual growth alone but also ethical and character development as well as building a faith-based support system that should follow parents into the community upon release.
- *Other Recommended Skills.* Healthcare (physical and mental), daily living skills, money management, leisure time skills, and accountability skills all can be helpful and even necessary for those who are in the prison system.[13]

In some correctional institutions, programs for incarcerated fathers have been able to collaborate with an outside agency or faith-based program to provide resources for the prison library, visiting room toys and materials, volunteers to mentor and tutor inmates, development of family day programs, and volunteers to support the prison staff responsible for implementing the program. The more broadly based the collaborative effort is, the stronger the program and its effects will be in shaping and supporting fathers in becoming better parents.

Conclusion

I believe programs to support incarcerated fathers and their families will be routinely offered by many states in the coming years. While incarcerated fathers have made mistakes and challenged the laws of society, they still continue to be fathers and family members. From within the walls of prison, there is great potential for them to connect with their children and take steps forward in strengthening their relationships and looking toward a better future. Incarcerated fatherhood programs are having a positive impact on fathers, their families, and the institutions that provide these programs. I believe the impact of these efforts will be even more significant as word of the success of these programs begins to make its way through the correctional community.

After finishing this paragraph, I will begin preparing for this evening's support groups. I will facilitate two groups of approximately 20 men, mostly fathers who are on parole or probation from state or local prison. Our focus tonight will be on developing healthy relationship skills. Since most of these men did not have healthy role models growing up, many are learning what a healthy relationship looks like for the first time. More important, they really want to change but have never had anyone they trusted to teach them what they needed to know to be loving, nurturing men and fathers. Tonight, in the safe environment of the group, they will learn, grow, and begin applying what they have learned. Each week I hear about small successes from various men as they check in and share their experiences—small steps, but significant ones. It will take time and learning, and they will need to be patient with the process, but it will be well worth the journey.

Perhaps, as these better educated, more skilled, loving fathers reenter their communities, we will begin to see fewer and fewer of the next generation going to prison. Maybe one day we will hear of a state having to close a few prisons because they are no longer needed. That is my hope and my dream.

Endnotes

1. Bureau of Justice Statistics Correctional Surveys, November 2004, U.S. Department of Justice, Office of Justice Programs; Harrison, P., and Beck, A.J., 2005, "Prisoners in 2004," *Bureau of Justice Statistics Bulletin*, Washington, DC: U.S. Department of Justice.

2. Ibid.

3. Mumola, C.J., 2000, "Incarcerated Parents and Their Children," *Bureau of Justice Statistics Special Report*, Washington, DC: U.S. Department of Justice.

4. Harrison, P.M., and Karberg, J.C., April 2003, "Prison and Jail Inmates at Midyear 2002," *Bureau of Justice Statistics Bulletin*, Washington, DC: U.S. Department of Justice.

5. Jefferies, J.M., Jenghraj, S., Finney, C., February 2001, "Serving Incarcerated and Ex-Offender Fathers and Their Families: A Review of the Field," Vera Institute of Justice, prepared for the U.S. Department of Justice.

6. Johnston, D., and Gabel, K., 2005, "Incarcerated Parents," in *Children of Incarcerated Parents*, edited by K. Gabel and D. Johnston, New York: Lexington Books, pp. 3–20.

7. Center for Organizational Research and Evaluation, 2001, "Process Evaluation of the Long Distance Dads Program," Erie, PA: Penn State–Erie, the Behrend College Center for Organizational Research and Evaluation.

8. Travis, J., Solomon, A.L., and Waul, M., 2001, *From Prison to Home: The Dimensions and Consequences of Prisoner Reentry*, Washington, DC: The Urban Institute; Hull, K.A., Forrester, S., Brown, J., Jobe, D., and McCullen, C., 2000, "Analysis of Recidivism Rates for Participants of the Academic/Vocational/ Transition Education Programs Offered by the Virginia Department of Correctional Education," *Journal of Correctional Education*, 51(2), 256–261.

9. Center for Organizational Research and Evaluation, 2003, "Outcomes Evaluation of the Long Distance Dads Program," Erie, PA: Penn State–Erie, the Behrend College Center for Organizational Research and Evaluation.

10. Personal participation and observation by author.

11. Missouri Department of Correction, Office of Child Support Enforcement Demonstration Project 2003.

12. Turner, Robin, December 2004, "Helping Offenders Parent Effectively, H.O.P.E. Final Report," the Father's Workshop of York County, Pennsylvania, Department of Community Corrections.

13. Gaes, G., and Kendig, N., January 2002, "The Skill Sets and Health Care Needs of Released Offenders," in *From Prison to Home: The Effect of Incarceration and Reentry on Children, Families, and Communities*, U.S. Department of Health and Human Services, The Urban Institute.

Fathers and Contexts of Involvement

The six chapters in this section address specific contexts of involvement through which fathers and men support, relate to, and guide children, including working and providing for children, early childhood education, mentoring, assisting with education, religious settings, and leadership in the home.

In Chapter 18, "Working Fathers: Providing and Nurturing in Harmony," authors E. Jeffrey Hill, Giuseppe Martinengo, and Jenet Jacob outline fathers' issues in harmonizing work and family needs and expectations. Introducing the metaphor of musical harmony as a paradigm for working fathers, they explore the significance of work for fathers in their role as parents and the frequent conflicts that occur between work and family contexts. The authors offer a set of in-depth, concrete suggestions for dealing with work-family conflicts such as limiting work time as possible, "bundling" activities, staying in touch from a distance, and using flexible work options.

In Chapter 19, "Men Teaching and Working with Children: A History and Future," Bryan Nelson writes about men working with children in early childhood and elementary education. Using personal examples, historical research, and findings from contemporary studies, Nelson documents the history of men teaching children and identifies some critical issues related to why so few men are found teaching children in today's society. He debunks myths about men teaching children and suggests ways to move toward a brighter future for men's involvement in teaching and working with children.

Mentoring as a topic of interest in father-child relationships is explored in Chapter 20, "Fathers as Mentors: Bridging the Gap between Generations." Frank Pleban and Keri Diez present ideas about mentoring's definition and context. The authors show how mentoring by fathers and other caring adults can bridge the gap between generations. They also suggest potential contributions of a father's mentoring efforts including protection against risk behaviors, development of a nurturing relationship, formation of prosocial behavior, and development of mastery. The chapter concludes with observations about how men and fathers can become good mentors in the lives of children.

In Chapter 21, "Strong Fathers as Strong Teachers: Supporting and Strengthening a Child's Education," Mike Hall of Strong Fathers–Strong Families shares his insights on fathering and supporting a child's education. As a former middle school teacher and principal and a current fatherhood practitioner, Hall brings much experience to his treatment of the topic of academic achievement and fathers' influence. He provides insight on what fathers bring to their involvement in the educational context and then focuses on how fathers' involvement can complement and reinforce schools' efforts. In addition, he documents and highlights the positive outcomes on a child's educational achievement when fathers are positively involved.

Yet another context of meaningful involvement for fathers is discussed in Chapter 22, "Turning the Hearts of Fathers to Their Children: Why Religious Involvement Can Make a Difference." Loren Marks and David Dollahite fashion a framework for understanding the role of religious contexts on fathers and fathering. The authors outline briefly the religious contexts in which fathers and children often exist in family life. They also address ways in which religious beliefs, religious practices, and faith community support may help turn the hearts of fathers to their children, assisting them to be more responsible and connected with their families. They conclude by examining some key applications this topic may have for fathers, families, and those who wish to strengthen father involvement.

A final context of involvement is addressed in Chapter 23, "Serving in Order to Lead: Fathers as Leaders at Home," in which Kevin Galbraith and Sterling Wall argue for the importance of fathers serving children and families in the home setting. The authors assert that fathers ought to provide effective leadership in family life and begin with an exploration of different types of leadership. The chapter's central argument is a further exploration of the concept of servant leadership and related principles that can be carried out in home and family life.

This section highlights the varying contexts of involvement in which fathers and men in general may engage as they associate with and care for children, ranging from the workplace to the school ground. Each context offers meaningful opportunities for men to mentor, lift, support, and guide children in positive ways that make a difference in children's well-being. Whether through mentoring, service, or religious instruction, fathers can work in a variety of involvement contexts to care for children.

Author E. Jeffrey Hill with his daughter Abigail on her wedding day

Working Fathers:
Providing and Nurturing in Harmony

E. Jeffrey Hill, Giuseppe Martinengo, and Jenet Jacob

Today's ideal father is now expected to do it all. As always, he is supposed to be a good provider and supply the necessities of life for his family by working at a good-paying job.[1] He often feels compelled to work long hours to ensure a successful career so he can provide well for the needs of his children. At the same time, however, the culture of fatherhood prescribes that he be more nurturing and involved in child rearing than ever.[2] He ought to be changing diapers, singing lullabies, reading stories, wiping runny noses, washing dishes, and helping with homework. Juggling all of these responsibilities is not easy. There is growing recognition that many fathers experience conflict as they attempt to manage the demands of work and family life.[3]

Perhaps a musical metaphor of harmony might help fathers think in productive ways about how to manage this work-family conflict more effectively. It is empowering for a father to think of himself as the composer, lyricist, orchestrator, and performer of his work and family life. Using a harmony metaphor, pertinent questions are not necessarily "How can I limit my work time so that I can attend to my family life?" or "How can I get out of the house more so I can have more time at work?" More helpful questions come to mind, like "What am I learning at work that can help me have a better family?" or "Are there possibilities for overlapping work and family time in harmony?"

The purpose of this chapter is to help fathers learn how to find harmony in work and family life in ways that make work less detrimental to their involvement with their children. The chapter is divided into two major sections. First, we offer evidence that many fathers are working hard to contribute to the well-being of their children: they are working longer hours to become better providers, and they are more involved in everyday family living than they ever have been before.[4] However, this increased involvement engenders a higher level of conflict between work and family.[5] Hence, the second and longer section of this chapter provides perspectives, ideas, thoughts, and suggestions for how working fathers can simultaneously provide for and nurture their children in ways that harmonize rather than conflict with each other.

Working Fathers: The Forgotten Half of Work and Family Life

For many years the underlying assumption in society was that the actual behaviors of fathers lagged behind the culture of fatherhood that called for more involvement in family life.[6] The perception was that, even in dual-career families, mothers assumed the lioness's share of childcare and household tasks, with home life providing the onerous "second shift" of their unending work.[7] By and large, a deficit perspective prevailed, which assumed that men habitually devoted less time and energy to the work of the home. Men as a group were often vilified for not assuming their fair share of household responsibilities.[8] Researchers pointed to the small number of men taking paternity leave as evidence that men were fundamentally uninterested in greater childcare responsibility.[9] As a result, there was little discussion of work-family conflict because most fathers seemed to simply not be as involved in the activities of home life.

Most work-family research has focused on mothers' challenges for finding harmony in their work and family lives. Feelings of stress over work-family issues are presumed to be a woman's domain. In parenting workshops, Levine and Pittinsky found that people estimated that twice as many women as men experienced a significant amount of work-family conflict.[10] Studies on work and family life have rarely looked at fathers discretely or acknowledged the degree to which they experience work-family conflict. Work-family programs for employees appear to be less accessible to fathers, largely because men are typically expected

The Mexican Fishing Story

An American entrepreneur, father of two young children, was standing at the pier of a small coastal Mexican village when a small boat with just one fisherman docked. Inside the small boat were several large yellowfin tuna. The American complimented the Mexican, also the father of two, on his fish.

"How long did it take you to catch them?" the American asked.

"Only a little while," the Mexican replied.

"Why don't you stay out longer and catch more fish?" the American asked.

"I have enough to support the needs of our home," the Mexican said.

"But," the American asked, "What do you do with your time?"

The Mexican fisherman smiled and said, with a twinkle in his eye, "I fish a little, but then I do a lot at home, *señor*. I play with my *niños*, lend a hand with the *comida* (meal), and then take a siesta with my wife, Maria. After helping the kids with their *deberes* (homework), we stroll to the plaza in the evening where we listen to the guitar and sing with our amigos. I have a full and wonderful life, *señor*."

The American scoffed, "I am a Stanford MBA and could help you a lot. You should spend a lot more time fishing, and with the proceeds you can buy a bigger boat, and with the proceeds from the bigger boat you could buy several boats; eventually you would have a fleet of fishing boats. Instead of selling your catch to a middleman, you could sell directly to the consumers, eventually opening your own can factory. You would control the product, processing, and distribution. You would need to leave this small coastal fishing village and move to Mexico City, then L.A., and eventually New York, where you would run your expanding enterprise."

The Mexican fisherman asked, "But *señor*, how long will this all take?"

To which the American replied, "Not long, maybe 15–20 years."

"But what then, *señor*?"

The American laughed, "That's the best part. When the time is right, you would announce and sell your company stock to the public and become very rich; you would make millions."

"Millions, *señor*? Then what?"

The American said slowly, "Then you would retire and move to a small coastal fishing village where you could do a lot at home. You could fish a little, then play with your grandkids, help with the *comida*, take a siesta with your wife, and stroll to the plaza in the evenings where you could listen to the guitar and sing with your amigos."

(Adapted from www.noogenesis.com/pineapple/fisherman.html)

not to use them.[11] If they do, they are at risk for being considered less committed to the organization.[12] As this indicates, society as a whole seems to assume that fathers simply do not care to be as involved in family life, making efforts toward resolving conflict between work and family life unnecessary for fathers.

Research from the National Study of the Changing Workforce (NSCW) challenges these assumptions by demonstrating that the behaviors of working fathers are quickly catching up to the culture of fatherhood.[13] For example, in 1977, fathers in dual-earner households spent just 46 percent as much time in household chores and childcare as mothers did (3.2 hours/workday for fathers versus seven for mothers). By 2002, they had increased their contribution to 72 percent as much time (4.7 hours/workday for fathers versus 6.5 for mothers), quite a dramatic change, especially in a nationally representative data set. NSCW results also show that working fathers' average work hours increased from 43 per week in 1992 to 48 in 2002.[14] Working fathers employed full-time report 15 percent more work hours than mothers employed full-time (48 hours/week for fathers versus 41 for mothers). Fathers are now working their own "second shift" with combined employment and home work hours of more than 80 hours per week. It is not surprising that fathers now report just as much work-family conflict as working mothers do.[15]

There is growing recognition of the challenges of work-family conflict that occur when fathers attempt to both provide for and nurture their children in an environment of limited support. An important question, then, is, How can working fathers be successful on the job while at the same time being meaningfully involved in the lives of their children? How can they find harmony? It now seems apparent that the cultural ideal of the "super mom" has transferred to fathers, with many experiencing the tension between being a "good company man" and a "good family man."

Approaches to Dealing with Work-Family Conflict

Fathers, employers, and family members can benefit from many practical suggestions designed to help fathers find more harmony between demanding work and family responsibilities. This chapter is for working fathers who want to be more involved with their children. It is also for those who provide the institutional support and environment that enable fathers to make choices to prioritize their family relationships.

One word of warning before you start reading: do not try to implement these suggestions all at once; it could be overwhelming and frustrating. Think of them more as a buffet of ideas from which you may pick and choose those that fit better in your current situation. Also, you may start planning and organizing your life so that more of these suggestions (or others you will eventually find) will become part of your life later on. In any case, we offer eight approaches for fathers and those supporting them to consider in managing work-family conflicts and improving fathers' sense of commitment and involvement.

(1) Don't work longer than is truly necessary.

Perhaps an obvious suggestion for increasing father involvement is to decrease the time spent at a job. Too many fathers spend so much time providing material resources—far beyond the necessities—that they have little time to go for a leisurely walk, fix dinner, play catch, read, do yard work, or any of the other seemingly unimportant but essential activities of everyday living. There is an old saying: "Children need our presence more than our presents." This fact especially applies to working fathers.

One father learned this important lesson when he stayed at work a little later than he had planned to finish up an inconsequential work assignment. Because traffic was a little heavier than expected, he missed his oldest son's first swim meet. He arrived just as his son was getting out of the water. He vowed he would never again let his job keep him from missing important events in the lives of his children. George Durrant, author of many books on family life, poignantly wrote to fathers:

> At your place of work, you are needed. But, sad as it may seem, there has never been a man who, when he leaves his daily job or when he retires, is not adequately replaced. As one man said, "I felt that if I left the company, it would take a month or so and then I'd be replaced and they wouldn't even miss me. But," he said, "I was wrong. It only took a week." ... But there is a place where a man has no substitute. Not after a month or a year or a generation. That is the place where they call him "Father." When he leaves home [for work], he's missed. And until he returns, there will be an empty, unfilled space in the hearts of his family.[16]

In setting work and family priorities, it is important to remember that the meaning experienced in spending more time together can never be replaced by material goods. There is no real substitute for time spent playing and working with children: it is one of the most important ways to express love and commitment.

(2) Choose a vocation that optimizes opportunities for father involvement.

All honest jobs and professions are necessary in our society. However, not all jobs and professions give you the same amount of money, time, or flexibility. If it is important to you to have time to spend with your children, carefully investigate how father-friendly each alternative career is that you may pursue. If you are still planning your life, make sure you choose a vocation that may facilitate involvement with your children. Think about the advantages and disadvantages of possible careers and include in your decision what are the explicit and the hidden requirements of different professions and trades. If you have already chosen a vocation but still have many years in front of you, think how much better off you and your children could be if you were to make a career change, even if this change were going to affect your finances somewhat. Finally, if you honestly realize that a vocational change is not possible anymore, think about going to work for an organization that is more sensitive to working fathers' difficulties and desires for family involvement. Also, you can try to change the way your employer organizes your work, so that you may still improve your situation.

(3) "Bundle": Do two things at once in harmony.

"Bundling," or doing two or more things simultaneously, can be a useful concept for working fathers who want to be more involved with their children. There are many opportunities to bundle work and family activities in harmony without dissonance.[17] For example, I (Jeff) recently brought my 16-year-old daughter, Hannah, to the university campus in the morning. While I engaged in my primary activity of writing a boring scholarly article (not this one!), she enthusiastically organized all the books in my office library. Every few minutes we interacted briefly, and then at noon I took her out to lunch. Using bundling, I got a full morning's work done, had my library organized, and created a memory with my daughter, all at the same time.

The same concept may be applied when running errands around home or in the community. For example, when you need to go to the store, one way to be a more involved father is to take a child along with you. While getting your shopping done, you bundle time to connect with a child one-on-one while you travel to and from the store. In our home we have modified a famous credit card slogan: "Children: never leave home without them."

(4) Make the best of it when you travel out of town on business: keep involved at a distance.

In today's mobile society, a growing number of fathers have to travel away from home many nights each year. Latest U.S. figures estimate an increase of 4 percent in the number of business trips, a total of 122 million trips taken by 34 million business travelers.[18] Fathers are disproportionately represented among corporate executives—those who travel the most. While it is certainly more difficult to be an involved father when you have to visit a distant city, it is not impossible. Here are some suggestions from fathers who frequently travel:

- Inform your children of the trip as far ahead of time as possible.
- Be clear about your departure and return dates.
- Show your children on a map where you will be going.
- Phone a different child each night for a personal one-on-one chat.

- Have your children fax you homework to the hotel where you are staying.
- Exchange e-mails or fax messages with your children each day.
- Write your children post cards from the city where you are each day.
- Buy a speaker phone. Talk to your whole family at once.
- Call your children to family prayer. They can use the speaker phone.
- Use frequent flyer miles to bring your kids on business trips.
- Purchase souvenirs of the trip or other gifts for your children.
- Upon your return, take individual time with each child to debrief.

With a little creative and intentional thought, you can build in opportunities for meaningful connections from a distance. In this way, family members are assured that thoughts and desires, though far away, are focused on them. It may be surprising to watch how these connecting experiences open the doors for building even deeper relationships.

(5) Use some of your commute time as a time for enhancing father involvement.

The average commute to and from work in the United States is about 50 minutes per day. It ranges from a high of 62 minutes in New York to a low of 30 in North Dakota.[19] Instead of making this a stressful time away from your children, think of ways to enhance family involvement. Here are some suggestions:

- Bring along a voice recorder and record value-based stories about your life. Your children can listen and learn from you over and over again at bedtime, even when you are away from home.
- Use a hands-free cell phone to talk to your children while you drive home.
- Listen to inspirational books, music, or other materials on tape to create energy for being with your children.
- Deliberately think about your children and say of them, "This is my most important work."

(6) Create more family time by using flexible work options.

Perhaps a personal story may illustrate how fathers might leverage job flexibility in order to increase the quantity and quality of time with their children.[20] In 1990, I was working for IBM, and the company offered me an excellent promotion to New York. However, the commute would be horrendous and the cost-of-living out of sight. I hated to turn it down, but it just wouldn't work for our family, which included seven children at the time. Then, in a quiet moment, I got the idea to propose to take the job but stay in my home and telecommute. I reasoned with my future boss that I could better do my job through a modem from my home in the West than from an expensive office in the East. To my surprise, she agreed to try it out, even though telecommuting was virtually unknown in those days.

My Experience with Paternity Leave

In December 1988, my wife, Juanita, and I discovered she was expecting our seventh child. She had given birth to twins less than a year before, and the responsibility for this new baby would be just too much. While struggling with how we should cope, I got an inspiration to request paternity leave from IBM, my employer. This was a new program that enabled fathers to take time off for their children without risk of losing their job. Thousands of IBM women took maternity leave each year, but only a handful of men took paternity leave.

Early in January 1989, I approached my new manager with the leave request. He chuckled and thought I was playing a practical joke on him. I convinced him I was serious. He apologized and, after some give-and-take, my leave was approved. My manager explained I could take up to six months' leave without pay.

After a difficult labor and delivery, our 10-pound, 11-ounce Emily was born the first week of June. My first day on leave was a great eye-opener. During my entire career, I had never before been present when my children came home from school. I could not believe the kids' energy as they burst through the door anxious to share the experiences of the day. Listening to them was like opening a fire hydrant of enthusiasm. I came to realize I must have missed most of their school lives by never having been at the crossroads before.

With me at home full-time, we defined new duties. Juanita was now responsible for the baby, and I was responsible for the other children. We shared household chores. The haphazard rhythm of everyday living at home was much different than the regular cadence of office work. I would just get started with breakfast when Hannah would need her diaper changed and Aaron would be yelling that his older brother Jeffrey wouldn't give back a toy. I was suddenly baptized with a great wave of appreciation for what Juanita had been doing all those years while I was a casual occupant of our home.

In the past, Juanita had often talked to me about the kids, saying things like, "We've got to do something about Jeffrey ... or Aaron ... or Abigail...." My standard reply was, "Don't worry—they'll grow out of it." Now, when I saw Jeffrey do the same obnoxious thing 50 times a day, I understood her exasperation! Before, I had been the easygoing parent the kids came to when Juanita's patience had worn thin. Now the kids would say, "Oh, Dad, you're just like Mom!" Juanita would just smile at me, and sometimes I'd respond, "It's not funny" and walk away.

While Juanita was caring for the baby, I took the responsibility for toddler Hannah, who required constant supervision. We jogged together an hour every day, me pounding the pavement and her taking in the world from the vantage point of her stroller. She would excitedly give me a play-by-play description of her view: a dog here, a cat there, a flock of birds in the sky. In just a few weeks, Hannah began to display almost constant exuberance toward me. It warmed my heart and soothed my soul.

During the leave, I kept a low profile in the outside world. I did not tell our friends or anyone in the neighborhood I was staying home full-time. I refrained from answering the phone during the day. Sometimes I would forget, and the person on the line would say something like, "Jeff, is that you? What are you doing at home?" I felt a sense of guilt—as if I should look over my shoulder for the truant officer, who might try to haul me back to work. I felt better when I overheard Abigail talking to one of her friends. "Why is your daddy home?" the friend asked. "He's taking a leave," Abby responded cheerfully, "because he *loves* me."

As my leave drew to an end in late November, I met with my manager to discuss my return to IBM. I realized how pale the work world was compared to the richness of the family realm. I didn't want to go back to work—I wanted to stay home. I came to understand that, although I had taken the leave because I felt my family needed it, really *I* was the one who had needed it.

When I discuss this leave with others, many say something like, "Oh, that's nice, but I could never do that." That may or may not be true. When I took paternity leave in 1989, very few companies offered it. Now, U.S. law requires that all companies with more than 50 employees offer fathers at least 12 weeks of unpaid leave in conjunction with the birth of a new baby, while protecting their job.

This leave changed my life for the better. I am more in tune with my children and feel a tender bond with each of them. It affected me so much that I changed my employment. I went from being a systems engineer at IBM to being an expert on work and family issues to getting a Ph.D. in Family and Human Development to becoming a professor in Home and Family Living at Brigham Young University. To you fathers, I strongly encourage you to take some time off when your babies are born. Your life may never be the same again!

(Adapted from Hill, E.J., 2000, "Balancing Family and Work," in *Strengthening Our Families: An In-Depth Look at the Proclamation on the Family*, edited by D.C. Dollahite, Salt Lake City: Bookcraft.)

The increase in both my productivity and level of father involvement was immediate. Instantly I gained an hour and a half a day because I didn't have to drive to and from work. Instead of dragging myself to work and needing to unwind after a "fast-lane" commute, I could roll out of bed early with an exciting idea and immediately type it into the laptop. So what if I was still in my pajamas? A little later, I could get the kids up, and we could share breakfast and a family devotional. Because I was working from home, I could listen for baby Amanda while my wife went to an aerobics class, did shopping, or ran other errands. When work got frustrating and I needed a little break, I could put toddler Emily in the jogging stroller and go for a quick run or play a 10-minute game of one-on-one basketball with teenager Jeffrey. Then I could go back to work refreshed. We set up two extra computers in the den so the children could do their homework while I worked on tasks for IBM. Sarah, Abby, and Hannah particularly liked to work side-by-side with me. Some questioned whether I could be effective in such an environment; however, my children's interruptions were less frequent and more satisfying than the interruptions of coworkers.

One morning while I recorded my daily voicemail greeting, my wife, Juanita, was folding clothes in the laundry room across the hall. My six-year-old daughter Emily had just taken a shower upstairs and could not find the clothes she wanted to wear. She came downstairs draped in nothing but a towel. When Juanita saw her, she said in a loud, giggly female voice, "Look at you! You have no clothes on!" After several colleagues commented with a chuckle about my voicemail greeting, I listened to it, and this is what I heard:

Male Voice: This is Dr. Jeff Hill with IBM Global Employee Research . . .
Giggly Female Voice: Look at you! You have no clothes on!
Male Voice: . . . . I'm not available right now.[21]

In ways that perhaps only other telecommuters can understand, this experience is a humorous reflection of the challenges that arise as we work to build a more harmonious relationship between work and family life. Telecommuting and other work flexibility programs are not available in all jobs, but they are becoming more accepted. In particular, fathers are more likely to use such options when they do not result in loss of pay.[22] Such options effectively address an important need by enabling fathers to more effectively harmonize work and family life.

Other possibilities to consider in creating a more harmonious work-family relationship by taking advantage of flexible work options include:

- When possible, use flextime to be home when your children return from school.
- Use family leave to be home full-time for several weeks after babies are born.

- Once a month, come in to work early, then volunteer at your child's school.
- Work four days, 10 hours a day, to create three-day weekends with your kids.

These options provide unique opportunities for family-unifying experiences at particularly important times.

Job flexibility is especially valuable for working fathers with special-needs children. In the United States, about nine million children have special healthcare needs.[23] A father's initial and ongoing response to this challenge significantly affects the well-being of family members.[24] Researcher David Dollahite has written, "Most men desire to be good fathers, yet they face significant challenges stemming from increasing economic, societal, and familial changes, demands, and complexities."[25] To have children with special needs while trying to keep up with an overly demanding job that does not allow for flexibility may be overwhelming for a father. A flexible job environment may enormously improve the family life—and substantially increase the productivity—of a working father who needs to face this type of challenge. In fact, usage of flexible work options can benefit any father who takes advantage of such opportunities to focus on family time and involvement.

(7) Let your children whisper to you while you are in the workplace.

As a father, you can be more involved with your children even while you are in the workplace. One suggestion is to display recent family pictures prominently in the space where you work. When you need to be rejuvenated, take a minute or two to look at the pictures and remember a positive experience with each child. When chatting informally with coworkers, talk about your children, not sports.

You may be able to communicate briefly with your children several times a day while you are on the job. During lunch or breaks, you might call home to visit for just a minute or two. Some working fathers routinely telephone their children right after they arrive home from school. The kids have a lot more to say about their school day at midafternoon than they will later in the evening when the father physically returns from work. Other fathers like to send e-mail messages to family members.

If you involve your children in your job, you will be more involved with them. One way to get your children involved is to explain at their level what you do all day and why you do it. You may even be able to occasionally bring them to your workplace or have them assist you with work tasks. Many working fathers do not have a lot of options when it comes to flexibility on the job. However, as you plan and organize your work efforts, try to think of your family members and take small opportunities to connect with them regularly.

(8) Do your best!

In our lives, we are not always able to do what we know would be the ideal for us and for our families. In many cases, circumstances may limit our choices and constrain us so that we take paths that are not what we dreamed. However, we can always strive to do our best to improve our family life even if we may never reach our ideal.

A few years ago, I sat in an auditorium with several hundred other men as we listened intently to George Durrant, a wise and caring speaker, motivate us to be better fathers. A middle-aged, working-class man with muscles and a mustache gathered courage to speak and then stood up. He emotionally asked, "What you say sounds great in the ideal world, but what do you expect me to do when I have nine kids and a wife to feed and I have to work 14 hours a day at two jobs just to keep body and soul together?" He went on to list many additional reasons why his job situation made it impossible for him to have the time or energy to be the unhurried, sensitive, and playful dad being described to the group. He glared at Dr. Durrant as he concluded with the terse question, "So just what do you expect me to do?" Dr. Durrant took a deep breath, paused, and then with emotion in his voice replied simply, "I would think that your wife and children would expect you to do your best. My friend, just do your best."[26]

Conclusion

In today's world, it is not easy to be a good father. Many conflicting demands are competing for fathers' attention, energy, and time. Our society still expects fathers to be their families' providers but at the same time pushes them to increase their involvement with children and household chores. We believe it is a positive trend that fathers are more involved in their children's lives. Children need the distinctive influence of fathers to grow harmoniously. However, in order to be effective fathers, men need to evaluate their priorities and take into consideration their limitations. Their time and energy are not unlimited, and fathers need to make choices. Working fathers need to carefully consider the implications of their present employment for their family life and make changes when necessary or possible.

According to research, father involvement—more than mother involvement—is strongly influenced by institutional practices, employment opportunities, and cultural expectations.[27] The well-being of our children requires businesses and other employment providers to take into consideration the exigencies of working fathers. More flexible and father-friendly policies may benefit employees' families and, indirectly, workers' job satisfaction and productivity.

In conclusion, we believe it is in the best interest of all segments of our society to foster a better and more flexible work environment for working fathers.

Fathers need to be able to satisfy all their responsibilities without unnecessarily sacrificing their jobs or their children. Finally, we think fathers should consider it a duty to take advantage of present opportunities or push for change so that, with their children and spouses, they may live better lives together as families.

Endnotes

1. Christiansen, S.L., and Palkovitz, R., 2001, "Why the 'Good Provider' Role Still Matters," *Journal of Family Issues*, 22, 84–106.

2. LaRossa, R., 1988, "Fatherhood and Social Change," *Family Relations*, 37, 451–457.

3. Hill, E.J., Hawkins, A.J., Martinson, A.J. and Ferris, M., 2003, "Studying Working Fathers: Comparing Fathers and Mothers' Work-Family Conflict, Fit, and Adaptive Strategies in a Global High-Tech Company," *Fathering: A Journal of Theory, Research and Practice*, 1, 239–261.

4. Bond, J.T., Thompson, C., Galinsky, E., and Prottas, D., 2003, *Highlights of the 2002 National Study of the Changing Workforce*, New York: Families and Work Institute.

5. Hill et al., 2003.

6. Coltrane, S., 2000, "Research on Household Labor," *Journal of Marriage and the Family*, 62, 1209–1233; LaRossa, 1988.

7. Hochschild, A.R., 1997, *The Time Bind*, New York: Metropolitan Books.

8. Hawkins, A.J., and Dollahite, D.C. (Eds.), 1997, *Generative Fathering: Beyond the Deficit Perspective*, Thousand Oaks, CA: Sage Publications.

9. Hyde, J.S., Essex, M.J., and Horton, F., 1993, "Fathers and Parental Leave: Attitudes and Experiences," *Journal of Family Issues*, 14, 616–641; J.C. Hood, (Ed.), 1993, *Men, Work, and Family*, Newbury Park: Sage Publications.

10. Levine, J.A., and Pittinsky, T.L., 1997, *Working Fathers: New Strategies for Balancing Work and Family*, Reading, MA: Addison-Wesley Publishing Company, Inc.

11. Levine, S.B., 2000, *Father Courage: What Happens When Men Put Family First*, New York: Harcourt, Inc.

12. Meiksins, P., and Whalley, P., 2002, *Putting Work in Its Place: A Quiet Revolution*, Ithaca, NY: Cornell University Press.

13. Bond et al., 2003.

14. Bond et al., 2003.

15. Hill et al., 2003.

16. Durrant, G., 1976, *Love at Home Starring Father*, Salt Lake City: Bookcraft.

17. Sandholtz, K., Derr, B., Buckner, K., and Carlson, D., 2002, *Beyond Juggling: Rebalancing Your Busy Life*, San Francisco: Berrett-Koehler Publishers, Inc.

18. Cendant, December 11, 2003, *Trends and Information: Hospitality Services*, retrieved January 29, 2005, from www.cendant/com/media/trends_information.cgi.

19. U.S. Census Bureau, 2002, *American Community Survey*, retrieved July 22, 2004, from www.census.gov/acs/www/Products/Ranking/2002/R04T040.htm.

20. Hill, E.J., 2000, "Balancing Family and Work," in *Strengthening Our Families: An In-Depth Look at the Proclamation on the Family*, edited by D.C. Dollahite, Salt Lake City: Bookcraft.

21. Shellenbarger, S., September 24, 1997, "Work and Family: These Telecommuters Just Barely Maintain Their Office Decorum," *Wall Street Journal*, p. B1.

22. Hill et al., 2003.

23. Family Voices, 2004, "Who Are Children with Special Healthcare Needs?", retrieved February 1, 2005, from www.familyvoices.org/cshcn.htm.

24. Dollahite, D., 2003, "Fathering for Eternity: Generative Spirituality in Latter-Day Saint Fathers of Children with Special Needs," *Review of Religious Research*, 44, 339–351.

25. Dollahite, D.C., 1998, "Fathering, Faith, and Spirituality," *Journal of Men's Studies*, 7, 3–15, at 3–4.

26. Hill, E.J., October 7, 1999, "Parents Must Just Do Their Best to Juggle Work, Family," *Deseret News*, p. C02.

27. Dollahite, D.C., 1998; Doherty, W.J., Kouneski, E.F., and Erickson, M.F., 1998, "Responsible Fatherhood: A Review and Conceptual Framework," *Journal of Marriage and the Family*, 60, 277–292.

The author's parents, Charmaine and Captain Ronald E. Nelson, USAF, are pictured with their children, Teresa and Richard (back row) and Bruce, Karen, and Bryan (front row). In the inset are Bryan (center) with children Emma and Otto.

Men Teaching and Working with Children: A History and a Future

Bryan G. Nelson

When I was growing up, my dad played with my brothers, sisters, and me whenever he could. Though his position in the military kept him away for months at a time, my dad stayed involved in our lives, and when he was home, he clearly loved being with us and nurturing us. From camping trips to cookouts to playing together with us at the local gym or just rolling around on the floor wrestling, my dad clearly enjoyed his children and wanted to be involved in their lives. He even attended Parent Teacher Association (PTA) meetings and got involved in our school as often as he could. His mother and father never finished high school, and so, understanding the value of education, he encouraged all of us in school and wanted us to attend college.

Because my dad so naturally assumed and deeply enjoyed, along with my mother, the role of nurturer and guide as his children's primary educator, I was surprised to discover when I eventually became a teacher that there were so very few other men (except for the janitor) working in schools. I wondered where all the men were. Was my father unusual among men because of his talent for and clear joy regarding nurturing children? I had grown up with a dad who loved being with kids, and *I* loved being with kids, so it seemed natural to me that other men would want to enter the teaching profession or work with children as well.

Where were all the men?

In this essay I briefly share a few of my experiences coming to work with children and the practical realities of men working with children that I have learned from research and professional experience.

Becoming a Teacher of Children

Before I became a teacher, I worked as a back deckhand on a ship, a radio disc jockey, a newspaper reporter, a short-order cook, and a construction laborer. Even though I knew my father had always really wanted to be a history teacher, a career in teaching had never crossed my mind—until one fateful summer. I took a job at a summer camp in the former Soviet Union, in Russia. I found I loved it. Working with children was challenging, rewarding, and just plain fun. After that summer was over, I ended up working in different capacities as a caregiver for two different families, a coach at a school in Paris, and an assistant in an after-school program for children. Eventually, I was inspired to look for a full-time job working with children and found one at a parent-owned childcare program, working with children ranging in age from infancy to five years.

Looking back on my earlier experiences, I understand that I knew how to play with children, but I wasn't sure how to teach. I knew how to have fun, but there were times the job called for more than just having fun. It required guidance. Guidance of young children was something that would take further time for me to understand, but I was willing to learn. A woman who worked in the childcare program offered me new ideas for activities I could do with the children. She had me sit at a table and help some of the older children with scissors. The boys usually had a harder time cutting, and having the role model of a man taking the time to cut out designs with them provided the extra inspiration they needed to want to try. She had me sit in the book corner and read to the children. I'd have a group of children sitting all around me absolutely riveted to the story I was reading them. The first time I read to a group of children, I had a memory of my childhood: the first time I saw the word "cat" being written. I could see the letters being carefully written and then experienced a flash of understanding that those symbols, those three letters, had a meaning. I realized as I sat with the group of children that they could have that same flash of insight into the world of words, books, and language. It was thrilling. I had found work that fascinated me: teaching and working with children.

I began taking classes to get my teaching certificate and degree, and I soon found that the profession and the classes were filled with women. At this point I first began to question: *Where were all the men?* It felt strange being the only man in class, and it felt strange being one of only a few men working with children at my employer's childcare center. As I continued working with children while attending university, I also traveled to state and national conferences on early childhood and elementary education. At these professional gatherings, I would tower over the crowds of women (I'm 6'3"), and only occasionally would I see another man. In fact, the professional gatherings were so chock-full of women that often the men's bathrooms had been converted for women's use during the conference. I'd typically have to ask a janitor or someone at an information desk where the nearest available bathroom was for men. On several occasions the small group of men that were in attendance at these conferences would post a man at the door to the bathroom so the women wouldn't walk in while we were using it!

Over my years of experience in working with children and families, I realized how important this work with children is to their future and well-being. And I knew how important fathers are to children. I knew this by seeing children's positive and enthusiastic responses to men. It didn't make sense to me that so few men were teaching and working with children. In the remainder of this essay, I recount a brief history of men teachers, discuss why there are so few men teaching in early childhood programs or elementary schools today, debunk myths and stereotypes regarding men in the classroom and other professions working with young children, and share my vision for changing the status quo.

A Brief History: Was There a Time When Men Taught?

My experience at the summer camp has turned into more than 20 years of working with children and families, attending conferences, and completing college and graduate work in the areas of child development, education, and men teaching. As my experiences working in the field of early childhood and elementary education grew, I continued to wonder: *Where were all the men?* I finally decided to do some research to answer this question. I learned some interesting things.

If you had walked into school classrooms in early colonial America, you would find men—a lot of men.[1] Nearly all colonial-era teachers were men. According to public records, from 1635 to 1750, almost all of the teachers on town payrolls were men. Often young men, some studying to be clergy, were hired by local school boards to teach. It wasn't until 1750 that the number of men teachers decreased to 85 percent, with the remaining 15 percent being women teaching primarily in summer programs.[2]

Over the next century, the male majority of teachers continued to decrease. During the 1800s, the proportion of men teachers in some states dropped to less than 25 percent. For example, by 1834 in Massachusetts, 54 percent of teachers were men, and by 1860 this figure dropped to 22 percent.[3] Obviously, there had been men teachers, and then the situation changed dramatically. What happened?

There are several explanations for the decline in the number of men teachers in the United States over the past two centuries. One of the primary reasons appears to be that men could earn higher wages in other occupations and women could replace the men teachers for lower wages, thereby making it cheaper for town school trustees. Demographic changes appear to be another reason why women began to enter teaching in greater numbers. In the mid-1800s, decreasing birthrates and an overall rise in the age men and women were getting married provided women a greater opportunity to attend school. With their newfound education, women wanted to work outside the home.[4] At that time, teaching was one of the few socially acceptable careers for middle- and upper-class women because teaching could be considered an extension of a woman's domestic role.

As Figure 1 shows, from the 1800s until the 1940s, the number of men teaching in school classrooms steadily declined.

Then, during a brief historical period from the 1940s until the 1980s, the percentage of men teachers again increased to a high of 34.3 percent in 1971. One of

Figure 1: Men Teachers in Public Schools: 1870–1999

Source: Statistical Abstracts, U.S. Department of Education, Bureau of Labor Statistics

the reasons for this temporary shift appears to be the unprecedented changes in society (e.g., wars and free postwar education) and in the roles of men and women during this time (e.g., women's movement). Since that 20th century peak, however, the percentage of men teaching has again steadily decreased to 25.1 percent in 1999. Currently, 18.9 percent of elementary and middle school teachers and less than 5 percent of early childhood educators are men.[5] If this trend continues, the percentage of men working with and teaching children will continue to

---

Successful Programs Supporting Men Teachers

These programs and websites offer programs, information, and support about recruiting and retaining men teachers:

- **MenTeach.** A national clearinghouse for research, education, resources, and advocacy with a commitment to increase the number of men teaching children in early, elementary, and secondary education: www.MenTeach.org
- **Call Me Mister.** A teacher training scholarship program with the goal of training 100 black men to be elementary school teachers: www.callmemister.clemson.edu/
- **Troops to Teachers.** A resource for men who served in the military to get support becoming teachers: www.proudtoserveagain.com/index.html
- **Teach for America.** A teacher training program for men (and women) who want to become teachers: http://www.teachforamerica.org/
- **Minority Recruitment Project.** A teacher training program in Kentucky for minority men: www.louisville.edu/edu/MTRP/mtrp.html

If you do an Internet search, you'll find additional programs being offered by universities and colleges. Also, these other websites offer information throughout the world about men teaching:

- **Canada.** A website about male teachers in Ontario, Canada: http://maleteachers.com/
- **Europe.** A website hosted from the United Kingdom: www.meninchildcare.com/
- **New Zealand.** A government-sponsored site in New Zealand: www.teachnz.govt.nz/training/providers/men.html
- **Australia.** A government-sponsored site from Queensland, Australia: http://education.qld.gov.au/workforce/diversity/equity/male-teachers.html

decrease unless action is taken to recruit more men teachers and retain the few currently working in the field.

Though my research provided me with a historical understanding of why so few male teachers worked with children, my curiosity was not yet satisfied. At the same time, I was eager to take some sort of action to draw more men into the field of education, so I did two things. First, I started an organization called MenTeach (www.menteach.org). I also applied for and received a fellowship to attend Harvard University to further explore through graduate research why men *in this day and age* were not only choosing not to enter careers working with children but also in fact abandoning their already established teaching careers.

The Harvard University Study: Why Are So Few Men Teaching Today?

Interestingly enough, but I guess not surprisingly, in 1997 when I applied to and was accepted at Harvard, I was admitted through the Maternal-Child Health department because there was no department devoted to *fathers, men, and children.* No *paternal*-child health department existed or any department remotely close that could house my research aims. So it was through the Department of Maternal-Child Health that I conducted a first-of-its-kind study of men teachers in the field of early childhood education. Using a random national sample survey of 1,000 early childhood educators (equal numbers of men and women), I researched the answer to these questions: *Are men important to children as teachers, and if so, why are so few men teaching?* With a statistically sound response rate of 507 participants (64 percent female and 36 percent male), the study provided a foundation for understanding more about men teaching and working with children.

The most interesting finding revealed in the study was that almost all (98 percent) of the early childhood educators surveyed strongly agreed or agreed that men were important to the growth and development of children in their roles as teachers. But less than 5 percent of early childhood teachers are men. Many survey respondents included written comments about the positive influence men have working with young children:

- "In the setting I am currently working in there are a couple of male college workstudy students—the children respond well to them—it has been wonderful—hopefully the numbers will increase."
- "Men need to be encouraged to be with children. . . . Men can be as nurturing as women. They can be an important factor in the growth and development of children. Men need to encourage men!!!"
- "I've only met one male kindergarten teacher in my life, and I've had one male student kindergarten teacher. Both were exceptional teachers."

■ "This country as a whole does not value, support, or encourage men to work with young children. In spite of some progress in the home, the general population, especially males themselves, do not recognize the value of the contributions they can make and the profound influence they can have in the early childhood population."

Thus, the study supported my own experience validating the importance of men teaching and working with children.

The study not only showed a highly positive response regarding the value of men working with children but also revealed why so few men were teachers. The current and most common barriers to men teaching and working with children identified by survey respondents are as follows.

■ **Stereotypes.** Some people believe that working with young children is "women's work," that men are not nurturing, and that there must be something wrong with any man who would want to teach young children.
■ **Fear of accusation of abuse.** Some people fear that men will harm children or be accused of abuse.
■ **Low status and low wages.** Working with young children has low status and low wages.

Later, through subsequent analysis, I looked more closely at these findings around barriers men face and barriers that employers face in recruiting, hiring, and retaining men teachers. Further research revealed that survey respondents had hit on three of the many stereotypes and myths about why so few men are working as teachers of young children. Such perceptions make it difficult for men to enter or remain in careers working with children. In order to make progress, efforts must be made to challenge stereotypes, acknowledge people's fears or concerns, and work for better compensation for both men and women who care for young children. Organizations such as MenTeach and others in the field of education now must work strategically to bring our culture and society, ironically, out of the 21st century "dark ages" into the "light" of colonial America, where men not only taught but were valued, trusted, and highly regarded as teachers of children.

Debunking the Myths and Stereotypes: What's the Truth?

As my children were growing up, I would visit their schools. Invariably, teachers and other school staff would stop me in the halls on my way to the classroom to visit or volunteer. Staff would ask who I was and what I was doing in the school. I felt immediately suspect. I could tell by the way they acted toward me that women, and often men principals, feared I would harm the children or that there was something odd about a father wanting to visit his child at school or volunteer. There were times that school staff welcomed me, but that was typically after they got to know me. Though I hoped that my experience—getting stopped in the hall on my way to volunteer—was my own isolated experience, my Harvard and post-Harvard research into men teaching and fathers working with children in childcare or school settings suggested otherwise.

There are many myths about why so few men work with young children and many stereotypes about men who do. Some of the myths are addressed below, and perspectives based on more accurate information are offered instead.

Myth #1: Men and Harm to Children

- **Myth.** Men who work with young children may be prone to atypical feelings for or dangerous intent toward children and may sexually molest them.
- **Truth.** A child is just as safe in a childcare program or school classroom as he or she is at home with parents.

If abuse of a young child occurs, it is most likely to occur in the child's home.[6] In 90 percent of reported cases of child abuse in the United States, the perpetrators of abuse on young children were parents or other relatives.[7] There is no question that our children must be safe from harm, but being suspicious of all men or instituting "no-touch" policies for only men teachers does not protect children. Actions, rather than suspicions, are what protect children. Actions designed to avoid harm and minimize possible occurrences of abuse include carefully screening, recruiting, and supervising staff and volunteers; providing staff with training on child abuse; designing the environment to control access by visitors; reducing hidden places in which abuse may occur; and building close partnerships with parents.[8] These are the things that keep all children safe and allow all staff members to work in an environment without suspicion.

Myth #2: Men and Money

- **Myth.** Men won't work with young children because of the low wages.
- **Truth.** Men can be found working in many low-wage jobs, such as the fast food industry, general labor jobs, and temporary or seasonal work.[9] Men work in these low-wage jobs because men are accepted in these settings and a number of other men also work there.

Another way of understanding this myth is to look at the number of men teaching in the primary and secondary grades. In school districts where teachers have similar levels of experience and education and are represented by a union, the salaries are the same. In these settings, only 16.2 percent of primary grade teachers are men compared to 42.5 percent of secondary grade teachers. If money were the only reason men don't work with young children, there would be more men teaching in the primary grades.

Myth #3: Men Don't Apply for Teaching Positions

- **Myth.** Men do not apply for jobs to teach or care for young children.
- **Truth.** Men apply for teaching positions but often are not hired.

A survey of early childhood education programs in Ohio found that center directors would not consider hiring a man without an early childhood degree, even though they had hired women without degrees.[10] And in a national study of National Association for the Education of Young Children (NAEYC) members, eight out of 10 administrators/directors indicated that men have applied, at some point, to teach in their programs. An owner of a childcare program from a Midwestern state commented, "Many women administrators will not hire men."[11] It is important to work toward creating incentives for men to apply for these positions and an atmosphere that encourages them to be hired and retained for positive performance.

Myth #4: Men Lack Interest in Teaching Children

- **Myth.** Men who teach children will leave the profession for something else.
- **Truth.** Men often want to stay in their jobs as teachers but face many pressures to move into administration.[12]

Many men see administration, such as an elementary school principal position, as something very different from teaching. It is often not something they are primarily interested in doing. However, men, like women, face pressures to move into another aspect of the profession because the wages in early education are often at or below the federal poverty level.[13] When men and women leave the profession, it is typically because they cannot earn a living wage.

Myth #5: Men and Sexual Orientation

- **Myth.** Men who teach young children are often gay.
- **Truth.** There is no information available about the sexual orientation of men who teach young children.

Men who teach young children are a diverse group, which includes men who are heterosexual, bisexual, and gay, just like the population of women who teach young children. These men are performing a job that in more recent decades has traditionally been considered more appropriate for women. If men do this, people often assume there must be something different about them. Women often face a similar myth when performing a job traditionally considered more appropriate for men. In an inclusive profession that serves a diverse population of children and families, sexual orientation has no place in determining the appropriateness of a person to be a teacher of young children.

Myth #6: Men and Capacity for Nurturing

- **Myth.** Men are not nurturing or patient enough to work with young children.
- **Truth.** Men have been caring for children as fathers, uncles, brothers, grandfathers, and teachers for generations.

The way men have cared for children has varied by culture and throughout history. However, no reliable research indicates men are any less capable of nurturing children than women are. Men may at times nurture children differently than women do. For example, fathers tend to engage in more physical play, allow a greater degree of independence, and engage in more open forms of verbal interaction than mothers.[14] Studies of men teachers show they are also patient, nurturing, and similar in their practices to women teachers.[15] Also, many kinds of work that require great amounts of patience have been traditionally done by men, such as being a counselor or a coach of a sports team.

Myth #7: Men and Capacity for Teaching

- **Myth.** Men who teach young children can't make it in other professions.
- **Truth.** Many men who enter early education often do so after they have had successful careers in other fields.

The myth that men who work in the field of teaching children cannot make it in other professions discredits the value of teaching as a profession and devalues the contributions of those who labor to teach and guide children. Men have become teachers of young children after careers in the military, insurance industry, banking industry, and law enforcement.[16] The men who work with children do so because they have chosen this career and typically have excellent abilities in the field of teaching children.

Myth #8: Men and the Needs of Children

- **Myth.** Men are not wanted or needed to work with young children.
- **Truth.** Most people want children to have loving men involved in their lives and recognize the value of such involvement.

According to the author's study, 98 percent of NAEYC members believe it is important for men to work with young children.[17] In another study, one respondent to a survey of licensed childcare providers in the state of Washington wrote this comment about men teachers: "The children are really thrilled to have the attention, nurturing, and care of men. And we happen to know that the benefit of male influence is wonderful and critical."[18] Most people believe it is important for children to experience having men as teachers and caregivers. This is unlikely to happen until the myths and stereotypes about men teachers are challenged. Only when men are encouraged, supported, and accepted as teachers and caregivers of young children will they enter and remain in the field of education and care of young children.

Toward a Brighter Future: What to Tackle First?

My father was a very important influence in my life. His nurturing and love for playing with his children, his participation in my education and school, and his involvement in my life affected me deeply. He made a huge difference in who I am today, the father I'm proud of being, my intrinsic love for working with children in the classroom, and my work with fathers (and mothers) as the primary educators of their children. The stereotypes that keep fathers and men out of the classroom need to be challenged—but what to tackle first?

Our fears about men hurting children, being uncaring or incapable of nurturing, or having interest only in money or status must be acknowledged, and the stereotypes should not be perpetuated. This mindset alone, among men, women, and institutions, is discouraging positive, caring men from spending time with children and entering the teaching profession. With few positive models of men in our schools, children learn about men either at home or through the media. Movies repeatedly depict men as using physical force to resolve problems or too incompetent to care for young children, and newspapers often run headlines about men arrested for violence. Tragically, media portrayals of men spring from some ugly realities. Children need loving men in their lives to balance the distorted and negative image of men in the media. The solution to protecting our children from harm isn't fewer men but stronger, caring, nurturing men in their daily lives.

Next, it is important to fight for paying our teachers—both men and women—well for the important work they do. Institutions demonstrate through the wages they offer the underlying values and shared beliefs of society as a whole. That our society values, through pay, our professional athletes, business consultants, and even waste management employees (garbage men) more than we do our children's teachers is unacceptable. I am not devaluing these services to society but simply putting our values into perspective. In the past year especially, economists have stepped up to the plate in an effort to draw attention to the value of early childhood education, showing that for every $1 spent there is a $16 return on investment.[20] If we pay teachers more and respect the important work they do, additional highly qualified, smart, trained, nurturing individuals with a talent for working with children—men included—will become teachers.

As a father and a teacher, I encourage men to consider teaching in early child-hood programs or schools. I also encourage those in hiring positions to recruit men to teach and care for children. An individual might start as I did, by working at a summer camp or coaching a sports team, or a father could volunteer in his child's classroom to read a story, play with blocks, or help children learn to write their name. Children need strong, caring men in their daily lives. What better time to offer that care than when children are young and eager to learn and play? What better place than the learning environments children experience as they grow and develop?

When I get discouraged or wish to remember what needs to happen to change the status quo and bring men into the challenging, rewarding profession of teaching young children, I imagine walking into a school classroom in the future. The build-ing is modern and clean with the latest equipment and supplies that are readily available. The air is filled with the laughs and comments of young children. In every room you enter, there are equal numbers of men and women, teaching, reading, or playing with the children. And those teachers, educated and well paid, are as diverse in characteristics as the children in each classroom. I know that with time, resources, and persistence, this vision for the education of young children and the involvement of men in children's daily lives can come true.

Endnotes

1. Youcha, G., 1995, *Minding the Children: Child Care in America from Colonial Times to the Present*, New York: Scribner Press.

2. Tyack, D.B., and Hansot, E., 1992, *Learning Together: A History of Coeducation in American Public Schools,* New York: Russell Sage Foundation.

3. Clifford, G.J., 1991, "Daughters into Teachers: Educational and Demographic Influences on the Transformation of Teaching into 'Women's Work' in America," in *Women Who Taught: Perspectives on the History of Women and Teaching,* edited by A. Prentice and M. Theobald, Toronto: University of Toronto Press, pp. 115-135.

4. Ibid.

5. For data about percentages of men and women working in various industries, see www.bls.gov/cps/cpsaat11.pdf (Bureau of Labor Statistics, July 2005).

6. Finkelhor, D., and Ormrod, R., June 2000, *Characteristics of Crimes Against Juveniles,* Juvenile Justice Bulletin, Washington, DC: U.S. Department of Justice, Office of Justice Programs, Office of Juvenile Justice and Delinquency Prevention, www.ncjrs.org/pdffiles1/ojjdp/179034.pdf.

7. U.S. Department of Health and Human Services, National Center on Child Abuse and Neglect, Child Maltreatment 2003 report, retrieved July 2005, http://nccanch.acf.hhs.gov/pubs/factsheets/canstats.pdf.

8. National Association for the Education of Young Children Position Statement: "Prevention of Child Abuse in Early Childhood Programs and the Responsibilities of Early Childhood Professionals to Prevent Child Abuse," retrieved July 2005, www.naeyc.org/about/positions/pdf/ChildAbuseStand.pdf.

9. Bureau of Labor Statistics, July 2005. For data about percentages of men and women working in various industries, see http://stats.bls.gov/pdf/cpsaat11.pdf. Also see www.bls.gov/oes/. For a listing of the lowest-wage jobs in the United States, see http://ftp.bls.gov/pub/news.release/History/ocwage.11142001.news. To compare the percentages of men and women in those low wage jobs, see www.bls.gov/cps/.

10. Masterson, T., 1992, "A Survey: Attitudes of Directors towards Men," in *Men in Child Care and Early Education: A Handbook for Administrators and Educators,* edited by B. Nelson and B. Sheppard, Minneapolis, MN: MenTeach.

11. Nelson, B.G., 2002, *The Importance of Men Teachers and Reasons Why There Are So Few: A Survey of the National Association of the Education of Young Children (NAEYC) Members,* Minneapolis, MN: MenTeach.

12. Sargent, P., 2001, *Real Men or Real Teachers: Contradictions in the Lives of Men Elementary School Teachers,* Harriman, TN: Men's Studies Press.

13. Center for the Child Care Workforce, 1998, *Worthy Work, Unlivable Wages,* Washington, D.C.

14. Cox, M.J., et al., 1992, "Prediction of Infant-Father and Infant-Mother Attachment," *Developmental Psychology,* 28, 474–483; Krampe, E.M., and Fairweather, P.D., 1993, "Father Presence and Family Formation: A Theoretical Reformation," *Journal of Family Issues,* 14(4), 572–591; Nord, C.W., Brimhall, D., and West, J., 1997, *Fathers' Involvement in Their Children's Schools,* U.S. Department of Education, Office of Educational Research and Improvement, Washington, DC.

15. Robinson, B.E., July 1981, "Changing Views on Male Early Childhood Teachers," *Young Children,* 36, 27–32; Seifert, K., 1992, "The Culture in Early Childhood Education and the Preparation of Male Teachers," in *Men in Child*

Care and Early Education: A Handbook for Administrators and Educators, edited by B.G. Nelson and B. Sheppard, Minneapolis, MN: MenTeach, pp.17–27.

16. Nelson, B.G., and Sheppard, B., 1992, *Men in Child Care and Early Education: A Handbook for Administrators and Educators*, Minneapolis, MN: MenTeach.

17. Nelson, 2002.

18. Cunningham, B., and Charyn, S., Summer 2002, "Men in Child Care," *The Link*, Office of Child Care Policy, Washington State Department of Social and Health Services.

19. Retrieved July 2005 from www.census.gov/prod/www/statistical-abstract-04.html.

20. Retrieved August 2006 from http://minneapolisfed.org/research/studies/earlychild/.

Author Keri S. Diez and her father, Jerry

Fathers as Mentors:
Bridging the Gap between Generations

Francis T. Pleban and Keri S. Diez

"One father is more than a hundred schoolmasters."
—English Proverb

The concept of adult males mentoring children is not a new concept or phenomenon. In fact, the existence of mentoring relationships has been documented dating back to Homer's *Odyssey*. The *Odyssey* depicts the mentoring of Odysseus's son, Telemachus, by his friend and elder, Mentor. Mentor leads Telemachus through the journey from childhood to adulthood and, along the way, authenticates his identity as an adult. Now, as then, the hallmarks of an adult mentor—for example, a father—are the genuine sincerity, caring, understanding, patience, enthusiasm, trustworthiness, and compassion he communicates to a child as they set out on their journey together throughout the child's life. Children, in order to grow up healthy, need such mentors, and adults, in order to stay healthy themselves, need such positive interactions with children.

In today's challenging world and throughout history, youths have desperately needed positive adult role models and support networks. Mentors can help to fill the void that sometimes occurs when parents, especially fathers, are busy or absent. Fathers and other responsible men should be attentive to the needs of children, their own and others, who can benefit from positive adult mentoring. The void in a child's life that sometimes occurs when parents and other caregivers do not provide adult leadership can become a source of pain and problems. For some children, such a void may become a principal part of their family environment. According to researchers, this type of atmosphere may spur destructive risk-taking behaviors by children and youths that carry over into adulthood.

As in the story of *Odysseus*, the gentle guidance and friendship of an adult mentor can make all the difference in a child's journey through life. Voids can be filled by those who step forward to give adult leadership and provide necessary support: a coach, a pastor, a friend's parent, a teacher, or a youth leader. Mentors help children find the guidance they seek and overcome the tendencies toward risk-taking behavior that can leave them vulnerable or in danger. To highlight the value of mentoring, this chapter explores how mentoring is defined, its context, and how mentoring by fathers and other caring adults can bridge the gap between generations. It also shares ideas on how mentoring is important in the lives of children and how fathers and others can make it more meaningful in their own lives.

What Mentoring Means

To date, no unanimous definition of the term *mentoring* has been adopted, but certain identifiable themes regarding adults and continuing education or guidance with youth have been assembled that provide a context for defining the mentoring relationship between adults and children in other environments.[1] Scholars Galbraith and Cohen state that mentoring involves the following components:

- a process within a contextual setting (e.g., teaching how to catch a ball);
- a relationship of a more knowledgeable individual with a less experienced individual;
- provision of networking, counseling, guiding, instructing, modeling, and sponsoring;
- a developmental mechanism (personal, professional, or psychological) for growth of an individual;
- socialization and reciprocal relationship; and
- an identity transformation for both mentor and mentee.[2]

Mentoring thus involves a certain set of core elements: teaching skills or ideas, a tutoring relationship, support or guidance, and personal growth. Regardless of the personal or professional context in which mentoring occurs, mentoring, in all of its forms, can be viewed as a positively sustained relationship between two individuals (e.g., a child and father).

A "positively sustained relationship between two individuals" can begin in many contexts. Mentoring relationships usually take some time to grow and produce fruit. A young girl who wishes to become an artist may learn under the direction of a caring aunt who teaches art. An uncle may guide his nephew in learning the finer points of catching and throwing a baseball. A youth pastor may become a familiar figure and friend for a teenager who returns over the years for personal talks about growing up and making life decisions. Fathers are natural mentors in the lives of their own and other children. One of the greatest sports athletes today, Tiger Woods, has pointed again and again to the mentoring efforts of his own father in preparing him for his success in the world of golf. To be sure, he was born with natural gifts and a desire to play the game, but his preparation for success took root and matured in his mentoring relationship with his own father.

Mentoring provides a safe and supportive environment for children and adults alike to address key personal issues or challenges in a child's life together. Addressing challenges such as death, divorce, developmental changes in maturation or health, friendships, academics, athletics, and other life obstacles or events can be positively assisted through a helpful mentoring relationship. If it is true that a father or father figure can be more than a hundred schoolmasters, as our proverb suggests, then a man's influence as a mentor can have a pivotal influence on a child's well-being. Such mentoring relationships are generally viewed as powerful tools against academic failure, teen pregnancy, drug abuse, and youth gang activity. Furthermore, mentored youths have been shown to improve their view of themselves, their social relationships, and their communication and conflict resolution skills.

Mentoring involves a social relationship, with the adult, or mentor, assuming two main roles: (1) someone with expertise, skill, or knowledge as the result of training or experience and (2) a positive role model in a particular behavioral or social role for another person to emulate. In mentoring, adults contribute their knowledge, skills, and experience in order to assist and nurture children in working toward the achievement of their own objectives through guided developmental learning. The adult serves as an influential presence and an advocate, providing specific guidance and advice to the child in overcoming challenges or reaching specific goals. As an example, when individuals travel on river rafting expeditions, they are typically led and assisted by an experienced river guide who knows how to handle the equipment and navigate the currents. When men or fathers act as mentors, they are also guides, steering children or youths on their specific expeditions, helping them reach their specific goals in a safe, healthy manner.[3,4]

This communal relationship historically has taken two forms: typically, it occurs in the context of either natural or planned mentoring. *Natural mentoring* has commonly been defined as a relationship between an adult and child that occurs through bonds of friendship, collegiality, teaching, coaching, or counseling. For example, a child's swimming teacher becomes a natural mentor in teaching the skills associated with swimming. *Planned mentoring* occurs through structured programming, in which mentors and participants are selected and matched through a deliberate and formal process (e.g., Big Brothers/Big Sisters). Structured mentoring programs can pair children or youths with specific needs, such as learning challenges, with an individual who is prepared to assist with those needs.

What positive benefits accrue that indicate mentoring really counts in the lives of children? Regardless of the mentoring approach that occurs, three common outcomes have been studied and documented among mentoring relationships:

■ educational/academic development,
■ career development, and
■ personal development.

Growth and development in all three of these domains is typically addressed at one time or another throughout a child's life and into adulthood. Educational or academic mentoring is demonstrated by helping and steering youth to improve their overall scholastic achievement. Similarly, career mentoring helps youth to develop necessary skills to enter, continue on, or advance on specific career or vocational paths. A young man who participated in the scouting program did the work to complete a badge for expertise in radio and broadcasting and subsequently went on to train and work in a related career in the radio industry. This is an example of career mentoring. Perhaps most important, personal development mentoring supports youth during times of personal and social stress and provides guidance for critical thinking and informed decision making. Personal development mentoring, as frequently seen between a father and his child, has historically been termed *intergenerational mentoring*. Characteristic of many father-child relationships, this is part of the process by which adult men help youth to bridge the gap between generations and learn specific skills needed for their own transitions to adulthood.

Intergenerational Mentoring:
Bridging the Gap between Adult and Child

Intergenerational mentoring is a process of encouraging, teaching, sponsoring, and guiding the development of children and youth by people of older generations. This mentoring approach is a unique way of bringing two groups together to share their strengths. This mutually beneficial relationship often appears to profit the adult as much as, and in some respects even more than, the mentored child. One older gentleman, Ed, reminisced about his role in a mentoring relationship:

> I was in my 60s and wanted to give something back to the community. I was recently retired and wanted to keep busy. I became a mentor to a young man. I thought it was going to be something that I could do from time to time and really help a young person through a tough period in his life. Boy, was I wrong! It was me who really benefited. I mean, he did start to do better in school and stay out of trouble more. So I guess I helped him, too. But I learned so much from him. I stayed involved in his life for many years, and now he brings his family to visit me, like I am part of his family. Who knew that a person could receive so much by giving a little?

Reading about Ed's experiences with intergenerational mentoring illustrates how vitally important and mutually beneficial the mentoring relationship can be to both mentor and mentee. For example, the benefits of being a mentor in a child's life can help adults feel more productive, experience an enhanced sense of purpose, and become more involved in their community. Mentoring helps men feel valued and invested in both their own future and that of the child or adolescent. Mentoring benefits both generations. Young people receive additional attention, guidance, and support from a compassionate adult while learning new skills and ideas.

The gap that can occur between generations as children grow up can be bridged by this kind of involved mentoring. Men, in particular, have a central role to play in guiding youth. It is interesting to note that some naturalists have observed the wild and unruly behavior of young bull elephants that have grown up without the example and guidance of older male elephants in a herd. Young male elephants unmentored in the wild by older bull elephants have at times become destructive of property and life in rural African villages, banding together to go on sprees of wild behavior. What does this suggest? Naturalists are not entirely sure of the answer, but some researchers have indicated that perhaps these young elephants who have seen no model of restraint from older adult males are victims of a lack of mentoring. This suggests again, by comparison, that men play an important intergenerational role in mentoring and raising the next generation.

Intergenerational mentoring has been shown to promote an understanding of shared values, respect for individuals in all stages in life, and empowerment of communities by facilitating community collaboration. Additionally, intergenerational mentoring can promote cooperative problem solving and an appreciation for rich cultural traditions, values, and family heritage. Fathers, working in this capacity as mentors, have the ability to bring multiple family generations together, building a sense of individuality in a child while at the same time providing a sense of "family ownership" and identity through their impact on future generations.

The Essence of Mentoring

Forest Witcraft, in *Within My Power*, wrote, "One hundred years from now, it will not matter what my bank account was, how big my house was, or what kind of car I drove. But the world may be a little better, because I was important in the life of a child."

I am sometimes asked by concerned parents and other adults about specific unhealthy, aberrant, and destructive behaviors exhibited by today's youth (i.e., alcohol and drug use, sexual promiscuity, gang involvement, etc.) and what they can do to protect their children from partaking in such behaviors. These are not always easy questions to answer. I believe one undeniable fact remains evident and consistent in understanding and addressing such concerns, for these are not health issues specific to just boys or girls; urban or rural youth; youth of one socioeconomic status, race, or religion; or youth from dual or single parents.

The basic premise is that these are human problems affecting human beings, so there is no "one size fits all" answer. However, certain needs keep reappearing across the environments youth live in—their family, school, community, and peer groups. Children look to adults in their lives—fathers, mothers, school teachers, or other adults acting in a mentoring capacity—to obtain guidance for healthy development. There are six basic needs that all youth (and adults) strive to fill through their personal connections with others, specifically adults. The needs, which are interrelated and equally important, are as follows, in no particular order:

- to be accepted,
- to receive affection,
- to belong,
- to receive love,
- to be recognized, and
- to feel safe.

Finally, regardless of the characteristics of the adult and the amount of interaction, personal and social growth can occur in conjunction with youth only in an environment in which you as an adult mentor reiterate: "You are safe, I care about you, and I care about what you have to say. I am here to listen to you, and I am here to help you in any way that I can. You may stumble, you may falter, but I will not let you fall."

—*F.T. Pleban*

The Role of Fathers and Father Figures as Mentors

In the past, fathers were typically seen as the "forgotten contributors to child development."[5] All too often, this paternal description seems to hold true today. Fathers in the past were generally expected to provide household income; give emotional support to their wives, who traditionally took care of the children; ease the workload of their wives; and contribute to the education of their children.[6] Frequently these expectations were ill-defined and left interpretive room for errors or shortcomings, such as being absent or unavailable in a child's life. Unfortunately, those shortcomings gave the impression of failure for many fathers. However, this impression of failure is in contrast to what is actually reported by many of today's fathers and their true feelings concerning their children. The contributions of a father's mentoring efforts can include protection against risk behaviors, development of a nurturing relationship, formation of prosocial behavior, and development of mastery.

Protection against Risk Behaviors

It is common today for many fathers to report spending more time with their children than their fathers did with them.[7] Tina describes one such situation in which her husband stepped in to be the primary caregiver for their two children when he was injured on his job:

> Ever since my husband was injured at work and became a stay-at-home dad, this bond has been created between him and the kids that is so strong. I know they are better suited for the world because he has turned into so much more than a dad. He's their mentor as well.

Men consistently report that they are frightened by accounts of crime, alcohol and drug use, sexual promiscuity, and accidents that befall youth and feel their presence may help to curtail some of the problems plaguing young people.[8] Comments from youths themselves support this notion that a father's presence can be a protective influence. One young person, Chris, said of his father:

> He took the time to be there for me, and I did not want to disappoint him by getting involved with drugs and the old gang. I stayed out of trouble for him and am so much better for it now.

This young person's comment is telling. He notes that, because his father was there for him, he specifically "stayed out of trouble for him" and tried not to disappoint him, in this case, through drug use or being involved in a gang. Such is the power of a man's mentoring influence. As a response to the concerns they see young people facing, many fathers are choosing to spend more time with their families in lieu of professional or career opportunities such as making more money or taking a promotion.[9]

Development of a Nurturing Relationship

Fathers have sometimes been left out of the developmental process of their children's lives. This may be due, in part, to the bond that develops between mother and child and the important maternal role in a child's development. In effect, the attachment and closeness that fathers need to develop toward their newborn child is not predicted by previous experience (i.e., carrying the child in the womb). However, research has shown that fathers, when compared to mothers, are equally able to interpret their child's behavioral cues and respond appropriately. In other words, fathers have the capacity and ability to nurture and bond with their infants in the same way mothers do.[10] While this capacity has too often been misunderstood, it is the formation of this relationship in a child's early years that paves the way for men to become a positive mentoring influence over a child's lifetime. However, men who do not have this early opportunity may also establish productive and caring mentor relationships with children and adolescents. As one example, this is evidenced by the nurturing relationship between a father and his adopted twin daughters. One daughter, Jamie, revealed this about her relationship with her dad:

> My dad adopted my sister (twin) and me when we were seven years old. He raised us all by himself. I am having my own baby now, and I pray that my husband can bond with our baby as well as my dad did with us.

What a lovely sentiment regarding a subject, adoption, that is cloaked in uncertainty. It seems that even fathers who did not spend the very early years with a child can form a real and lasting bond with their adopted children.

Formation of Prosocial Behaviors

Male adult involvement in children's lives has been linked to positive outcomes for infants, children, and adolescents alike. Throughout his or her developmental years, a child continues to benefit from high levels of paternal involvement. During this time, youths need support and guidance in shaping their emotional and behavioral autonomy. In fact, it is the presence of a strong male mentor that seems to be responsible for the development of many prosocial behaviors, as opposed to antisocial behaviors that commonly arise during youth and adolescence and subsequently can disrupt a potentially healthy life. The maternal role seems to be somewhat less consequential than the paternal role in this particular aspect of development, although both are important.[11] This influence of paternal mentoring on prosocial youth behaviors extends from involvement in play to increasing cognitive capabilities and empathy.

Development of Mastery

Fathers as mentors tend to spend more time encouraging exploration in play with children and less time utilizing play as a form of entertainment or distraction. Additionally, adult males tend to encourage children to endure frustration, support children in mastering tasks before offering assistance, and utilize real-life consequences with children as a disciplinary style.[12] What are the practical consequences of such patterns for children and youth? One young man, Frank, recalled his father's mentoring influence:

> My fondest and most precious memory of my dad was when he took me out behind the railroad track to teach me to ride my bike on two wheels. I was scared, but he promised to be right there with me. Suddenly, I realized that I was really moving and looked back to smile at my dad, and he was standing back there watching me ride away. I was riding on my own. My dad's encouragement and confidence made it okay for me to ride on my own. I'll never forget the sunset that afternoon or the look on my dad's face as I rode along the tracks.

The sense of mastery and support his father encouraged in this scenario portrays the value of a father's mentoring touch. The positive effects of fathers' patterns for children, as described above, tend to include increases in adaptive and problem-solving abilities, cognitive abilities, and empathetic feelings. Additional positive effects of involved fathers include a decrease in gender-role stereotyping, an increase in self-control, and better physical development.

Children mentored by adult males have been shown to be less psychologically maladjusted, less likely to participate in substance use and abuse, less likely to be depressed, and less likely to exhibit overall conduct problems. Johnson and Sullivan stated, "Mentoring someone . . . a young adult . . . is a complex task and not to be underestimated; which takes a set of difficult skills that run the gamut from patience and perseverance to openness and self-reflection."[13] Yet there is great value in such mentoring, as children develop mastery and new skills, form positive social abilities, and learn to avoid behaviors that can put themselves and others at risk.

What Makes a Good Mentor?

An example of a great mentoring relationship between a father figure and a young adult was portrayed in the popular 1976 film *Rocky*. *Rocky* is a film depicting Rocky "The Italian Stallion" Balboa (played by Sylvester Stallone) as a struggling small-time boxer who lives in a tiny, dilapidated apartment in Philadelphia. Mickey, a boxing trainer (played by Burgess Meredith) believes Rocky can make it to the top of the boxing world, but only if he is willing to work hard and with conviction for the title shot against Apollo Creed (played by Carl Weathers).

In this film, Rocky wants to know why Mickey always tries to make his life difficult and insists on being tough with him, as recounted in the following dialogue:

Rocky: I been comin' here for six years, and for six years ya been stickin' it to me, an' I wanna know how come!

Mickey: Ya don't wanna know!

Rocky: I wanna know how come!

Mickey: Ya wanna know?

Rocky: I WANNA KNOW HOW!

Mickey: OK, I'm gonna tell ya! You had the talent to become a good fighter, but instead of that, you become a leg-breaker to some cheap, second-rate loan shark!

Finally, Rocky comes back with, "It's a living." And Mickey responds, "It's a waste of life." This scene is a pivotal moment in the movie. At this point things begin to change for Rocky, and he and Mickey go on to have one of the closest mentoring relationships ever portrayed in film. They form a bond that subsequently benefits both men. This is a wonderful, heart-warming example of how two people who are very different in age, knowledge, and experience can come together and form a mentoring relationship that is mutually beneficial and extremely potent. This happened in the movie, but it can also happen in real life.

Mentors come from many backgrounds, socioeconomic and educational levels, and religious affiliations. What's important is the human being, not his demographic characteristics. It is the human relationship that makes a mentor special and his contributions so important. Each mentoring relationship is different, just as each child and adult is different, but there are a number of personal characteristics that seem to contribute to successful mentoring relationships, regardless of the situation:

- **Commitment.** A person considering developing a mentoring relationship should be ready to invest enough personal effort and time—at least a year— to actually have an impact. Before all else, a successful mentor first must have a very real desire and commitment to be a part of another person's life.
- **Respect**. Mentors must show genuine respect for mentees and their decisions in order to win their trust. Mentors have to realize their way may not be the best for the mentees and respect them enough to offer support even when they make their own decisions—sometimes contrary to the mentor's beliefs.

- **Ability to Listen.** The ability to listen is one of the most difficult parts of verbal communication to master. Often help comes in the form of listening, asking pertinent questions, and helping the mentee think situations through on their own. Mentees are not always looking for advice but want to learn personal and social skills to make informed decisions on their own.
- **Empathy.** Mentors do not need to have had the same life experiences to "feel for" the mentees. When mentors empathize with the personal situation of a mentee, they are feeling their pain but not feeling pity for them. Pity—concern aroused by the misfortune, affliction, or suffering of another that often implies a feeling of sorrow that inclines one to help or show mercy—does nothing toward bringing two people together. Empathy, however, indicates a sense of shared compassion and a willingness to be supportive.
- **Problem Solving.** Mentors should be able to help their mentees make sense of confusing and complicated situations. This will enable the mentee to make good judgments and informed decisions free of confusion.
- **Flexibility and Openness.** Communication and an appreciation for diversity are vital in the mentor/mentee relationship. The mentor must be willing to experience new things—such as music—in this relationship. Mentors may find they actually enjoy hip-hop or country music. Mentors should remember that change is usually good for any individual in any relationship.

Any number of other characteristics could benefit a mentor in this type of relationship, such as enthusiasm, patience, perseverance, reliability, and, of course, a genuine interest in young people. None of these guarantees a successful mentoring relationship, but without them failure is almost guaranteed.

Conclusion

Mentoring has been a popular area of both practice and research in the past two decades. At the same time, the topic of mentoring has generated some controversy concerning its practice and research validity. Nevertheless, mentoring has come to be viewed as a poignant interpersonal interaction leading to personal growth and development for all involved. It is a type of interaction and support that makes a difference for children and provides men with the opportunity to be involved and contributing partners in children's lives and well-being.

Mentoring and the array of mentoring relationships and opportunities can still be looked at as somewhat uncultivated terrain. Opportunities abound for men to make a difference in their families and communities through mentoring. Individuals, communities, and public and private institutions can promote and realize the potential growth and development of children and youth through the variety of planned and natural mentoring opportunities. Quality mentoring programs will be advanced as practices are refined and further developed based on sound research and evaluation. Such programs can open the door for men and fathers to make a larger difference in their communities and bring children across the threshold to the next generation. Fathers mentoring children should not be viewed as a "quick fix" for developmental or behavioral problems in children and youth but one aspect that should work in conjunction with the overall family, school, and community environments. Mentoring relationships need time to develop and grow, slowly and positively, for them to bear fruit. If mentoring is started early in a child's life, a father will learn, through the child's actions and words, that it is the least he can do . . . and the most he can do.

Endnotes

1. Cohen, N.H., and Galbraith, M.W., Summer 1995a, "Mentoring in the Learning Society," in *Mentoring: New Strategies and Challenges* (New Directions for Adult and Continuing Education, No. 66), edited by M.W. Galbraith and N.H. Cohen, Jossey-Bass Publishers, San Francisco, CA, pp. 5–14.

2. Galbraith, M.W., and Cohen, N.H., Summer 1995b, "Issues and Challenges Confronting Mentoring," in *Mentoring: New Strategies and Challenges* (New Directions for Adult and Continuing Education, No. 66), edited by M.W. Galbraith and N.H. Cohen, Jossey-Bass Publishers, San Francisco, CA, pp. 89–93.

3. Cohen and Galbraith, 1995a.

4. Galbraith and Cohen, 1995b.

5. Lamb, M, 1975, "Fathers: Forgotten Contributors to Child Development," *Human Development*, 18, 245–266.

6. Strom, R.D., Beckert, T.E., Strom, P.S., Strom, S.K., and Griswold, D.L., 2002, "Evaluating the Success of Caucasian Fathers in Guiding Adolescents," *Adolescence*, 37, 131–149.

7. Gleick, J., 1999, *The Acceleration of Just About Everything*, New York: Pantheon.

8. Strom et al., 2002.

9. Popenoe, D., 1999, *Life without Father*, Needham, MA: Addison-Wesley.

10. Parke, R.D., 1996, *Fatherhood*, Cambridge: Harvard University Press.

11. Shek, D.T., and Keung Ma, H., 2001, "Parent-Adolescent Conflict and Adolescent Antisocial and Prosocial Behavior: A Longitudinal Study in a Chinese Context," *Adolescence*, 36, 545–555.

12. Parke, 1996.

13. Johnson, A.W., and Sullivan, J.A., Summer 1995, "Mentoring Program Practices and Effectiveness," in *Mentoring: New Strategies and Challenges* (New Directions for Adult and Continuing Education, No. 66), edited by M.W. Galbraith and N.H. Cohen, Jossey-Bass Publishers, San Francisco, CA, pp. 43–56.

Author J. Michael Hall with his wife, Sabra, and their sons, Jacob and Joshua

Strong Fathers as Strong Teachers: Supporting and Strengthening a Child's Education

J. Michael Hall

The scene is very familiar. Most of us have been in a public school cafeteria with white walls, tile floors, and drab, laminate-covered tables. These cafeterias usually have windows, are flooded with fluorescent lights, and, as if by federal law, have exposed stainless steel somewhere close to the kitchen. On one particular morning, one of these familiar cafeterias held more than 100 fathers and their children. There were book-laden backpacks everywhere, and most of those in attendance were in some stage of donut, juice, or coffee consumption.

One such dad-and-kid team consists of Juan and his daughter, Carmen. Juan is wearing a denim uniform shirt, a NASCAR cap, jeans, and dirty work boots. Carmen, a third grader, is dressed in her favorite outfit and smiling a huge, chocolate-donut smile. She is almost completely off her cafeteria stool as she leans in as close as possible to her dad. Most mornings Juan, who pours concrete for a living, is already at the worksite by this time of the day. However, today Juan's job is to be at school for Carmen. Her smiles, giggles, and attention to her father are what let him know that being at school this morning is well worth the time spent away from the job. Another dad, Marvin, is sharing a donut with his son, Marvin Jr. Marvin is also in a uniform shirt and somewhat cleaner work boots. Marvin is normally in bed at this time of the morning after working all night loading trucks for a parcel delivery company. Junior is just as happy as Carmen and perhaps even happier since he doesn't live with his dad all the time. Marvin Sr. knows that this time with his son is more important than his much-needed sleep. Marvin also comes to school quite often to see Junior at lunch since his joint custody agreement and weekend work schedule limit the amount of time he can see his son.

This scene is played out over and over again in public schools all over the United States during the annual Dads and Donuts Day. Typically for this event, men are invited to come with their child to school one morning, eat a donut, have pictures taken, shake hands with the principal, deliver their children to the classroom, and then go to work to show off their new picture. As this event concludes, everybody leaves with a nice little "Kum Bah Yah" warm and fuzzy experience, yet many of the participants and hosts do not understand the unharnessed potential of what they have just witnessed.

The schools hosting these "donuts and dads" events are working tirelessly to educate children so they will have the necessary skills to become wage-earning, productive citizens in our democratic society. To educate children from a million different backgrounds with amazing emotional and cognitive challenges is an almost insurmountable task. Staff members at these schools spend an enormous amount of time wondering how to help these children reach the specified academic standards. The fathers who attend these events wonder how they, as fathers, will help their children reach their fullest potential.

The schools and fathers that come together in these pastry-based events seldom realize that if they would get better acquainted with each other they would exponentially increase the potential of the very children who keep them both up at night. This simple morning of donuts could actually be a catalyst in drastically improving home life for children and the academic bottom line for schools.

The described scenes have been a part of my everyday experience over the past few years. As a speaker and facilitator of fatherhood workshops, I have the privilege of actually being a part of bringing fathers into public and private schools, Head Starts, and early childhood programs three or four days a week throughout the school year. I see literally hundreds of fathers who look just like Marvin Sr. and Juan showing up at schools on any given day to support their children and the programs that are educating them. In these events I always see kids who are excited, fathers who are proud (and a bit scared), and schools that are instantly better off. As a former special education teacher and a "recovering" school principal, I have been part of several campuses where we failed to see or tap into the incredible potential for kids that exists in truly involving fathers in the education of their children. Over the years, I have become a believer in this effort as I have had the opportunity to work with thousands and thousands of fathers who keep showing up at schools in large numbers in order to become a bigger part of their child's life and educational experience.

The thousands of real fathers I have encountered provide the basis for this chapter. Tremendous research on this subject is validated by all of these fathers who have entered their child's school and this very important discussion. These fathers, as men and parents, have shown us they bring a totally different set of skills and perspectives into the educational environment. This very different perspective can have a tremendous impact on the educational outcomes for their children. This chapter will focus on how fathers' involvement can complement and reinforce school efforts, the particular focus fathers can bring to supporting children's education, and the positive outcomes on a child's education when fathers are positively involved.

Schools and Fathers: Same Goals, Different Roles

According to the U.S. Department of Education's National Center for Educational Statistics, there are 14,559 public school districts representing more than 94,000 school campuses in our country. Those public schools represent approximately 48 million students enrolled in elementary and secondary campuses. Those 48 million students are from 25.8 million married-couple families, eight million single-mother families, and 1.9 million single-father families.[1] Even though they may approach it differently, these schools and families are both in the business of helping the same 48 million children.

Fathers and schools play incredibly similar roles in the lives of children. Both care for children and are interested in their becoming independent and successful in the adult world. Fathers and schools both spend an incredible amount of time working to prepare children to possess the skills necessary to be successful. When they do their best work, both fathers and schools are involved in the same endeavor from different angles but working for the same outcomes.

How do schools, fathers, and mothers relate to each other in raising children and helping them become successful? As a parent, fathers play the role of the person "other than the mother" who is there to help the child grow and develop as a human being. Schools play the role of the institution "other than the family" that helps that same child grow and develop. Just as the child is born of one parent to actually be raised and nurtured *between* two parents, the same child comes from one family, regardless of family structure, to reside between the family and the school that work together to raise the child into competent adulthood. Fathers, mothers, and schools can interact to assist children in ways that overlap and are unique to each relationship.

Typically, mothers provide the "safe place" for children to be nurtured and cared for as they grow in life. Mothers are attentive to the security and well-being of children and bring this focus to their efforts as parents. Although they also care about children's sense of security, many fathers play the role that encourages the child to push, explore, and take more risks in order to grow.[2] From these different perspectives, mothers and fathers work together in creating an atmosphere that nurtures a child's security while also encouraging initiative and independence. In a similar way, the family generally plays the role of establishing a safe place for the child, and the school often becomes the trusted entity outside the family to help children expand and grow away from the safety and confinement of the home. As fathers and mothers need to work cooperatively to create such an environment for children, the family system and the school need to work cooperatively to facilitate healthy learning and growth for children.

How do fathers and schools, in particular, share similar goals in their relationships with children? The father and the school are both in the job of preparing children to possess competencies to independently take on adult challenges in the world outside both the family and the school. In order to develop these competencies in children, fathers and schools pursue particular approaches that have much in common. Both fathers and schools:

- encourage children to explore, take risks, and push themselves in learning and growth,
- teach children to deal with the frustrations and challenges inherent in activities that challenge them and promote growth,
- set limits on a child's risk taking while providing room for appropriate and timely exploration, and
- provide various learning experiences (both safe and risky) that allow children to check their competencies in a real-world environment.

Fathers and schools simultaneously encourage, guide, and challenge children through various activities meant to help them learn and grow. The best schools and fathers also understand they not only have the job of providing challenges and learning experiences for the children under their charge but must also provide certain rites of passage that allow children to check themselves against real world standards and give them a feeling of tangible progress.

The entire process of going from one grade level to the next gives children the idea of accomplishment and progress. As children progress from grade to grade, fathers support those rites of passage by addressing such progress. Whereas a mom might say, "I can't believe my baby is a fourth grader!" the father might use that step to encourage further growth and tell the child, "Now that you are a big fourth grader, I'll bet you are ready to ride your bike to the park." A father may also set goals using those rites of passage by telling a child he or she can conquer some task like riding a bike, camping with friends in the backyard, or riding that ominous roller coaster by the time they are in a specific grade. Those grade-level demarcations that occur from fall to spring each school year are a huge impetus for goal setting in American culture. Parents and schools use both the age and the grade level of the child to spur them on to further progress as well as set parameters for certain activities and behaviors.

The Father's Role in Education

As fathers take on a collaborative role with the school in teaching children, a father's role can be defined by certain qualities and behaviors associated with being a man and a father. Three key components of a father's role in the growth and learning of his children include the actual quality of being a man and a parent, his expectations regarding the future path for his children, and the way in which he teaches and engages his children through play and interaction. These elements help to define a father's role as a teacher of his children and a strong supporter of their formal and informal education.

Fathers, Masculinity, and Learning in the Outside World

Fathers exert a significant influence on children simply by virtue of their masculinity and the interactions they engage in that frame a child's encounters with the larger world. Fathers and mothers come to their experience with a child somewhat differently, in the beginning, simply by virtue of their gender.

From the time a child is conceived, it begins its life in the body of the mother (stop me if you have heard this before) and even from the moment of conception prepares to move away from the mother for the rest of his or her life. The father, who had a role in the conception of the child, primarily has only to wait and furnish support while the child is formed inside the mother. At the birth of the child, the mother typically has a very strong bond and a profound basis for a relationship with this child: it is *of* her and *from* her. Mother and child have spent a significant amount of time physically together that has contributed to this tremendous personal bond. It is arguable as well that the mother acts as she does and bonds as a parent because she is feminine and has gone through the incredible physical, chemical, emotional, and perhaps spiritual change of childbirth. The father has a more limited basis for his relationship with the child to begin with, as he has been waiting on the outside of the two bodies that were joined together.

Once a child is born of the mother, he or she begins in amazingly minute steps to move away from her. The child very literally starts his or her life at the actual physical core of the mother and then begins to grow, explore, and learn ever so slowly to be less dependent on the mother. Mothers are used to carefully nurturing a child since this has been part of their experience from the beginning of the child's conception. However, fathers have functioned on the outside of that relationship and thus enter the life of the child from the outside world. The father comes straight to the child and basically begins to help with the journey of becoming less dependent on the mother. It is a common part of a man's masculinity to help children face and encounter the outside world because they come from that world into a child's life. In a sense, they represent much of that world to a child and have a role in guiding children as they learn about the outside world.

Fathers and father figures are more likely to play rough with a child, take the child into the outside world, and envision a time when the child makes his or her way into the outside world as an independent adult. However, fathers do not necessarily have to "tug" on a child to bring him or her away from the mother. Unless the mother has an unhealthy grip on the child, it is very natural for the child to begin to move toward the world outside of the mother and explore it. Thus, a main job for fathers is to be the one who decides how far into the real world the child may go. He sets boundaries for the child and allows or perhaps even encourages the child to take risks within those same boundaries. He also typically sets the boundaries further out than mom would. Dr. Kyle Pruett of the Yale Child Study Center found that fathers are much more likely than mothers to encourage their children, regardless of gender, to explore the world around them.[3] He and others also suggest fathers may support novelty-seeking behavior because the father himself is a novelty for the child just by being "not the mom."[4]

One of the father's most important, and perhaps easiest, jobs is to be another and hopefully the primary person the child can trust besides the mother. A father's different perspective and natural tendencies as a male parent give him strength in his role as the one who helps a child move into the outside world. The differing tendencies of mothers and fathers as parents allow them to assist children in broader ways as they work together. These tendencies do not dramatically change once men and women become parents and, if used in complementary tandem, can help parents become more effective as a team when they use these masculine and feminine traits in their parenting. To describe parenting traits as feminine and masculine may ruffle the feathers of some who falsely believe people with mostly masculine or feminine traits can parent androgynously. If boys and girls are different and men and women are different, then surely fathers and mothers are different and can work together in ways that are both complementary and effective for the children they are to raise.

The influence of a father's masculinity and perspective is important for both sons and daughters as they grow up. Boys and girls may spend their early years with a mother and father who are both involved but then enter the environment of the public elementary school, which is primarily populated by females. Continuing interaction with fathers and other men, who may express different worldviews and ways of dealing with both the child and the outside world, allow children to experience other viewpoints and ways of interacting with the world around them. For example, a father's actions and reactions to his environment can teach a child how to deal with stressful situations, new people, and new environments from a male perspective. Both male and female children benefit from seeing this diversity of approaches because it can help them understand themselves as well as the opposite gender. According to scholar Norma Radin,[5] just by being "Dad" (masculine and different from a mother), a man possesses tremendous teaching potential.

Typically, fathers (and men in general) are expected to live in the "real world" and help children to prepare for it. This is, for good or ill, one of the expectations associated with masculinity and being a man. For women, there are expectations associated with being the center of home life for children. Even though a majority of women in the United States work outside the home, typically children often still see their mothers as the center of home and family life and look to their mothers to take care of their needs when they come through the door after working. It is a role that children associate with mothers because mothers have met their needs since birth and before. To a child, a mother exerts the gravitational pull of mothering that is, in its essence, based on caregiving and meeting their needs because that has been the child's experience. The key point here is that children may look to mothers and fathers for differing types of experience, and this has implications for how fathers and mothers relate to and interact with their children.

To observe how a father's masculinity plays a role in his parenting, you simply have to watch the reaction of children when a father enters the door at the end of his workday. Many times children will approach or even "attack" the father, and then the children or father will try to activate each other through some sort of physical contact—it might be hugs, high fives, or a new wrestling move. Outside of the physical interaction, children typically want to know what he *did* outside the home that day. He may cook supper on a consistent basis or take care of other household needs for his children, but they want to know what happened "out there" and how he reacted to it. The father can enter from a high-powered, influential job or back-breaking manual labor, but regardless of socioeconomic status he is seen as a representative of the outside world to his children. Children want to see how their father reacts to the outside world, to see both how he does things and why he interacts with them the way he does.

When a father brings the outside world into his home for his children, so they can experience it through his eyes, it gives him strength as a teacher. Since children are naturally headed into the real world, they want to know how to deal with it. A father's role as the bridge for his children to the larger world provides him with both a huge opportunity and responsibility. It is a responsibility to help his children develop skills to deal with the real world they will inherit someday. It is also an opportunity to validate the reasons for working hard in school: the world that challenges him every day is more easily navigated by those with an appropriate education.

Many of the fathers I encounter in schools and Head Start programs during a "Bring Your Dad to School Day," a "Math Morning," or a "Dad and Kid Reading Day" are hard-working men who are proud of the blood, sweat, and tears they put into supporting their families. However, even as they encourage and teach their children to possess a strong hands-on work ethic, they are also usually the first person to articulate the benefits of gaining an education that will allow their children to choose the type of work they will do to support themselves. Fathers are very quick to emphasize the idea that the children must support themselves. The vision they cast for their children regarding the importance of gaining a good education plays a tremendous role in the future success of their children.

Fathers as Visionaries for Their Children

Fathers enter a child's life from outside the sphere of the mother. Fathers thus take on the role of one who prepares a child for life outside that same sphere. A father tends to look at a child not only as a small, helpless human being but also as one who will not always be helpless and small. Fathers have expectations for their newborn babies as well as tangible hopes and dreams for the child and adult they will become. Even as a father may dream of his child becoming a sports star or astronaut, he also envisions the type of toddler he wants this newborn to become. For example, he may envision his child as a bright-eyed baby, an inquisitive toddler, an early reader, a high school honor student, or a successful, educated adult. Fathers who become active and engaged in the life of their young child usually do so because of a vision they have developed for their child. This vision may change as time passes, but by simply having a vision the father begins to develop in his role as the one most likely to help that child flesh out that vision.

A father's vision for a child is usually infused with a variety of expectations. This vision and the related expectations are also what help children understand how their interaction with their father actually works. A father's expectations for his child are what furnish structure to his interactions with his child. For example, a father may help a daughter study for a social studies exam because he knows she needs to develop the willingness and discipline to study for many future exams. Or a father might encourage a child to keep practicing on the basketball court in the driveway because he envisions the time his son or daughter will be in a game and need the skill to make a lay-up. Because fathers hold and set expectations for their children as adults, their actions as fathers are determined in some part by how it will affect the child's future outcome.

The vision a father has for his children can powerfully affect their education. To help children succeed, a father's mindset and expectations should not be based so much on particular future occurrences as on what type of person their child will become. Should children try to do well on a spelling test? Of course, but fathers often focus less on what will happen to their child and are more concerned about how their child will react if certain things happen. In other words, success on the spelling test is not as important to the father as is the success of achievement that comes through hard work and preparation. The father knows a good spelling grade is helpful in the child's future but real life success is not determined by grades so much as acquired skill and experience. Having expectations about how the child will *be* instead of what the child will *do* makes the father a strong influence on the child's education. Because he cannot predict what will happen to his children, he works to prepare them to have the character and skills that will make them successful on their own both in school and in the unpredictable real world.

Fathers' expectations that their children will become competent also become apparent to children when their fathers are active and engaged in their lives. As fathers express this expectation, it lets children know they are seen as competent and they hold a special place in the future. This knowledge helps children persevere in challenging academic situations because they begin to understand they are not only capable of handling the challenge but, if they persevere through it, they will be rewarded in the future. Fathers who have high expectations for their children's educational efforts and actively assist them tend to have children who do much better educationally.

Fathers as Teachers through Play

Play is perhaps the primary method of learning that children use to encounter the outside world in their early years. Research and observation has shown us that, because of their masculine nature, fathers interact with their children in a more playful manner. They tend to encourage children to explore.[6] This playful and sometimes rough style of interaction is seen by some as second-class parenting because it is different from the interaction most mothers have with their children. However, from the time their children are very small, fathers want to *do* something with their child. The father-child interaction is exactly that—*interactive.* It is active, engaged involvement between two people.

Fathers tend to engage and activate a child through play even at young ages. As the child grows and the father gains caregiving competencies, play becomes a little rougher and more unpredictable. This rough-and-tumble play not only is a way for children and fathers to make deep personal connections but also allows the father to gain confidence to take the child out into the further expanses of the neighborhood and community. Play is the vehicle that engaged fathers use to teach children about their own abilities and about what the child will someday be able to do. When children "win" or "conquer" the dad in physical play, they learn they truly have abilities. When children "lose" or "falter" against the old man, they can also develop the idea that, as capable as they are, they still need more skills and help. Fathers need to balance the amount of success and frustration children must handle in any given "teachable moment." These moments may include pulling themselves up on the couch, walking across the room, their first solo bike ride, or even conquering quadratic formulas. Play allows fathers to better control the laboratory that helps children learn to deal with the frustration and anxiety that accompany true learning. Play interaction is not the only way fathers engage a child, but it is a way for fathers to teach their children to fulfill the expectations fathers have set for them. A father who expects his child to be physically and emotionally resilient will allow a child to take certain risks and play in this rougher manner while also providing the guidance and support needed along the way.

In many of my educational workshops, I describe a scenario in which a child is running across the front yard and trips and skins his or her knee on the sidewalk. I ask the participants what would happen if only the mother were in the yard at the time. Almost to the person, they respond that surely the mother would run (or sprint like the Six Million Dollar Man) to respond to and care for the child. I then describe to many folks who are nodding their heads that moms typically not only respond to the child but clean the wound, apply antibacterial spray and a cartoon-character bandage, and then apply a kiss and an ice cream bar. Once all this is done, then the child stops crying because he or she is comforted.

In this same workshop, I describe the same scenario with the same child skinning the same knee, but this time the father is in the yard. Again almost to the person, they respond that the father would respond by encouraging the child thus: "Get up! You are fine." Though this story is humorous, it resonates with most parents. Because fathers expect their child will be a resilient adult, they expect that same child can and should be resilient right now! I reassure the workshop participants that fathers will attend to a child's needs but may not necessarily use antibacterial ointment (unless you count WD-40) or a bandage (unless you count duct tape). However, fathers will many times use humor to diffuse the child's anxiety and pain. Mothers would often think this is cruel except for the fact that most children will respond to it if the father has already been engaged with the child.

The point is that children need to be nurtured and cared for by either the mother or father when they experience physical and emotional pain, and sometimes when they are experiencing pain they need to be encouraged to endure it. Fathers are much more likely than mothers to help the child endure minor pains. For children to be resilient in an academic setting that can be painful both physically (remember dodgeball?) and emotionally (remember junior high?), the father needs to play with his child and view that play as an optimal teaching opportunity. My experience as a middle school principal taught me that fathers who did not interact (through play or caregiving) with their child at an early age often did not have enough connection with their child to help them navigate math class, reading problems, lunchroom traumas, or most of the trials and tribulations that come with pre-adolescence and the teen years. Too often, the child who has not been taught by the father through play does not know how to deal with adverse conditions that often accompany gaining an education in a building of 400 or 500 other children. Additionally, the father who has not played with his child has not had the opportunity to be taught by both the child and the fatherhood experience how to help the child as he or she faces minor and major adversities.

Why Fathers Count in the Education of Their Children

Although a discussion of fatherly traits that are required for the positive development of our children is necessary, it is also critical to see why those traits make a difference in the education of our children. The father's own masculinity and engagement with his child, high or low expectations of his child, and ability to teach and challenge through play are three important traits in helping children become educated learners. When fathers become involved in the daily lives and education of their child, they can make a huge difference in the outcomes for that child. Long observation, anecdotal information, and a strong and growing body of research evidence over a period of almost 50 years confirm the value of fathers' involvement in the education of their children. Researchers have done a tremendous amount of work to show us how fathers continue to count in the education of their children. To illustrate, I have chosen to highlight a few key research findings regarding the influence of father involvement on school readiness, academic performance in the classroom, and social behavior.

Children Are Ready for School

Being ready and able to enter the classroom, participate in school, and relate to other children is important for a child's educational beginning. Research on children and school readiness has illustrated some of the following points:

- Children of involved fathers tend to have a greater tolerance for stress and frustration. They are able to be one of many in a classroom, deal with not being the center of the universe, maintain their focus on their class work, and have the confidence to work on their own.[7]
- Children with fathers who are more active in their play initiation and give less immediate support in the face of frustration are more competent in being adaptive and solving problems.[8]
- When fathers are involved in the early life of children (18 months to three years of age), children are less likely to have separation anxiety from the mother or the father when they begin school.[9]

Children Perform Better in the Classroom

How do children perform academically when their fathers strive to be involved and engaged with them? Research findings suggest father involvement is a real and powerful factor in improving children's classroom performance:

- Boys who have nurturing fathers score higher on intelligence tests than do boys with less involved fathers.[10]
- Preschoolers with involved fathers have stronger verbal skills than those with less involved fathers.[11]
- Children with positively engaged fathers have a higher cognitive competency on standardized intellectual assessments.[12]
- Girls who have a close, warm relationship with their father have a stronger competence in mathematics.[13]
- Children whose fathers are highly involved in their schools are more likely to do well academically and enjoy school and less likely to have ever repeated a grade or been expelled than children whose fathers are less involved in their schools.[14]
- Children whose fathers share meals with them, spend leisure time with them, or help them with reading or homework do significantly better academically than children whose fathers do not.[15]
- Students with highly involved fathers have a more positive perception of their academic ability, which results in higher grades in secondary school.[16]
- Boys with highly involved fathers in their life receive superior grades and perform a year above their expected age level on achievement tests.[17]

- Fathers who support their children in less conventional ways have daughters who are more successful in school, work, and career and sons who eventually achieve more academically and in their careers than do children with less supportive fathers.[18]

Children Are Better Behaved

A child's educational experience is as much about social learning and growth as about learning to read, write, and do math. Research on child behavior in school settings shows father involvement is also a positive influence in this area:

- Father involvement correlates with fewer behavior problems exhibited by children, and this holds after controlling for the level of maternal involvement.[19]
- When both boys and girls are reared with engaged fathers, they demonstrate "a greater ability to take initiative and evidence self-control."[20]
- For predicting a child's self esteem, it is sustained contact with the father that matters more for sons but physical affection from fathers that matters more for daughters.[21]
- The higher a child rates acceptance by his or her father, the higher teachers rate the child on social competence and positive conduct.[22]
- Children who have fathers who regularly engage them in physical play are more likely to be socially popular with their peers than children whose fathers do not engage them in this type of play.[23]

Fathers' involvement with children strengthens the support system for children in their preparation for school, performance in academic situations, and social behavior with their peers and other adults.

Conclusion

We could fill several volumes with stories abut what great dads do to help their children get the education they want them to have. However, once we understand the *why* of fathers, we begin to better understand how we can lead fathers into being even more effective in the lives of their children. As indicated by research and observation, fathers play a very important role in the development of their children. However, we have to understand further that, due to their unique contributions, fathers' involvement is absolutely essential for children to reach their highest potential in education.

My organization, Strong Fathers–Strong Families, provides facilitation for school-based father and child interactive events. One of our most effective events is what we simply call "Bring Your Dad to School Day." I explain to people that this event is like the aforementioned Dads and Donuts Day on steroids. While the traditional Dads and Donuts Day events are always well attended, this version, in which we tell fathers there will be a workshop, are many times better attended than previous events. School administrators and teachers are amazed that many fathers will take time out of their workday to be at school to attend a workshop. The consistently high attendance is a testament to the fact that fathers around the country care for their children and will be involved if they are *invited*. Many of these workshops are at least two hours long, and although campus staff members predict the fathers won't stay that long, fathers consistently tell us in our evaluations they wish it were longer. It has been our experience that this willingness to be involved can have a *huge* impact on the school culture and student outcomes if schools and families will take advantage of the concern they *both* have for the children at stake.

While we invite fathers into the school and feed them a donut, we also take them a step further into the actual classroom to observe their children in their "natural" school habitat. Even though I am sure teachers are on their best behavior, we ask that fathers get a chance to see what happens on a regular school day. When these fathers visit the classroom, they gain a better understanding of what is expected of their children, how they are being taught to meet those expectations, and what their children and the teacher encounter in a given school day. After fathers are able to observe for a while, we pull them out to discuss what they saw in the classroom. They are amazed at the high level of academics being presented in the classroom, they are typically amazed at their child's abilities, and they are also concerned about the level of work that is being asked of their child. Once we describe the world into which their child will go upon graduation, they begin to set their resolve to do an even better job of helping their child gain an education.

In follow-up activities and interviews, we have found that fathers have gone home and begun to check the homework every night, taken over the job of helping their child review for tests, and become very involved in the various special projects that are sent home. Every father I have talked to has spoken of a better relationship with his child, a better rapport with his child's teacher, and an improvement made by his child in some academic area such as test scores, homework completion, or getting assignments from school to home and vice versa. Fathers have proudly told us about a child making the honor roll for the first time or making great improvement on report cards since they have become more involved. Fathers of children whose behavior was not up to par prior to their involvement have consistently reported that their children's behavior has improved since they have become more involved in their children's school. When we have involved fathers in the schools in a positive manner, we have also found that teachers are more receptive to involvement by both mothers and fathers and mention the same positive changes the fathers have described.

One of the reasons I presently work with schools to increase father involvement is that I saw what a difference it made when I was a teacher and administrator. Children with actively engaged fathers were always better behaved and had high levels of academic achievement. The inverse was also true that children who struggled the most with academic and behavior issues came from fatherless homes or a home where father and mother lived in chaos with their children.

As a father of two boys, I also know that I have a big impact on how well my sons do in class. By setting high expectations, checking on their classroom progress, and helping with class projects, I have seen my children maintain a high level of academic success. My wife, who is a third grade teacher, plays a huge role in their education as well, but I have seen the difference when I do not hold up my end of the bargain. I also see the confidence level of my sons change when I speak of their great abilities, and they have an even stronger resolve to do well when I inform them of how those abilities will help them achieve whatever they wish in the world outside our home and their school.

There is tremendous scientific and anecdotal data to confirm that a father's involvement in the education of his child is imperative to that child's success. When a family and a school work together to prepare a child to become an educated, productive adult, the father can assume a very powerful role in that child's education. By simply being male, being the masculine parent that is very different from the mother, and being a representative of the outside world, a father helps a child reach the fullest potential possible with the education he or she has received. Schools are dealing with a myriad of challenges as standards are constantly being raised while the traditional structures that have supported children and families have consistently been eroding. In order to develop an appropriately trained workforce for an ever-changing world economy, schools are scrambling to do more work with less time and money. It has been known for several years that children with parents involved in their education do better in school. However, schools have failed to do a good job of involving those families in order to improve student outcomes. The time and money would be well spent bringing families into the school as partners. An even more focused approach to exponentially improving social and academic outcomes for students would be to strengthen the role of fathers within the home, on the school campus, and invariably within the life of the child. Time and money would not only be well spent in such an effort but would pay dividends in human, social, and financial capital tenfold. If we will commit to such a worthy effort, our children, homes, and communities will be all the stronger for the effort.

Endnotes

1. U.S. Department of Education, National Center for Education Statistics, 2003, *Projections of Education Statistics to 2013*, and unpublished projections and estimates.

2. Pruett, K., 2000, *Fatherneed: Why Father Care Is As Essential as Mother Care for Your Child*, New York: Free Press.

3. Pruett, 2000.

4. Radin, N., 1981, "The Role of the Father in Cognitive, Academic, and Intellectual Development," in *The Role of the Father in Child Development*, edited by M. Lamb, New York: Wiley, pp. 379–428; Belsky, J., 1980, "A Family Analysis of Parental Influence on Infant Exploratory Competence," in *The Father-Infant Relationship: Observational Studies in the Family System*, edited by F.A. Pedersen, New York, Praeger, pp. 87–110.

5. Radin, 1981.

6. Pruett, 2000.

7. Biller, H.B., 1993, *Fathers and Families: Paternal Factors in Child Development*, Westport, CT: Auburn House.

8. Pruett, 2000.

9. Cox, M.J., et al., 1992, "Prediction of Infant-Father and Infant-Mother Attachment," *Developmental Psychology*, 28, 474–483.

10. Radin, N., 1972, "Father-Child Interaction and the Intellectual Functioning of Four-Year-Old Boys," *Developmental Psychology*, 6, 353–361.

11. Radin, N., 1982, "Primary Caregiving and Role-Sharing Fathers," in *Non-Traditional Families: Parenting and Child Development*, edited by M. Lamb, Hillsdale, NJ: Erlbaum, pp. 173–204.

12. Lamb, M., (Ed.), 1997, *The Role of the Father in Child Development*, 3rd ed., New York: Wiley.

13. Radin, N., and Russell, G., 1983, "Increased Father Participation and Child Development Outcomes," in *Fatherhood and Family Policy*, edited by M.E. Lamb and A. Sagi, Hillside, N.J.: Lawrence Erlbaum, pp. 191–218.

14. Nord, C.W., 1998, *Students Do Better When Their Fathers Are Involved at School* (NCES 98-121), Washington, D.C.: U.S. Department of Education.

15. Cooksey, E.C., and Fondell, M.M., 1996, "Spending Time with His Kids: Effects of Family Structures on Fathers' and Children's Lives," *Journal of Marriage and the Family*, 58, 693–707.

16. Grolnick, W.S., and Slowiaczeck, M.L., 1994, "Parents' Involvement in Children's Schooling: A Multidimensional Conceptualization and Motivational Model," *Child Development*, 65, 237–252.

17. Biller, 1993.

18. Snarey, J., 1993, *How Fathers Care for the Next Generation: A Four-Decade Study*, Cambridge, MA: Harvard University Press.

19. Amato, P.R., and Rivera, F., 1999, "Paternal Involvement and Children's Behavior Problems," *Journal of Marriage and the Family*, 61, 375–384.

20. Pruett, K., 1987, *The Nurturing Father,* New York: Warner Books.

21. Duncan, G.J., Hill, M., and Young, W., October 10-11, 1996, "Fathers' Activities and Children's Attainments," paper presented at the Conference on Father Involvement, Washington D.C., pp. 5–6.

22. Forehand, R., and Nousianen, S., 1993, "Maternal and Paternal Parenting: Critical Dimensions in Adolescent Functioning," *Journal of Family Psychology*, 7, 312–321.

23. Carson, J., Burks, V., and Parke, R.D., 1993, "Parent-Child Play: Determinants and Consequences," in *Parent-Child Play: Descriptions and Implications*, edited by K. MacDonald, Albany, NY: State University of New York Press, pp. 197–220; Parke, R.D., 1995, "Fathers and Families," in *Handbook of Parenting, Vol. 3: Status and Social Conditions of Parenting*, edited by M.H. Bornstein, Mahwah, NJ: Erlbaum, pp. 27–63.

David and Jonathan Dollahite on June 3, 2006, the day David baptized Jonathan

Turning the Hearts of Fathers to Their Children: Why Religious Involvement Can Make a Difference

Loren D. Marks and David C. Dollahite[1]

Charles Dickens, the English author and keen observer of human affairs, wrote of revolution-era France: "It was the best of times, it was the worst of times." In many ways, Dickens' dichotomy regarding "the best of times" and "the worst of times" captures the state of contemporary American fatherhood.[2] Many fathers are more highly involved with their children than the fathers of past generations.[3] Conversely, many other fathers are disconnected from or uninvolved with their children.[4] For many of the fathers who are highly involved in their children's lives, their religious faith is a motivational influence.[5]

The sphere of religion, like fathering, is also seeing the best and worst of times. On one hand, news reports of "holy war" casualties arrive with tragic regularity—often involving slain children, fathers, or both. On the other hand, data indicate that religious involvement strengthens marriage and supports men's ties to their children.[6] Religious belief and practice is a common influence in the lives of men across the world. Little empirical research, however, has examined *how* religion affects fathers and *why* religion is influential and meaningful to many fathers and their families.

As we study fathering and family life, this question of why religion is influential is central to our research on families. In our efforts to answer this and other related questions, we interview highly religious fathers and their families in their homes. We ask them about the meaning their religious faith holds for them; why they are willing to sacrifice significant time, money, and energy for their faith; and how their faith influences their beliefs about and approach to fatherhood and family life.

In our current research project involving religion, fathering, and families, we have conducted qualitative, in-depth interviews with an ethnically and economically diverse sample of more than 130 Christian, Jewish, Latter-day Saint (Mormon), and Muslim families from several regions of the United States. In our research, we emphasize that it is vital to consider three dimensions of religious experience—*spiritual beliefs*, *religious practices*, and *faith community*—if we are to understand the influence of religion in connection with fathers and families.[7]

In this chapter, we outline briefly the religious contexts in which fathers and children often exist in family life. Then we address ways in which religious beliefs, practices, and community support may help turn the hearts of fathers to their children. Finally, we conclude by addressing some of the key applications this topic may have for fathers, families, and those who wish to strengthen father involvement.

An Overview of Religious Involvement in America

Recent polls indicate that 90 percent of American adults report a belief in God and a similar number desire spiritual education and training for their children.[8] Most of this number attend worship services at least occasionally, and many highly involved persons report that their religious involvement has a significant influence on their personal and family lives. Indeed, for a substantial minority of Americans, religion is reportedly "the single most important influence in [life]."[9]

What evidence do scholars have that religious involvement is a salient influence in American life? In a landmark book titled *Handbook of Religion and Health*, Koenig, McCullough, and Larson critically review and analyze more than 1,200 empirical studies and 400 reviews on the connection between religious involvement and mental and physical health.[10] In sum, the book documents that religious involvement is linked with higher levels of functioning in a variety of areas. Perhaps most striking is the finding of one national study that people who attend worship services more than once a week live 7.6 years longer than non-attenders—and among African Americans, frequent attenders average a 13.7-year lifespan advantage over their nonattending counterparts.[11] Since religious involvement affects mental and physical health in measurable ways, might it not also affect relational health—particularly family relationships? The empirical answer is "yes," but as mentioned earlier our research effort is centered on discovering how and why family relationships, especially father-child relationships, are influenced by religion.

Turning the Hearts of Fathers to Their Children

The Old Testament is recognized and accepted as scripture by all four major faiths represented in our study (Christian, Jewish, Mormon, and Muslim). The last two verses of the Old Testament offer these words from Deity:

> Behold, I will send you Elijah the prophet before the great and dreadful day of the Lord: And he shall turn the hearts of the fathers to the children, and the hearts of the children to their fathers, lest I come and smite the earth with a curse. (Malachi 4:5-6)

A connection between the hearts of fathers and their children is thus suggested as an important divine concern. The influence of faith communities on such family connections is at the heart of our interest in understanding fathering. In the next portion of this chapter, we address ways in which spiritual beliefs, religious practices, and faith community involvement may help turn the hearts of fathers to their children.

Spiritual Beliefs and Fathering

Many fathering scholars have emphasized that father-child ties are typically more fragile and tenuous than mother-child ties.[12] Therefore, influences that support and motivate positive father involvement are especially valuable. Wade Horn, former president of the National Fatherhood Initiative, has pointed out that an important element of many religions is their capacity to hold men personally accountable to their God for their responsible (or irresponsible) fathering.[13] Indeed, many spiritual beliefs encourage the view that human beings, family relationships, and family responsibilities are *sacred*. In this section, we will discuss three spiritual beliefs the fathers we interviewed discussed in connection with their efforts to be honorable parents for their children. These beliefs are that (a) a child is a gift from heaven, (b) fathers are accountable to God, and (c) fathering should reflect God and His attributes. It is important to note that each of these beliefs promotes father responsibility and involvement; each belief will be addressed and illustrated.

A Child Is a Gift from Heaven
If a father believes God has called fathers to teach, bless, protect, and provide for the child God has placed in his care, then fathering becomes a sacred service for God, not just a socially prescribed role. Daniel,[14] a Jewish father of two, noted:

The miracle of watching your kids be born—if that doesn't make you religious, I can't comprehend it. If that doesn't give you faith in God, I don't
know what else there is in the world that could possibly move someone. I
go up at night and look at my kids sleeping in bed as if two angels were
lying there. I have faith then. I can't thank the Lord enough for the blessings I've received, that He's bestowed upon me—a great wife, two
extremely healthy children—I [need] someone to thank for that.

William, a Mormon father of six, explained his belief in his children's (and
his own) divine origin:

Our faith teaches us who we are, and it teaches us something very different from what the world teaches us, and that has a profound impact on
our lives, the things we choose to do, the way we choose to spend our
time, the circles that we get drawn into, and the circles that we stay out
of. I think that knowing [I am] a child of God and that I am not just a biological aberration . . . has had a profound impact on me and on the things
I have wanted to do. My faith tells me far more than the world tells me
about who I am. . . . [Subsequently, we believe] our children are an inher-
itance unto us from the Lord. In our case, none of them are "accidental"
or unwanted; they came as a gift and as great blessings.

The spiritual belief that "children are an heritage of the Lord" (Psalm 127:3),
as illustrated by Daniel and William, is a principle that motivates loving, involved
fathering by framing the father-child relationship as a divine trust.

Fathers Are Accountable to God

A second central spiritual belief for the fathers—closely related to the conviction that a child is a gift from God—was the spiritual belief that fathers must
account to God for their efforts in their fathering stewardships. A Christian father
of five explained:

[My faith] gives me a sense of accountability to someone other than just
me and (my wife). [I am accountable to] God above.

Several Muslim fathers we visited referred to a teaching regarding the importance of faithfully raising righteous children (particularly daughters). As Dawud,
a father of two, articulated:

There's a saying by our Prophet: whoever [has] been blessed with two
daughters . . . and raises them [to be] good and faithful . . . God will grant
him Paradise. . . . Now I'm the father of two daughters, so that's the way
my religion influences me—trying to raise them [to be good and faithful].

Many Muslim fathers also referred to their belief in the Day of Judgment, when they will be brought before Allah to answer for their deeds, including their fathering.

Nader (father of two): You're supposed to teach [children] at a certain age. . . . At the day of judgment, [an untaught child] will be asked about his bad deeds; he will point to his parents . . . and say, "Hey, my father didn't raise me right. He did not teach me this. He did not teach me that." So, if you actually did not teach your kids, you will be blamed for it.

Omar (father of two): When you stand before God on Judgment Day, you will have your book in your hand. You will be given your book in your left hand or in your right hand—right hand, you're good; left hand, you're [not]. It's everybody, not just Muslims. . . . [However,] the Koran always says God's mercy came before His anger. So before He gets angry with you, He has mercy on you.

Although Omar addressed accountability and judgment, this judgment is not necessarily harsh and punitive. Notice that Omar also emphasized God's "mercy before anger" approach as a divine parent.

A belief in God's patience and mercy for our parenting efforts was also recognized and echoed by Malik, a Christian father who was incarcerated for several months and had to plead with his wife for a second chance to be a "good husband and father." Discussing the issue of divine judgment, Malik explained:

[God]'s just waiting there with loving arms and says, "Come on, I understand. I understand what you're going through, because I've been there," . . . and I believe that's what people need to know. And God is not . . . sitting there with a black robe, pounding his gavel, but He's there with open arms, just waiting to take you in.

Malik's image of a God without a gavel who stands instead "with open arms, just waiting to take you in" seems to capture and embody what many of the participants believed about God and the ways they reportedly related with God. This point brings us to a third spiritual belief that was meaningful to the fathers in their relationships with their children—namely, fathers should strive to emulate their Creator.

Fathering Should Reflect God and His Attributes

Joseph, a Christian father of four, emphasized God's patience and mercy and explained how he tried to extend this model to his own fathering:

The whole meaning of life is to get to know God and to become like Him and to do the same sorts of things that He is invested in. And I'm sure that

I fall way short and still have a lot that I don't see and mess up on, but as a Dad you see your kids make efforts to please you and to do what you want and to imitate you; you don't get upset that they didn't do better. It's just amazing that they even want to, you know? So rather than focus on the [kids'] shortcomings, it's just about trying to [help them] relate to God and to get to know Him better.

Choi, a Christian father of two, similarly related his beliefs regarding God's love for him and his conviction that this provides a template for his relationships with his children:

One thing [from having a child] is that we know how God loves us . . . how we treat our children [lovingly] is how He treats us. The good thing is that I understand how God feels about me. . . . I [am] always thinking that I have to be a good parent for my child in terms of faith in God. This keeps pushing my efforts to keep growing in my faith for my children.

These examples highlight how these fathers' belief in a God who demonstrates caring and patience also informs their own parenting efforts as fathers.

A particularly striking example of a father reflecting God's attributes was offered by one of the mothers we interviewed. She said of her husband:

I've seen him changing over the years; he loves the Lord and wants to do what pleases Him . . . modeling what he sees as being valuable for the kids to see. . . . A lot of our understanding of who God is comes through fathers, because God is presented as a father in the Bible. If a kid grows up having a father who is loving and kind and supportive and strong in disciplining them, I think it is easier for them to understand God and who He is. A lot of the attributes he is striving for are aspects of God; it's all connected. So the kids see in their father aspects of God, a perfect God.

In sum, the highly religious fathers in our sample emphasized several connections between their spiritual beliefs regarding God and their personal responsibilities as fathers. A representative summary regarding this linkage was offered by a Jewish father (Jacob), who stated, "I don't know how to draw a line . . . between my [family] values and my religious values." Religion can thus build a powerful and unifying bridge between a man's spiritual beliefs and values and his parenting beliefs and values. Indeed, they may often be one and the same. The ties between spiritual beliefs and family practices can be strong, as fathers seek to live and do what they reportedly believe. Next, we will consider ways in which fathers applied and *practiced* their reported spiritual beliefs with their families.

Religious Practices and Fathering

As we pushed beyond spiritual beliefs to question fathers and their families, we found that the fathers we interviewed engaged in a variety of meaningful religious practices with their children. These activities include offering volunteer service together, praying together, reading scripture together, or participating in a variety of sacred family rituals. Instead of focusing on the variety of practices, however, we would like to focus on three recurring themes that explain *why* these practices were meaningful to the fathers and their families. The themes are that (a) sacred rituals bring meaning and order to family life, (b) sacred family time unifies the family, and (c) family prayer promotes connection.

Sacred Rituals Bring Meaning and Order to Family Life

Sacred rituals and practices have received recent attention from both clinicians and researchers as ways to create meaning and restore structure, order, and connection in a fast-paced and chaotic world that tends to ignore sacred and familial relationships.[15]

Many of the fathers and families we interviewed resonated with this notion, particularly those who were Jewish. Seth, the father of three, said:

Judaism gives meaning to the passing of time, and I think we need that as people. . . . From bris [circumcision], to bat/bar mitzvah, to marriage, to [the ritual associated with] death, it gives meaning to the passing of time. . . . Judaism gives meaning to that time and pauses the rat race. [It] fills certain needs that we have.

Many of us think of ourselves and our families as too busy or absorbed with life's frenetic pace to have a slow-paced family evening of ritual, but according to many of the families in our study, this is a core reason *why* family ritual is so vital. It is an oasis of time and reflection in the time-crunched and frequently meaning-parched existence outside the home.

Daniel, a Jewish father of two, said of his family's weekly Shabbat ritual:

We have Friday (Sabbath) nights at home together. Even when I worked unbelievably crazy hours and at crazy times in life, we always had Friday nights together. . . . I don't know that the Sabbath meal is a religious experience for most people, but for me, it's the heart of religion.

Deborah, the wife of Jacob, offered similar insights regarding the importance of ritual:

We do the same rituals for our holidays and all our Sabbath activities, and a lot of times we have to nag them [the kids] and pull them into things, but if we *don't* do something, or if something is missed, or if we say, "We are not going to do Shabbat," they say, "What do you mean we're not doing it!?" [with animation] They'll get mad that we don't do it. They're upset because it's not the way it usually is. They get upset if we don't hallow [the Sabbath]. It's very interesting. Sometimes they act like we are annoying them by dragging them through the ritual, but if we don't have it there for them, they get upset by it. . . . [Sacred ritual] provides a lot of strength and comfort and structure.

For these families, sacred rituals demanded work, preparation, and the hassle of "pulling" children into involvement. However, the meaning-filled punctuation of these rituals outweighed the associated costs and challenges. Perhaps the great effort that is often required to bring the outside world to a halt for the sacred and for family *is* the work that infuses these rituals with poignancy and meaning.

Sacred Family Time Unifies the Family

While the potential of sacred rituals to restore order, meaning, and structure to family life is evident, it was not the only benefit families described from sacred practices. These practices also strengthened and reinforced relationships. Several of the Latter-day Saint (Mormon) families we interviewed discussed Family Home Evening, a practice that in some ways parallels the Jewish Sabbath meal. Consuella, a mother of two, discussed this ritual and her husband's role in it:

Family Home Evening is a meeting we have, the whole family, parents and the children. We have the meeting every week, we sing a hymn, and we have a prayer. My husband or I will prepare a short lesson or teaching from the Gospel. Sometimes my husband, Alberto, prepares a longer lesson, and [then] our older daughter Maria [will] retell the lesson in her words. This has had a tremendous impact on her [and her sister].

Patricia, a Mormon mother of six, also commented on her husband's efforts to make sure their family had Family Home Evening each week and partially attributed the families' close relationships to this practice. However, like the Jewish families mentioned earlier, this "unifying" required overcoming the children's resistance. Patricia recalled:

When our children were very young, we used to think, "Why are we doing this [Family Home Evening]? This is crazy; they are not listening to a word." And now, as adults, the [older ones] will come back and say, "Family Home Evening was so wonderful!" [Laughs]. You don't realize the impact a lot of things have when you are doing them. . . . They are all very close to each other, and family is the most important thing in their lives . . . because of the kinds of things that we did, because we spent a lot of time together and still do.

In these examples, fathers and mothers who committed to family time with their children found that this type of religious practice has been highly beneficial despite the challenges of maintaining the practice at times.

The value of sacred family time was also apparent in other examples. Ibrahim, like many Muslim fathers, discussed the unifying power of the Ramadan fast for his family:

> [During the month of Ramadan] we all come together as a family, and we eat together and we thank God together, we pray together, after we break the fast. And then we do more prayers. So the whole month of Ramadan is a very unique experience. We do a lot less of the worldly things and a lot more of godly things. . . . When you do those kinds of things together every day, from day to day, it tends to bring people together, and it strengthens our beliefs and family.

In sum, for many families and fathers we interviewed, sacred rituals involving the whole family were meaningful in a number of ways and offered a context in which relationships were strengthened. As we will see next, sacred rituals are not the only (or even most salient) religious practice mentioned by these fathers and their families. Shared prayer was also a positive and spiritual influence in many of their lives.

Shared Prayer Promotes Connection

Another important religious practice fathers and mothers described to us was prayer as a family or between parents and children. This religious practice provided a context of meaningful connection and support for fathers to give children. Khalid, a Muslim father of three, referred to evening prayer with his children and discussed this practice as a context in which he could express and exemplify the care and concern he feels for his wife and children. He explained:

> We have five prayers a day [in Islam] . . . and once a day I get the kids to pray *with* me, in the evening. . . . [T]his is the central activity for our daily life. We start our day in the morning with a prayer, we pray all during the day, and there's one in the evening. . . . [At prayer time, we say to] the kids, "Let's quit the TV and pray, and you go back to the TV later," [so at] the end of the day I have my kids around me, and [I] thank God that they are healthy and safe. . . . My intention [is], I'm caring about my wife and my kids because my God asked me to care about them . . . my God asked me to do that.

David, a Christian father of five, also prays with his children each night. His wife, Annie, reported:

We pray together as a family. David is so good about bedtime. He has never missed a night, praying with the children, the boys in their room, because they're in the same room, and then the girls. I think for them it's routine . . . [it] evens their day out. It's something they've learned to expect . . . . Daddy's always going to be there. I feel like it de-stresses the home.

Prayer thus seems to be a religious practice that gives families a consistent platform for connecting with each other, often on a daily basis.

Other parents we visited talked about the value of prayer in family life as a means for resolving family problems. Wyman, a Christian father, expressed it this way:

We believe in the power of prayer in our family, and we pray every day together as a family. And then we believe that when we take any issue to God, He says that He'll fix it for us, because we believe that He's a God who hears our prayers and who answers our prayers. So as a family, we strongly believe in prayer, and so we encourage one another with prayer. Issues come up, and we pray together.

Wyman's belief that shared prayer helps solve problems was echoed by many other fathers. These problems often involved conflicts within the family, as Thomas illustrated:

There are many times when we don't see eye to eye, and my kids will be the first to tell you that. . . . But the important thing is that when you have an authority, a loving God in your life whom you're trying to emulate, then you can go to the Word that describes his love and his way of dealing with others. And you can measure yourself against that. And that generally brings us back to a common ground. . . . I personally feel that, when you have a conflict, the most important thing to do is go to God together with it [in prayer] and lay it on the table and ask for some spiritual direction [and] to reorient your own attitude toward the conflict.

For Thomas and his family, prayer frequently served as a source of conflict resolution between himself and his spouse or children. For Wyman's family, shared prayer is a time to seek help for issues that need to be fixed as well as time to encourage each other. For Khalid, the evening prayer is a time to thank Allah for his wife and children and to convey his desire to care for them. As one Jewish father expressed it:

There's three kinds of prayer: public prayer, private prayer, and family prayer. . . . In each case, you are trying to connect with God, which is *very* important for people who believe in God; we all want to connect with God.

For many of the fathers and families we interviewed, prayer *did* foster connection—connection with their wives, their children, and their God.

In our experience with fathers and families we have studied, learned from, and observed in meaningful religious engagement, their sacred religious practices provided a religious context that promoted father-child relationships and family closeness. Further, these practices often offered reprieve and solace from the hassles of daily life in ways that helped offer and maintain a sense of meaning and a sense of the sacred in family relationships.

Faith Community Involvement and Fathering

Spiritual beliefs and religious practices have been presented as two rich contextual influences for father-child relationships. Spiritual belief tends to be personal. Religious ritual and practice, as presented in the preceding section, is often familial. The final religious context we will address, however, is broader than the individual father and his own family. This context is *faith community involvement.* Wade Horn has emphasized that "there is no secular organizational network that has [the] degree of contact with as many men as do churches and synagogues" and that faith communities may have the capacity to influence fathers in ways that no secular institution can.[16]

In connection with our sample, faith community involvement is more than nominal affiliation with a religious group or what some participants called "pew warming" (e.g., occasional attendance with minimal contribution to the faith community). The fathers in our sample contributed an average of eight percent of their incomes and spent an average of nine hours a week engaged in religious activities and involvement. A concern is that in some cases these efforts by fathers to contribute money, time, and energy may be counterproductive. Rashaad, a Christian father of three, explained:

> [In connection with my church involvement] sometimes my wife lets me know, "Honey, I think you're overdoing it. I can just tell with your demeanor. You're just stressed out." Sometimes I've just had to break away and say, I just need a break. . . . I mean, I'm burned out, overloaded, and sometimes you feel like people don't appreciate you. . . . [S]ometimes you do just get overloaded.

Variations on Rashaad's expression of strain were quite common among the fathers (and mothers) in our study, implying a need for balance. However, these strains were ultimately voluntary. Sociologists Stark and Finke argue that when individuals invest in a faith community it is because the perceived benefits outweigh the perceived costs.[17] Consistent with this notion, the fathers and families we interviewed also emphasized many benefits they felt their faith communities provided to them and their children. We will mention and address three of these benefits: (a) the faith community is a support in overcoming or avoiding addiction, (b) the faith community "family" helps to raise children, and (c) the faith community offers fathers brotherhood and belonging. The fathers' own illustrative comments are included.

The Faith Community Is a Support in Overcoming or Avoiding Addiction

A few fathers from varying faiths discussed the important role of their faith and faith community in overcoming alcohol and drug addictions, and others mentioned that they felt their faith-based associations had prevented them from such addictions. James, a father of five, discussed this at considerable length and then summarized:

> [I could not have beaten my addictions without my] church. . . . I've been to rehabs, to AA and NA (Alcoholics Anonymous and Narcotics Anonymous) meetings; I tried everything you can basically try to quit. Now I'm not saying that these places don't have good foundations, because they do. But for me, I found something that was true to me and what I needed [in my church]. It took me a long, long, long road to find it. I mean [I had] to really soul search and find it. It took a long time, but I did. The answer was the church that I go to now.

Personal reports like the one above from James are consistent with a recent scholarly review that found:

> [M]ost of the nearly 150 studies on the relationship between religious involvement and substance abuse suggest less substance abuse and more successful rehabilitation among the more religious [and that] persons who are religiously involved—whether adolescents, young adults, or older adults—are less likely to use, abuse, or become dependent on alcohol or other drugs.[18]

These findings related to faith community involvement are especially relevant to fathering for three reasons: (a) substance abuse, especially alcohol abuse, is a disproportionately "masculine" problem;[19] (b) fathers' employment and provision capabilities increase when alcohol and drug abuse decrease;[20] and (c) an estimated 65–80 percent of domestic abuse is related to alcohol abuse.[21] Thus, by promoting recovery and preventing addiction, faith communities like the one described by James contribute to the physical, financial, and relational health of fathers *and* their families.[22]

The Faith Community "Family" Helps to Raise Children

An additional benefit of faith community involvement reported by a majority of the fathers and families was a sense of shared ties and social support that was often deep enough to be compared with "family." Abe, a Jewish father of three, commented that "the sense of community and continuity is [strong] . . . the extended Jewish community has become our family." One Mormon father addressed how his church "family" had been influential with his children:

> There's an old adage, "It takes a village to raise a child." Our congrega- tion is the [village] that we have chosen to focus our energies on, and I think our kids felt comfortable in that community and have drawn a lot of strength from it. . . . A lot of things that the church provides as part of its standard program are faith-initiated, and it's only because [so many] persons of faith are involved that there is enough energy around to make them happen. I think that they [our church family] have had a big impact [on our children].

Jose, a Christian father of four, commented:

> Our [involvement in our] faith allows us to separate ourselves from the world and to spend time together and with our children. . . . For me, faith and family and raising children [go] hand in hand. I can't imagine doing it without our religion.

Saul, like several fathers we interviewed, had become more involved in a faith community *because* of his children. Saul, who is Jewish, explained:

> There's a term in Judaism called *tikkun olam*. Loosely translated, it means to heal the world. [Our synagogue uses] that as a model, teaching the [children] charity, teaching them to do volunteer works. . . . The [Sunday] school, and the people we have at the synagogue, are a big piece of that. They create a lot of opportunities and environments to train the children . . . [but] I think we're involved in it, too, so that helps strengthen the family. It's kind of funny—*they teach us more than we teach them.* We have an extremely active religious school, and they learn a number of things, and through the bar and bat mitzvah process, *they've taught us.*

Saul's narrative underscores the important point that, although many of the fathers were involved in a faith community at least partly because of the benefits they felt their children received, they also reported benefits for themselves. Their faith communities had become for them and their children a place of support and instruction that enhanced their opportunities in family life.

The Faith Community Offers Fathers Brotherhood and Belonging

Compared with men of previous generations, today's fathers are far less likely to be engaged in community clubs, fraternal organizations, sports leagues, or other contexts that promote meaningful social and personal ties outside of work.[23] Further, a variety of modern forces combine to make stable employment with the same colleagues the exception rather than the rule.[24] These changes have served to leave many contemporary fathers without deep and supportive personal relationships, including relationships with role models and mentors for fatherhood and family life. Active faith community involvement was reported to us as profoundly important in filling these needs that are increasingly difficult to fulfill elsewhere.

Bryce, a Christian father of four, explained that key benefits of church involvement for him included models and parenting "references":

[Our faith community is important to us] as a support group, as a sounding board, as an advice group, which is why we chose to belong to a church. People who are 70 years old went through the [marriage and parenting] stuff, [so] we thought [it] was real important that we ask them what they did. They say, "This is how we handled it. This is how our friends handled it." [We've] got 20 references, [and] we can either consider their way or be hardheaded and try to do it our own way. On the other side of that coin, [we can] tell somebody 20 years our junior, "Been there, done that." That's the beauty of a congregation, you have people from one to 99, and wherever they are, you've either been there or are going to be there. You can solicit their input, whatever the situation.

For Bryce, the faith community gives opportunities both to learn from others about parenting and to share with others his own thoughts and insights. An active community of "models" to rely upon for parenting counsel and support is a benefit to fathers, who are often less apt than mothers to seek out formal sources of parenting support or instruction.

Other fathers referred to a sense of brotherhood among fathers in the faith community that was meaningful to them. Michael, a Jewish father, explained how this has helped him:

At our synagogue, they have services every morning and evening, and to have services, you need a quorum of 10 men. So I started going once a week and made a commitment to do that, to be one of the 10. [I]t feels, most of the time like [we are] making a difference [together]. . . . At the end of December, I was laid off from work, and it was amazing how supportive everyone was at the synagogue, helping me, giving me tips, checking to make sure I was okay. So that's a social support system that I have. And now that I have another job, everyone is friendly and congratulating me. There's that personal level of contact [among the men in the quorum].

Omar, a Muslim father, similarly commented on the brotherhood he felt at mosque:

Prayer in Arabic is called *salah*. What does *salah* mean? It means connection; it is your time to connect with God. When you go to pray at the mosque . . . everyone is equal. The poor person is standing next to the rich man; the sick is standing next to the healthy, the white is standing next to the black. There is an equality. From a societal standpoint, that brings the society together. No one is better than another, except by his good deeds. . . . Everyone stands in line. Before prayer, the prayer leader tells you to close the gaps (so your shoulders are touching your neighbor) . . . and then we pray together. This brings [us all] together.

The sense of togetherness, community, and support mentioned by Bryce, Michael, and Omar was simply but powerfully communicated by one immigrant Muslim father from the Middle East, who reported that worship at the mosque was the only time and setting in American culture where he felt he truly "belonged."

This sense of belonging is important on an individual level, but it can have profound implications on fatherhood. Steven Nock has emphasized, "As a member of a congregation . . . a man is known for how well he fulfills his obligations and responsibilities."[25] This means that an implied cost of men's "belonging" to such a faith community "family" is a continued effort to be the best father that his circumstances permit. We have now come full circle, because this contextual expectation of many faith communities is rooted in the first contexts we addressed in this chapter—the spiritual beliefs that a child is a gift from heaven, that fathers are accountable to God, and that fathering should reflect God and His attributes. In a phrase, fatherhood is sacred.

Conclusion

Contemporary images of deadbeat dads and news reports of global, religion-based violence are not the whole picture when it comes to faith and fathering. While these "worsts" are all too prevalent as realities, the fathers in this study present us with a more positive and hope-filled image. These fathers who value their religious involvement and its benefits report their efforts to integrate sacred beliefs and practices in ways that bless the lives of their children, their wives, themselves, and their communities.

In the social sciences we often become focused on problems in families and communities, almost to the exclusion of examining healthy fathers and families. Practitioners, researchers, and fathers themselves need more than an awareness of paternal pitfalls and pathologies. We need a vision of how to establish deep, generative, sacred relationships with our children and those of their generation, particularly those who lack involved fathers. For the fathers we have discussed and many others across the world, vital rays of that vision are provided by their religious faith. As William, a father of six, reflected on his 30 years as a father, he summarized:

Faith points a different direction than [selfishness and "the world"]. Faith gives you the patience to spend the time and the energy [your child needs] . . . and a lot of that is one-on-one time. Faith drives you to be involved [with your child] and [to] live outside yourself, to live beyond yourself.

In other words, faith turns the heart of the father to his child.

Endnotes

1. We are grateful for funding for this research provided by the LSU Faculty Research Grant and by the Family Studies Center and the Religious Studies Center at BYU.

2. Doherty, W.J., 1997, "The Best of Times and the Worst of Times: Fathering as a Contested Arena of Academic Discourse," in *Generative Fathering: Beyond Deficit Perspectives*, edited by A.J. Hawkins and D.C. Dollahite, Thousand Oaks, CA: Sage, pp. 217–227.

3. Hawkins, A.J., and Dollahite, D.C., 1997, *Generative Fathering: Beyond Deficit Perspectives*, Thousand Oaks, CA: Sage.

4. Popenoe, D., 1996, *Life without Father*, New York: Free Press.

5. Horn, W.F., 2001, "Turning the Hearts of Fathers: Faith-Based Approaches to Promoting Responsible Fatherhood," in *Clinical and Educational Interventions with Fathers*, edited by J. Fagan and A.J. Hawkins, New York: Haworth, pp. 191–214.

6. King, V., 2003, "The Influence of Religion on Fathers' Relationships with Their Children," *Journal of Marriage and Family*, 65, 382–395; Lehrer, E.L., and Chiswick, C.U., 1993, "Religion as a Determinant of Marital Stability," *Demography*, 30, 385–403; Mahoney, A., Pargament, K.I., Tarakeshwar, N., and Swank, A.B., 2001, "Religion in the Home in the 1980s and 90s: A Meta-Analytic Review and Conceptual Analyses of Links between Religion, Marriage, and Parenting," *Journal of Family Psychology*, 15, 559–596; Marks, L.D., and Dollahite, D.C., 2001, "Religion, Relationships, and Responsible Fathering in Latter-day Saint Families of Children with Special Needs," *Journal of Social and Personal Relationships*, 18, 625–650; Wilcox, W.B., 2004, *Soft Patriarchs, New Men: How Christianity Shapes Fathers and Husbands*, Chicago: University of Chicago Press; Wilcox, W.B., 2002, "Religion, Convention, and Father Involvement," *Journal of Marriage and Family*, 64, 780–792.

7. Dollahite, D.C., and Marks, L.D., 2005, "How Highly Religious Families Strive to Fulfill Sacred Purposes," in *Sourcebook of Family Theory and Research*, edited by V. Bengtson, P. Dilworth-Anderson, D. Klein, A. Acock, and K. Allen, Thousand Oaks, CA: Sage, pp. 533–541; Dollahite, D.C., Marks, L.D., and Goodman, M., 2004, "Religiosity and Families: Relational and Spiritual Linkages in a Diverse and Dynamic Cultural Context," in *The Handbook of Contemporary Families: Considering the Past, Contemplating the Future*, edited by M.J. Coleman and L.H. Ganong, Thousand Oaks, CA: Sage, pp. 411–431.

8. Harris Poll #11, 2003, *The Religious and Other Beliefs of Americans 2003,* retrieved March 29, 2004, from www.harrisinteractive.com/harris_poll; Nock, S.J., 1998, *Marriage in Men's Lives,* New York: Oxford University Press.

9. Miller, W.R., and Thoresen, C.E., 2003, "Spirituality, Religion, and Health: An Emerging Research Field," *American Psychologist,* 58, 24–35.

10. Koenig, H.G., McCullough, M.E., and Larson, D.B. (Eds.), 2001, *Handbook of Religion and Health,* New York: Oxford University Press.

11. Hummer, R., Rogers, R., Nam, C., and Ellison, C.G., 1999, "Religious Involvement and U.S. Adult Mortality," *Demography,* 36, 273–285.

12. Doherty, W.J., Kouneski, E.F.. and Erickson, M.F., 1998, "Responsible Fathering: An Overview and Conceptual Framework," *Journal of Marriage and the Family,* 60, 277–292.

13. Horn, 2001.

14. All names are pseudonyms.

15. Doherty, W.J., 2001, *The Intentional family: Simple Rituals to Strengthen Families,* New York: Quill; Imber-Black, E., Roberts, J., and Whiting, R.A. (Eds.), 2003, *Rituals in Families and Family Therapy,* New York: Norton; Marks, L.D., 2004, "Sacred Practices in Highly Religious Families: Christian, Jewish, Mormon, and Muslim Perspectives," *Family Process,* 43, 217–231.

16. Horn, 2001.

17. Stark, R., and Finke, R., 2000, *Acts of Faith: Explaining the Human Side of Religion,* Berkeley, CA: University of California Press.

18. Koenig et al., 2001.

19. Ibid.

20. Burger, W.R., and Youkeles, M., 2000, *Human Services in Contemporary America,* Pacific Grove, CA: Brooks/Cole.

21. Gallagher, B.J., 1987, *The Sociology of Mental Illness,* 2nd ed., Upper Saddle River, NJ: Prentice Hall.

22. Marks, L.D., 2005, "Religion and Bio-Psycho-Social Health: A Review and Conceptual Model," *Journal of Religion and Health,* 44, 173–186.

23. Putnam, R.D., 2000, *Bowling Alone: The Collapse and Revival of American Community,* New York: Simon and Schuster.

24. Hochschild, A.R., 1997, *The Time Bind,* New York: Owl Books.

25. Nock, 1998.

Author Sterling K. Wall, second from right, with his father, Elwood (right), and sons Sterling (second from left) and Taylor.

Serving in Order to Lead: Fathers as Leaders at Home

Kevin A. Galbraith and Sterling K. Wall

A few years ago, one of us was involved in providing counseling services in rural communities. Through this work, it became apparent there was an underlying problem affecting many individuals, couples, and families—the absence of good leadership within the family. An absence of good and caring leadership both directly and indirectly influenced a variety of problems many of these families were experiencing. For example, rather than working together for a common purpose, couples often pulled in different directions from one another, even though they generally had the same basic goals and desires in life. Roles between children and parents were often reversed. Out of necessity, some children were obligated to assume a primary role of caring for younger siblings. In other families, children imposed and dictated rules, limits, and terms to their parents. In many cases, parents seemed to be completely uninvolved in the details of family life. It became apparent that many problems within families (i.e., loneliness, depression, substance abuse, financial difficulties, divorce, parenting problems, etc.) could have been prevented or eliminated early on but instead grew larger because they were ignored or pushed aside. In too many instances, it seemed as if no one was "steering the ship." Simply put, good leadership was desperately needed in many of these families.

For instance, I, Kevin, recall working with a young teenager in junior high school, whom I will call Andy (name changed). It was obvious that Andy wanted and sought the attention of his father. However, no matter what Andy did, he was unable to get the attention he so desperately wanted. His father was not a bad man but did not have time for his son because he was too busy running his own business. Andy's father seemed to have the belief that as long as he provided for his son's temporal needs he had met his obligation as a father. Andy's mother was worried about Andy and took the initiative to schedule therapy appointments for him; however, she too was busy with the family business. Needless to say, Andy lacked motivation and the excitement for life that characterized many other young men his age. He was talented, bright, and had an ability to excel academically and in other activities, yet he was depressed and found little meaning in life. He was disinterested in school, and his mother was especially concerned about the early age at which Andy began experimenting with drugs. I, too, was concerned. Unfortunately, I was unable to provide counseling services for the family because the father believed it was unnecessary. Because of Andy's apathy about life, he reluctantly attended two to three counseling sessions to "get his mother off his back" before he quit coming. It was evident that many of Andy's problems related to the unwillingness of his parents to be parents. I believe they cared about Andy but were unwilling to provide needed leadership and invest themselves in his life. Andy seemed to especially need validation and involvement from his father.

Tragically, this account is too common and experienced by too many children today. Children want and need the leadership and involvement of their parents. Not long ago, I was reminded of how quick parents can be to disregard the needs of their children. My son's friends (from several different families) were invited to join our family to swim at the public pool, which they had done many times. On this particular occasion, however, we suggested that the friends invite their parents, who had never joined in on the fun. Although invitations were extended, parents were "too busy" to swim. It was surprising that the boys did not seem to be bothered that their parents declined the invitation. It seemed as if they had become accustomed to their parents' lack of involvement and grown to accept it. Building lasting relationships by spending time with their children seemed to be low on their list of priorities.

We assert that fathers can make a difference in their children's lives and that the most important leadership fathers will ever render will be within their own homes. Given the responsibilities associated with fatherhood, we also assert that fatherhood is synonymous with leadership. Fatherhood is all about teaching, nurturing, correcting, and providing for children, all of which are aspects of leadership. Families are in need of exemplary leadership from fathers, yet unfortunately, not all fathers are exemplary leaders. Moreover, it is not just the presence of fathers but *how* they are present that matters.[1] Many fathers are completely removed or detached from the lives of their children. Other fathers may be present but provide leadership that is stern, dictatorial, or authoritarian. While these types of fathers reflect the extremes of ineffective fathering, there are other fathers who are nurturing and involved. These fathers provide positive, encouraging, creative, humble, and firm leadership through their examples and understand what it means to be a father and live lives of service for their families.

Much evidence provided in this book supports the importance of father involvement both in the home and in the lives of children. This chapter focuses on fathers as providers of effective leadership for their families. Given the critical role men play in providing good leadership for their families, this chapter encourages fathers by describing different types of leadership, exploring the concept of servant leadership, and sharing principles associated with servant leadership that can be carried out in home and family life.

Different Types of Leadership

There is a large range of ideas and images that have been associated with the concept of leadership. As stated by Bass, "There are almost as many different definitions of leadership as there are persons who have attempted to define the concept."[2] One may think of leadership as a combination of personality traits, the power to force compliance, the ability to persuade or influence others, a set of behaviors or actions, the privilege to make decisions, or the amount of power one holds relative to others.[3] Not surprisingly, the definition one assigns to leadership, including the type of leadership one exercises, is generally related to one's philosophy, theory, or concept of what a leader is. Hence, there are stern, authoritarian leaders concerned with structure and the exercise of power.[4] To an authoritarian leader, leadership is all about establishing strict rules and enforcing compliance in order to maintain a strong task orientation. Power is used to ensure that others follow as the leader deems necessary. There are also democratic and egalitarian leaders, who, unlike authoritarian leaders, are concerned with relationships and joint decision making.[5] Rather than trying to control and dominate, these leaders encourage participation and are more concerned with supportive relations and building consensus. There are also laissez-faire leaders, who tend to remain detached and uninvolved.[6] These leaders tend to avoid making decisions or dealing with problems and generally avoid maintaining responsibility.

Each of these types of leadership can be found throughout history and across a variety of settings. However, not every type of leadership is most suited for the patterns of home and family living. Kouzes and Posner stated this principle well:

> Traditional management teachings suggest that the job of management is primarily one of control: the control of resources, including time, money, materials, and people. Flesh-and-blood leaders know, however, that the more they control others, the less likely it is that people will excel. They also know that the more they control, the less they'll be trusted. *Leaders don't command and control; they serve and support.*[7] (emphasis added)

This is especially true within family relationships. Power-assertive and uninvolved, laissez-faire leadership styles tend to be ineffective and can even create lasting family problems. Family leadership is most effective when it is nurturing and based on kindness, service, and a willingness to further the growth of others. One particular type of leadership that is especially relevant and applicable to the home and family is servant leadership.

Servant Leadership and Fathering

Amid the many theories and types of leadership, Robert Greenleaf's (1904-1990) teachings and writings on servant leadership have influenced and transformed leadership in many organizational settings, including businesses, charitable foundations, churches, and universities. Greenleaf's work was introduced at a time when scholars argued there was a crisis of good leadership in our society.[8] Accordingly, the ideals of servant leadership have been valued and continue to "create a quiet revolution in workplaces around the world."[9] Principles associated with this style of leadership stand in sharp contrast to the many self-serving styles of leadership so prevalent today. Servant leadership is not only applicable in organizational settings but has the potential to elevate the positive influence of fathers in the home and create a lasting influence on the quality of family life. Given their role as parents and leaders, servant leadership is especially relevant to fathers who are willing to go the extra mile to make a difference within their family relationships.

What exemplifies servant leadership? Robert Greenleaf described it accordingly:

> The servant-leader is servant first. . . . It begins with the natural feeling that one wants to serve, to serve *first*. Then conscious choice brings one

to aspire to lead. . . . The difference manifests itself in the care taken by the servant—first to make sure that other people's highest-priority needs are being served. The best test, and difficult to administer, is: do those served grow as persons; do they, while being served, become healthier, wiser, freer, more autonomous, more likely themselves to become servants? And, what is the effect on the least privileged in society; will they benefit, or, at least, will they not be further deprived?[10]

As stated by Greenleaf, servant leadership begins with a willingness to be of service. However, other characteristics and attributes associated with such leadership are nurtured when in the service of others, including humility, patience, self-discipline, compassion, and love. The core aspects of servant leadership might be summarized in the following points:

- The individual begins with a willingness to be of service.
- Once an individual begins to serve others, he or she then makes a conscious, deliberate choice to lead.
- The power behind this type of leadership is the willingness to serve. Service to others transforms the leader into an individual who is respected, admired, loved, and followed by others.
- The willingness of others to follow is voluntary, rather than forced.
- Individuals follow the servant leader willingly because the servant leader is genuinely concerned with furthering the growth of those he or she serves.

Therein lies the power behind servant leadership. Individuals respond to the leadership of those who serve them because they come to respect and love them.

Robert Greenleaf further expounded on this process of leadership in the following statement:

A new moral principle is emerging which holds that the only authority deserving one's allegiance is that which is freely and knowingly granted by the led to the leader in response to, and in proportion to, the clearly evident servant stature of the leader. Those who choose to follow this principle will not casually accept the authority of existing institutions. *Rather, they will freely respond only to individuals who are chosen as leaders because they are proven and trusted as servants.*[11]

We have witnessed practical examples of this in our own family experiences. For example, in Sterling's family there are five children. Living in Wisconsin, the oldest children periodically have the "privilege" of shoveling snow from a 100-foot driveway and chopping and hauling wood to heat the home. I have learned that when I arrive home and insist that they go outside immediately to get the task done I am met with a number of complaints and sullen resistance. However, when

I say "*Let's* go outside and shovel the driveway," I am met not necessarily with perfect cooperation but with much more open and willing attitudes (especially since they look forward to throwing snow on Dad when he is not looking).

A father's ability to lead his children is tangibly increased by the amount of time he spends in their direct service. However, that service often consists of simple things we don't ordinarily think of as service, like playing one of their favorite board games with them, reading them a book (even older teenage boys like this), or playing catch. The most powerful impact seems to come from the little interactions when we are doing nothing but sitting and talking. Children appreciate knowing that fathers are there to listen to them and serve them by being present and attending to their interests rather than using them to serve their own needs.

On one occasion, while passing through the kitchen, I (Sterling) whispered to my wife to join me in the other room for a moment. We went into the living room and sat down. I told her to just wait. Within a few minutes, all of the children had come into the room, like butterflies to pollen, each talking about different things. We made a conscious effort to attend to them and their interests. The energy and life that was infused into them and our family was amazing! We ended up playing charades later that night with all of the children enthusiastically participating.

What does this have to do with leadership? Everything! As previously stated, the servant leader serves first. We had served our children in the ways they, and many children today, are eagerly looking for—attention from someone who cares about them. For example, after spending time listening to our children, it was time to set the table for dinner. When they were "invited" to help with this chore, cooperation and teamwork rather than sullen resistance followed, with Dad tossing dishes to the kids to put on the table. Fathers find they carry a more powerful influence and increased ability to lead their children when serving their children first.

The ethic of servant leadership dates back many years. One approach in the study of leadership is to examine historical models of individuals that provide specific examples of leadership styles. Not surprisingly, the figure most often associated with servant leadership as a model is Jesus, the originator of the Christian faith tradition.

Jesus, whose leadership has had a profound influence on humanity, fully understood the power of servant leadership. This is evident in the accounts of his love, example, and life of service. He also taught the principle of servant leadership. For instance, in one account his disciples had been disputing among themselves who should be the greatest among them. Jesus provided loving correction by teaching them, "If any man desire to be first, the same shall be last of all, and servant of all" (Mark 9:35). On another occasion, Jesus taught a multitude and his disciples, "But he that is greatest among you shall be your servant. And whosoever shall exalt himself shall be abased; and he that shall humble himself shall be exalted" (Matthew 23:11–12). Jesus also modeled the principle of servant leadership in very specific ways, for example, by washing his disciples' feet (John 13:5). In that particular instance, Jesus taught his followers that if he, whom they called Lord and Master, should wash their feet, then they "ought to wash one another's feet" and follow his "example" and "do as I have done to you" (John 13:14–15).

These accounts of Jesus are noteworthy because they illustrate true servant leadership, as described by Greenleaf. First, Jesus served others actively and consistently. Second, he led, as is evident by his desire to teach, correct, and inspire those he served. Moreover, he taught and led in a way that elevated his followers so they grew as individuals. Through his service and leadership, his followers worked to become more wise, more autonomous, and better servants themselves. It should be noted that principles of servant leadership are also found across many other faith traditions and life philosophies. For fathers, the key point is to define the central principles of such leadership and pursue them in family living.

For fathers, then, who wish to pursue this type of leadership in the home, their task is to become of service to their spouses, children, and other family members and to merit the trust and willing support of those they wish to lead and serve. Furthermore, servant leaders must provide leadership by actively teaching, guiding, and correcting those they lead. It is thought provoking to imagine the impact of the servant leadership of a trusted, loving father who leads by example in comparison to a father who uses an authoritarian approach. Rather than following or obeying out of contempt or fear, children would be more likely to trust and follow the leadership of a father out of love, respect, and appreciation. In such a context, mentoring from an admired role model takes place, and close bonds between fathers and family members can form. For instance, Sterling's children were much more willing to shovel the snow when their father grabbed a shovel, too, especially when he helped them build a fort with the snow they removed.

As husbands and fathers ourselves, we understand some of the challenges and demands associated with fatherhood and are fully aware that neither fathers nor family relationships are ever perfect. We also realize some children may choose to turn from the leadership of their parents, even when the leadership is closely aligned with servant leadership. However, we are confident that the closer fathers come to implementing true servant leadership, the happier and more satisfied each member of the family will be. In a sense, their influence will, in the words of Greenleaf, act as "a leaven" for the whole family.[12]

Becoming a Servant Leader

What can fathers do to become better servant leaders? Larry Spears, who has written extensively on servant leadership, has observed:

It is important to note that servant leadership is not a "quick fix" leadership approach. . . . At its core, servant leadership is a long-term, transformational approach to life and work—in essence, a way of being—that has potential for creating positive change throughout our society.[13]

In other words, a servant leader is something one becomes. It is a way of being. When a father consciously and regularly serves his family, the motives behind his service and leadership change so that the service and leadership become more genuine and are a natural response to helping others grow as individuals. Spears also observed, "True leadership emerges from those whose primary motivation is a deep desire to help others."[14] Developing a sincere desire to serve and lead is a process that may need to be acquired over time. However, two practical steps can help fathers to develop this desire and provide servant leadership within their families.

First, an important step for a father is to consciously adopt a new vision of himself as a servant to the family. Picturing or envisioning himself in his role as a servant and a leader sets the stage for kind acts of service and active leadership to follow. Without the ability to envision oneself as a servant leader, providing this type of leadership will be especially challenging. Fathers must envision their fatherhood role in a new light. Perhaps a personal example from one of us will clarify this principle.

I, Sterling, recall a time several summers ago when my wife and children had left for a few weeks to visit grandparents while I stayed home to finish my dissertation. With the empty house and quiet evenings, I spent a considerable amount of time reading, pondering, and reflecting on our family and what I could do to make our interactions more positive. After a time I realized I was there to serve my family and that through service both my family and I would experience the joy we were seeking. I anxiously waited for their return as I committed to begin each interaction with this simple thought in mind, "How can I serve you?" They returned, and it was a night-and-day difference. The relationship with my wife was strengthened immensely, and in turn she responded with increased service of her own toward me and the children. There was great cooperation between our children as well. Such a powerful change came from simply shifting my attitude to serving my family rather than expecting them to fit around my schedule and needs.

To cement this kind of vision, fathers can take action by serving and making an effort to provide caring leadership. In other words, fathers will be more able to see themselves as servant leaders in family life when they are engaged with their children and contribute in caring ways. Such efforts should continue even when a father makes mistakes and feels he is not reaching the ideal of a servant leader. This type of leadership is not developed overnight. Rather, it is created by forming a vision and, over time, working toward becoming a more committed servant leader. It requires time, patience, and a sustained effort. Through leadership marked by service, fathers may overcome the disposition to be unkind or use power in a self-serving or coercive manner. Service encourages the development of virtues such as love, appreciation for others, cooperation, persuasion, patience, and understanding. In other words, as fathers provide service in the home to family members, those traits and attributes specifically associated with servant leadership increasingly become part of their character. A father's motives for helping others will not only be more genuine but will be recognized as such by those being served.

A second key step for fathers in becoming servant leaders is to consistently perform small and simple acts of service to family members on a daily basis. Reflecting on our own lives, we have observed that small acts, when applied on a daily basis, can leave a lasting impression and have a profound impact on children and spouses. Our own fathers provided larger acts of service that were greatly appreciated (i.e., assistance with the purchase of a car, going on an exciting family trip, etc.). However, the greatest impact in our lives came from a pattern of small and simple acts of service over time. Kevin was influenced by fishing trips with his father (even though he was not particularly fond of fishing), games on the front lawn, his father's humor and excitement for life, time spent working together, little tips on how to make the "world's finest chocolates," long-distance runs together, and most important, the example his father set as a dedicated and involved father. Sterling recalls time with his father hauling wood, bucking hay, and playing catch in the field. He also remembers his father taking the family to the downtown movie matinee and seeing his father sleeping through the show because of the sacrifice he made working on the family car for several nights.

These examples do not exemplify just service but also leadership and being actively involved in family life. The family was the highest priority of our fathers, and this was evident in their actions. This deep commitment is illustrated by a simple story, as told by Sterling:

> I caught a glimpse of the sacrifice a servant father makes when I asked my own father what he liked most about his career. He said, "I get my summers off." I asked, "Yes, but what do you like about it?" To which he responded, "I have hated it for the last 20 out of 30 years, but I stuck with it to support our family." Now, I realize my father could have switched careers, but in his mind, he was there to support the family, and not the other way around.

Because of their example and vested interest in our growth and development, we admire our fathers and have sought to follow their leadership. We observed that the little things our fathers did that left a lasting impression on us are the same types of things that mean so much to our own children today. Bedtime stories, piggyback rides to bed, helping a child repair a bike, assistance with homework, taking an interest in a child's hobby, working with a child to accomplish a task—these are among the little things appreciated by our children. Such small and simple acts of service bless all children.

Overcoming Discouragement as a Father

We recognize that this vision of servant leadership for fathers is idealistic and sets a high standard. Some fathers may feel overwhelmed and even discouraged from trying to live up to this standard. A father's efforts in this manner may not bear fruit immediately. His children may be unappreciative at first, and he may be impatient. However, there is a line of research that provides encouragement in spite of the personal shortcomings or limitations fathers may have. John Gottman found that those fathers who are emotionally open and sensitive to their wives and children have happier, more stable marriages and children who are more socially adapted.[15] Gottman also found that, even though negativity existed, married couples were more likely to have happy, stable marriages if their relationships were characterized by more positive than negative interactions.[16] Happily married couples had a ratio of five positive interactions to every negative interaction, whereas distressed couples had a ratio of one to one. This finding was the underlying difference between the two types of couples. An expression of appreciation, laughter, humor, a shared ritual or activity, a smile, or a meaningful discussion—all have important implications for couples. Likewise, we believe this principle has important meaning not only for couples but also for fathers and children. Fathers are not perfect; they make mistakes. In spite of their deficiencies and limitations, if fathers will do their best by getting involved in the lives of family members and increasing the number of positive interactions through kind acts of service, we are confident they will be respected and appreciated as fathers and leaders. We are also certain they will be instrumental in furthering the development of each member of the family.

Conclusion

The influence of fathers is needed in the home. Families need good leadership. Given its emphasis on serving for the betterment of others and leading in a caring manner, the ideal of servant leadership can be especially relevant and applicable to fathers and families. Through good leadership, fathers make a difference both in helping the family and showing their children what it means to be a father.

When we think of fatherhood and leadership in family life, the image of a trim tab on a ship comes to mind (as related by Covey).[17] Ships are directed by the rudder, which can be very difficult to turn when currents in the ocean are strong and when a ship is large. However, turning the large rudder is manageable with a trim tab—a small rudder connected to the big rudder. The trim tab, which is small and easily turned, forces pressure from the current onto the large rudder, causing it to turn to direct the destination of the ship. Similarly, fathers can act as trim tabs within their families. Through caring leadership and service, fathers can create a family environment that supports the growth of family members while enriching their own lives and experiences as fathers.

A father's decision to serve might be called the trim tab for his family. Andy's father, mentioned at the beginning of the chapter, had not made that decision, and Andy seemed to drift as a ship at sea without the constancy provided by a rudder. It is our hope that more fathers will choose to serve and meet the often overlooked needs of their families. As they do, bonds will be formed, love will be increased, and they will provide leadership that has a lasting influence among those they serve.

Endnotes

1. Gottman, J., 1998, "Toward a Process Model of Men in Marriages and Families," in *Men in Families: When Do They Get Involved? What Difference Does It Make?* edited by A. Booth and A.C. Crouter, Mahwah, NJ: Lawrence Erlbaum Associates, pp. 149–192.

2. Bass, B.M., 1995, "The Meaning of Leadership," in *The Leader's Companion: Insights on Leadership through the Ages*, edited by J.T. Wren, New York: The Free Press, pp. 37–38, at 38.

3. Bass, B.M., 1990, *Bass and Stogdill's Handbook of Leadership: Theory, Research and Managerial Applications*, 3rd ed., New York: The Free Press.

4. Ibid.

5. Ibid.

6. Ibid.

7. Kouzes, J.M., and Posner, B.Z., 1995, *The Leadership Challenge*, San Francisco: Jossey-Bass, at 16.

8. Bennis, W., and Nanus, B., 1985, *Leaders: The Strategies for Taking Charge*, New York: Harper and Row; Burns, J.M., 1995, "The Crisis of Leadership," in *The Leader's Companion: Insights on Leadership through the Ages*, edited by J.T. Wren, New York: Free Press, pp. 8–10; Gardner, J.W., 1990, *On Leadership*, New York: Free Press.

9. Spears, L.C., 1998, "Introduction," in *The Power of Servant Leadership*, edited by L.C. Spears and P.B. Vaill, San Francisco: Berrett-Kohler Publishers, pp. 1–15, at 2.

10. Frick, D.M., and Spears, L.C., 1996, "Introduction," in *On Becoming a Servant-Leader*, edited by D.M. Frick and L.C. Spears, San Francisco: Jossey-Bass Publishers, pp. 1–10, at 1–2.

11. Greenleaf, R.K., 1977, *Servant Leadership: A Journey into the Nature of Legitimate Power and Greatness*, New York: Paulist Press, at 10.

12. Frick and Spears, 1996, at 5.

13. Spears, 1998, at 4–5.

14. Spears, L.C., 2003, "Introduction," in *The Servant-Leader Within: A Transformative Path*, edited by H. Beazley, J. Beggs, and L.C. Spears, New York: Paulist Press, pp. 13–27, at 15.

15. Gottman, 1998.

16. Gottman, J.M., and Silver, N., 1999, *The Seven Principles for Making Marriage Work*, New York: Three Rivers Press.

17. Covey, S.R., 2002, "Servant Leadership and Community Leadership in the Twenty-First Century," in *Focus on Leadership: Servant-Leadership for the Twenty-First Century*, edited by L.C. Spears and M. Lawrence, New York: John Wiley & Sons, pp. 27–33.

Fathers and Contexts of Support

T he three chapters in this section furnish understanding about mechanisms of support for fathers and their involvement with children. Parenting is an experience that demands much of individuals and involves ongoing obligations over a long period of time. Fathers and mothers both benefit from support as parents, and these chapters identify contexts that can be beneficial in providing such support to fathers and father figures including community initiatives, small groups, and parent and family education.

In Chapter 24, "Fatherhood in the Community Context: A Grassroots Approach to Engaging Communities to Support Responsible Fathering," Joseph White addresses the issue of community support for fathers and their involvement with children. He provides a case for the importance of strengthening father involvement and then utilizes a case study approach to examine key practices in a grassroots, community-based effort to support responsible fatherhood. As founder of the Sioux Falls Fatherhood Initiative and a university scholar, White brings both practical experience and research findings to bear on his discussion of the community context as a support system for meaningful father involvement. His discussion includes exploration of themes and outcomes from interviews with key leaders in the community and a leadership summit on fatherhood.

Chapter 25, "The Big Benefits of Small Groups for Fathers," introduces the concept of small group support for fathers in their involvement with children. Author and scholar Ken Canfield, founder and president of the National Center for Fathering, describes the potential of small groups for providing meaningful support to fathers in their efforts, shares real-life examples of the benefits of small groups for men, gives a detailed rationale for the power of small groups for fathers, and suggests ideas for making them work.

Parent and family education as a source of support for fathers in their efforts is explored in Chapter 26, "Supporting Fathers through Educational Programs: Promising Strategies and Positive Successes." As a family life specialist and educator, Sean Brotherson develops, implements, and evaluates educational resources and programs for parents. In this chapter, he challenges the deficiency mindset about fathers' involvement in parent education, discusses issues related to supporting fathers through educational programs, and suggests a series of best practices for implementing such programs. Such practices can make a meaningful difference by supporting fathers' involvement.

This section provides an introduction to some of the contexts of support that can be mobilized to encourage more responsible and meaningful father involvement. Community-based initiatives, small groups, and parent and family education each offer unique components that can facilitate healthy fathering in important ways. These contexts of support continue to grow and become more influential as efforts expand to empower fathers and provide them with more resources and support. Such contexts of support may be the primary means of creating and sustaining long-term, focused efforts to address ongoing concerns about responsible fathering and assist men in becoming more fully engaged and responsible in their family lives.

Author Joseph M. White with his son, Joseph, Jr.

Fatherhood in the Community Context: A Grassroots Approach to Engaging Communities to Support Responsible Fathering

Joseph M. White

By the end of the past century (2000), three out of four Americans believed fatherlessness was among the most significant problems facing the United States.[1] This belief stemmed largely from the prevalence of father absence in family life, the rate of out-of-wedlock births, and the continuing difficulty of divorce. There are 25 million children living without their biological father in the United States (more than one-third of all children in this country). More than 1.3 million children annually are born outside of marriage (one-third of all births). Up to one million children are involved each year in divorce. There are pervasive negative outcomes associated with each of these factors.[2] Such statistics should be all too familiar by the time you get to this point in the book. However, these statistics also bear repeating and help to make the case for community-level action in strengthening father involvement.

The problem of father absence exists in cities both large and small. For example, Sioux Falls, South Dakota, is a small to moderately sized community in the Midwest and has similar rates of children under 18 living in mother-only families (21.7 percent) as the state (18.6 percent) and nation (22.4 percent).[3] The challenges associated with this reality in family life can be many. Children in father-absent homes are at least two to three times more likely to be poor; use drugs; experience educational, health, emotional, and behavioral problems; be victims of child abuse; and engage in criminal behavior than peers with married, biological (or adoptive) parents. Many single mothers make heroic efforts and sacrifice, and as a result, their children are often well adapted. But these statistics highlight the challenge they face when carrying the load by themselves.

Children with loving, involved fathers are more confident, sociable, and likely to have healthy self-esteem, do well academically, and engage in prosocial behaviors. They are more likely to avoid problem behaviors such as drug use, truancy, and criminal activity. While the problems associated with fatherlessness affect families and individuals at alarmingly high rates, they also affect communities in dramatic ways. Problems associated with father absence create significant strains on local social and human service agencies, educational systems, police departments, judicial and legal systems, and other community entities. Father absence or underinvolvement affects nearly all aspects of community life. Community context is critical to understanding family life,[4] and scholars have called for community strategies that include responsible fathering.[5]

Local, community-based fatherhood efforts have great potential and may be one of the most important keys in turning the tide of father absence and changing the culture of fatherlessness in society. Community-based efforts have wide support in a variety of areas including full-service schools,[6] alcohol abuse prevention,[7] and marriage.[8] There are a variety of well-designed programs to assist fathers and families. However, they often operate at a group or organizational level with little collaboration among community leaders who could enhance and facilitate the services offered. Collaborative, community-based efforts should begin by establishing a clear mission statement, goals, and objectives that set the standard of what is expected of fathers; what healthy, involved fathering looks like; and how fathers will be treated. Such a process will help organizations and individuals work with fathers based on those standards and pay huge dividends in collaborative efforts designed to promote responsible fatherhood.

A wise and trusted leader in his final years said, "When you get to be my age, nothing else in life will matter so much as how well your children turn out." The purpose of this book has been to make the case for why fathers count in the lives of their children in a variety of settings, from early childhood to marriage, from fathering to grandfathering, from attachment to psychological development, from divorce to incarceration, from small fathering groups to education, from diverse ethnic backgrounds to religious and spiritual settings. It is the purpose of this chapter to highlight how all these settings and more can come together and work for the greater good, how representatives from each of these areas can unitedly bring their knowledge and expertise to bear in promoting responsible fatherhood. More specifically, this chapter will show how leaders in one Midwestern community recognized the importance of this issue and rallied together to develop collaborative action plans intended to turn the tide of father absence. An overview of our community fatherhood coalition approach will be followed by information on a series of interviews I conducted with community leaders and conclude with insights and recommendations from a community leadership summit on fatherhood.

Overview of a Grassroots Approach to Strengthening Fatherhood

It is often best to place the tools for solving a community issue in the hands of local people who can develop or use local resources and find local solutions. In strengthening fatherhood, there must be a willingness for local agencies and individuals to step forward and collaborate in providing services and programs that can aid fathers and families. This chapter highlights lessons from a collaborative effort between the Dakota Fatherhood Initiative and the Sioux Falls Area Community Foundation (SFACF), begun in 2003, to develop a local fatherhood initiative that would serve fathers and their families within the Sioux Falls area.

The general plan for developing our grassroots community-level movement called for several steps leading up to a Leadership Summit on Fatherhood (LSF): developing a media campaign, identifying and interviewing community leaders from various sectors, writing a report of findings, recruiting key players from throughout those community sectors, organizing and hosting a leadership summit, and writing a final report summarizing the LSF, each sector's action plans, and general recommendations to the community for the work to continue.

To begin the work for our community-based effort, the SFACF stepped forward with funding support and encouragement. The SFACF provided financial support and assistance in identifying potentially interested leaders from various sectors of the community. Without the leadership, guidance, and support of this organization, particularly from Marsha Englert, the foundation's program officer, who had the vision of developing a local fatherhood program, the project would have struggled to succeed. This basic approach to beginning a community-based fatherhood effort was initially designed by the National Fatherhood Initiative, which also provided important technical assistance as the work began.

Connecting with Community Leaders

For any community-based effort to succeed, there must be communication with leaders and groups within the community, and steps must be taken to invite their support and involvement. For the effort in Sioux Falls, this developed through a series of interviews with community leaders. The community leader interviews were designed to assess perceptions of fathering issues, gather feedback, and build support for a local fatherhood effort. This series of interviews was conducted in the summer of 2003, and through it I was able to gain a fairly clear picture of how fathers count in the eyes of a diverse group of community leaders.

In the 39 community leader interviews, I asked men and women about perceptions of father absence, benefits of father involvement, and suggestions for promoting father involvement within their sector and in the community at large. I also asked about specific resources available for fathers and barriers to promoting responsible fatherhood. Three out of four interviewees were male, and together they represented 11 different sectors of community life, including business, nonprofit, social service, faith, education, health, civic, legal, media, and government sectors. Positions of those interviewed varied widely and included president, vice president, director, general manager, lieutenant governor, city councilor, county commissioner, sheriff, state attorney, judge, pediatrician, family therapist, childbirth education coordinator, superintendent of schools, station manager, financial advisor, public affairs officer, and youth and family pastors. Community leaders who participated in the interviews reflected a wide cross-section of community life and provided the basis for a strong grassroots movement.

One of the initial objectives of the interviews with community leaders was to identify current resources available to help fathers in the community. We wanted to create a community-level assets map that identified where services for fathers were physically located and how far they were from those who needed them. Unfortunately, with the exception of a new "Dad and Baby" class at Avera McKennan Hospital and an Even Start fatherhood program, there were no programs with which to create a map, so that part of the project was put on hold.

In addition to the assets, we wanted to identify leaders interested in supporting responsible fatherhood within their organizations and realm of influence. Several prominent organizations stepped forward right away: Krispy Kreme offered a monthly Donuts with Dad day for fathers to come in with their children and receive free donuts; the Sioux Falls Skyforce (semiprofessional basketball team) donated 2,000 tickets for dads and their children to attend a home game at the Sioux Falls Arena; and the local semipro hockey team, the Sioux Falls Stampede, donated tickets for fathers and youth to attend a home hockey game.

There was general consensus that fatherhood was a critical community issue. Almost all the community leaders I interviewed were anxious to identify effective strategies for promoting responsible fathering. However, at the same time, some expressed concerns about (1) not knowing where to start and (2) feeling over-whelmed by time constraints and other commitments. Several clear and pressing themes emerged from the interviews, each of which provided key insights and meaningful recommendations.

Community Leaders and Understanding Fatherhood

Initially in connecting with community leaders, I also wanted to get a sense of the leader's perception of and concern about father absence in Sioux Falls (and how it compared to the state and nation). Community leaders were asked about the benefits of involved fathers to children, mothers, and the community; about resources that could be used to address father absence; about commitment to the problem; about programs and services directed toward fathers; and about gaps in those services. Finally, they were asked about strategies and barriers to promoting responsible fatherhood, the extent of collaboration within the community, and whether or not existing programs could be expanded to include a fatherhood component. I ended the community leader interview by asking if they or someone from their organization would be willing to help with the planning committee for a leadership summit on fatherhood. This was very helpful, as it led us to the individuals who would shape our summit and provide concrete support in the community.

Community leaders struggled with estimating the level of father absence in Sioux Falls. Responses ranged from 10 percent to 60 percent (average response was 31.7 percent). The actual percentage was 21.7 percent.[9] Most (97 percent) said a father was very important to the healthy development of his children. Nearly 100 percent rated their level of concern about father absence in Sioux Falls as very high or somewhat high but felt that other leaders in their area had significantly lower levels of concern. Almost 100 percent rated the level of awareness in the community at large as somewhat low or very low. This is significant because it suggests that most leaders recognize the problem of father absence and the need for father involvement but do not believe the community understands or appreciates the depth and magnitude of the dilemma. This perspective sets the stage for the themes that emerged from the ensuing questions about benefits of, barriers to, and strategies for promoting responsible fathering.

Community Interview Themes on Strengthening Fatherhood

In building support for a community-based approach to strengthening father-hood, it was important to connect with leaders, familiarize them with the issues, and assess the available community resources and support. Using a community leader interview process to facilitate this approach was very helpful. Leaders provided concrete feedback on benefits and meaning of fatherhood, resources and strategies to strengthen fatherhood, and how to adapt existing programs or opportunities for assisting fathers and families.

Benefits of Involved Fathers

When asked about the benefits children receive from a father's participation, most leaders said they benefit from a role model who teaches them morals and character. Others said it "promotes increased self-esteem and self worth" and "provides a balanced perspective." Mothers were said to benefit from father involvement through the shared responsibility of parenting (one leader called it "load sharing"). They said this contributed significantly to a mother's decreased stress (economic, emotional, physical, etc.), enhanced communication, and increased time with children. Some recognized that having an involved father also contributes to an enhanced support network for mothers.

Some noted that communities benefit from father involvement through lower crime rates and fewer problem behaviors (alcohol, drugs, pregnancy, and delinquency). Leaders also suggested that involved fathers would ultimately contribute to decreased demand for many public services including after-school programs, childcare, criminal courts, supervision, and welfare. Several leaders said involved fathers would help children to develop increased levels of citizenship and community involvement.

Resources and Strategies to Support Fathers

More than 92 percent of leaders said it was important or very important to mobilize resources to address father absence in Sioux Falls and they were personally committed to addressing the issue. However, only 72 percent felt other leaders in their sector and 56 percent of leaders from the community at large were committed to it. Perhaps one of the more poignant comments came from the state's lieutenant governor. When I asked whether he was personally committed to addressing the issue of father absence, he said, "Yes, as long it doesn't detract from my family time." Although it was an unrehearsed and direct response, it was profound! The value of a community-based approach to father involvement is that it allows responsibility to be spread across a wide number of persons and organizations.

Several types of resources were identified and suggested as important avenues for addressing father absence, including financial (fund raisers, sponsors, in-kind donations), educational (parenting classes, counseling, anger management), spiritual (support classes/groups, religious groups/church), business policies (flex time), and social services (Big Brothers/Big Sisters, mentoring programs, etc.). Although resources exist that could be mobilized to address father absence, few leaders were able to identify already existing programs or services specifically directed toward fathers. A few identified programs they were aware of through their workplace, which included Even Start (fathers and literacy) and Avera

McKennan Hospital (a new "Dad and Baby" class). Some recognized religious men's support groups that may focus on responsible fathering as one component of their program.

Leaders suggested that gaps in programs and services for fathers were "everywhere" and that strategies for increasing awareness and providing support and services were important. Strategies that involved different sectors of the community to promote responsible fatherhood were identified, including:

- working with local businesses to promote fun, engaging activities like Golf with Dad, Donuts with Dad, etc.;
- involving city government and the Parks and Recreation Department by hosting a city-wide Father's Day picnic;
- developing an effective and sustained media campaign to increase awareness (e.g., Public Service Announcements);
- providing policy-related support, such as promoting a family-friendly workplace through flex time; and
- conducting specific fathering workshops in educational settings and encouraging fathers' participation in the educational system and at parent-teacher conferences.

Gathering specific strategies for supporting father involvement from local community leaders allowed them to identify local resources, provide potential solutions, and make a commitment to local support for a grassroots effort.

A logical issue we explored in community leader interviews was whether existing programs could be expanded to include a fatherhood component. Suggestions from leaders included forming partnerships with local groups such as Big Brothers/Big Sisters, Boy Scouts, McCrossan's Boys Ranch, daycare providers, and spiritual organizations (Promise Keepers). Also, educational initiatives could be formed with public schools and preschools, libraries, Extension Services, or other community education projects. Additional suggestions included the use of healthcare providers (prenatal classes, the Avera McKennan Lecture Series), charities (United Way, Lutheran Social Services, Children's Inn), and collaboration with the Parks and Recreation Department's programming committee (sports and hunting, etc.). Action plans that seek to expand existing programs to include fatherhood components will minimize startup costs and maximize outcomes. In addition to finding ways to build on existing programs, such efforts will inevitably uncover important gaps that remain and identify new and innovative approaches through which those gaps can be closed.

Community Leadership Summit on Fatherhood

Following the community leader interviews conducted to connect with the community on the topic of strengthening fatherhood, we developed a planning committee for a community leadership summit on fatherhood. We did this to establish the direction for the leadership summit, determine whom to invite from the community and state, and assist with preparations. In initiating our community-based effort, we envisioned a phased approach to strengthen fatherhood. Phase I involved the community leader interviews and creating macro-level awareness of the issue, and Phase II focused on micro-level activities in many sectors of the community that could be applied to strengthen fatherhood and families. The community leadership summit was intended to be the culminating event of the Phase I macro-level activities, thus setting the stage for Phase II micro-level applied activities.

The focus of this chapter is on the initial (Phase I) activities we engaged in to launch a grassroots community-based effort to strengthen fatherhood. Phase II involves service activities that necessarily move into the hands of practitioners and local service providers. Such services should eventually include workshops, counseling, education, training (e.g., prenatal care specific to new dads), mentoring, targeted father support groups (e.g., spirituality, recovery, employment, divorce), and community-wide activities for fathers and their children.

The vision behind the community leader interviews and community leadership summit on fatherhood was to get the movement started so that community leaders would be informed, inspired, and encouraged to get involved with promoting responsible fatherhood within and across their realms of influence. The leadership summit on fatherhood was held at a local conference center over a prolonged, catered lunch hour. We asked for a couple of hours to visit with community leaders so they could begin to see how they could support fathers in devoting hours each day to becoming better men and better parents.

Leadership Summit Activities

The Sioux Falls Leadership Summit on Fatherhood began with a luncheon attended by more than 60 individuals from the community. Representatives from all major community sectors were present. The mayor, chief of police, county sheriff, fire chief, and lieutenant governor participated. Participants attended the luncheon and then a 90-minute breakout session. The event was designed as a working lunch, in which all who attended provided important insight, feedback, and support in developing a working set of plans for supporting father involvement within their sector of the community.

The summit began with a performance by a local musician followed by the reading of a letter of support from Governor Mike Rounds, who said that "all

---

Examples of Participating Organizations by Community Sector

Following are examples of the types of organizations that participated in the fatherhood initiative from differing community sectors:

- **Nonprofit and Social Service Sectors.** Child Protection, Children's Inn and Children's Home Society, Volunteers of America, Family Services, United Way, and Lutheran Social Services Refugee and Immigration.
- **Media Sector.** KSFY television station and Flynn Advertising.
- **Legal and Government Sectors.** Sheriff's office, state attorney, city council, county commission, state legislator, judicial circuit court, and the governor's office.
- **Health Sector.** McGreevy Clinic, Alpha Center, Avera McKennan Hospital, and Sioux Valley Hospital.
- **Faith Sector.** Sunny Crest Methodist Church, First Lutheran Church, Memorial Lutheran Church, North American Baptist Seminary, and the Catholic Archdiocese.
- **Education, Civic, and Grassroots Sectors.** Augustana College, Sioux Falls School District, Sioux Falls Development Foundation, and the Optimist Club.
- **Business Sector.** Krispy Kreme Doughnuts, Naps BBQ, Dakota King Inc., Wells Fargo Bank, Skyforce basketball team, Billion Automotive, and CNA Western Surety.

---

good men want life to be better for their children than it was for them." The governor's letter explained that fathers who are positive role models provide "a set of core values" and "skills necessary to succeed in life" and noted that "when a father takes an active role in his children's life" he will "discover strength within himself that he never knew he had." Participants next heard a brief presentation from me (as interim director of the Sioux Falls Fatherhood Initiative) on the importance of supporting responsible fatherhood from a variety of avenues across community life. We then premiered a new video, *Fatherhood: Making a Difference* (developed by Dakota Video and Post), which highlighted the positive impact fathers have in the life of their children and featured commentary from community leaders along with children's voices sharing thoughts about fathers' influence. Copies of this video were made available to all in attendance as an example of what could be produced as a resource in our own local community.

The lieutenant governor provided the keynote address regarding the importance of responsible fathering from both personal and professional perspectives. The vice president of a local college presented research evidence relating the impact of father absence and the benefits of father involvement. The luncheon concluded with the local director of the Sioux Empire Marriage Savers presenting a father involvement resource package. Materials included information on developing a Father of the Year essay, CDs, brochures, and various fatherhood programs. We also shared the report on community leader interviews to highlight the community's insight and level of concern about fatherhood issues.

Planning in Community Sectors

The next portion of the leadership summit involved planning by leaders representing different sectors of the community (business, education, etc.). Participants were led to breakout sessions for different community sectors; sessions were divided into eight distinct groups, including public safety, education, business (including health), media, social services, nonprofits, faith, and government. The focus of this activity was to generate ideas and action steps for follow-up in the launch of Phase II of the community fatherhood initiative.

Sector leaders (facilitators) were members of their respective sectors, and most had participated on the planning committee. Facilitators led the discussion, in which participants developed a set of objectives, activities flowing from those objectives, and specific action plans for accomplishing those activities (including identification of responsibilities, deadlines, and resources). Additionally, sectors were asked to identify indicators of success. Of course, the groups, having widely varying dynamics, completed their objectives in different ways. The action plans created by the sectors were not set in stone but represented a solid beginning step the community could then build on and adapt over time in strengthening fatherhood.

Conclusion of Leadership Summit

To end the leadership summit on a strong note, a local business leader provided support and encouragement in our efforts to follow through and make a difference in the lives of children, fathers, and their families. He noted the challenges ahead—dealing with resources and funding, for example—but that the next step would be to follow through and find ways to resolve those challenges. The summit meeting concluded with participants turning in evaluations and collecting additional resources from the display booth. The committee felt it was important to use the summit to raise awareness, plan strategies, and create follow-up mechanisms to more fully implement a grassroots effort to strengthen fatherhood and families. Outcomes associated with Phase I of the community initiative and the leadership summit assisted that process.

Sector Action Plans for Strengthening Fatherhood

Business
- *Objectives*
  - Increase public/employee awareness of need to balance work and family.
  - Increase administrative and executive awareness.
  - Collaborate with other entities.
- *Action Steps*
  - Develop and implement family-friendly policies.
  - Recognize father-friendly businesses.
  - Distribute father-friendly review guidelines to businesses.

Faith
- *Objectives*
  - Increase awareness of father importance with congregations.
  - Develop networks to promote father involvement.
  - Promote fathers' spiritual development.
- *Action Steps*
  - Provide resources on father importance to congregations.
  - Host interfaith breakfast on the topic.
  - Make presentation on efforts at fall ministerial meeting.

Government
- *Objectives*
  - Promote use of flex time.
  - Introduce father-friendly legislation.
  - Upgrade Bright Start program to be supportive of fathers.
- *Action Steps*
  - Encourage flex-time policies in government settings.
  - Develop father-friendly legislation package with Legislative Resource Center help.
  - Upgrade Bright Start program to include new information and training for fathers.

Media
- *Objectives*
  - Review national PSAs in support of fatherhood.
  - Develop ideas for local PSAs.
- *Action Steps*
  - Promote relevant national PSAs.
  - Produce and promote local PSAs.

Initial Outcomes to Strengthen Fatherhood

Several immediate outcomes occurred as a result of the summit, which reflected the growth of interest within different community sectors. For example, a large breakfast was planned for various leaders in the faith community to share the vision for fatherhood within their community and to identify proactive efforts they would take within their sector to promote responsible fatherhood. Also, a staff member who worked as a parent educator within the South Dakota penal system and had been working with inmates for years to promote responsible fathering found out a few days after the summit that her administrators, who had attended the summit, had approved giving her organizational and financial support to begin training for and offering the Long Distance Dads program (for incarcerated fathers). Additional outcomes emerged as leaders continued talking and making plans, and many further developed their sector action plans with specific objectives, timelines, and anticipated outcomes. Sector leaders in one area of the community provided a presentation at a regional conference to highlight their project and assist other leaders and practitioners interested in replicating their experience.

Follow-Up and Collaboration to Strengthen Fathers and Families

One of the most critical elements in initiating a grassroots effort at the community level is follow-up. In our Sioux Falls effort, community sector leaders were identified and encouraged to follow through with their action plans, make sure information was disseminated, and hold follow-up meetings. A follow-up meeting was also held with all sector leaders a month following the summit to address concerns, provide feedback, and determine future meetings and plans.

If efforts to support responsible fatherhood are to be long-term, broad-based, and successful, cross-sector collaboration within communities is essential. Without it, individuals typically continue in normal patterns with little knowledge about what other individuals and organizations in the community are doing. Community collaboration provides them with the advantage of supporting and being supported by others with similar interests and objectives. Therefore, a final point of emphasis was for those community leaders who chose to carry the flag of fatherhood within their realm of influence to engage in cross-sector dialogue and initiate joint participation with other community groups in a variety of related and mutually beneficial activities to support fathers and families.

The potential for collaboration is exciting. For example, the public safety and social service sectors might collaborate on developing targeted mentoring programs for fatherless children as well as new and disconnected fathers. There is a wide array of collaborative possibilities. The challenge for community leaders is to take advantage of this information and begin collaborating in effective and beneficial ways to strengthen families (including efforts that directly include fathers or father figures) in their community. As an example of one outcome from our effort, an invitation was extended for collaboration on a community-wide Father of the Year essay contest that would require coordination across many sectors of community life (see the National Center for Fathering website: www.fathers.com/).

It became evident throughout Phase I of this project that the community would need to support an individual who could devote a considerable amount of time to the community fatherhood movement and serve as its director. With continued effort, the Sioux Falls initiative hired an individual as director to play a key role in promoting collaboration to support responsible fathering within and across each sector of community life. This individual has visited community leaders as well as practitioners working on the front line with fathers and their families; been an advocate for promoting father-friendly policies and practices across business, government, and educational entities; and served as an important community resource in facilitating and supporting the activities and projects that have evolved.

Recommendations to Strengthen Fatherhood

Those who participated in our effort agreed that the summit provided positive insights, resources, and motivation for supporting responsible fatherhood. A number of key recommendations emerged as important next steps for our community initiative:

- Identify an individual to fill the position of director of the Sioux Falls community fatherhood initiative, and identify funds to support him or her and to assist with program and operating costs.
- Sector leaders should continue to meet and identify collaborative approaches for accomplishing sector objectives and action plans, including work that expands the participant base within each sector and follow-up within and across sectors.
- Sector leaders should collaborate to bring the Father of the Year essay contest to our community.
- The media sector should collaborate with others to develop and disseminate local public service announcements. All sectors should distribute the *Fatherhood: Making a Difference* video. Distribution of media messages in support of fatherhood will facilitate the goal of increased community and individual awareness of the need for positive father involvement.
- Community leaders should plan a second community leadership summit on fatherhood for the following year that would include an evaluative progress report since the first meeting.

Conclusion

The process of developing a community-based, grassroots movement to support responsible, involved fathering may be one of the most important and high-impact approaches available to strengthening families. Such an effort must begin at the community level if both micro- and macro-level changes are to occur in community and family life. In our experience, using a community-based approach to strengthen fathers and families received strong support from community leaders throughout various sectors of community life. The process also illustrated how important fathers were in the eyes of those leaders for varying reasons. The perspectives and strategies that emerged from our process provided an important first step in developing a comprehensive, community-wide fatherhood program.

The community leader interviews brought to light many specific needs within the Sioux Falls community. They identified overwhelming gaps in programs and services to fathers, considered the potential barriers to efforts designed to encourage father involvement, explored strategies that could be used to address those gaps and barriers, and suggested the need for leaders to come together and commit, as one business person said, "time, talent, and treasure" in a concerted effort to address the problem of father absence. Success only comes to those who act, and our community leaders recognized the unique opportunity they had to do something about this problem. A key strategy for action was needed in order to help them move forward and take the next step.

The next important step we took was to develop the Leadership Summit on Fatherhood (LSF), which provided leaders with an opportunity to learn more about the problems related to father involvement, collaborate with others in developing effective action plans, and network with others interested in addressing this problem. One of the unplanned benefits of the process came from developing a nucleus of supportive individuals willing to put the community summit together. That group saw the process through to the end and provided leadership, guidance, and invaluable community connections. As community leaders seriously consider recommendations that emerge from such an effort and invest time, talent, and treasure in supporting fatherhood in their community, significant changes will occur, not only in improving the human condition but, perhaps more important, improving the family condition across their community.

Across the board, fathers count in so many areas of life. It is important to find ways that men make a difference across the various sectors of community life and coordinate efforts that support those activities and recognize and celebrate the good that men do.[10] These efforts can best be accomplished by identifying community leaders who champion the cause of fatherhood and by carefully developing a grassroots movement that promotes and supports responsible fatherhood throughout the community.

Communities who accept this invitation will need to develop their own, tailored approach to addressing fatherhood issues, but it is our hope that these insights from our project will provide a good foundation from which to begin. This approach is not a quick-fix strategy, but rather it is designed to establish a sustainable, effective, broad-based approach to addressing challenges that families face, with a specific emphasis on supporting fathers and families. In our community, we worked methodically through this approach for more than a year to get the Sioux Falls project up and running; as of this printing, it is still going. It has found an organizational home that supports its work (www.sf-fathers.org/). While there is still much work to do (like strengthening cross-sector collaborations), the potential for long-term sustainability is promising. We invite you to take the challenge of engaging your community in a proactive effort to promote responsible, involved fathering and turn the tide of father absence. As you bring all sectors of

---

Recommendations for Starting a Community-Level Fatherhood Initiative

While approaches will vary, following are a few key recommendations for communities interested in promoting father involvement (not in order):

- Be fully committed to the process and willing to see it through to the end.
- Develop a reasonable set of goals and objectives, short- and long-term.
- Identify the movers and shakers in the community who would be willing to meet with you and provide their insight and support for moving the project forward. You may want to meet with them individually at first to share your passion and excitement about the project and invite their participation.
- Host a few meetings to get them together so they can share what they think needs to be done. They also can help identify key players from their organizations or other community sectors who may be good contacts.
- Begin planning a fatherhood leadership summit. Put together a strong planning committee who can help with details, promote it, and carry it off.
- Identify someone who can write follow-up reports of events and see the project through to the end. This can be an interim director.
- Funding is key. It will be critical to find good funding streams from community organizations to help sponsor the project.
- Find a way to support a permanent director. For long-term sustainability, it will be critical to develop funds to support a permanent position and staff who can help move the effort forward and maintain collaboration between sectors.

community life to the table, you will send a profound message across your community that fathers count, and this message will help your community change for the better the lives of fathers, children, and families.

Endnotes

1. National Center for Fathering, 1999, *Fathering in America*, retrieved December 15, 2005, from www.fathers.com/research/1999GallupFathAmerica .html.

2. Horn, W., and Sylvester, T., 2002, *Father Facts*, 4th ed., Gaithersburg, MD: National Fatherhood Initiative.

3. U.S. Census Bureau, 2000, *Fact Sheet*, from http://factfinder.census.gov/ servlet/SAFFFacts?_sse=on.

4. Mancini, J.A., Bowen, G.L., and Martin, J.A., 2005, "Community Social Organization: A Conceptual Linchpin in Examining Families in the Context of Communities," *Family Relations*, 54(5), 570–582.

5. Brotherson, S.E., and White, J.M., 2002, "Federal and State Policy Initiatives to Strengthen Fatherhood: Issues and Implications for Practitioners," *Professional Development: The International Journal of Continuing Social Work Education*, 4(3), 16–34; Levine, J.A., and Pitt, E.W., 1995, *New Expectations: Community Strategies for Responsible Fatherhood*, New York: Families and Work Institute.

6. Dryfoos, J., and Maguire, S., 2002, *Inside Full-Service Community Schools*, Thousand Oaks, CA: Corwin Press, Inc.

7. Holder, H.D., Saltz, R.F., Grube, J.W., Voas, R.B., Gruenewald, P.J., and Treno, A.J., 1997, "A Community Prevention Trial to Reduce Alcohol-Involved Accidental Injury and Death: Overview," *Addiction*, 92(6s2), 155–171.

8. Doherty, W.J., and Anderson, J.R., 2004, "Community Marriage Initiatives," *Family Relations: Interdisciplinary Journal of Applied Family Studies*, 53(5), 425–432.

9. U.S. Census Bureau, 2000.

10. Hawkins, A.J., and Dollahite, D.C. (Eds.), 1997, *Generative Fathering: Beyond Deficit Perspectives*, Thousand Oaks, CA: Sage.

Author Ken R. Canfield, top center, with his children, left to right, Micah, Sarah, Rachel, Hannah, and Joel

25

The Big Benefits of Small Groups for Fathers

Ken R. Canfield

I am inspired by Paul Revere, the patriot of American history. During a pivotal moment in history, he awakened the countryside to an approaching danger and emphasized the need for action. "The Regulars are coming out! The Regulars are coming out!" he called. Contrary to popular legend, historians tell us that he *didn't* cry, "The British are coming!" In Revere's day, the majority of New Englanders still thought of themselves as British.

Whatever the case, his warning served its purpose. In a matter of hours, the King's men (the Regulars) and the American militia were battling in Lexington, and the American revolution was under way. The time was ripe for a Declaration of Independence and the birth of a nation.

There is a parallel here for those of us who seek to help fathers be more actively engaged in the lives of their children. The threat of fatherlessness is very real and imminent. Its effects are ravaging families all across our nation. It's time to sound the alarm, gather the troops, and respond to the need of the hour.

Increasingly, fathers are responding to this call. There is a new generation of courageous men in America who believe that success is measured more by *posterity* than by *prosperity*. Recognizing that children deserve much more than just the leftovers of their time and energy, these millennial men are not allowing their past or their current pursuits and aspirations to keep them from developing deep, abiding bonds with their children. One dad at a time, a fathering movement is upon us. But I believe those men gaining the most ground against the enemy are the dads in groups, gathering for mutual support, wisdom, and encouragement. It's critical to their success that they meet with other men on a regular basis and openly discuss the issues they are facing as fathers. Among all the efforts we engage in at the National Center for Fathering, I believe the most beneficial and lasting influence will come from the establishment of small groups that help fathers come together and better their fathering.

The Potential of Small Groups for Fathers

My colleague, George Williams, has noted the benefits of group meetings for the urban dads in his 12-week fathering course. He has assessed the critical aspects of what has made the efforts of these fathers more successful. These dads, most of whom were challenged by complex family and economic situations, helped one another by:

- challenging each other's behavior,
- influencing each other's reasoning,
- motivating each other to achieve,
- exchanging resources and information, and
- giving and receiving feedback on task work.

George concluded that gathering men in small groups to process the challenges of fatherhood is one of the most effective ways to bring dignity and strength to the urban father.

I believe *small groups* have the greatest potential of any strategy to create lasting positive change in fathers' behavior. Over the years I have had the privilege of speaking to some 50,000 men during our two-day training events designed to inspire and equip men to be more committed fathers. At each event, I spend about seven hours describing the best practices of effective fathers. I can "blow in" on a Friday afternoon; "blow up" with facts, ideas, and illustrations to motivate the attendees; and then "blow out" on Saturday afternoon to get back to fathering my own family. The sequence is all too familiar. Yet, for all my efforts, I realize that the real goal of the events is to stimulate what I believe is the long-term solution—small-group interaction. If we can provide local organizations with small-group curricula and a framework for getting the men into the groups and then provide a large event to help stir men's hearts to action, those small groups have the most potential for life change.

Practical Benefits of Small Groups for Dads

What is it about small groups for dads that makes them so potentially effective? Small groups offer men three vital elements: companionship, assistance and insight, and accountability.

Companionship

The average man cannot identify three men he knows well enough and trusts enough to share absolutely anything. Few men realize the value of friendships, but other men can serve as sounding boards and companions who can identify with struggles, rejoice in victories, and challenge each other to be better husbands and fathers. Honest and caring companionship is a strength for fathers and a primary benefit of small-group interaction.

Small-group friendships provide a safe place to be honest and vulnerable. A dad might tend to portray himself as better or more "together" than he really is, but other men who know him well won't put up with that; they'll force him to be honest and face reality. They'll also allow him to share about personal issues without the threat of having that information disclosed to the world. And sometimes he just needs to be able to vent an emotion or relate a struggle so he can move forward and think more clearly about his family. He learns the truth behind the saying: "Shared joy is double joy; shared sorrow is half sorrow."

Every man needs a brother—a battle buddy—who will stand with him in times of need. These aren't superficial relationships with golfing buddies or softball teammates that may actually take time away from his family but close friends he knows he can call at any hour who will be eager to help. More important, they'll be committed to helping him be the best father he can be.

Assistance and Insight

Typically, when moms get together for coffee, one of them will say something like, "You should have seen what that girl of mine did last Friday." The members of that informal small group share joys and struggles, swap tips, and tell each other, "Be encouraged; you're not alone." Women are wonderful at finding encouragement and support by gathering together in informal ways.

For some reason, men usually need a more formal arrangement for this type of assistance and insight to take place, and that's a good reason for them to be in a "fathering small group." Other dads are walking treasures of experiences and insights. Some have kids who are hard to handle or have strayed from the path their fathers intended for them. Or maybe there's an older man with grown children who is actually eager to help a younger dad. He's been through his children's teen years; he's dealt with the mixed emotions of seeing his daughter bloom into a woman; he has learned how to balance his career and family life; he's overcome his fear of talking to his children about difficult matters. Such fathers can provide meaningful assistance, insight, and support to one another in walking the roads of family life.

Talking with other fathers can produce new ideas and perspectives and a fresh optimism when men fall into a rut with their families. Bouncing ideas off other men is invaluable as a dad seeks to keep his thinking grounded in practical reality. Why should he learn by trial and error when help is so close? Another father who has "been there" in the trenches with a sick child, a shy teenager, or a stressful job can offer much meaningful perspective and insight. Small groups provide a ready-made venue for fathers to make such connections with each other.

Accountability

A committed father *should* feel a natural sense of accountability to his wife and children. His promises and vows should keep him motivated to be there for them, express his love often, and work on his weak areas in those relationships. Unfortunately, many dads need more than that. Small groups provide a regular fathering checkup with other dads who are like-minded, trustworthy, and have permission to ask difficult questions or make brutally honest observations. That may sound intimidating at first, but it's really a valuable form of protection from potential pitfalls.

Author and speaker Howard Hendricks has said, "A man without a small group is an accident waiting to happen." All dads sometimes get off track, whether in their marriages, with their children, in business, or in their morality. When a man knows he'll be held accountable, that gives him extra motivation to make better choices. If Bob knows that on Thursday morning Tony is going to ask him how he handled his anger this week, Bob has one more reason to count to 10 before responding to his teenage son. And since Tony is a trusted friend, he won't reprimand Bob if things didn't go so well. He'll be disappointed, but he'll encourage Bob and help him come up with strategies that will work. (And Bob would do the same for him.)

Accountability will help a man maintain his integrity. Next time he's leaving on a business trip, if he has a couple of close friends to answer to when he gets back—friends who will expect an honest answer when they ask what he did with his free time or how he handled himself in that business meeting—that can make a big difference. Fathering requires action. It's more than knowing the right information; it's *applying* that information. It helps when a man has someone putting pressure on him each week by saying, "So what did you do about what we discussed last week?"

Real-Life Examples of Small Group Influences on Men

I would like to share examples of three men I know who have seen positive changes because of their involvement in a small group. These men are not numbers on a statistical chart but real men with real families who have made real strides forward in their family lives.

Ron and his wife, Trisha, have three children and a nice house and are active in their community. For several years, their lives seemed to be on cruise control, but as time passed, Ron couldn't seem to keep it together. Balancing family and work was tough, and he was often sullen and irritable. One day, Trisha told him he was losing touch with her and their children. She couldn't take it anymore, and he needed to either get his life together or get out.

During his childhood, Ron had watched four different stepfathers come and go, and he always said he wouldn't be like that. And yet now his own family appeared to be headed down a similar path.

So when Ron was approached about a fathering small group at his church, he was motivated to get involved. As the first meeting approached, though, and he found out who else would be there, he wanted to run and hide. He thought, "These guys have it all together! I'll be the only one who's struggling."

Somehow he forced himself to go—and the next few months changed his life. He discovered the other guys weren't perfect. They confronted each other about questionable habits and applauded each other when they succeeded. They shared joys and frustrations and affirmed and empowered each other. Ron realized he wasn't alone in the battle, and that was exactly what he needed. The other fathers held his feet to the fire to apply what he had learned, and their support helped him to change.

Several months later, Trisha told one of the small-group leaders, "This is the best thing that has ever happened to us. Ron is different now. Thank you!"

John saw the benefits of a small group in an unusual and memorable way. He wasn't a great husband and father. Like many men, growing up he never had someone model for him what a good father was. So he fumbled along through life and soon found himself married with children. For several years, John's wife, Susan, would have told you they were struggling, but John really didn't know how to make things better.

Then John joined a small group, where he was challenged, encouraged, and supported. It was hard going at first. However, after several weeks of opening his heart to other men about his strengths and weaknesses in his family, there were signs of a transformation. One day after work, on an evening that seemed pretty average to John in every other way, Susan made this observation: "Honey, during the past few months, I've seen a huge change in your life. I just want you to know I'm proud of you."

John glowed, of course, and he wanted more details. "What do you mean? What have you noticed?" he asked.

"Well, lots of things," she said, "but probably the biggest change is the way you treat the dog. Have you noticed how he approaches you? He's seen the change, too."

It wasn't exactly what John was expecting to hear, but there's something to that. We know dogs are sensitive to tone of voice and body language. And you could even say that, for a young couple, getting a dog is like early training for parenthood. They learn about being an authority, giving praise, being consistent, and being responsible for another's well-being. Of course, having a child raises the stakes exponentially, but pets can be good training and, as John found out, give us good feedback on our behavior. A small group can bring about that kind of noticeable, lasting life change that will benefit a man's wife, his kids, and even his dog.

Another father, **Roger**, diligently monitored his son Ryan's educational and sports achievements but failed to stay connected with Ryan's other activities. As a sophomore, Ryan had a new group of friends, and though he continued to do well in school and sports, Roger knew something wasn't right.

One night during Ryan's senior year, Roger overheard his son's friends making jokes about stealing cars, but because he didn't understand the power of peer influence, he let the comment slide. A few days later, when Ryan was picked up for car theft, Roger was devastated.

Roger learned a lot about being a father of a teenager, including how critical it is to monitor the friends they spend time with. But perhaps no lesson was as powerful as the one in the courtroom. As his son was being charged, Roger was surprised to see another group of peers in the room—his own. Several fathers from his small group came to silently support Roger, and they have continued to be there for him throughout the process. It has made a big difference.

Roger discovered the value of peer support from other fathers in a small group. Gaining insights, sharing accountability, and receiving positive support can be a major asset for men in their fathering efforts, especially during difficult times.

Why Small Groups for Fathers?

I'm bullish about the notion that, more than anything else, getting dads in groups will help the fathering movement take deep roots. Although my convictions about the power of small groups are grounded in both experience and research, I offer this evidence from the world of research to bolster my argument about small groups for fathers.

Most Social Behavior Occurs in Groups

It is a reality that most social behavior occurs in groups. We live with families, travel in car pools, work as teams, worship in congregations, are entertained as audiences, learn in classes, and socialize with friends. Therefore, having fathers meet together in a small group to learn fathering skills is a natural experience. Small groups provide structure to most of life's activities and can reinforce social behavior in both positive and negative ways.

Research Demonstrates the Importance of Groups

For more than a century, research has revealed the importance of groups in the lives of individuals. There have been more than 700 studies concerning groups in the past century. In fact, the earliest studies in social psychology concerned performance in groups (such as Triplett, 1898; Allport, 1920; etc.).[1] Later work by Sherif and Asch focused on conformity in groups.[2] Kurt Lewin, a renowned scholar in the social sciences, spent the majority of his later years studying behavior in groups and is considered the founder of the "group dynamics" movement.[3]

While early work on small groups tended to focus on basic social-psychological processes in an attempt to generate general theories, more recent work on small groups has tended to focus on practical issues. Much of this research follows trends in the use of groups in such domains as industry, education, and community relations.[4]

Research has repeatedly shown that groups are important and exert powerful influences on the lives of individuals. Applied to training and support for fathers, small groups provide us with the opportunity to help another father who may face challenging economic or personal issues. This was the idea Vice President Al Gore had in mind when he called for a Father-to-Father initiative in 1994. Fathers would meet together for mutual support and extend that outreach to specific fathers in need. In his words, "I'm calling for the mobilization and national movement of fathers meeting together to mutually support and reach out to one another."

Individuals tend to find their identity as they identify with others in particular groups, such as families, fellow workers, faith groups, and a multitude of other group contexts. Groups provide a network of relationships and a meaningful atmosphere of support or guidance. When individuals gather in groups, they can share resources, monitor each other's lives, and give needed feedback.

Small Groups Can Strongly Influence How Individuals Learn

Small groups can have a powerful impact on how individuals learn. In fact, one of the great success stories in the development of learning theory is the widespread use of what has come to be called "cooperative learning." I have listened to hundreds of testimonies over the years from fathers who report that the small-group experience helped them prepare and execute new actions in their fathering. Why? Because they were learning and taking such actions together with a number of other fathers.

Social psychologists have also confirmed that *members of a group have higher achievement, greater retention, and greater cooperation than individualistic efforts in learning.* In comparing group members with individuals learning a subject, they discovered that group members had more:

- willingness to take on difficult tasks and persist, despite difficulties, in working toward accomplishing goals;
- long-term retention of what is learned;
- higher-level reasoning and critical thinking (groups tend to promote more frequent insight into and use of higher-level cognitive and moral reasoning strategies than do individualistic learning experiences);
- creative thinking (members in groups more frequently generate new ideas, strategies, and solutions than they would on their own);
- transfer of learning from one situation to another (group to individual transfer—what individuals learn in a group today they are able to do alone tomorrow); and
- positive attitudes (cooperative efforts result in more positive attitudes toward tasks being completed and greater continuing motivation to complete them).[5]

With these patterns in mind, it is important to devise learning strategies to enhance the learning potential of fathers. It seems obvious that the use of small groups is one strategy that can take advantage of these benefits and maximize a father's learning and application of ideas in his parenting.

Small Groups Promote Positive Interdependence

Another key is that small groups tend to create positive interdependence between group members. This fosters "promotive interaction," which occurs as individuals encourage and facilitate each others' efforts to reach the group's goals (such as maximizing each member's learning). For fathers, having other individuals to encourage and even facilitate their efforts to become better men and better parents can be the difference between failure and success.

According to researchers, group members promote each other's success by:

- giving and receiving help and assistance;
- exchanging resources and information;

- giving and receiving feedback on tasks (in cooperative groups, members monitor each other's efforts, give immediate feedback on performance, and, when needed, give each other help and assistance);
- challenging each other's reasoning (intellectual controversy often promotes curiosity, motivation to learn, reconceptualization of what one knows, better decision making, and greater insight into a problem);
- advocating increased efforts to achieve (encouraging others to achieve increases one's own commitment to do so);
- mutually influencing each other's reasoning and behavior (group members actively seek to influence and be influenced by each other—if a member has a better way to complete a task, group members usually quickly adopt it); and
- engaging in the interpersonal and small-group skills needed for effective teamwork.[6]

Ultimately, small groups encourage the interdependence of fathers so modeling and transformation can take place. In my limited experience, creating courses that promote interdependence of fathers through small groups is the most efficient way to foster a large grass-roots movement. A small group is one of the optimal settings in which a father can learn new fathering behaviors.

Support for the Power of Small Groups

Our research at the National Center for Fathering confirms that small groups make a difference for dads. In our surveys, when we isolated the men who are involved in a regular small group and compared them to those who are not, we discovered some noteworthy distinctions. For example, the men in small groups scored higher on family involvement indicators like eating meals with their families, had fewer sexual struggles, reported fewer problems with dishonesty, and were more connected with their families on a spiritual level.

If a father fails to connect with others who can provide support and accountability, then the likelihood of his achieving his goals as a father is greatly diminished. But the typical father doesn't realize how much he'd benefit from honestly and openly sharing joys, dreams, and challenges with other dads; how much other men need his listening ear and support in their quests to become the best dads they can be; or the encouragement he'd feel from sharing a meal with other dads and reflecting on how fatherhood influences their purpose in life.

Our research confirms the firsthand testimonies we have heard over and over from fathers: *Meeting with other men for mutual support and encouragement is one of the best investments they can make as fathers*. They discover that it isn't just one more obligation on their calendar—it's actually liberating to discover there are other men who care about them and their fathering journey.

Simply put, small groups are extremely effective tools to help fathers learn information and apply it to personal life scenarios. Therefore, at the National Center for Fathering, we have invested significant resources in developing curricula using small groups to enhance fathers' acquisition and application of fathering skills.

Recruiting Fathers into Small Groups

For those who are trying to recruit men for fathering small groups, let me offer some brief suggestions from Bill Beahm, Ph.D., a former member of our staff. Bill calls these "guerrilla tactics" because reaching out to dads needs to be active and somewhat aggressive. But, considering the benefits, it's well worth it.

- **Target your captives.** Identify men you think would benefit from being in a small group—and would fit well in a particular group.
- **Give a personal invitation.** The old line "If you build it, they will come" doesn't work for men's groups. You can't rely only on printed fliers and posters. Contact each man personally, and tell him how excited you are about his joining the group.
- **Pursue, pursue, pursue.** Keep after them, and be ready for any excuse they could possibly come up with. Be so flexible in the details that they can't say "no." Say, "Well, when *can* you meet?" Also, try approaching their wives to explain how the group will benefit their families.
- **Don't lose heart.** That fathering group could very well be a cure for the cancer that plagues the families in your community. Don't let nervousness, procrastination, or busy schedules stand in your way.

Another Kind of Teamwork

While not the core issue of this discussion, I would be remiss not to mention perhaps the best "small group" team: a father and a mother. I believe unmarried men can be fantastic fathers, and I encourage a broad and redemptive view of fatherhood that can address the needs of all dads—married, divorced, or single— and help them make the best of their situations. Still, the ideal situation for children clearly involves a father and a mother in the home. Marriage is an important, potentially divisive issue, but it plays a significant role in our quest to promote responsible fatherhood. While some social commentators have concluded that the most prudent way to promote fatherhood is to restore marriage, our discussions will be more successful if we include unmarried fathers and describe marriage as a great asset to a father's efforts to stay connected to his children. In that context, it would be wise to consider new strategies that seek to reverse the tide of divorce and strengthen the marriage bond. This fathering movement can be broad enough to encourage all men to be responsible father figures and redemptive enough to admit there are no perfect fathers.

We have asked thousands of fathers across the country, "Who has most influenced you in your fathering?" A vast majority of them have said, "My wife." Encouragement from a spouse provides dads with strength to persevere through mistakes and provides support to get through the teenage years when the rewards of fathering aren't nearly as apparent. Children face a wide range of physical, social, and emotional challenges, and what's best for the child isn't always crystal clear. Sometimes she'll need to be protected and comforted by her parents; at other times, she'll need encouragement and opportunities to work out problems on her own. When it isn't clear how to handle each situation, it helps if a dad knows he has a partner who cares for the child just as much as he does. Being part of that team makes a huge difference.

A mom and a dad complement each other, employ mutual respect, share struggles, discuss options, and brainstorm courses of action. They combine their strengths and work together for their children's benefit. This small group also deserves attention and support from fathers as they seek to engage their children.

Conclusion

I don't have a horse, but I still want to proclaim in the street like Paul Revere, "The real heroes are coming out! Look at the needs in the families around you! You can make a difference!"

We all know how vitally important children are to the future of this nation. The research is clear that children stand a much better chance of reaching their full potential when they have actively engaged fathers.

I believe the strategy of getting dads in small groups is one of the most important ways to change the world, one father at a time. These dads will benefit from companionship, assistance and insight, and accountability. Could this be another pivotal moment in the history of our nation? It can be if you and the dads around you take action and continue the revolution.

Endnotes

1. Triplett, N., 1898, "The Dynamic Factors in Pacemaking and Competition," *American Journal of Psychology*, 9, 1898, 507–533; Ringelmann, M., 1913, "Recherches sur les moteurs animes: Travail de l'homme [Research on Animate Sources of Power: The Work of Man]," *Annales de l'Institut National Agronomique*, XII, 1–40; Allport, F.H., "The Influence of the Group upon Association and Thought," *Journal of Experimental Psychology*, 3, 1920, 159–182.

2. Sherif, M., 1936, *The Psychology of Social Norms*, New York: Harper.

3. Lewin, K., 1951, *Field Theory in Social Science,* New York: Harper.

4. Tindale, R.S., Heath, L., Edwards, J., Posavac, E., Bryant, F., Suarez-Balcazar, Y., Henderson-King, E., and Myers, J., 1998, *Theory and Research on Small Groups*, New York: Plenum Press.

5. Ibid., at 17.

6. Johnson, D., and Johnson, R., 1989, *Cooperation and Competition: Theory and Research*, Edina, MN: Interaction Book Company.

Author Sean Brotherson (right) with his father, Jack, and sons Ethan and Mason

Supporting Fathers
through Educational Programs:
Promising Strategies and Positive Successes

Sean E. Brotherson

Eagles Kindergarten Center sits on the edge of a quiet residential neighborhood in Fargo, North Dakota, not far from the flowing waters of the Red River. It seems an unlikely place for a revelation. And yet, it was in this small educational community that I first saw the potential for supporting fathers through education truly materialize in a remarkable way.

In February of 2000 I received a phone call at my office at North Dakota State University from the school principal at Eagles Kindergarten Center, Michelle Vannote, and she inquired whether I would be interested in working with the center on a project to involve and support fathers in their children's lives. I jumped at the chance. At the time, my own child was a student there. Principal Vannote explained that the U.S. Department of Education had produced an educational program and video entitled "Fathers Matter" on the value of a father's involvement in a child's education and academic achievement, and the center wished to use this resource to encourage more reading with its kindergarten children. She asked whether I would be willing to assist in teaching the educational portion of the program at a school-sponsored event for fathers and father figures. I agreed. Having some experience with fathers and parent education, I hoped we could get 20 fathers to come out and participate in the event.

Two months passed, and the morning of the event arrived. I drove to the site of the school, arriving a few minutes before the program was scheduled to begin. What I saw as I pulled into the area made me stop and rub my eyes.

Delivery vans, police cars, cement mixers, motorcycles, pickup trucks, and numerous other vehicles were parked up and down the streets surrounding Eagles Kindergarten Center for blocks in every direction. I had to park a quarter-mile away from the school. When I walked into the school auditorium, I was astonished. Every chair was filled, and men were standing, packed along the sides and back of the room: men in business attire, men in construction outfits, men wearing baseball caps, and men in military uniforms—nearly 150 men who were fathers, grandfathers, uncles, stepfathers, and other father figures.

The men listened intently for 30 minutes to a presentation on the importance of their involvement in a child's education and then moved for the next hour to the classrooms. Scattered about the school, they sat with their own children and others and read out loud in strong, caring voices. A low rumble sounded throughout the halls of the school outside the classrooms. The principal and I met and talked, pleased with the success of the event but also a little surprised at the high level of participation. As we talked about lessons to be learned from our experience, I was forced to ask myself some questions as a family scholar that would lead me to new understanding of how to support father involvement through educational efforts.

What had been my assumptions about fathers' involvement, and how did those shape my expectations for their participation in an educational program? Why did these fathers and father figures come to learn and participate? How could educational efforts be best designed to truly reach and engage fathers in meaningful ways?

Challenging the "Deficiency Mindset" about Father Involvement

When considering educational efforts to support fathers, it is valuable to explore whether past challenges have been due to deficiencies in fathers, deficiencies in educational approaches and assumptions, or both. I would argue that a "deficiency mindset" based on pervasive and negative assumptions about fathers has contributed in real ways to the limited response of fathers to educational opportunities in many circumstances. For example, I watched a recent episode of the highly popular TV sitcom *Everybody Loves Raymond* in which the title character and father, Ray Barone, makes an earnest commitment to his wife to do more at home and help with dinner. Inevitably, he sets the kitchen on fire, ruins dinner, and must be rescued by the quick thinking and easy competence of his wife. Although quite funny, it was also somewhat painful. We observe constant portrayals of men as bumbling and incompetent fools who are rescued from their parenting failures by mature and confident wives, bossy mothers or mothers-in-law, or even sassy teenage daughters. This is not an empowering model for men.

While the effects of such media portrayals should not be overemphasized, at the same time they do shape a cultural mindset about fathers and father figures. In a recent Father's Day article in our local newspaper, the *Fargo Forum*, reporter Tom Pantera pointed out that past icons of fatherhood in the media, such as Ward Cleaver (*Leave it to Beaver*) or Cliff Huxtable (*The Cosby Show*), were "paradigm[s] of fatherly wisdom and gentle discipline," but that "modern-day TV dads—people like Ray Barone, Homer Simpson, and Al Bundy—are paradigms of paternal ineptitude and apathy."[1] Do such assumptions have an effect on the typical interactions of average adults in society with fathers as parents? The effects may be subtle but important. For example, when a child becomes sick at school, it's almost standard procedure to call the child's mother. Often, the father is hardly considered. A cultural mindset that assumes the worst about fathers and their involvement can do little to bring out the best in men.

Scholars Alan Hawkins and David Dollahite have critiqued the influence of what they call a "deficit perspective" on the involvement of fathers and father figures in family life. They suggest that far too many scholars, practitioners, and garden-variety citizens "approach their work [and family life] ... within a perspective of fathering that focuses on the deficiencies of some fathers and the struggles of many fathers, ending up with a mind-set in which most fathers are viewed as uninvolved, uninterested, unskilled, and unmotivated to perform their proper paternal role."[2] In other words, it is assumed that fathers are probably *un*likely to be very interested in educational materials or programs that wish to engage them as fathers—or so the thinking has been.

Before mobilizing educational support on behalf of fathers, it is critical to examine and at times readjust the assumptions we bring to interactions with fathers. James Levine, head of the Fatherhood Project in New York City, has written that "the single most powerful contributor to effectiveness—at least the one place where effective strategies start—is with a change in expectations about fathers on the part of agencies that deal with families."[3] It can thus be beneficial to reexamine and, if necessary, change the assumptions we sometimes bring to our educational efforts to target and support healthy father involvement. This may require recognizing our "deficiency" assumptions and replacing them with "strength-based" assumptions.

To truly engage fathers through educational support and services, it is necessary to challenge and change our own assumptions about the deficiencies of men

Assumptions about Fathers and Involvement

The assumptions we bring to our interactions with men and their children shape the manner in which we engage them in educational efforts. Contrast the following deficiency and strength-based assumptions about men as fathers or father figures.

Fathers and Motivation
- *Deficiency Assumption.* Fathers are generally uninterested in better parenting and usually unwilling to change to become better parents.
- *Strength-Based Assumption.* Fathers genuinely care about being good parents and are usually willing to be involved when they understand the benefit to their children.

Fathers and Parenting Ability
- *Deficiency Assumption.* Fathers generally don't have the sensitivity and care needed to be effective in their parenting efforts with children.
- *Strength-Based Assumption.* Fathers generally have both the competence and care that is needed to be effective and loving parents.

Fathers and Caregiving
- *Deficiency Assumption.* Fathers are inadequate in being emotionally sensitive to children, meeting basic needs, and nurturing with affection.
- *Strength-Based Assumption.* Fathers are very capable in engaging children with play and physical activity, fostering independence, and teaching limits to children.

Fathers and Parental Growth
- *Deficiency Assumption.* Fathers have moved too slowly in sharing family work with women and being more involved as parents like the "new father" should do.
- *Strength-Based Assumption.* Fathers are learning new expectations about parental involvement and developing the understanding and skills needed for good parenting.

As efforts are made to support father involvement through educational outreach, it is critical to examine the assumptions we use and replace deficiency assumptions with strength-based assumptions. Healthy parenting begins with healthy assumptions about parents.

and their motivations. Mental images of dad as dunce, dad as danger, or dad as deadbeat equal one outcome in educational efforts with fathers—failure. If we have been "infected" by a lack of success in the past or poor experiences with fathers, then it is likely that our level of expectations will rise no higher than striving not to be too disappointed. We can do better.

Fathers and Education about Parenting

Educational efforts to support fathers as parents must take into account how fathers access information on parenting and what men focus on regarding their parenting needs and interests. It is not surprising that men differ from women in several ways in this context.

Where do men gain their knowledge about parenting? Lowell Johnson asked a group of fathers this question and found that men look at their immediate relationships for such information. These men rated their own fathers (4.4 out of 5) as having the most influence on their knowledge of parenting, followed by experiences with children (4.3 out of 5), mothers (3.6 out of 5), wives or partners (3.5 out of 5), and other fathers (3.4 out of 5). In other words, fathers rely heavily on "experiential sources" of knowledge that include "the modeling of one's own parents, one's spouse, other fathers, and 'hands-on' experiences of raising children."[4] More formal or "institutional" sources of information, such as books, magazines, churches, educational classes, or the Internet, are less commonly used by men.

This pattern of valuing informal or experiential sources of knowledge about parenting over formal or institutional sources suggests that how to reach fathers with educational support is a critical issue. Promising strategies may involve efforts to utilize the network of relationships that fathers use for such information and inserting knowledge about parenting that can be easily communicated and discussed. In our work, we are attempting to reach men directly by creating educational resources, such as parenting newsletters for fathers, that fathers can discuss with their spouses, parents, or other fathers. In addition, this pattern indicates that more formal information sources on parenting must be adapted to meet the needs and interests of fathers as parents.

Parents come to educational programs with a variety of needs and goals. Fathers tend to focus on creating a close relationship with the child; mothers tend to seek support and connection with other parents. I recently was asked to assist in evaluating a parenting program entitled "Circle of Support." The program is excellent, but it was immediately clear to me that the weekly focus on "supporting each other as parents" and sharing feelings about parenting while seated in a circle was not likely to attract a lot of fathers, who tend to emphasize different things. In an interesting study by scholar Glen Palm on fathers' goals for parent education, he found that fathers were "most interested in obtaining the specific skills to build a close relationship with their child"[5]—things like activities together, discipline techniques, and teaching skills. In contrast, the goal of "build[ing] a support system with other men" ranked last among fathers' desires if they participate in parent education.

Is parent support unimportant? Not at all. But fathers may bring differing styles of engagement with their children to family life, and educators should recognize and build on the strengths in these differences.

Best Practices in Educational Efforts to Support Father Involvement

The mindset in parent education for many years seemed to be that fathers are "tough customers" to reach and respond only in small ways, if at all, to educational appeals for their involvement and improvement. Glen Palm, who studies fathers and parent education, has noted that fathers are sometimes seen as "assistant parents" and that he "frequently [has] been invited to parent education sessions to talk about father involvement to a group of mothers."[6] He points out, however, that in the past two decades a "revival of interest in fathers and potential new resources and educational services for them" has occurred and that new approaches are being pioneered to "help program implementers adapt to the needs of men, making programs more father friendly."[7] We list five "best practices" for working with fathers in educational settings and use the Eagles Kindergarten Center experience as a case study to highlight these.

Best Practice #1: Promote Awareness of Educational Resources and Programs.

Topping the list of best practices in educational efforts to support father involvement is the reality that effective efforts vigorously and repeatedly promote awareness of their educational resources or programs. Fathers and father figures are often less connected to the social networks that highlight information for parents or family members, such as school settings or healthcare systems. Therefore, efforts to reach fathers with awareness of educational opportunities must be systematic, strategic, and constant. In this context, it is imperative to both (a) identify the male(s) involved in a child's life who can be targeted with educational support and (b) ensure consistent efforts to deliver awareness of educational opportunities to such fathers or father figures.

Brent McBride and Thomas Rane, two fathering scholars, suggest first that "the key for educators will be to identify which men in the lives of children can be effectively targeted for outreach efforts."[8] After identifying such men, it is important to send them information directly or contact and invite them to an educational event in addition to communicating with them through other avenues.

Providing plenty of notice about educational programs can enable men to make needed schedule adjustments to be able to participate.

Case Study Example: Why did so many fathers and father figures attend the annual "Fathers Matter" educational program at Eagles Kindergarten Center? One key was that the staff planned and highlighted the educational program well in advance. Held annually in March, the event was planned by teachers and school administrators and inserted in the school schedule at the beginning of the year (the preceding August). Regular reminders were sent home through school newsletters, and children designed personal invitations to give to their fathers or other responsible male figures in their lives. Staff worked to ensure that each child would have an appropriate male figure available to share the event and participate in the educational program. Fathers and father figures were motivated to participate because they were aware of the event well in advance and received personal invitations.

Best Practice #2: Utilize a Strength-Based Approach with Fathers.

Educational efforts with men too often falter because programs make two fundamental mistakes. First, many educators or practitioners begin with negative assumptions about fathers' motivation and capacity rather than assuming that most men desire to be good parents and can develop the needed skills and understanding to be effective as fathers. Second, program efforts often focus on correcting men's deficiencies rather than identifying their strengths as fathers and building the program from that solid foundation. Jay Fagan and Alan Hawkins have suggested that "[educational] interventions that focus on fathers' deficiencies may discourage fathers from participating in the intervention."[9] If fathers or father figures sense an implicit judgment that they are inadequate parents before beginning an educational process, their motivation to participate may be somewhat diminished. Hawkins and David Dollahite, another scholar in this area, have written that a "strategy that consists mainly of holding up a mirror to men's faces so they can see their paternal warts more clearly is neither visionary nor empowering."[10]

How, then, can programs overcome this tendency to focus on deficiencies and instead build on strengths? First, they must accept the assumption that most fathers and father figures love their children and wish to be good parents. Programs marketing their offerings should state the clear expectation that they anticipate fathers will rise to the occasion and be involved and responsible parents. This informs fathers and other male figures that a high standard of expectation regarding their motivations and behavior is assumed and encourages them to live up to that standard. Educational efforts must also work to identify fathers' interests and capacities with children and then develop program resources and offerings based on those areas. One male involvement coordinator with Head Start in South Dakota found that the men in his program were interested in attending a NASCAR event with their children. They made appropriate arrangements, and 57 men showed up with their children for the event. They built on an identi-fied interest and developed it into a strength.

Case Study Example. The event at the Eagles Kindergarten Center demon-strated success because it built on strengths. First, the school set a high expecta-tion for father involvement and trusted that fathers and father figures would desire to be present for the sake of their children's happiness. Second, the school under-stood that men prefer to actively interact with children and made this a corner-stone of the experience. And finally, the school focused on one primary activity (reading) that fathers could enjoy and participate in with relative comfort and ease.

Best Practice #3: Define a Clear, Male-Friendly Focus for the Educational Effort.

Efforts to reach fathers with educational support have more potential for suc-cess when practitioners strive to define a clear, male-friendly focus. This means simply that you think about your assumptions, goals, potential barriers, delivery methods, content, and types of involvement and consider how they will be received by fathers and father figures. Your focus in any of these efforts can open or close the door of invitation to men. James Levine and Edward Pitt have referred to this as attention to building the "on-ramps to connection" for fathers in the lives of their children.[11]

One on-ramp that is simple to include in a program is the specific emphasis on inclusion of fathers. In developing a parenting newsletter resource specifically for fathers called *Father Times,* I have been thanked time and again by men who said they were grateful to be singled out and included as parents. Another on-ramp may be the type of involvement modeled in the program. Fathers often thrive in educational settings where activity and involvement, rather than discussion or support, is the focus. Glen Palm, in his experience with fathers and parent educa-tion, has noted that "we have found parent-child interaction time to be an essen-tial component for parenting programs for fathers" and suggested this is because "men appreciate both the active involvement as well as the opportunity to spend time with their child."[12] These and other methods for defining a clear, male-friendly focus in educational programs can bear much fruit in reaching fathers.

Case Study Example: One reason the educational event "Fathers Matter" at the Eagles Kindergarten Center succeeded, I think, was its clear focus on fathers making a difference. It did not apologize for focusing on men and highlighting their contributions to children's academic achievement. It provided a concrete, interactive activity that fathers could engage in with their children both at the event and afterward. It defined fathers and father figures as the target audience and focused on giving them an experience that would be meaningful and comfort-able to them.

Best Practice #4: Target Barriers and Reach Men Where They Are.

Many educational efforts have traditionally required the participants to be involved at a location, time, and manner of the program's choosing. However, this also has resulted in limited opportunities for reaching some target populations, such as fathers and father figures, and diminished the effectiveness of outreach efforts. Glen Palm identified time and work-related constraints as major factors that limit men's involvement with parenting programs.[13] Efforts to support fathers through educational outreach and resources must take such barriers into account and work to reach them where they are. This may mean being carefully attentive to how educational opportunities are scheduled so men can participate. Also, rather than continuing to compete for men's time with other priorities such as work or family responsibilities, new strategies involve reaching out to men at work sites, on the Internet, and in their homes to emphasize their importance as fathers.

How does one reach men directly and overcome the barriers of work and time? By going to them directly. One fatherhood educator, James Levine, described a 1996 presentation he gave to 40 men at the towering headquarters of Merrill Lynch and Company in the World Financial Center on Wall Street in New York. He was not there to talk "about emerging markets, which might be expected, but about an emerging issue with unexpected consequences for both their work and family lives: fatherhood."[14] A man named Joe Kelly runs an electronic newsletter for men about fathers and daughters called *Dads and Daughters* that reaches thousands across the country. I have been involved with developing a parenting newsletter that targets fathers and father figures of young children. Fathers can read this material in their own homes at their leisure. All of these are examples of trying to reach men where they are.

Case Study Example. The example of the Eagles Kindergarten Center takes the concept of reaching men where they are and enhances it simply by reaching men where their children are. On any given day, several hundred fathers have children in attendance at the kindergarten school—all in one place. The school program dealt with the challenges of time and work schedules by planning the event well in advance and encouraging fathers and father figures to arrange their work schedules so they could attend and participate. The timing brought all of them together with their children at a convenient, arranged time. Identifying possible barriers, such as time and work constraints, and making the effort to overcome them through planning and outreach can pay good educational dividends.

Best Practice #5: Invite and Educate Women and Staff to Provide Support to Father Involvement Efforts.

Despite the emphasis on reaching out to fathers and supporting them with educational resources, in reality little happens without educating women and staff to also provide a supportive setting for father involvement efforts. The research literature on supporting fathers through educational efforts is clear and compelling: if you want fathers to matter, mothers and other women must matter, too. The desire to engage fathers and father figures in meaningful ways with their children cannot become a zero-sum game in which men win and women lose. Father involvement occurs in a contextual framework in which mothers, female staff, children, institutions, and other influences all influence the support setting for such efforts. Attending to this reality and turning it into a strength is critical if educational efforts are to succeed.

James Levine and Edward Pitt argue in their book on strategies to enhance responsible fatherhood that attending to the influence of women in father involvement is vital for success. They state: "In every promising approach we have identified, women are a key factor as mothers of men's children, as marriage partners, or as staff members."[15] Lack of support from women in such roles as mother, spouse, teacher, staff member, or administrator will place a large stumbling block in the path of educational efforts to support fathers. Other scholars have commented on the need to involve mothers and other women in developing educational initiatives, continuing to meet the needs of mothers, providing a clear rationale for father involvement efforts, and developing an ongoing dialogue with women to receive input and create educational partnerships that work.[16]

Case Study Example. The Eagles Kindergarten Center is staffed primarily by women in teaching and administrative roles, and yet these women willingly worked to create an educational opportunity for the fathers and father figures of children in their classrooms and made room for that involvement to occur. They sought to engage the help and support of men, and their support and commitment on a yearly basis has made this a continuing educational effort. In the end, father involvement is not about men or women primarily but about the children in our lives and the way we meet their needs and enrich their lives.

Conclusion

At my fourth "Fathers Matter" educational event at the Eagles Kindergarten Center, I was stopped by a woman who was a teacher at the school. She asked if she could relate a story. She mentioned coming home on a recent night and finding her husband sitting by their young daughter's bed and whispering to her. He was holding a tape recorder and playing sounds from it at intervals and then asking her to identify them. Father and daughter were laughing and enjoying themselves. This teacher asked him where he got the idea to engage their daughter in this way, and he informed her that he had read about the activity in the parenting newsletter she had brought home. He had read the newsletter, he said, because it was called *Father Times* and was obviously for him as a father.

Think of the five best practices listed previously. They are not exhaustive but provide a departure point for thinking about educational efforts to support father involvement. In this incident, the father became aware of an educational resource for him as a father. The resource focused on strengths he could use as a father. The material was clearly intended for fathers and father figures and reached him in his home, where he could access it at his convenience. And finally, the opportunity was advanced by a woman, his wife and a teacher, who had cared enough to bring the material home and make it available to him.

Fathers may bring differing styles of engagement with their children to family life and the educational settings designed to support families. Educators and others should recognize and build on the strengths men bring to these interactions. We must sometimes challenge our assumptions in order to begin thinking of new and creative strategies for engaging fathers and father figures in educational efforts. A better starting point is the creation of new opportunities and more effective approaches to helping men realize that the most important work they will ever engage in will be within the walls of their own homes.

Endnotes

1. Pantera, T., June 20, 2004, "Daddy Do-Right," *Fargo Forum*, pp. B6–7.

2. Hawkins, A.J., and Dollahite, D.C., 1997, "Beyond the Role-Inadequacy Perspective of Fathering," in *Generative Fathering: Beyond Deficit Perspectives*, edited by A.J. Hawkins and D.C. Dollahite, pp. 3–16, at 6–7.

3. Levine, J.A., with Pitt, E.W., 1995, *New Expectations: Community Strategies for Responsible Fatherhood.* New York: Families and Work Institute, at 8.

4. Johnson, L., and Palm, G.F., 1992, "Planning Programs: What Do Fathers Want?" in *Working with Fathers: Methods and Perspectives*, Stillwater, MN: nu ink unlimited, at 68.

5. Ibid., at 66.

6. Palm, G.F., 1997, "Promoting Generative Fathering through Parent and Family Education, in *Generative Fathering: Beyond Deficit Perspectives*, edited by A.J. Hawkins and D.C. Dollahite, pp. 167–182, at 171.

7. Ibid., at 171, 174.

8. McBride, B., and Rane, T.R., 2001, "Father/Male Involvement in Early Childhood Programs: Training Staff to Work with Men," in *Clinical and Educational Interventions with Fathers,* edited by J. Fagan and A.J. Hawkins, pp. 171–190, at 185.

9. Fagan, J., and Hawkins, A.J. (Eds.), 2001, *Clinical and Educational Interventions with Fathers,* New York: Haworth Press, Inc., at 12.

10. Hawkins and Dollahite, 1997, at 12.

11. Levine with Pitt, 1995, at 41.

12. Palm, G.F., 1992, "Building Intimacy and Parenting Skills through Father-Child Activity Time," in *Working with Fathers: Methods and Perspectives*, Stillwater, MN: nu ink unlimited, at 79.

13. Palm, G.F., 1994, *Working with Fathers: Involving Men in Parenting Programs,* Minneapolis, MN: Family Information Services.

14. Levine, J.A., and Pittinsky, T.L., 1997, *Working Fathers: New Strategies for Balancing Work and Family,* New York: Harcourt Brace and Company, at 1.

15. Levine with Pitt, 1995, at 9.

16. McBride and Rane, 2001.

Concluding Thoughts: Where Fathers Count Most

The final section and chapter of this book concludes with a look at the most important setting and context in which fathering occurs, within the walls of a father's own home, whether he is married, single, divorced, or cohabiting. It is here that fathers "really" father by the way they treat their children, spouses, parents, ex-spouses, and other people who may be involved in his child(ren)'s life. It is here that fathering comes to life. It is, indeed, *where* fathers are born. We close with this chapter because it speaks to the heart of fathering. It offers a meaningful yet fun and enjoyable perspective on *how* and *where* fathers can count the most in the lives of their children.

In Chapter 27, "Within the Walls of Home," Joseph White provides a key argument for why home is the best place for men to learn to be fathers and why it is *the* place for building lasting lifelong relationships with children. The type of father a man is will be most evident at home where he is not watched or monitored by society, where he makes choices about how he spends his time and the way he interacts with his family. Home is the place where a father's messages, spoken and unspoken, are heard the loudest. Home is a father's ultimate school ground where his children learn the values and lessons of life that he has to impart.

This chapter explores how fathers spend their time at home, suggests ways to involve children in the tasks of home life, and explores opportunities for improving father-child communication. It also highlights the joy that can come from participating in child-centered projects like building a "backyard playland" and spending quality one-on-one time with children. Obviously, most discipline occurs in the home, and this chapter also calls on fathers to be kind, loving, firm disciplinarians and to be in tune enough with their children to know how to provide the specific guidance and instruction each one needs.

Finally, the author concludes with a personal note about how reconnecting with his own father has had important implications for his own children in their personal growth and identity as they have developed a bond of trust and love for their grandfather. This reconnecting process is tied to fathering in the home, as it illustrates the impact that forgiveness and relationship building can have across generations, with the potential of ultimately leading to a grandfather relationship that is spoken of kindly in the home. Home is truly where men can build lasting legacies that will benefit generations to come.

Author Joseph M. White reading to his daughters, from left, Sarah, Hannah, Victoria, Alexandria, and Isabella.

Within the Walls of Home: A Man's Most Important Work

Joseph M. White

As I sit here looking out my office window at the rain coming down, I realize that I have little influence with my children at this very minute in this very place. They are at home, and I am at work. I often long to be involved in their lives more frequently but am unable to do so because of work and other activities. Some may question my priorities about the "other activities," but it doesn't really matter. That is a topic for another discussion. What matters is the fact that I really want to be more involved in the lives of my children. The strange thing is that I already am fairly involved as a parent, but it doesn't seem like it is enough. It doesn't satisfy the longing within me to do more. My wife and I have even discussed rearranging our lives so that I could stay home with them full-time.

However, that is not practical for our current situation. The point? I really want to be with my children and spend time with them. I resonate with Robin Williams's line in the movie *Mrs. Doubtfire*: "I am addicted to my children." That is how I feel about my children. I believe many men have similar feelings.

One of the most important places all men—whether single, married, divorced, or remarried—need to address the challenges of fatherhood is within the walls of their own homes. This is especially true during the formative years of a child's life, but it is also important during later childhood and adolescence. As men put more effort into being good fathers within their homes, they will experience rewarding changes in both the quantity and the quality of time with their children. Simply put, we recommend that fathers spend more time with their children, particularly in the home and related settings. This chapter is about fathers' involvement at home, where men spend the majority of their time with their children, why that involvement is important, and what fathers can do to be more engaged at home.

It seems obvious that home is the most important place for responsible, involved fathering to occur. Fathers may include biological fathers, stepfathers, adoptive fathers, grandfathers, and other father figures. It is primarily in the home that fathers begin a pattern of interaction with their children that sets the tone for the rest of their mutual lives together. It is here that fathers begin to build that initial bond with their children that is meant to last a lifetime. It is here that fathers establish a routine of play and joyful contact that children will carry in their hearts as they grow and mature into manhood or womanhood. It is here that children learn about spirituality and values. It is here, in the home, especially during the formative years, that a positive connection with a father will have a long-lasting effect on a child's mind, heart, and soul. If a father is absent or uninvolved, then these experiences and caring bonds will also be absent, and their protective effect on children will not become real in the life of the child.

Why Home is the Best Place

Why is it that such important experiences between a father and his children occur within the walls of his own home? Of course, "within the walls of home" is inclusive of general experiences men have with their children in and around their home, including outside. Such experiences may take place in the yard, garage, garden, car, or around the neighborhood, as long as it is a place where father and child spend significant amounts of interactive time together. It is not inclusive of work settings or shopping malls (although these can be good places to spend time with your children).

Why do children need experiences with their father in their own home? Why not at the daycare center or the public school? Why not at Head Start or on the baseball diamond? Why not at the park or in a restaurant? Certainly these are places where fathers can and do engage in many wonderful fathering behaviors. Fathering in these settings is vital and constitutes an important aspect of the father-child bond, but fathering in the home is different.

Home is the place where fathers are most likely to play and frolic in a spontaneous manner and they are not judged, monitored, or critiqued by others. It is the place in which men will most likely provide "quantity" time rather than just "quality" time. And there is a much higher likelihood that those all-important "teachable moments" will occur in the home when a father is investing in quantity time with his children. A few minutes of quality time each day hardly sets the stage for a child to open up to his or her father in a deep and meaningful way. A few minutes of time hardly provides the setting for long and detailed personal discussions. The "quality time" mentality sends a message of limit to a child, a message that there is only so much of it to go around, so it had better be valued. Giving oneself over to free play or unstructured time with one's children can result in glorious, unexpected experiences of bonding and growth.

Home is typically the place children observe their father in normal, everyday living. It is the place children learn by the three most effective teaching methods: example, example, and example. There is no greater lesson a father can teach his children than to show his children something by his own actions. It is within the home, unfettered by social expectations, that a father can freely show his love and admiration for his children, his spouse, and his world. It is here that a father sends deep and abiding messages about what kind of place the "world out there" is, but more important, what kind of place home is meant to be and can be for a family. Such messages are transferred, almost imperceptibly, into the hearts and minds of a father's children, whether he realizes it or not. The "messages from home" that children receive about how a father loves and values them occur in many ways, and they are mostly received within the walls of home. This discussion will explore "value messages" that typically occur in the home through distinct concepts like prime time, child-friendly backyards, father-child personal time, "fix-it dad" experiences, discipline, enjoying the journey, and small talk.

Prime Time Is Personal Time

A child's "prime time" always occurs within the walls of his or her home. Prime time typically refers to that time of day when parents come home from work and sit down to watch the evening news or read the paper. I am embarrassed to say that I used to nudge my sweet little children away when I got home and tell them I would play with them later. I wanted to see what was going on in the world. But my observant wife, Alice, helped me learn that the most important prime time really wasn't about what had happened out in the world as much as it was about what was going on with our children at that moment. It was precisely at the time when I got home from work in the evening that our children were most anxious to share with me the day's events in their world. My wife gently nudged me away from the television and newspaper and toward them. She helped me learn to set aside that time, undivided and undistracted.

It is my experience that children want more than anything to have their father's attention and for him to validate them by spending time with them. Prime time can be an important and even critical bonding time that may be missed if one is not aware. Try it out. Turn off the television or radio, put down the newspaper, and focus on your children. Perhaps your children are not that vocal or outspoken with their needs, but if you persist you will find that most children will relish that time with you if you ask them about their day and explore things together that they like to do. Maybe it involves what we call "Daddy tackle time" where I get on the floor and my children jump on top of me and tackle me. Of course, I have to defend myself by tickling my way out of it. This humbling of oneself to frolic on the floor at the child's level sends a lasting impression. It tells them that you want to be a part of their world and communicate with them at their level. Maybe it involves jumping on the trampoline or going on a bike ride. It all depends on the child's age and interest. It is your job as a father to find out what those interests are and, in some cases, to help them explore new ones. Prime time is where some of the great bonding moments between you and your children will occur. They will happen almost imperceptibly if you will be willing to turn the television off, put down the paper, and jump into their world.

Fix-It Dad

There is no reason why children cannot be part of most activities fathers do around the home. Living in a home provides parents with an endless stream of projects to do, ranging from pulling weeds to preparing dinner. Such home activities furnish a ready-made menu of opportunities to involve and connect with your children.

Perhaps you have a lot of home repairs to do. Include children in the process. Ask them to help you fix the leaky sink or change the oil. I have had a lot of fun including my children in our projects around the home. When I make them "Daddy's helper," they feel validated and a part of their dad's life and activities. I often try to find ways to involve them at their level in whatever projects I am working on. They love to be a part of Daddy's world. Depending on their age, they love to get dirty, to get sawdust on themselves from a woodworking project, or to get oil on themselves from a car repair job. *This is a great secret to finding quantity time with your children.* Most farmers I know understand this secret and include their children in the daily routine and process of maintaining and managing the farm.

Regardless of whether or not men are good at fixing broken appliances or preparing a healthy meal, it is valuable to include children in home activities.

Fathers may sometimes feel they do not have the time to spare for such involvement, because it requires more of them and may seem more complicated. However, children benefit immensely from successfully solving problems and being involved with their fathers. Fathers who learn to be patient, intuitive, and resourceful teach their children great problem-solving skills and life lessons that can be transferred to the life challenges they will inevitably face.

Small Talk with Kids

Small talk will usually occur within the walls of your home. Being able to engage in small talk with your children is extremely important. Letting children know that you value them enough to talk with them about the little things and to listen to their trivial intrigues and smallest concerns sends a message that they are important. It says, "I value all things in your life, not just the major events." And it is through listening to the small talk that big and important things will come out. The more we listen to the small talk of children, the more we begin to hear the deep concerns of their hearts. The more we pay attention to the little things in their lives, the more prepared we will be when the big things accidentally or intentionally surface.

Small talk should go both ways between dads and kids. Fathers shouldn't feel like they always have to say something important or meaningful. Recently I discovered the beauty of postcards. During a period when I was traveling a lot, I began sending my children postcards. Postcards are great because you can't really say a whole lot. I started writing silly little things that were unique to each of my children. It wasn't much, but it was amazing to see how much they treasured those cards. They would carry them around all day and read them over and over. It was humbling to realize how "so little" could mean so much to a child.

Child-Friendly Back Yards

A critical consideration in home life is whether the space you live in is truly friendly and inviting to children. One of the great joys I have had as a father has been to develop an exciting "playland" in the back yard for our children. It was, as they would say, the coolest back yard in the neighborhood. The neighbor children always played in our yard. My daughters would tell me they would rather invite friends to our home than go away to their friends' homes because there were so many things to do.

Of course, part of the fun was planning, creating, and building the back yard playland with them. They were part of the brainstorming process. Once we decided what to do, I found tasks that were appropriate for their ages and included them along the way. I was amazed to see how much they enjoyed pounding nails into lumber (and then into scrap lumber, long after the projects were done). They had learned some important tasks and were busy practicing them. Some of the great projects we participated in building together included a clubhouse, a zipline (which they called the pulley slide), a play system that one friend called the only five-swing system in the city, a trampoline, and a two-story playhouse with a loft.

The zipline was probably one of the coolest things we have ever designed. It put fear into the heart of every mother who set foot in our back yard. But after seeing their children scream with delight as they sat on the seat and sped down the 50-foot steel cable toward the eyebolt attachment at the other end, they smiled as well. My hope was that mothers would relax when they saw the stopper at the lower end of the zipline that kept their children from slamming into the garage (where the pulley slide was attached) and that they would realize it was "perfectly safe." In the end, it was often hard for parents to pull their children away from it. Kids would often say, "Just one more time, please, Mom." A few mothers have paid me the highest compliment by bringing their husbands over to check it out and figure out how to build one for their kids.

Of course, our children also enjoy digging in the dirt, so we always set aside a corner of the garden just for them. We decided early on if we wanted them to stay out of the garden we had to give them their own patch of dirt in which to play. We also put up little wading pools or "slip and slides" during the summer when it is hot. The ideas for your back yard or home environment will be limited only by your imagination and the imagination of your children. You may have challenges of limited space or a lack of resources. However, think of it as a mission and brainstorm with your children to find ideas to work within those constraints. This may be one of the most important missions you accept as a father. When children grow up after having such experiences, their minds will not reflect so much on the clothes they wore or the nice furniture in their home but more on the fun and engaging things they did in and around their home. Their memories will be filled with the joys of creating and building their own little world in their back yard or room or garage and, most important, of the times they spent with their father in the process.

Enjoy the Family Journey

When we were younger as a couple and used to travel with our children, we typically drove like there was no tomorrow. We acted like we had to get to our destination in the quickest and cheapest way possible. Now we take things more in stride. We have learned to stop and smell the roses, in a sense, even if there happen to be many along the way. By so doing, our children have begun to enjoy the trips we take much more and are willing to sit for six to eight hours in the car if they know there is a pool waiting for them at the other end of the day. In fact, whenever we travel, the two uncompromising amenities (for the most part) are a pool and a continental breakfast. This approach has evolved into a common family theme we call "Enjoy the family journey."

Whether we are traveling for vacation, building a backyard playhouse, or planning a weekend barbeque, living by this value has helped relieve some of the stress of family life. It has also encouraged us to look to each other for our joy and enjoy the time we spend "getting there." Such an attitude has provided us with a more relaxed approach to life and a greater sense of wonder and gratitude for the experiences we have along the way as a family. Fathers should learn to enjoy the journey of parenting with their children so the message is received that it is the time and experiences shared, not the final destination, that is most important.

Father-Child Personal Time
Children need to feel they are special, especially to their fathers. They need this assurance, unconditional love, and attention more than we realize. They need to know their father is absolutely crazy about them and to experience "alone time" with dad so they can learn to feel comfortable enough to communicate with him.

One of the ways we have done this in our family has become fondly referred to as "Daddy-daughter dates." These alone-time experiences can range from getting a soft drink or going out to lunch to simply going to Dad's office. It can involve going shopping or visiting friends. It really doesn't matter so much *what* it is, as long as it involves just spending time together at some point in the process. A point of clarification is in order. I found out recently, when my oldest daughter moved into her teenage years and discovered shopping, hair, and Hillary Duff, that going with Dad to Menard's (a large home building supply store in the Midwest) was not cool. It was no longer an acceptable form of Daddy-daughter dates. I was crushed. She informed me that it was boring and that we spent way too much time there. This required that I explore new options for our one-on-one time as we developed and grew in our relationship. How grateful I am for this time with my daughters. It has been a wonderful part of our mutual development.

An important caveat about one-on-one time between fathers and children is that it doesn't have to be formal or even planned on a regular basis, although this can be very helpful. It should, however, be frequent (weekly or monthly, depending on ages and number of children) and involve considerable interest and discussion about what is important in that child's life, especially as they get older. Informal dialogue can often be rich and rewarding and produce memorable discussions and powerful teaching moments.

Discipline
Discipline is another dimension of parenting that generally occurs in the home. It is in the home that fathers provide structure and establish patterns of interaction about expected behaviors. It is here that fathers provide discipline and help establish consequences for unacceptable behaviors. It is here that fathers show compassion, love, and understanding in response to discipline. It is here,

then, that children learn and grow in developmentally appropriate and functional ways. Of course, the opposite is true, also. When children do not experience fathering that is both firm and kind (either through authoritarian or permissive parenting styles or because father is absent), then a child's development and functional growth are often thwarted.

Each individual has a unique parenting style, and each couple must negotiate these differences. I have been the more stern parent in our parenting partnership. An important part of our parenting journey has been our communication regarding disciplining our children. We have spent countless hours, late into the night, discussing the needs of different children. This has been very important to us because each child is different and has required slightly different techniques and approaches in order to learn and grow.

A root word in discipline is "disciple." This conveys the meaning that we are to help our children not only do the right thing but actually learn to follow parental guidance or the appropriate guidance of others. Used in this context, the term discipline sets a high standard for fathers. It highlights why it is critical for men to realize the importance of their examples. Being a responsible father requires a willingness to practice discipline with our children, but it also means, at its root, a desire that our children be willing to follow. If fathers don't live up to that which they require from their children, then hypocrisy ensues. This sets the stage for children to justify decisions not to follow their fathers and the good things they have taught. Although the standard for responsible fathering is high, it is worth it when children follow that standard and are willing to follow a life path that includes good and responsible choices themselves. There is great wisdom in the belief that good parenting is difficult and time-consuming, but the fruits of good parenting are well worth the effort. A wise leader who had reached his 90s once said that after people get to his age nothing else in life will matter more to them than how well their children turn out. The future well-being of children depends to a significant degree on how they respond to a father's example and guidance during the earlier years of life.

Fathers and Adult Children: Reconnecting with Each Other

Of course, there are fathers who, for whatever reason, do not make that meaningful bond and connection with their children early in life. Does that mean the child is doomed? Of course not. There are many stories of fatherless children who succeed, but the odds are often stacked against them. On the other hand, many fathers and children who did not have a strong or meaningful early relationship find ways to reconnect later in life.

There was a long period of my own life where I thought I would never have a good relationship with my father. I simply wrote it off as a lost cause. I even, in all seriousness, called him Darth Vader. However, my own experience has been one of great growth and change, because today not only do I have a great relationship with my father but my children do as well. When people ask me if they, as adults, can and should try to reconnect with their fathers or when older men ask about their children, my immediate response is simple: "It is never too late!" It is important to make the best of the time you have available in life and not to get caught up in distracting details or things that created pain or distance in the past. It is important to let some things go.

For the first few years after my father and I reconnected, in any conversation I learned to simply listen and keep my mouth shut as he would go on for the first five to 10 minutes about how terrible my mother was, even though they had been divorced for more than 10 years. Once he got it off his chest, we went on to other things. We had great conversations on the phone that would last for hours. I learned many things from him and am grateful for the wisdom and life experience he has shared with me. If I had gotten hung up on the fact that he was criticizing my mother, we would never have been able to move on to the great discussions we were yet to have and the next stage of our relationship, in which a deep bond was formed.

What does this have to do with fathering in the home? This process with my father has had an important impact on my own children, because they have now grown up knowing him fairly well and hearing his name spoken of kindly and respectfully in our home. Their grandfather is a loved and respected person and plays an important role in their lives. Because we went through the forgiveness process, my father and I have reconnected. Because we have reconnected, he is a welcome figure in our home. Although my father hated his own father until the day he died, it is my hope that our experience will serve as a catalyst for change across future generations in which our children will have strong, positive relationships with their fathers and grandfathers throughout their life and then pass that legacy on to their children and so on.

Conclusion

As we consider the impact of fathering in the home, we should also address the impact fathering has on fathers themselves. The benefits of fathering to men are varied and absolute. Not only does good fathering benefit children but it has a profound and critical place in a man's development in the adult stages of his life. In general, men will feel a profound sense of loss if they get to the end of life and have not done what they could to develop relationships with their children and then nurture those relationships to the best of their ability. All may not go as planned in a man's life, and he may have difficulties in being the kind of father he wants to be or should be. However, men need to make the very best efforts they can and go to great lengths to do the work of fatherhood in supporting their children's spiritual, mental, emotional, and physical development.

As I look out my window, it is still raining, but barely. Soon I will go home and see my beautiful children. As I walk through the door, the little ones will run up to me, grab my legs, and hug me, shouting "Daddy, Daddy, Daddy." The older ones will come around on their own time and say hello in a more calm and controlled manner. If they have been involved in some kind of project or if it was library day, they will run and grab their new adventures and share them with me, often all at once. As I sit down on our couch and listen to them speaking a collective language that only a father can understand, a language that blends different voices and levels of articulation and enthusiasm, I will simply smile and express my love for each of them and share in their interests.

Perhaps one of the older ones will start to play *Canon in D* on the piano. As I sit, I will lean forward into the prime-time events of their world and send a subtle message: they are valued beyond measure. The unspoken message will convey their importance and the meaningfulness of what they say, and they will feel loved. This loving scenario will take place, not in an executive suite or on a beach in Cancun, but within the walls of our home. Home is the place where my children's hearts have turned to their father and where their father's heart has turned to them. Home is the place where I have become a father and where my children have come to love their father. Home is the place where *most* fathering occurs, and may it be the place where the *best* fathering occurs.

About the Contributors

William D. Allen, Ph.D., is a licensed marriage and family therapist and owner of Healing Bonds, a private practice located in the Uptown neighborhood of Minneapolis, MN. Allen is an adjunct professor in the Family Social Science Department of the University of Minnesota and consults with both public and private sector institutions on a range of subjects related to family mental health and well-being. He has written and presented nationally on several topics including cultural influences on parenting practices, cultural competence, males in families, and, more recently, practical approaches for building healthy marriages. (ballen@umn.edu)

Sherri S. Bair and her husband, Dave, are the parents of one son and four daughters and also have two beautiful granddaughters. She is working on a master's degree in child and family studies and has a B.S. in family and consumer sciences, both from South Dakota State University. (sherri.bair@sdstate.edu)

Andrew O. Behnke, Ph.D., is an assistant professor of human development and an extension Latino parent specialist at North Carolina State University in Raleigh. Though a native Texan, he holds master's and doctoral degrees in family science from Utah State University and Purdue University. He conducts applied research on marginalized (i.e., poor, rural, [im]migrant) families, academic achievement among Latino youth, parental involvement in academics, stress and parenting, Latino fatherhood, poverty, and family and community partnerships. He is working to create a coalition to address the disparities in healthcare, nutrition, financial awareness, housing, and academic youth outcomes among Latinos in North Carolina. He is married to his best friend and has three adventuresome boys and one little princess of a daughter. His life mission is bringing better attention to those factors that help immigrant Latino families succeed and thrive in the U.S. (andrew_behnke@ncsu.edu)

Sean E. Brotherson, Ph.D., is an associate professor of child development and family science and an extension family science specialist at North Dakota State University in Fargo. He received his doctoral degree in human development and family studies from Oregon State University and holds bachelor's and master's degrees in family science from Brigham Young University. His research work and interests include generative fathering, healthy relationships in the home, marital reconciliation, and family life education and policy approaches to strengthening family relationships. His work has been published in *Fathering*, *Family Relations*, *Journal of Family Psychotherapy,* and *Marriage and Family Review*. He is the founder and co-director of the Dakota Fatherhood Initiative, a two-state grassroots fatherhood initiative focused on facilitating healthy father involvement in family life. He is the author of the *Bright Beginnings* parenting curriculum on parenting young children and coauthor of the *Father Times* parenting newsletter for fathers and father figures. He and his wife, Kristen, are the parents of six children. (sean.brotherson@ndsu.edu)

Ken R. Canfield, Ph.D., is a research scholar specializing in the area of fatherhood and the history of the family. He is founder and president of the Kansas City–based National Center for Fathering—the only national organization focused on equipping men to be the involved fathers their children need. Dr. Canfield is the author of *They Call Me Dad, The Heart of a Father, The 7 Secrets of Effective Fathers*, and other books on fatherhood as well as numerous academic and popular articles. He also writes the center's weekly *fathers.com* e-mail newsletter and has a daily "Today's Father" radio commentary (heard on some 500 stations nationwide). Canfield earned his B.A. degree in philosophy from Friends University (Wichita). He has an M.C.S. degree from the University of British Columbia–Regent College (Vancouver, B.C.) and a Ph.D. in education from Kansas State University (Manhattan). His dissertation reported on his innovative research on the life course of fathers. Ken and his wife, Dee, reside in Kansas City. They have been married for 29 years and have five children. (kencanfield@fathers.com)

Shawn L. Christiansen, Ph.D., is an associate professor in family life and human development at Southern Utah University. He has an M.S. from Brigham Young University in family life education and a Ph.D. from the University of Delaware in individual and family studies. He has taught at Central Washington University and Penn State Worthington Scranton. Although his scholarship has been mainly in the area of fathering, he is currently studying family wellness and health. When not working or riding his bicycle, he enjoys spending time with his supportive wife, Tiffiney, and their four convivial children (Chris, Camilla, Emma, and Elsa). (christiansen@suu.edu)

David Clay, M.A., is completing his doctoral degree in clinical psychology at the University of South Florida, where he earned his master's degree. He earned his bachelor's degree at Morehouse College. He recently completed his clinical internship at the Florida State Hospital, where he has accepted an offer for employment. David and his wife are raising their young niece. (David_Clay@dcf.state.fl.us)

Nate Cottle, Ph.D., is an assistant professor of development and family studies at the University of North Texas in Denton. He received his Ph.D. from the University of Texas at Austin in human development and family studies. He earned his master's and bachelor's degrees from Brigham Young University. His research has focused on healthy marital and family relationships, specifically in the areas of mate selection, marriage, and fathering. He is a faculty fellow at the Center for Parent Education and Family Support at UNT. He is also a member of the National Council on Family Relations and the International Association for Relationship Research. He and his wife have two daughters.

Keri S. Diez, Ph.D., is an assistant professor of health studies at Southeastern Louisiana University in Hammond. She holds a master's degree in counseling and a doctorate in education. Her areas of specialization are adult and higher education and gerontology. She teaches graduate and undergraduate courses in aging, worksite health promotion, human sexuality, and research methods. She has conducted research, presented, and published in the areas of intergenerational mentoring, older adults and self-efficacy in regard to physical activity, risk behaviors in college athletes, and cinema education. She is the 2004 Louisiana Association for Health, Physical Education, Recreation and Dance (LAHPERD) Taylor Dodson Young Professional award winner. (kdiez@selu.edu)

Paul Dixon, Ph.D., professor of educational psychology at the University of North Texas, is the author of more than 60 books, monographs, and articles reflecting a variety of interests. His research includes program evaluation, scale development, and learning and personality of children and adults in social interactions. As a university administrator, he contributed to the development of several national initiatives for support of urban school districts. His teaching experiences range from courses in statistics to courses in developmental psychology and parenting. (dixon@unt.edu)

David C. Dollahite, Ph.D., is a professor of family life at Brigham Young University, where he was awarded an Eliza R. Snow University Fellowship for his work on faith and family life and where he has served as associate director for outreach education in the School of Family Life. He has been a visiting scholar at the University of Massachusetts–Amherst, at Dominican University of California, and at the Maharaja Sayajirao University of Baroda in India under the Jawaharlal Nehru Visiting Scholar Chair. His scholarship focuses on religion and family life in the Abrahamic faiths, Latter-day Saint family life, and faith and fathering. He is coeditor of *Helping and Healing Our Families* (Deseret Book, 2005), editor of *Strengthening Our Families* (Bookcraft, 2000), and coeditor of *Generative Fathering* (Sage, 1997). He is a scientific advisor for the Center for Spiritual Development in Childhood and Adolescence, funded by the John Templeton Foundation. He has served on the Utah Commission on Marriage, on the Board of Scholars of the Sutherland Institute (a nonpartisan public policy think tank), and as president of the Utah Council on Family Relations. He and his wife, Mary, have seven terrific kids—Rachel, Erica, Camilla, Kathryn, Spencer, Jonathan, and Luke. (david_dollahite@byu.edu)

Tera B. Duncan, M.Ed., teaches part-time in the Marriage, Family, and Human Development Department at Brigham Young University. She has been teaching at the college level for more than 20 years. She is also a Ph.D. candidate in family psychology at Capella University, where she is researching adult attachment and value orientation in marriage. She has published the textbook *Gospel Perspectives for Family Theories*. She enjoys collaborative projects that support and strengthen family relationships. Tera and her husband, Gary, have a blended family of six children. (Tera_Duncan@byu.edu)

Kevin A. Galbraith, Ph.D., is a professor at Brigham Young University–Idaho in the Department of Home and Family. His specific area of interest is marriage and family relations. He received a bachelor's degree in psychology and a master's degree in counseling at Idaho State University. After working at various human service positions, he completed a Ph.D. at Utah State University in family and human development. Kevin and his wife, Kristin, have seven wonderful children and love spending time as a family. (galbraithke@byui.edu)

H. Wallace Goddard, Ph.D., CFLE, is a professor and family life specialist for the University of Arkansas Cooperative Extension Service. Wally is well known for his innovative programs such as the *Parenting Journey* and the *Great Self Mystery*. He is a member of the National Extension Marriage Education Coalition. Dr. Goddard coauthored *Family Life Education: Principles and Practices for Effective Outreach* with Stephen Duncan. Wally and his wife, Nancy, have three children as well as a growing gang of grandchildren and have cared for about 20 foster children over the years. (wgoddard@uaex.edu)

Stephen D. Green, Ph.D., is an associate professor and extension child development specialist with Texas Cooperative Extension at Texas A&M University in College Station. A central focus of his work is the unique contributions fathers bring to the parenting role. He has published numerous journal articles, extension publications, and educational curricula, including *Families First: Keys to Successful Family Functioning* and *Fathers Reading Every Day (FRED)*. His education consists of a Ph.D. in family and child development from Virginia Tech University, an M.S. in marriage and family therapy from Harding University, and a B.A. in psychology from the University of California, Davis. He is married and has two children. (s-green@tamu.edu)

J. Michael Hall, M.Ed., is executive director and founder of Strong Fathers–Strong Families. He holds a master's degree in school administration from Abilene Christian University. He has worked as a special education teacher in elementary and middle schools and is now considered a "recovering" middle school principal. He is the husband of a wonderful elementary school teacher and the father of two strong young men. He is considered a gifted speaker and work-shop facilitator and has worked with thousands of fathers and educators promoting the strengthening of fathers and families. He has spoken across the country in regional and national conferences on education, fatherhood, and family strengthening. He spends almost every morning of the school week working with dads and their children in Head Starts and public and private schools. He continues to use this extensive experience to develop projects and products that help those educational environments work better with fathers and families to benefit the children they serve. (www.strongfathers.com; mikehall@strongfathers.com)

Scott S. Hall, Ph.D., CFLE, is an assistant professor of family relations and child development at Ball State University. He has a master's degree in marriage and family therapy from the University of Nebraska–Lincoln, a doctorate in family studies from Purdue University, and certification from the National Council on Family Relations as a family life educator. Scott has focused on a variety of fatherhood issues as a father of three young daughters and a family scholar. He has been particularly interested in exploring predictors of fathers' involvement with their children, fathers' allocation of work and family roles, and fathers' influence on the long-term psychological and social development of their children. (sshall@bsu.edu)

E. Jeffrey Hill, Ph.D., CFLE, is an associate professor of family life at Brigham Young University. Before coming to BYU in 1998, he was an expert in work and family issues at IBM. Jeff received a master's of organizational behavior from BYU in 1984 and a Ph.D. in family and human development from Utah State in 1995. He teaches a variety of courses in the School of Family Life as well as a Work and Family class in the Marriott School of Management. He was the lead researcher on IBM's 2004 Global Work and Life Issues Survey with 98,000 invitees in 76 countries and 12 languages. He has published numerous scholarly articles on the topics of work and family, job flexibility, telecommuting, and reduced-hours employment options. Jeff and his late wife—the proud parents of nine children and five beautiful grandchildren—were married for 28 years. (jeff_hill@byu.edu)

Erin Kramer Holmes, Ph.D., is a visiting scholar in the School of Family Life at Brigham Young University. She received her doctoral degree in human development and family sciences from the University of Texas at Austin. She holds a bachelor's degree in family science from Brigham Young University and a master's degree in individual and family studies from the University of Delaware. She has studied and published on how fathers and children create meaningful relationships, the changes in marriage that accompany the transition to parenthood, how parents try to share home and work responsibilities, the influence of parenting relationships on children's social development, and how everyday life events shape home life. Erin and her husband, Chris, are the happy parents of two little girls. (erin_holmes@byu.edu)

Jenet Jacob is a Ph.D. student in the Department of Family Social Science at the University of Minnesota. She has studied and published on the topics of mothering, family systems theory, work/family conflict, learning in the home, and nonmaternal childcare. In 2004, she worked as a research fellow studying domestic policy in Washington, D.C. Prior to her Ph.D. work, she taught English as a second language for three years at the Brigham Young University English Language Center, where she served on the executive council. Jenet received a bachelor of nursing degree in 1997 and a master's degree in teaching English as a second language in 2000, both from Brigham Young University. She is the fifth child in a family of 11 children, of which all but nine are boys.

Loren Marks, Ph.D., is an assistant professor of family, child, and consumer sciences at Louisiana State University. His research efforts center on a national qualitative study of more than 130 families. Specifically, he examines the influence religion and spirituality have on parenting and marriage relationships and has authored or coauthored several publications on these topics. He received the 2004 Paper of the Year award from the Religion and Family Life section of the National Council on Family Relations and the Jack Shand Research Award in 2005 from the Society for the Scientific Study of Religion. Loren and his wife, Sandra, have four delightful but boisterous children. (lorenm@lsu.edu)

James P. Marshall, Ph.D., LMFT, is an assistant professor and extension family life specialist with the University of Arkansas Cooperative Extension Service in Little Rock. James is a native Virginian who received B.A. and M.S. degrees from Brigham Young University and a doctorate in marriage and family therapy from Texas Tech University. He and his wife, Kathie, are the proud parents of five children. He conducts applied research and does curriculum development and programming in the areas of marriage strengthening, parenting, individual development, and childcare. His work focuses on helping people create and maintain quality relationships. (jpmarshall@uaex.edu)

Giuseppe Martinengo is a Ph.D. student in the marriage, family, and human development program at Brigham Young University (BYU). He holds an undergraduate degree in social sciences from Universidade Estadual de Londrina (Brazil) and a master's degree in business administration from BYU. He is married and has four children. He is conducting research in the area of work and family with a special emphasis on working fathers and job flexibility. (giuseppemartinengo@gmail.com)

Bryan G. Nelson has worked with young children, men, fathers, and families for more than 30 years, including high school students, early/elementary education, Head Start, and other programs. He is the father of two children and continues to work with children and families. Since 1979, he has served as founding director of MenTeach, a national nonprofit organization with a mission to increase the number of men teaching children. He serves on the faculty at Metropolitan State University, teaching early childhood development and consulting with teacher recruitment programs. He has received various awards, including a leadership fellowship to Harvard University to research men, fathers, and children. A founding board member of the National Practitioners' Network for Fathers and Families and a founding father of the Festival of Fathers, he also served as president of the Minnesota Association for the Education of Young Children. (BGNelson@ MenTeach.org)

Terrance D. Olson, Ph.D., is a professor in the School of Family Life at Brigham Young University. He has been vice chair of the Family Science and Education and Enrichment sections of the National Council on Family Relations (NCFR). He co-created a character-citizenship program he used to implement a series of federal grants in the public schools as a tool for preventing self-destructive choices among adolescents. He is a member of the Association for Moral Education and examines how the concepts of moral agency and individual responsibility affect the quality of life, resilience, and competence of family members. He studies the intersection of philosophies of science with the content and delivery of family life education programs. Terry's doctoral degree from Florida State University emphasized marriage and family therapy, social-psychology theory, and family life education. He grew up in Albuquerque and taught at the University of New Mexico before joining the faculty at BYU. He and his wife, Karen, formerly of Stockton, CA, have raised six children. They have been unsuccessful in passing legislation that makes it illegal for grandchildren to be taken across state lines without grandparental permission.

Glen Palm, Ph.D., CFLE, is a professor in child and family studies at St. Cloud State University. He is a licensed parent educator and works with fathers of young children in a variety of parent education programs. As a researcher/practitioner, Dr. Palm has studied ethics in parent and family education, fathers' perceptions of attachment, parent education needs of incarcerated fathers, and the role of father-hood in influencing men's values and moral/religious beliefs. He has also served as a local program evaluator for Early Head Start, Even Start Family Literacy, and Early Childhood Family Education programs. He was a board member of the National Practitioners Network for Fathers and Families (NPNFF) from 1998 to 2004 and is a board member of the Minnesota Fathers and Families Network (MFFN). He has contributed chapters on fatherhood and parent education to a number of books. He is coauthor of *Fathers and Early Childhood Programs* (2004) with Jay Fagan and *Group Parent Education: Promoting Parent Learning and Support* (2004) with Deborah Campbell. He and his wife, Jane, have worked together as parent educators and have three children. (gfpalm@stcloudstate.edu)

Rob Palkovitz, Ph.D., is a professor of individual and family studies at the University of Delaware. His research interests are in fathering and intergenerational relationships and development, with a particular emphasis on the relationships between patterns of father involvement and men's adult development. He is currently studying transitions within fathering, characteristics of resilient fathers in challenging circumstances, and fathers in the "launching" phases of fathering. Along with his family, he regularly does volunteer work with inner city foster and fatherless children. Dr. Palkovitz received his bachelor's degree in psychology from the University of Virginia and both his master's and doctoral degrees in developmental psychology from Rutgers University. He and his wife, Judy, enjoy actively co-parenting their growing family. They have four sons and two daughters-in-law. (robp@UDel.Edu)

Vicky Phares, Ph.D., is a professor of clinical psychology and the director of clinical training at the University of South Florida. She completed her doctoral training at the University of Vermont. She has conducted research on fathers and developmental psychopathology and fathers' roles in the therapeutic process. She has published numerous articles and two books on the subject and has written a textbook on abnormal child psychology. She is married and has two grown step-daughters and a six-year-old son. (phares@cas.usf.edu)

Francis T. Pleban, Ph.D., CHES, is an assistant professor of health professions in the College of Health Professions at Grand Valley State University in Grand Rapids, Michigan. He holds master's and doctoral degrees in health promotion and health education, focusing on adolescent health issues, from Central Michigan University and Southern Illinois University, Carbondale. He has conducted research on environmental risk and protective factors affecting adolescent health and development, with particular attention to youth at-risk behaviors, juvenile delinquency, and youth gang involvement.

Jeffrey L. Stueve, Ph.D., is an adjunct professor in the Social Science Division at Bethel College in Mishawaka, Indiana. He serves as coordinator of family ministry at Trinity United Methodist Church in Plymouth, Indiana. He received his doctoral degree from the University of Illinois and was an assistant professor of family studies at the University of New Mexico. He is married and has two sons. Jeff has conducted research and written on fatherhood and co-parenting, with a special interest in paternal and co-parental identity. He is currently interested in understanding, promoting, and supporting loving father-child relationships, particularly, and loving family relationships, more generally. (jeffreystueve@yahoo.com)

Alan C. Taylor, Ph.D., is an assistant professor in the Department of Child and Family Studies at Syracuse University. He holds a master's degree in Family Life Education from Brigham Young University and a doctoral degree from Virginia Tech in child and family studies. He also obtained a certificate in gerontology at Virginia Tech. Alan and his wonderful wife, Kelly, have five tremendous children— Bronson, Holden, Camryn, Ethan, and Lauryn. He is also a Certified Family Life Educator, affiliated through the National Council on Family Relations. He has taught numerous courses relating to family development, gerontology and aging, and interpersonal communication skills. Alan has conducted research and published articles on grandfathering, grandparent-grandchild relationships, family theory, and family life education. Recently Alan has been involved in two large federal grants, one designated to disseminate information and resources on healthy marriage throughout the U.S. and the other to train graduate students to focus and integrate healthy marriage principles into child welfare community agency settings.

Neil Tift is the director of training at the National Practitioners Network for Fathers and Families (NPNFF) in Washington, D.C. Prior to his work at NPNFF, he was the director of the resource center at the National Fatherhood Initiative (NFI) in Gaithersburg, Maryland. From 1990 to 1998 Neil was the founding director of the Fathers' Resource Center in Minneapolis. For 21 years, he served as an adjunct professor of family studies at Metropolitan State University in St. Paul, teaching ethics, child psychology, and human service administration. Neil has written several chapters and numerous articles on fatherhood and related issues. He earned an M.A. in counseling psychology from the University of Saint Thomas. He is the father of three, the grandfather of five, and a foster father of many. (ntift@npnff.net)

Randell Turner, Ph.D., is a specialist in numerous categories of therapy programs designed especially for fathers, including programming for incarcerated, low-income, and teen fathers implemented through community-based organizations. He has published several fatherhood curricula, including *Foundations of*

Fatherhood for community-based programs, *FatherHOOD 101* for teen fathers, *Dr. Dad* to teach fathers how to care for sick infants and toddlers, and *Dads on Duty,* a program for military fathers. As part of his therapy for incarcerated men, Dr. Turner developed the "Long Distance Dads Program" for incarcerated fathers, now being utilized by the Pennsylvania Department of Corrections and in more than 300 federal, state, and county prisons nationwide. His latest work focuses on therapy for children with ADD and ADHD and the benefits of increased father involvement in the therapy process. Dr. Turner has a Ph.D. in psychology, and he and his wife, Robin, have seven children. (FathersWorkshop@att.net)

Sterling K. Wall, Ph.D., is an assistant professor of family and consumer sciences at the University of Wisconsin–Stevens Point. He holds a doctorate in family studies and human development from Auburn University, a master's in counseling from the University of Colorado–Colorado Springs, and a bachelor's of economics from Brigham Young University. Sterling was born and raised in Oregon City, Oregon. He and his beautiful wife, Natalie, have five children, one born in each state in which they have lived: Sterling M. (Utah), Taylor (Oregon), Mariah (Colorado), Meaghan (Alabama), and Hannah (Wisconsin). Sterling's research and scholarship focus on improving marital quality, exploring gender influences, and maintaining work-family balance. As he has said nightly to his children, "My favorite thing is to be your dad and for you to be my child." (swall@uwsp.edu)

Alice M. White received her bachelor's degree from Utah State University in elementary education in 1994. She is the mother of seven children, ages three months to 13. Alice has chosen a career as a homemaker and stay-at-home mom. In addition to her time as a mother and wife, she devotes significant time homeschooling her children. Alice married Joseph White in 1989. Her interests include music, gardening, reading, interior decorating, and Pilates. She also volunteers time and service to her church family. (connectsix@hotmail.com)

Joseph M. White, Ph.D., is a research assistant professor in the Department of Sociology at the University of Nebraska–Lincoln. He has taught graduate and undergraduate courses in marriage and family, adolescent and adult development, family assessment, and family public policy. He received his doctorate at Texas Tech University (1997) in human development and family studies and his bachelor's (1992) and master's (1994) degrees from Utah State University in psychology and family and human development, respectively. He has published in a variety of professional journals on topics ranging from fatherhood policy to fathering among American Indians and from identity development to recovery from substance abuse. He has served as founder and codirector of the Dakota Fatherhood Initiative, helped establish local fatherhood movements, and spoken on fatherhood at conferences and training workshops across the Midwest. He is collaborating with several Midwestern American Indian reservations to develop a culturally specific alcohol prevention program for youth and their families. His greatest work has occurred in his home, where he is a father of seven children (six girls and one boy), ranging in age from three months to 13 years. Joseph met his sweetheart, Alice, at Ricks College in Idaho in 1989. (jwhite.wfc@gmail.com)

George R. Williams, M.S., is executive director of the National Center for Fathering's Urban Father-Child Partnership. He has been a fathering practitioner for the past eight years and is a recognized fathering expert who has spoken and taught at numerous national conferences including PTA and Head Start. He is an approved National Head Start Consultant under four areas of expertise including fatherhood initiatives. He has authored five fathering curricula, including the *Coach Dads Play Book* and *R.E.A.D. (Reconnecting Education and Dads) to Kids* and is a contributing author for the textbook *Fundamentals of Early Childhood Education,* 4th and 5th editions. He has trained more than 400 trainers from coast to coast in his fathering curriculum *Quenching the Father Thirst.* He writes and records for the "Today's Father" radio program, which airs on more than 500 stations nationwide. He served on the expert panel of the Strengthening Families with Children Born Out-of-Wedlock research project conducted by Princeton University and has testified as an expert fathering witness before a Senate subcommittee. He earned his master of science degree from Friends University (Wichita, Kansas) in family therapy and is a lifetime member of Psi Chi, the National Honor Society in Psychology. George and his wife, Trudy, have three sons and one daughter. (gwilliamsfathers@aol.com)

Index